A SEMANTIC AND STRUCTURAL ANALYSIS OF MARK

SIL International®
SEMANTIC AND STRUCTURAL ANALYSIS SERIES

JOHN C. TUGGY, GENERAL EDITOR

A SEMANTIC AND STRUCTURAL ANALYSIS OF MARK

Ellis W. Deibler, Jr.

SIL International®
Dallas, Texas

© 2019 by SIL International®

Library of Congress Control Number: 2019947948
ISBN: 978-1-55671-451-1

The Greek text used in this SSA is from the fourth revised edition
of the United Bible Societies' *Greek New Testament*.

All Rights Reserved
No part of this publication may be reproduced, stored in a retrieval system,
or transmitted in any form or by any means without the express permission
of SIL International. However, brief excerpts, generally understood to be
within the limits of fair use, may be quoted without written permission.

Copies of this and other publications of SIL International®
may be obtained through distributors such as Amazon,
Barnes & Noble, other worldwide distributors and, for
select volumes, www.sil.org/resources/publications:

SIL International Publications
7500 West Camp Wisdom Road
Dallas, TX 75236-5629, USA

General inquiry: publications_intl@sil.org
Pending order inquiry: sales_intl@sil.org
www.sil.org/resources/publications

CONTENTS

Foreword	7
General Introduction to Semantic and Structural Analyses	9
Introduction to the Semantic and Structural Analysis of Mark	17
Authorship	17
Circumstances of Composition	17
Date of Composition	18
The Intended Audience	18
Mark's Purpose	18
Some of Mark's Special Interests	18
The Structure of Mark	19
Thematic outline of Mark	20
Constituent structure of Mark	28
The Gospel Of Mark 1:1—16:8	31
Book Constituent 1:1 (Book Title of 1:1—16:8)	32
Book Constituent 1:2–13 (Beginning of the Book 1:1—16:8)	35
Part Constituent 1:2–8 (Declarative Paragraph of 1:2–13)	36
Part Constituent 1:9–13 (Episode of 1:2–13)	41
Book Constituent 1:14—8:30 (Part I of 1:1—16:8)	43
Part Constituent 1:14–15 (Introductory Episode of 1:14—8:30)	43
Part Constituent 1:16—3:6 (Act I of Part I 1:14—8:30)	44
Act Constituent 1:16–20 (Episode of 1:16—3:6)	45
Act Constituent 1:21–45 (Scene of 1:16—3:6)	47
Act Constituent 2:1—3:6 (Scene of 1:16—3:6)	60
Part Constituent 3:7—8:30 (Act II of Part I 1:14—8:30)	77
Act Constituent 3:7–12 (Episode of 3:7—8:30)	78
Act Constituent 3:13—6:29 (Scene of 3:7—8:30)	79
Act Constituent 6:30—8:21 (Scene of 3:7—8:30)	124
Act Constituent 8:22–30 (Scene of 3:7—8:30)	151
Book Constituent 8:31—16:8 (Part II of 1:1—16:8)	154
Part Constituent 8:31—9:29 (Act I of Part II 8:31—16:8)	157
Act Constituent 8:31–33 (Episode of Act I 8:31—9:39)	158
Act Constituent 8:34—9:1 (Episode of Act I 8:31—9:39)	160
Act Constituent 9:2–29 (Scene to Act I: 8:31—9:39)	162
Part Constituent 9:30—10:52 (Act II of Part II 8:31—16:8)	171
Act Constituent 9:30–10:31 (Scene to Act II 9:30—10:52)	172
Act Constituent 10:32–52 (Scene to Act II 9:30—10:52)	189
Part Constituent 11:1—13:37 (Act III of Part II 8:31—16:8)	195
Act Constituent 11:1—12:12 (Scene of 11:1—13:37)	196
Act Constituent 12:13–44 (Scene of 11:1—13:37)	212
Act Constituent 13:1–37 (Scene of 11:1—13:37)	225
Part Constituent 14:1—16:8 (Act IV of Part II 8:31—16:8)	236
Act Constituent 14:1–31 (Scene of 14:1—16:8)	237
Act Constituent 14:32—15:41 (Scene of 14:1—16:8)	248
Act Constituent 15:42–47 (Episode of 14:1—16:8)	275
Act Constituent 16:1–8 (Episode of 14:1—16:8)	277

Book Constituent 16:9–20 (Part III: Conclusion of the Book 1:1—16:20).....................279
References..283

FOREWORD

My first involvement with Semantic and Structural Analyses (SSAs) was in 1973. SIL's International Translation Coordinator, John Beekman, called a number of us to Dallas from various parts of the world. We divided up the book of Colossians, and four teams of two each spent two weeks to work out an analysis of one chapter. Then, on the third week, we each shared our results with the others, and critiqued each other's work.

In 1979–1980, on a home leave from our work in Papua New Guinea, I worked on an SSA of Mark. I completed a draft of the propositionalization (i.e., the translation from the Greek) and three chapters of the relational structure, but no notes.

In 1989, I started work on the SSA of Romans. It was published in 1999. Then I started work on the SSA of Hebrews. It was sent off for publication in 2016.

John Banker was the chief editor for the SSAs until his death. After he died, at my suggestion, John Tuggy was appointed the chief editor for the series. He and I have worked closely together on this SSA. I have done the propositionalization, and all the notes, and he has done much of the relational structure, and written material on units larger than a paragraph.

It is my sincere hope and prayer that this work will be a great help to translators around the world. Any comments or suggestions can be sent to me: ew_deibler@sil.org.

Ellis W. Deibler, Jr.

ABBREVIATIONS IN THE DISPLAYS

[ANT]	anthropomorphism
[DOU]	doublet
[EUP]	euphemism
[HYP]	hyperbole
[IDI]	idiom
[IRO]	irony
[LIT]	litotes
[MET]	metaphor
[MTY]	metonymy
[RHQ]	rhetorical question
[SYN]	synecdoche
(desc)	descriptive
(emot)	emotive
(expo)	expository
(hort)	hortatory
(inc)	inclusive
(proc)	procedural
{MNG}	concept of the divine familial term in the context for comprehension checking

ABBREVIATIONS IN THE TEXT

20th Century	20th Century Bible
BAGD	Bauer, Arndt, Gingrich, and Danker
CEV	Contemporary English Version
EGT	Expositor's Greek Testament
GNT	Greek New Testament: UBS 4th Edition
GW	God's Word
JB	Jerusalem Bible
JBP	J.B. Phillips
KJV	King James Version
L&N	Louw and Nida
LB	Living Bible
NCV	New Century Version
NEB	New English Bible
NET	NET Bible
NIV	New International Version
NLT	New Living Translation
NRSV	New Revised Standard Version
REB	Revised English Bible
RSV	Revised Standard Version
SSA	Semantic and Structural Analysis
TEV	Today's English Version (Good News Bible)
THM	Bratcher & Nida, Translator's Handbook on Mark
TfT	Translation for Translators
TN	Translator's Notes
TR	The True Servant
TRT	Translator's Reference Translation
UBS	United Bible Societies
cf.	compare
ch.	chapter
e.g.	such as
i.e.	that is
p.	page
pp.	pages
v.	verse
vv.	verses

GENERAL INTRODUCTION TO SEMANTIC AND STRUCTURAL ANALYSES

The Semantic and Structural Analysis (SSA) series is designed to assist Bible translators and Bible translation consultants. Due to the careful attention to meaning at all levels of the discourse, they should also be useful for Bible scholars, teachers, preachers, and anyone interested in a thorough understanding of the biblical text. The analysis is firmly based on discourse linguistics and assumes that each New Testament book is an integrated whole. The analytical process involves detailed study of the grammar, lexicon and discourse structure of the Greek, with the aim of clearly presenting the meaning of the text and the linguistic evidence on which the meaning is established.

THEORETICAL BASIS

The theoretical basis of these studies is Beekman, Callow and Kopesec's theory of discourse analysis, presented in *The Semantic Structure of Written Communication* (1981) and further developed by Kathleen Callow in *Man and Message* (1998). However, other theoretical approaches have not been ignored. A large body of biblical scholarship has been considered, and some of the weaknesses in their works have been supplemented.

This work is called *A Semantic and Structural Analysis* because its primary interest is the organized meaning of the text. The aim is to present, as far as possible, the organization and meaning that the biblical author intended his audience to understand. The text is approached with several underlying assumptions about language as a communicative medium:

1. The writer used written language signals in his attempt to communicate meaning, emotion, and social relations to his readers.
2. The writer assumed a vast body of shared information with his audience, such as language, culture, world-view, social relations, socio-political circumstance, specific circumstances, and time of the writing. Beekman, Callow, and Kopesec call this the "communication situation".
3. The writer's own intended purpose and communication meaning were prior to and have priority over the written surface forms, but today our main access to the biblical writer's purpose and meaning is through the written text.
4. Communicated meaning consists of units of meaning logically related to other units of meaning.
5. Some meaning units are nuclear, or central, while others are satellitic or supportive to these nuclear units. These bundles of meaning are also bundled together within other, larger units of meaning. In other words, meaning units are organized hierarchically in a discourse, giving rise to the "natural prominence" of the units (so Beekman, Callow, and Kopesec).
6. The ways in which units are related to each other, that is, their "communication relations", are relatively few. These relationships are basic to human intelligence and makeup, and are used in all languages, whether or not there is a corresponding surface form expressing them. Moreover, even in the same language a specific relation is not always expressed by the same surface form, and conversely, one surface form may be used to express *more* than one semantic relation.
7. When two meaning units are related to each other, each unit in this relationship carries out a "communication role".
8. Every language has certain grammatical and lexical devices which may be used by an author to mark specific meaning units as prominent. This is called "marked prominence".
9. There are limited ways in which communication relations can be arranged so that a whole arrangement is a purposive and complete unit. Such an arrangement forms a communication paragraph, or "paragraph pattern".
10. Each unit has a "theme", that is, a central topic and an argument about that topic, understandable from the prominence structure of the unit. (This is not to be confused with *motif*, which is a prosodic and coherence feature that runs through units of various sizes.)

In order to present the meaning and structure of any written communication, the editors of the SSA series have developed their own metalanguage and diagramming devices, which are explained in what follows.

COMMUNICATION RELATIONS AND PARAGRAPH PATTERNS

Semantic relationships between propositions, "communication relations", are the basic joining elements at all levels of a discourse. "Paragraph patterns" are made up of these relations with the additional elements of purposiveness and completeness. (An explanation of the total array of semantic relations between propositions is available in Beekman, Callow, and Kopesec, also in 'A guide to the Semantic and Structural Analysis Series: theory and practice'.)

Of the two charts that follow, the first shows the paragraph patterns used in this analysis, and the second shows the communication relations and unit roles. Most of the terms in the charts are self-explanatory, but for further explanations see Tuggy (1992) and Beekman, Callow, and Kopesec (1981).

In the chart of communication roles, the relations are given in the usual order in which they are found in the Greek of the New Testament, e.g., reason–RESULT. Where there is no natural prominence on one part (i.e., where there is only *contextual* prominence), both relations are shown in lowercase letters, e.g., generic-specific.

		SOLUTIONALITY	CAUSALITY	VOLITIONALITY
I D E A S	EXPOSITORY −sequence	+problem(expo) +SOLUTION ±evidence^n ±(complication +SOLUTION)	+cause^n +EFFECT or +major +minor +INFERENCE or +evidence^n +INFERENCE^n or +application^n +PRINCIPLE	+justification^n +CLAIM
	NARRATIVE +sequence	+problem +RESOLUTION ±resolving incident^n ±(complication +RESOLUTION)	+occasion +OUTCOME	+step^n +GOAL
E M O T I O N S	EXPRESSIVE −sequence	+problem(emot) +SOLUTION ±seeking ±(complication +SOLUTION)	+situation^n +REACTION ±belief	+belief^n +CONTROL
	DESCRIPTIVE +sequence	+problem(desc) +SOLUTION ±experience^n ±(complication +SOLUTION)	+situation^n +REACTION	+description^n +DECLARATION
B E H A V I O U R	HORTATORY −sequence	+problem(hort) +APPEAL ±evidence^n ±(complication +SOLUTION)	+basis^n +APPEAL or +APPEAL +application^n	+motivation +ENABLEMENT^n or +motivation^n +ENABLEMENT
	PROCEDURAL +sequence	+problem(proc) +SOLUTION ±step^n ±(complication +SOLUTION)	+APPEAL +outcome^n	+STEP^n +accomplishment

STRUCTURAL FORMS OF PARAGRAPH PATTERN IN VARIOUS DISCOURSE TYPES

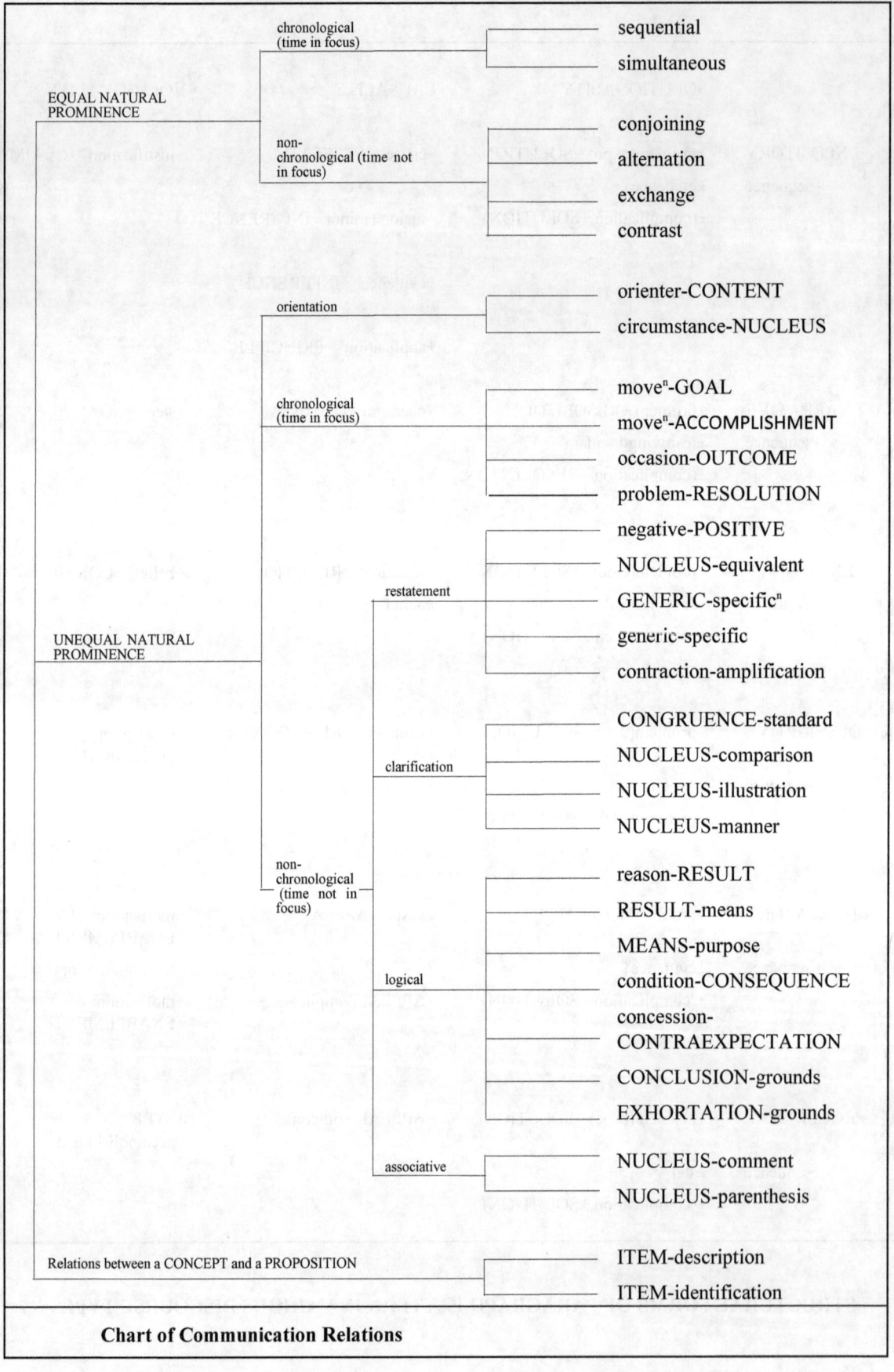

Chart of Communication Relations

THE FORMAT OF AN SSA

Following the General Introduction and a specific introduction to the book being studied, the main part of each Semantic and Structural Analysis (SSA) consists of displays and discussions of the semantic units which comprise the book. The displays are a translation of the Greek text plus a chart of the relations between those propositions. All units are considered, from the macrostructure or overall structure of the book, through the intermediate level structures such as parts and sections, down to the semantic paragraphs. Within each semantic paragraph smaller units are discussed, such as concepts, which relate to each other to form propositions (the basic units of meaning) and the relationship of the propositions to one another.

Each semantic unit, whether semantic paragraph or something larger, is presented in the following order: (1) a display of the unit, (2) an explanation of the structure of the unit and a statement of how the original author intended to affect his audience by it, (3) exegetical notes about specific words and phrases as presented in the display, and (4) arguments supporting the analysis of the unit under discussion as a whole.

THE DISPLAY OF THE UNIT

The display is a schematic representation of the structure of the meaning of the unit. It contains a number of elements, as detailed in the following example (from the SSA of the Gospel of John – not published):

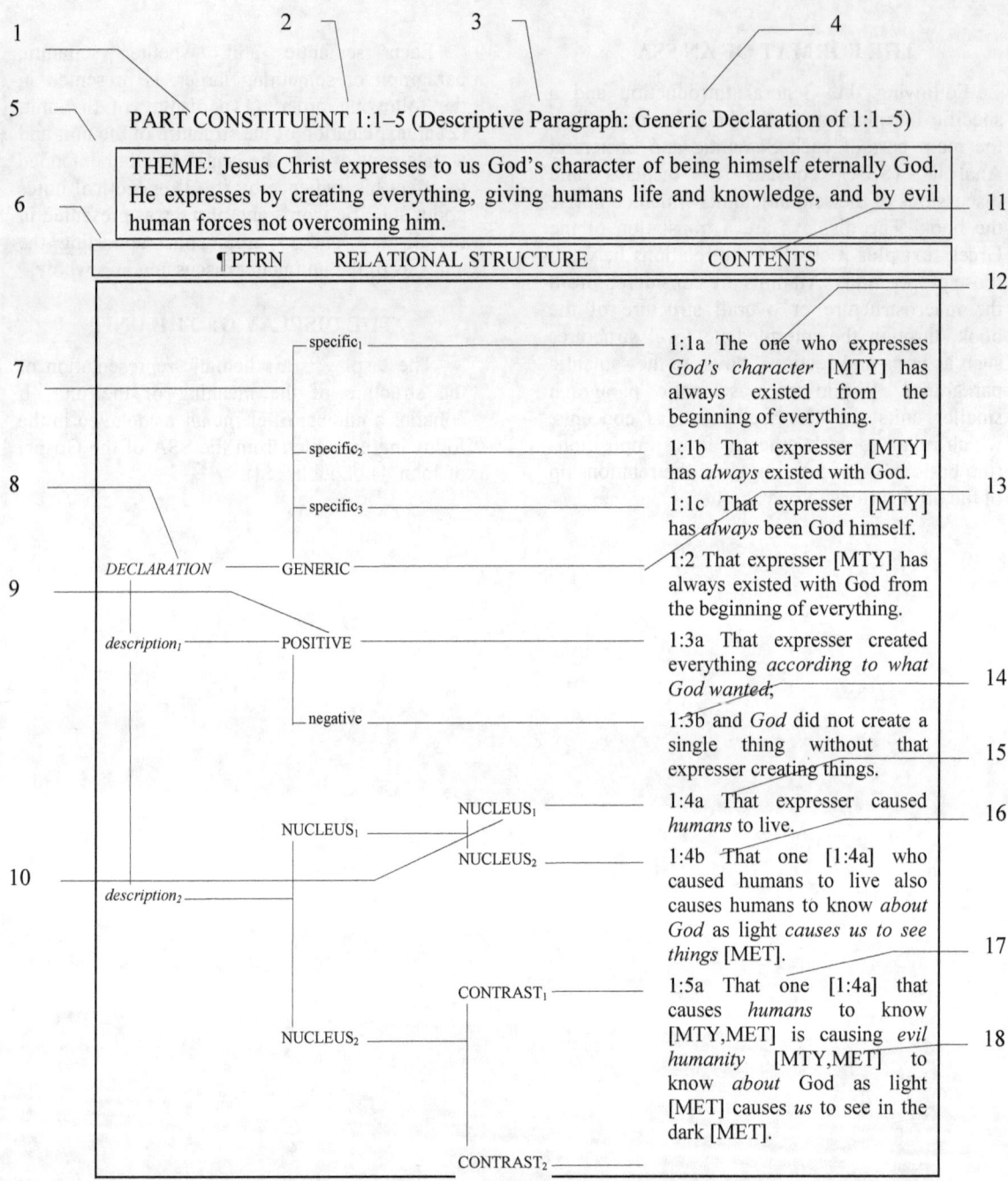

Key:

1. 'Part Constituent' shows that the unit goes together with some other similar unit(s) to form a 'Part'; i.e., it gives the broader context of the unit.

2. '1:1–5' defines the specific text span of the unit.

3. 'Descriptive Paragraph' shows that the author was describing something with the intent of affecting the emotions of his audience (see the chart of Structural Forms of Paragraph Pattern, above) within the specific semantic level of this unit, which here is a semantic paragraph.

4. 'Generic Declaration of 1:1–5' states that the unit functions as a generic declaration within the larger context of the text span identified.

5. The second line is a statement of what the unit is all about. The Theme Statement presents the most prominent, or nuclear parts of the unit, stating the topic and what is said about that topic.

6. The middle box contains column headers showing the type of information found below in the body of the display.

The main body of the display is in two main columns: on the left are the internal relations and structure of the unit, and on the right is the message content.

7. The text is assumed to be structured hierarchically, and is therefore displayed with a form of tree diagram showing levels of dependency and branching.

8. The labels farthest to the left show the interdependent highest level units.

9. The next level from the left shows the units that support the highest level units.

10. Each succeeding column shows a lower supportive level and branching of units.

Units with labels in upper-case letters (capitals) are prominent or nuclear. In this particular example, the highest level of interdependent units is a declaration (prominent) with two descriptions supporting the declaration. The declaration is made up of four units, a generic statement with its specifics, as shown by the second level from the left.

It should also be noted that although the vertical lines indicate direct interdependency between units, a dotted vertical line is used to signify a proposition's relationship to those that follow as a group. (This is used mainly for the orienter-content relationship.)

11. The right-hand column of the display, under the title 'CONTENTS', has its own characteristics.

12. This column shows the results of a careful study of the Greek text and its semantic significance. The meaning is stated here in propositions, with verbs in the active voice (as far as possible) and all participants made explicit. The Greek text from which these propositions are derived may be a clause, a phrase, a verb, an abstract noun, or some other grammatical unit.

13. In the example above, the declaration unit is made up of four propositional statements. Each propositional statement is numbered as a part of a verse (1:1a, 1:1b, 1:1c, and 1:2). However, propositions are not numbered separately unless they require separate treatment. Here 1:3a is made up of two separate propositions in one propositional statement.

14. At the beginning of most propositional statements, a conjunction is used to signify its relationship to some other proposition. In 1:3b the negation is a restatement of the previous positive statement, and is therefore given the conjunction 'and'. In 1:5b the contrastive statement is introduced by 'but'.

15. The meaning is expressed unambiguously, e.g., 'we are united to God'. In 1:4b the Greek term 'the life', is expressed as 'the one who caused humans to live'.

16. The referents of pronouns and demonstratives are made explicit. In 1:4b the Greek has 'he' referring back in the text to 1:4a. This is signaled unambiguously in square brackets: 'that one [1:4a]'.

17. Italic words represent implicit information which is judged to have been part of the message which the writer intended and expected to communicate. The exegetical notes give justifications for the inclusion of this information in the meaning of the message.

18. Abbreviations in square brackets indicate where a figure of speech (e.g., [MTY] = metonymy, [MET] = metaphor) was used in the Greek.

In addition, words in bold face indicate focal words or phrases in the Greek that cannot be appropriately reflected in the grammar of written English.

THE STATEMENT OF THE AUTHOR'S INTENT

Following the display is a section entitled 'Intent and Macrostructure' or 'Intent and rhetorical structure'. It deals with discourse type: how the biblical author intended the unit to affect his audience (in terms of the chart of Structural Forms of Paragraph Pattern, above). Where there are alternative ways of interpreting the author's intent, the reasons for the preferred analysis are given. Also, the unit's structure is discussed in terms of the author's strategy for accomplishing the intended effect on the audience.

THE EXEGETICAL NOTES

The section entitled 'Notes' contains comments on words and phrases from the display. Most of the notes consider the Greek text and its meaning, stating different opinions found in the commentaries and reasons for choices made in the analysis. In particular, discussion is focused on relationship with other units, prominence, purpose, meaning, plus historical and cultural matters required for understanding the text, implicit information, and translational problems.

THE EVIDENCE FOR THE ANALYSIS OF THE UNIT

The Notes are followed by two sections that present the textual and semantic evidence for the analysis of the unit.

In the section entitled 'Boundaries and Coherence' argumentation is given for the analysis of the beginning and ending points of the unit. In view of the wide variation in ways that commentaries and translations divide the material of biblical books into smaller units (sections, paragraphs, etc.) it is important to consider the linguistic evidence provided by discourse study of the Greek text. For each unit there need to be not only convincing indicators of its boundaries but also elements within it showing its coherence.

Under 'Prominence and Theme' the textual and semantic prominence features within the unit are set out. These include both the features of natural prominence, as in the relationships between propositions and sub-units, and the grammatical and lexical devices which are indicators of marked prominence, such as forefronting and emphatic words. In this section there is also an explanation of how these prominence features determine the unit's Theme Statement (as given in the display).

INTRODUCTION TO THE SEMANTIC AND STRUCTURAL ANALYSIS OF MARK

Authorship

Mark does not give his own name anywhere in the New Testament. But this is not surprising; Matthew wrote a gospel in which his name is given but not with a 1st person pronoun. Matthew is obviously one of the participants in the events mentioning 'the apostles', but he never says 'we/us apostles.' The same is true of John; he is obviously referring to himself when he writes 'the disciple whom Jesus loved', but he never gives his name or uses the 1st person pronoun. The same is true of Luke: he never gives his name. The writers of the epistles give their names (except for the author of Hebrews), but not the writers of the Gospels.

Mark's name is given eight times in the New Testament. Twice in Acts (12:12, 12:25) his name is given as 'John, who was surnamed Mark.' This is the same expression used in referring to Peter in Acts 10:32: 'Simon who is surnamed Peter'. In Acts 15:37 Mark is called 'John who is called Mark.' John was his Jewish name; Mark (Markos in Greek) is his Greek name (so Hendriksen). In Colossians 4:10 Mark is referred to as 'Mark the cousin of Barnabas.' The other three times Mark is mentioned (2 Tim. 4:11, Philemon 24, and 1 Peter 5:13) he is simply called 'Mark.'

Although Mark does not give his name as the writer, there is unanimous tradition that he was the author.

There is one other instance where it can be said that Mark is referred to: that is in Mark 14:51-52, in the account of the young man who ran away. The man's name is not given; but many scholars say this was Mark. Why? Because it doesn't make any sense to have it mentioned if it were some other unnamed individual. It does make sense if Mark is referring to himself, somewhat ashamedly, as the one who ran away naked. In this writer's words, 'this is Mark leaving his footprints in his Gospel.'

There are not many clues as to Mark's activities beyond that. In Acts 12:12 the believers were gathered in prayer in the home of Mark's mother. We can assume Mark was there. In Acts 12:25 we read that after Saul and Barnabas had delivered the gifts from the believers in Antioch to the needy believers In Jerusalem, they returned to Antioch, taking Mark with them. In Acts 15 (vv. 36–39) we read that Barnabas wanted to take Mark with them on their next journey, but Paul said 'no,' because Mark had deserted them in Pamphylia and returned home. Why Mark did this, we do not know. Was it because of concerns about his family? Was it from homesickness? Was it from weariness, or apprehension about the work that lay before them? We do not know. So they split; Mark went with Barnabas, and Silas went with Paul. But it is clear that subsequently Paul and Mark were reconciled, for at the end of Paul's ministry (2 Tim. 4:11) he asked Timothy to come and bring Mark with him, 'because he will be helpful to me in my ministry.' It seems that Mark was with Paul while Paul was in prison in Rome (Col. 4:10), but it is not stated that Mark was also in prison; more likely it meant that he was in Rome, carrying on a ministry there, but able to visit and encourage Paul. This was most likely during the years 61–63.

Circumstances of Composition

Many of the early church fathers testify that Mark's gospel was written in Rome. Peter was also there. And it seems that during that period, Mark spent considerable time with Peter, and from Peter he got all the information he needed to write the Gospel. Origen says that Mark wrote the Gospel "in accordance with Peter's instructions." Clement of Alexandria says "The occasion for writing the Gospel according to Mark was: After Peter had preached the word in Rome and by the Spirit had proclaimed the gospel, those present, being many, urged Mark, as one who had followed him for a long time and remembered what he had spoken, to write down what he had said. He did this and distributed the Gospel among those who had asked him [for it]. When Peter learned about it, he neither strongly forbade it nor promoted it." Tertullian wrote, "The Gospel which Mark published may be affirmed to be Peter's whose interpreter Mark was." Irenaeus wrote, "Mark, the disciple and interpreter of Peter, himself also handed down to us in writing what had been preached by Peter." Papias, writing about 95–110, said "Mark became Peter's interpreter and wrote down accurately, but not in order, all that he remembered of the things said and done by the Lord… Peter used to teach as the occasion demanded, without giving systematic arrangement to the Lord's sayings, so that Mark did not err in writing down some things just as he recalled them."

Date of Composition

There is no consensus among scholars as to the date in which Mark's Gospel was written. Three possibilities have been suggested: 1) In the mid 50s to early 60s, 2) mid 60s, 3) late 60s or early70s. We will try to summarize the evidence for each:

1) The early date. As noted above, Clement said that Mark wrote his Gospel while Peter was still preaching in Rome. This would mean it was written no later than the early 60s. Peter was martyred probably in 64 AD, so it could have been written before that time. However, granted that Mark got his information about the life of Christ from Peter, that doesn't prove the book was written before Peter's death.

2) The middle date. Two early writers claimed that Mark's Gospel was written after Peter's death. So the suggestion is that the gospel was written shortly after the persecution of Christians by Nero in 64 A.D., to encourage believers to maintain their faith. But there is no evidence from the Gospel itself that such was its purpose.

3) The late date. Most scholars suggest Mark wrote in the late 60s or early 70s, close to the time of the destruction of Jerusalem. Support for this date is an interpretation of Mark 13:14, 'Let the reader understand', which is the writer's interjection in the middle of Jesus' predictions of the coming persecution. It is suggested that this is Mark's warning that the destruction of Jerusalem was imminent, and his suspicion that attacks on believers in Rome would quickly follow.

The Intended Audience

Strauss (p. 32) says that since the middle of last century, "it has been assumed that each of the Gospels was written within a specific first-century church community to address the specific needs and concerns of that community." So it is presumed that Mark's Gospel was written in Rome for the church in Rome. That is still the majority view among biblical scholars. But more recently some scholars have suggested that the Gospels were written for the church at large. Since it is clear that Matthew and Luke used Mark for some of their material, it shows that Mark's Gospel must have been widely circulated. But even if it was thus circulated, it does not prove that such was Mark's primary motivation. One bit of evidence that his Gospel was intended for local believers may be in the fact that it has no author's name. The author was so well known that no name was needed. But more telling evidence is the occurrence of the names Rufus and Alexander (15:21) in such a way that it is apparent that the readers in Rome knew them. However, it is also true that the Gospel writers hoped that their writings would be copied and probably widely circulated.

Mark's Purpose

Biblical scholars have proposed a variety of purposes that Mark had in mind. Hendriksen says that "according to tradition, this Gospel was composed to satisfy the urgent request of the people of Rome for a written summary of Peter's preaching in that city." And there seems to be no good reason to try to come up with a better motivation. Strauss (and others) has given a wide variety of purposes for the book suggested by various biblical scholars. But then he says "Mark likely had a variety of purposes in writing, and it is more profitable to seek his general theological goals rather than a single or specific occasion or crisis in the church."

Some of Mark's Special Interests

In Bible commentaries, often times 'themes' or 'motifs' are mentioned. These are topics of special interest to the author that he keeps alluding to in the text. Mark has a few topics of interest which commentaries mention. Edwards in the introduction, has a section about 'Themes'. A section is presented with each of the following: *discipleship, faith, insiders & outsiders, gentiles, command to silence, journey, following Jesus*. Donahue & Harrington:27ff., and France:31 also detail many motifs or themes.

There are many motifs throughout the book and in certain concentrated areas which demonstrate how Mark intended to affect his audience. Motifs are concepts that are woven through the writing and appear at certain places in the book, giving marked prominence to that unit. The motifs that this study has observed are as follows:

- Jesus' hidden identity (1:25, 1:34, 3:11–12, 4:41, 5:43, 7:36–37, 8:29–30, 12:35–37, 16:8)

- Jesus spoke with authority (1:22, 1:27, 2:9–12, 3:13–15, 4:29–41, 6:7, 6:51–52, 11:27–29)
- Casting out demons (1:26, 1:34, 1:39, 3:15, 3:22, 6:13, 9:28)
- People were astonished (1:27, 4:41, 6:51, 10:24–26, 12:17)
- Jesus used his hands to heal (1:31, 5:41, 6:5, 8:22–23, 9:27)
- Jesus praying or teaching on praying 1:35, 6:46, 9:29, 11:17, 11:24, 11:25, 12:40 13:18, 14:32–39)
- Powerful effect of believing God/Jesus (2:5, 4:40, 5:34, 36, 7:28–30, 9:19–24, 10:48–52, 11:22–24)
- Only God/Jesus can save (2:5–12, 10:23–27, 14:36)
- Jesus is creating a new order 2:19–22, 7:5–23, 9:2–8, 10:41–45, 12:38–44, 14:22–25)
- People rejected Jesus and caused him to suffer (3:6, 6:6, 8:31–33, 9:9–13, 10:32–34, 10:35–40, 12:1–12, 14:63–65, 15:1–5, 15:6–15, 15:16–20, 15:21–47)
- Total commitment to Jesus (8:34–38, 10:21, 10:28–31, 10:32–37, 13:9–13, 38)
- Judas betrayed Jesus (3:19, 14:10–11, 14:17–21, 14:41–42, 14:43–50)

The Structure of Mark

Many commentators think of the Gospel of Mark as his reminiscences of Peter's teachings and the recounting of his experiences with Jesus. The idea is that Mark had accumulated bits and pieces of Jesus' life and just strung them together 'like beads on a string'.

While working on this project, it quickly became apparent that there were two halves in the book: one dealing with Jesus' ministry in and around Galilee, and the other with his ministry in Judea. No other Gospel has a dichotomy of this sort. Then it became apparent that the episodes were lumped together by some common topic, thus producing further groupings.

I trust that you will be convinced by the evidences set forth that the structure of Mark is indeed complex and has a message to present. This has all been presented in the analysis of the book that is given below.

As Wallis aptly stated, "Was Mark an epic poet? ... The author is doing more than 'threading pearls on string;' he is creating an exquisitely designed necklace. The crown jewel of Mark's literary creation is the deity of Jesus."

Thematic outline of Mark

THE GOSPEL OF MARK 1:1—16:8
THEME: Mark's account of the teaching and miracles of Jesus, leading up to his death and resurrection.

BOOK CONSTITUENT 1:1 (Book Title of 1:1—16:8)
Theme: This is the good message about Jesus the Messiah, the Son of God. It begins like this:

BOOK CONSTITUENT 1:2–13 (Beginning of the Book 1:1—16:8)
THEME: The good message about Jesus the Messiah begins when John the Baptizer appeared to announce Jesus' arrival, and when God audibly said that Jesus was his beloved Son when John baptized him.

    PART CONSTITUENT 1:2–8 (Declarative Paragraph of 1:2–13)
    THEME: After John was arrested, Jesus came and preached the good news which came from God.

    PART CONSTITUENT 1:9–13 (Episode of 1:2–13)
    THEME After Jesus was baptized by John, God showed him to be His Son by the Holy Spirit descending upon him; by Himself, God the Father, declaring it; by Satan testing him; and by the angels taking care of him.

BOOK CONSTITUENT 1:14—8:30 (Part I of 1:1—16:8)
THEME: By Jesus claiming to have the authority to establish a new order over the religious rituals teaching and healing in and around Galilee district, he was leading his disciples to answer his question, 'Who do you say I am?

    PART CONSTITUENT 1:14–15 (Introductory Episode of 1:14—8:30)
    THEME: After John was arrested, Jesus came and preached the good news which came from God.

    PART CONSTITUENT 1:16—3:6 (Act I of Part I 1:14—8:30)
    THEME: Jesus demonstrated his power and authority by summoning some followers, healing many sick people, and establishing a new order over the religious rituals fostered by the Pharisees which led to the religious authorities planning to kill Jesus.

        ACT CONSTITUENT 1:16–20 (Episode of 1:16—3:6)
        THEME: Jesus summoned four fishermen and they immediately went with him.

        ACT CONSTITUENT 1:21–45 (Scene of 1:16—3:6)
        THEME: Jesus demonstrated who he is by healing many sick people and people with evil spirits.

            SCENE CONSTITUENT 1:21–28 (Episode of 1:21–45)
            THEME: People were amazed at Jesus' teaching and also as a result of him expelling a demon.

            SCENE CONSTITUENT 1:29–31 (Episode of 1:21–45)
            THEME: Jesus healed Simon's mother-in-law.

            THEME: Jesus healed many people and expelled many evil spirits.

            SCENE CONSTITUENT 1:35–45 (Episode Cluster of 1:21–45)
            THEME: Jesus continued his ministry by telling God's message, expelling evil spirits, and curing a leper.

                EPISODE CLUSTER CONSTITUENT 1:35–39 (Episode of 1:35–45)
                THEME: Jesus traveled throughout Galilee, telling God's message and expelling evil spirits from people.

                EPISODE CLUSTER CONSTITUENT 1:40–45 (Episode of 1:35–45)
                THEME: After a leper pleaded with Jesus to cure him, Jesus cured him and arranged for him to be able to associate with people again.

        ACT CONSTITUENT 2:1—3:6 (Scene of 1:16—3:6)
        THEME: Jesus had some sharp discussions with the religious authorities about his authority over religious practices, culminating in the authorities planning to kill him.

SCENE CONSTITUENT 2:1–12 (Episode of 2:1—3:6)
THEME: While Jesus was teaching in a crowded house, men brought a paralyzed man to be healed, and Jesus demonstrated his authority to forgive sins by healing the man.

SCENE CONSTITUENT 2:13–17 (Episode Cluster of 2:1—3:6)
THEME: Jesus invited Levi to come with him as his disciple.

   EPISODE CLUSTER CONSTITUENT 2:13–14 (Episode of 2:13–17)
   THEME: Jesus invited Levi to come with him as his disciple.

   EPISODE CLUSTER CONSTITUENT 2:15–17 (Episode of 2:13–17)
   Theme: Jesus refuted those who objected to his associating with people like Levi.

SCENE CONSTITUENT 2:18–22 (Episode of 2:1—3:6)
THEME: John's disciples and others came to Jesus with a question about fasting and he answered them with parables.

SCENE CONSTITUENT 2:23–28 (Episode of 2:1—3:6)
THEME: When the Pharisees complained about Jesus' disciples plucking grain on the Sabbath day, Jesus replied that he is able to determine what people should do on the Sabbath.

SCENE CONSTITUENT 3:1–6 (Episode of 2:1—3:6)
After Jesus healed a man on the Sabbath, the Jewish leaders began to plan to kill him.

PART CONSTITUENT 3:7—8:30 (Act II of Part I 1:14—8:30)
THEME: By Jesus appointing his disciples to teach and heal people in and around Galilee district, he was leading his disciples to answer his question, 'Who am I?'

ACT CONSTITUENT 3:7–12 (Episode of 3:7—8:30)
THEME: Many people crowded around Jesus in order to touch him because he had healed many. Because of the crowd he got into a boat and taught from it.

ACT CONSTITUENT 3:13—6:29 (Scene of 3:7—8:30)
THEME: Jesus appointed his twelve apostles and involved them in his ministry throughout Galilee, where he became so popular that even King Herod began questioning who Jesus was.

SCENE CONSTITUENT 3:13–19 (Episode of 3:13—6:29)
THEME: Jesus appointed twelve apostles.

SCENE CONSTITUENT 3:20—4:34 (Episode Cluster of 3:13—6:29)
THEME: Although Jesus' family and/or others thought he had gone insane, Jesus taught about evil spirits and not speaking against the Holy Spirit, and several parables about how God's rule increases.

   EPISODE CLUSTER CONSTITUENT 3:20–35 (Episode of 3:20—4:34)
   THEME. Jesus told them that those who obey God are as dear to him as his close relatives.

   EPISODE CLUSTER CONSTITUENT 4:1–34 (Episode of 3:20—4:34)
   THEME: Jesus taught the crowds four parables about the various ways that people who hear his message react. He constantly used parables when he taught people.

SCENE CONSTITUENT 4:35—5:43 (Episode Cluster of 3:13—6:29)
THEME: Jesus performed various miracles in the Galilee region, from calming a storm to bringing a young girl back to life.

   EPISODE CLUSTER CONSTITUENT 4:35–41 (Episode of 4:35—5:43)
   THEME: Jesus and his disciples crossed the sea in a boat and, while Jesus slept, a storm arose, so the disciples woke him, and he calmed the storm, causing the disciples to be awestruck.

   EPISODE CLUSTER CONSTITUENT 5:1–20 (Episode of 4:35—5:43)
   THEME: Jesus expelled evil spirits from a Gerasene man and then allowed them to go into a herd of pigs which then ran down a hill and all drowned. As a result the local people asked Jesus to leave the area.

EPISODE CLUSTER CONSTITUENT 5:21–43 (Episode of 4:35—5:43)
THEME: Jesus healed a woman who had been suffering from hemorrhaging, and caused Jairus' daughter to live again.

SCENE CONSTITUENT 6:1–29 (Episode Cluster of 3:13—6:29)
THEME: Jesus' identity is brought to the foreground. The people of Nazareth town were offended by what he was teaching, he also sent out his disciples two by two, and Herod thought that Jesus was John come to life, whom he had beheaded.

EPISODE CLUSTER CONSTITUENT 6:1–6a (Episode of 6:1–29)
THEME: Jesus taught in the synagogue, and the people who heard him were astonished and offended.

EPISODE CLUSTER CONSTITUENT 6:6b–13 (Episode of 6:1–29)
THEME: Jesus began to send out his disciples two-by-two and gave them power and instructions.

EPISODE CLUSTER CONSTITUENT 6:14–29 (Expository Paragraph of 6:1–29)
THEME: King Herod heard about Jesus and mistakenly thought that John the Baptizer had come back to life after he had had John executed due to the insistence of his wife, Herodias.

ACT CONSTITUENT 6:30—8:21 (Scene of 3:7—8:30)
THEME: While Jesus was traveling outside of Galilee and Judea, he taught his disciples that he was powerful by what he did and by accepting persons whom the disciples considered unclean.

SCENE CONSTITUENT 6:30–34 (Episode of 6:30—8:21)
THEME: The apostles returned to Jesus to report what they had done. Then they all went off to a lonely place, but many people followed them. When they arrived, there was a crowd, and Jesus pitied them and began to teach them.

SCENE CONSTITUENT 6:35—8:10 (Episode Cluster of 6:30—8:21)
THEME: By Jesus performing miracles and teaching about what is or is not acceptable to God, he taught his disciples that the non-Jewish people were also to hear the good news about God's rule.

SCENE CONSTITUENT 8:11–21 (Episode Cluster of 6:30—8:21)
THEME: After the Jewish authorities demanded that Jesus perform a sign that would prove that God had sent him, and he refused to do so, Jesus taught his disciples to not imitate the authorities' bad influence of questioning what God was doing.

EPISODE CLUSTER CONSTITUENT 8:11–12 (Episode of 8:11–21)
THEME: Some Pharisees demanded that Jesus perform something that would demonstrate that God sent him. Jesus refused to do so.

EPISODE CLUSTER CONSTITUENT 8:13–21 (Episode of 8:11–21)
Theme: Jesus warned the disciples of the evil influence of the Pharisees and King Herod, and rebuked them when they worried about not having enough food with them.

ACT CONSTITUENT 8:22–30 (Scene of 3:7—8:30)
THEME: The episode of Jesus healing a blind man in stages is an analogy of how Jesus' disciples understood in stages that he was as the promised Messiah.

SCENE CONSTITUENT 8:22–26 (Episode of 8:22–30)
THEME: Jesus healed a blind man – in stages.

SCENE CONSTITUENT 8:27–30 (Episode of 8:22–30)
THEME: Jesus asked his disciples what people were saying about him and, then, what the disciples thought about him, and Peter replied that Jesus was the Messiah.

BOOK CONSTITUENT 8:31—16:8 (Part II of 1:1—16:8)

THEME: Jesus taught his disciples that he would go to Jerusalem to suffer and die, but his disciples thought all along that he would go to Jerusalem to reign as the Messiah king, liberating them from Roman rule.

PART CONSTITUENT 8:31—9:29 (Act I of Part II 8:31—16:8)

THEME: Jesus instructs his disciples about his death and resurrection, and their need to suffer for him in order to see his glorious rule.

ACT CONSTITUENT 8:31–33 (Episode of Act I 8:31—9:39)

THEME: Jesus rebuked Peter for objecting when Jesus spoke plainly to his disciples about his coming death and resurrection.

ACT CONSTITUENT 8:34—9:1 (Episode of Act I 8:31—9:39)

THEME: Jesus explained to the crowd and his disciples what is required of someone who wants to be Jesus' disciple.

ACT CONSTITUENT 9:2–29 (Scene to Act I: 8:31—9:39)

THEME: Jesus took three disciples to a high mountain to show them his glory, and later told them that he must be evilly treated. He also showed them that evil spirits can only be expelled through much prayer.

SCENE CONSTITUENT 9:2–8 (Episode of 9:2–29)

THEME: Jesus took Peter, James and John up a high mountain where his appearance became different, and Moses and Elijah appeared and talked to Jesus.

SCENE CONSTITUENT 9:9–13 (Episode of 9:2–29)

Theme: Jesus told them that the one like Elijah had come and had been evilly treated, and that the Messiah would also be evilly treated.

SCENE CONSTITUENT 9:14–29 (Episode of 9:2–29)

THEME: When Jesus and the three disciples returned to the other disciples, they saw a large crowd and some teachers of the Jewish laws arguing with them. A man spoke out that he had brought his son to be healed but the disciples were not able to do it; Jesus expelled the evil spirit and later explained to the disciples why they had failed to do so.

PART CONSTITUENT 9:30—10:52 (Act II of Part II 8:31—16:8)

THEME: On their way to Jerusalem, Jesus taught his disciples that he must die and become alive again; but even so, they thought he was going to be the ruling king in Jerusalem. So, James and John asked Jesus that they might be the most important in his kingdom.

ACT CONSTITUENT 9:30–10:31 (Scene to Act II 9:30—10:52)

THEME: Jesus taught his disciples various matters about living peaceably under his rule, but primarily that he must suffer, die and become alive again, and that they must be totally committed to him.

SCENE CONSTITUENT 9:30–32 (Episode of 9:30–10:31)

THEME: Jesus was teaching his disciples that he would be handed over to other men, killed and become alive again; but they did not understand what he was saying.

SCENE CONSTITUENT 9:33–37 (Episode of 9:30–10:31)

THEME: When Jesus asked his disciples what they had talked about while they were traveling, they were ashamed to answer. So Jesus taught them by illustration about what kind of person God considers important. He also taught them about who is for them and who against them.

SCENE CONSTITUENT 9:38–50 (Episode of 9:30–10:31)

THEME: Jesus taught his disciples to not reject those who were performing miracles even if they were not accompanying him, to allow fellow believers who are in other groups to function without hindrance, to not cause fellow believers to sin, and to live peaceably with each other.

SCENE CONSTITUENT 10:1–12 (Episode of 9:30–10:31)
THEME: Some Pharisees asked Jesus if the law permitted a man to divorce his wife. Jesus answered and supported his answer from scripture.

SCENE CONSTITUENT 10:13–16 (Episode of 9:30–10:31)
THEME: Jesus became indignant when he saw his disciples scolding people for bringing children for him to bless, because it is people who trust like children who will be part of God's rule .

SCENE CONSTITUENT 10:17–31 (Episode of 9:30–10:31)
THEME: A rich man ran to Jesus to ask what he should do in order to live eternally; After questioning the man, Jesus told him to sell all his possessions, which he refused to do, and the disciples were astonished that Jesus said that the rich had no advantage to be under God's rule.

ACT CONSTITUENT 10:32–52 (Scene to Act II 9:30—10:52)
THEME: Jesus told them what was going to happen to him in Jerusalem. However, James and John asked to be the most important in his ruling kingdom.

SCENE CONSTITUENT 10:32–34 (Episode of 10:32–52)
THEME: As Jesus and his disciples and others were traveling toward Jerusalem, Jesus took the disciples aside and began to tell them again about what was going to happen to him.

SCENE CONSTITUENT 10:35–45 (Episode of 10:32–52)
THEME: James and John requested to sit on the right and left of Jesus when he rules, and Jesus told them what will happen and how they should act.

SCENE CONSTITUENT 10:46–52 (Episode of 10:32–52)
THEME: As Jesus passed by, a blind man called out asking Jesus to have mercy on him; Jesus called for him and healed him.

PART CONSTITUENT 11:1—13:37 (Act III of Part II 8:31—16:8)
THEME: When Jesus entered Jerusalem as Israel's king, he had a final conflict with the Jewish authorities. Then, he foretold what would happen to Jerusalem before he returned later.

ACT CONSTITUENT 11:1—12:12 (Scene of 11:1—13:37)
THEME: Jesus entered Jerusalem as a king, cursed Israel (symbolized by the fig tree), cleansed the temple. The Jewish authorities asked Jesus by what authority he had done these things. When the fig tree that Jesus cursed withered, Jesus taught his disciples to expect God to do what they asked him to do.

SCENE CONSTITUENT 11:1–11 (Episode of 11:1—12:12)
THEME: Jesus sent two disciples to get a young donkey, which they brought to him; then people threw their cloaks on it, and Jesus mounted it and rode to Jerusalem with people shouting praise to him.

SCENE CONSTITUENT 11:12–14 (Episode of 11:1—12:12)
THEME: Jesus cursed the fig tree as a sign of what would happen to the people of Israel.

SCENE CONSTITUENT 11:15–19 (Episode of 11:1—12:12)
THEME: Jesus and his disciples went to the temple in Jerusalem, and there Jesus expelled those who were buying and selling goods in the temple and taught that the temple was to be a place of prayer. These actions angered the priests and teachers of the Jewish laws who, then, looked for a way to kill Jesus.

SCENE CONSTITUENT 11:20–25 (Episode of 11:1—12:12)
THEME: The next day when Jesus and his disciples passed the fig tree that Jesus had cursed, they saw that it had withered. Jesus used this as an illustration for trusting God to answer prayer.

SCENE CONSTITUENT 11:27—12:12 (Episode of 11:1—12:12)
THEME: The chief priests, teachers of the Jewish laws and elders asked Jesus by what authority he was doing these things. He, then, asked them a question which they would not answer; so he did not answer theirs. Instead Jesus accused the Jewish authorities of planning to kill him.

ACT CONSTITUENT 12:13–44 (Scene of 11:1—13:37)
THEME: Jesus had a final conflict with the Jewish authorities, and warned his disciples to not follow the haughty way of these authorities.

EPISODE CLUSTER CONSTITUENT 12:13–17 (EPISODE of 12:13–34)
THEME: The Jewish authorities took an aggressive role, but Jesus cleverly foiled various attempts by the Jewish authorities to trap him into saying something that would incriminate himself.

SCENE CONSTITUENT 12:35–44 (Episode Cluster of 12:13–44)
THEME: Jesus now takes the aggressive role by teaching publicly in the temple. Jesus warned the people and his disciples to avoid the teachers of the Jewish laws' haughty actions. Jesus said that he was more than just King David's descendant. Jesus also taught that God highly values a widow's unnoticed offering rather than the haughty actions of the Jewish authorities.

ACT CONSTITUENT 13:1–37 (Scene of 11:1—13:37)
THEME: Jesus foretold events that will happen to Jerusalem and the temple, and warned his disciples to always believe him and be ready for his return.

SCENE CONSTITUENT 13:1–2 (Episode of 13:1–37)
THEME: Jesus prophesied that the temple would be completely destroyed.

SCENE CONSTITUENT 13:3–37 (Episode of 13:1–37)
THEME: Jesus prophesied about the events that would precede his return, and commanded his disciples to be prepared for his return.

PART CONSTITUENT 14:1—16:8 (Act IV of Part II 8:31—16:8)
THEME: The Jewish authorities and the Roman authorities executed Jesus. He suffered, died, and came back to life again, just as he said he would.

ACT CONSTITUENT 14:1–31 (Scene of 14:1—16:8)
THEME: A woman and the Jewish leaders and Jesus himself foreshadowed his imminent death.

SCENE CONSTITUENT 14:1–11 (Episode Cluster of 14:1–31)
THEME: A woman beautifully symbolized Jesus being buried, while the Jewish authorities plotted with Judas to arrest Jesus without causing a riot.

EPISODE CLUSTER CONSTITUENT 14:1–2 (Episode of 14:1–11)
THEME: The Jewish leaders planned how they could seize Jesus without starting a riot.

EPISODE CLUSTER CONSTITUENT 14:3–9 (Episode of 14:1–11)
THEME: Jesus commended a woman who extravagantly anointed Jesus in anticipation of his death.

EPISODE CLUSTER CONSTITUENT 14:10–11 (Episode of 14:1–11)
THEME: After Judas negotiated with the religious authorities to help them seize Jesus

SCENE CONSTITUENT 14:12–31 (Episode Cluster of 14:1–31)
THEME: Jesus instructed two disciples to prepare the Passover meal. While eating the Passover, Jesus predicted that someone would betray him. He also changed the significance of that meal to be that God now accepts people because of Jesus' dying. Later he predicted that Peter would deny that he knew Jesus.

EPISODE CLUSTER CONSTITUENT 14:12–17 (Episode of 14:12–31)
THEME: Two disciples followed Jesus' instructions and prepared the Passover meal.

EPISODE CLUSTER CONSTITUENT 14:18–26 (Episode of 14:12–31)
Theme: During the Passover meal, Jesus prophesied that one disciple would betray him. He gave his disciples bread and wine which represented his body and blood which would be sacrificed to establish the new agreement with many people.

EPISODE CLUSTER CONSTITUENT 14:27–31 (Episode of 14:12–31)
Theme: Jesus predicted that Peter would deny three times that he knew him.

ACT CONSTITUENT 14:32—15:41 (Scene of 14:1—16:8)
THEME: Jesus enemies, the Jewish authorities and the Roman authorities, arrested Jesus, tried him, and then crucified him.

SCENE CONSTITUENT 14:32–52 (Episode Cluster of 14:32—15:41)
THEME: Jesus' disciples slept while they were supposed to be on guard. Judas came with an armed crowd and arrested Jesus. All the disciples and even Mark ran away.

EPISODE CLUSTER CONSTITUENT 14:32–42 (Episode of 14:32–52)
THEME: While the disciples slept, Jesus prayed that God would spare him from the coming suffering.

EPISODE CLUSTER CONSTITUENT 14:43–49 (Episode of 14:32–52)
THEME: Judas betrayed Jesus, and the armed crowd arrested Jesus.

EPISODE CLUSTER CONSTITUENT 14:50–52 (Episode of 14:32–52)
THEME: Mark ran away.

SCENE CONSTINUENT 14:53—15:20 (Episode Cluster of 14:32—15:41)
THEME: The Jewish authorities had an illegal mock trial of Jesus. Incidentally, Peter denied Jesus just as Jesus said he would. The Roman authority had a trial, but was swayed by the crowd so that he ordered Jesus to be executed. Then the Roman soldiers mocked Jesus as if he were a king.

EPISODE CLUSTER CONSTITUENT 14:53–65 (Episode of 14:53—15:20)
Theme: After witnesses accusing Jesus contradicted each other, Jesus said that he was the Son of God, the Messiah, after which the Jewish leaders decided that Jesus must be executed.

EPISODE CLUSTER CONSTITUENT 14:66–72 (Episode of 14:53—15:20)
THEME: As Jesus predicted, Peter denied three times that he knew Jesus.

EPISODE CLUSTER CONSTITUENT 15:1–5 (Episode of 14:53—15:20)
THEME: In the governor Pilate's presence Jesus refused to answer accusations against him.

EPISODE CLUSTER CONSTITUENT 15:6–15 (Episode of 14:53—15:20)
Theme: At the crowd's insistence (instigated by the Jewish religious authorities), Pilate released a criminal and ordered that Jesus be crucified.

EPISODE CLUSTER CONSTITUENT 15:16–20 (Episode of 14:53—15:20)
THEME: The soldiers ridiculed Jesus as being a king.

SCENE CONSTITUENT 15:21–41 (Episode Cluster of 14:32—15:41)
THEME: After the soldiers crucified Jesus, they gambled for his clothing, other people insulted him, and then Jesus died; the temple curtain split in two, and a Roman officer declared that Jesus was the Son of God.

EPISODE CLUSTER CONSTITUENT 15:21–24 (Episode of 15:21–41)
THEME: After the soldiers crucified Jesus, they gambled for his clothing.

EPISODE CLUSTER CONSTITUENT 15:25–32 (Episode of 15:21–41)
THEME: People passing by, as well as the Jewish leaders and two criminals being crucified with Jesus, insulted him.

EPISODE CLUSTER CONSTITUENT 15:33–41 (Episode of 15:21–41)
THEME: As several women who had accompanied Jesus watched, he died, after which the temple curtain was torn in two, and a Roman officer declared that Jesus was the Son of God.

ACT CONSTITUENT 15:42–47 (Episode of 14:1—16:8)
THEME: Several women watched as Joseph and others buried Jesus' body in a cave after getting permission from Pilate.

ACT CONSTITUENT 16:1–8 (Episode of 14:1—16:8)
THEME: Two days later, several women were astonished to find Jesus' tomb empty, but an angel told them Jesus was alive again.

BOOK CONSTITUENT 16:9–20 (Part III: Conclusion of the Book 1:1—16:20)
THEME: After Jesus arose from being dead on Sunday morning, his disciples did not believe he was alive. So, Jesus rebuked them for not believing and commanded them to preach the good news throughout the world. Jesus then ascended to heaven, and his disciples started telling God's message everywhere.

Constituent structure of Mark

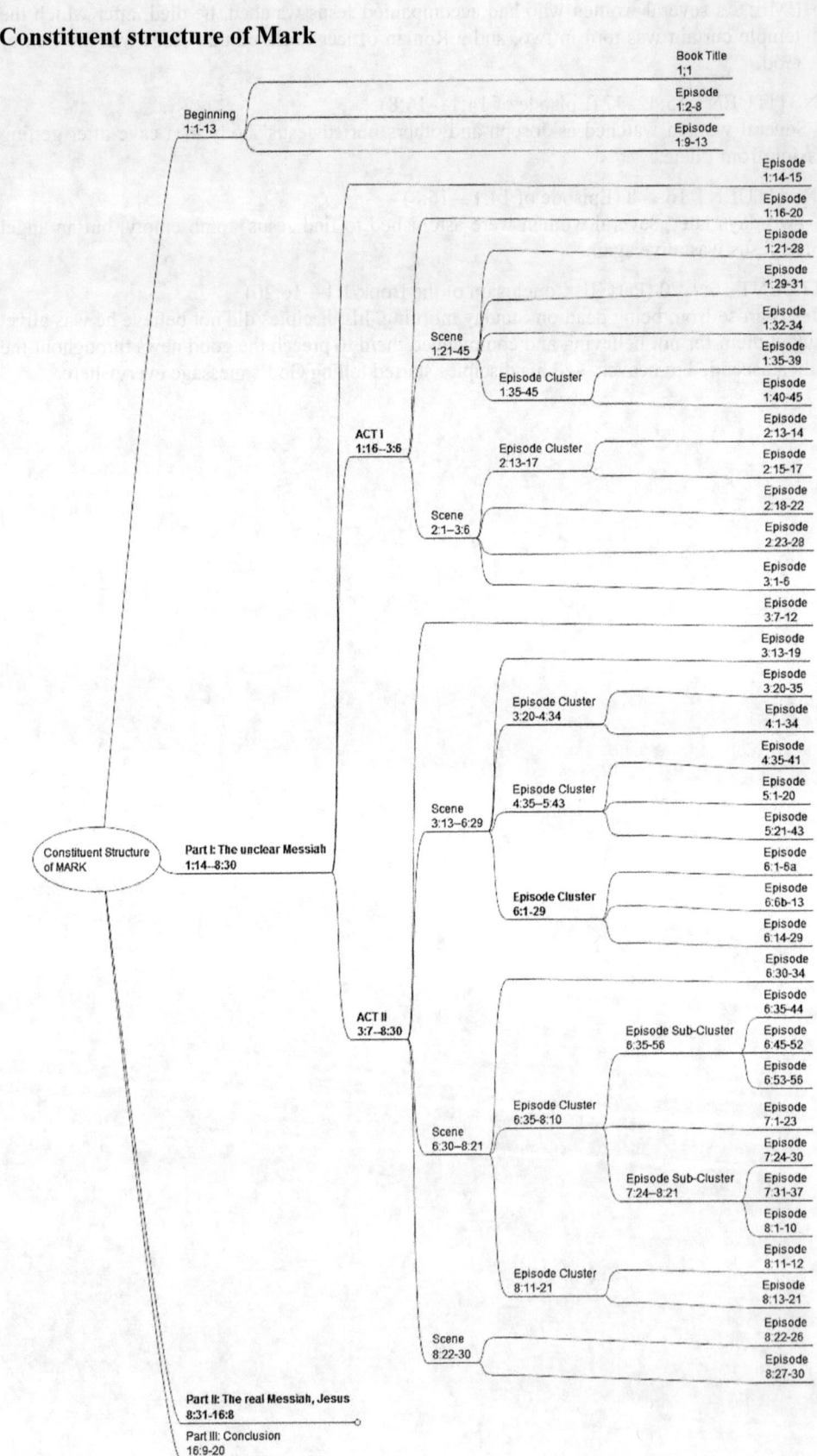

INTRODUCTION TO THE SEMANTIC AND STRUCTURAL ANALYSIS OF MARK

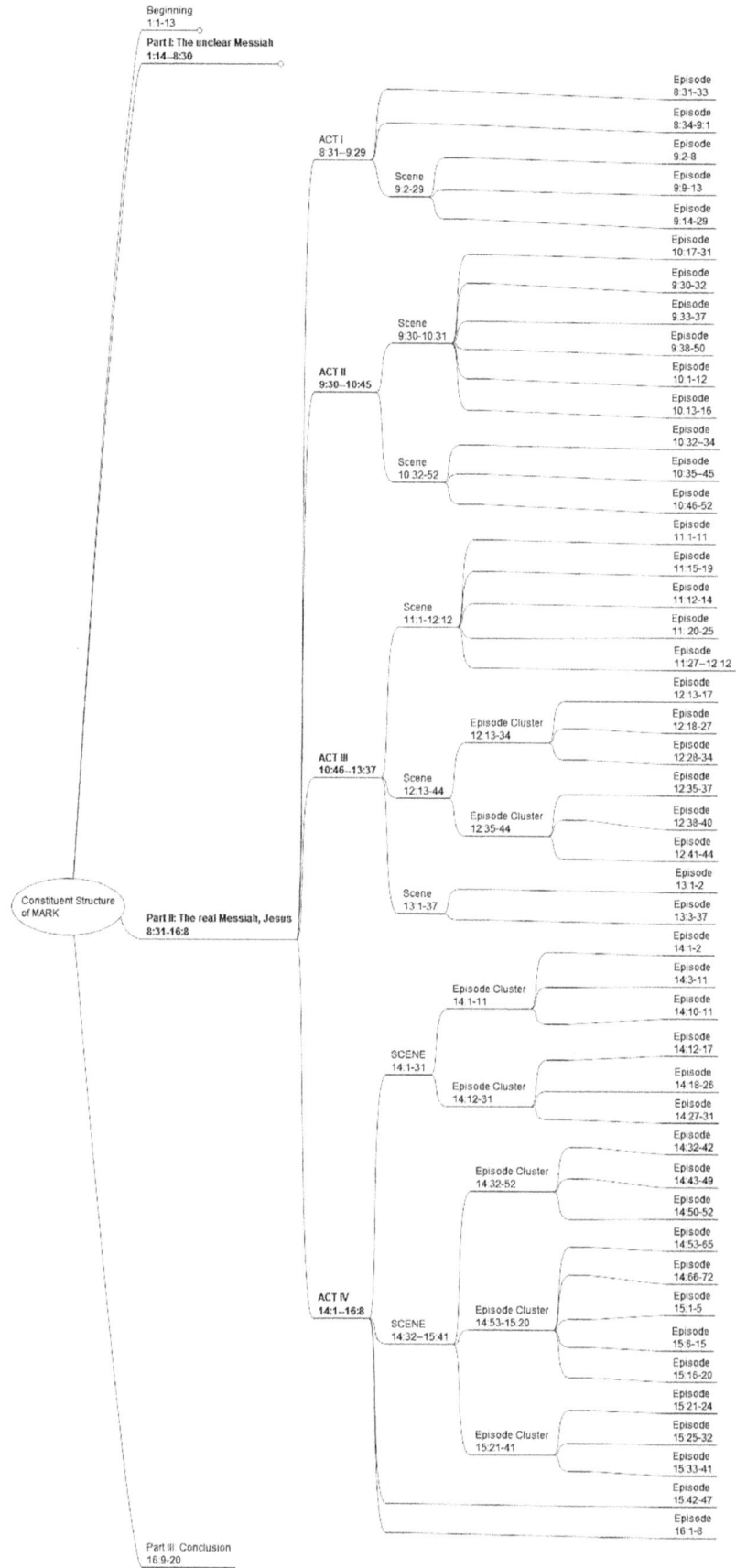

THE GOSPEL OF MARK 1:1—16:8

THEME: Mark's account of the teaching and miracles of Jesus, leading up to his death and resurrection.

MACROSTRUCTURE	CONTENTS
BOOK TITLE	1:1 This is the good message about Jesus the Messiah, the Son of God. It begins like this:
THE BEGINNING	1:2–13 The good message about Jesus the Messiah begins when John the Baptizer appeared to announce Jesus' arrival, and when God audibly said that Jesus was his beloved Son when John baptized him.
PART I	1:14—8:30 By Jesus claiming to have the authority to establish a new order over the religious rituals teaching and healing in and around Galilee district, he was leading his disciples to answer his question, 'Who do you say I am?'
PART II	8:31—16:8 Jesus taught his disciples that he would go to Jerusalem to suffer and die, but his disciples thought all along that he would go to Jerusalem to reign as the Messiah king, liberating them from Roman rule.
PART III THE CONCLUSION	16:9–20 [Not in earliest texts.] After Jesus arose from being dead on Sunday morning, his disciples did not believe he was alive. So, Jesus rebuked them for not believing and commanded them to preach the good news throughout the world. Jesus then ascended to heaven, and his disciples started telling God's message everywhere.

INTENT AND RHETORICAL STRUCTURE

We can only surmise how the author of this book intended to affect the readers by how he structured and put prominence throughout the book. In doing so, there are some significant markers along the way that point to his intent.

Most importantly, we could title the book, "Who is this man Jesus?" Commentators over the ages have consistently observed the "hidden identity" motif throughout the book. Quite unlike the other Gospels, the author does not explicitly repeat that Jesus is the expected Messiah of Israel. Except for the first 13 verses, there are no explicit hints as to who Jesus is. This hidden identity is explicitly expressed by:

1) Two episodes in which Jesus encountered demon-possessed people who declared who Jesus is, but Jesus always silenced them. (See episodes 1:29–31, 3:7–12.)
2) At the turning point of the book, Jesus asked his disciples who people say he is, and then who they believe he is (8:27–30).
3) Introducing the book's turning point, suddenly, without the usual introductory information of an episode, there is the healing of the blind man in stages. This is an analogy about Jesus' identity (Donahue & Harrington p. 258, France p. 322–323, Gundry p. 240 ff., Kopesec, Strauss p. 354–355). First they understand a bit, and then Jesus later causes them to understand more completely who he is.

Note what happens after the above mentioned turning point of the book:
1) The disciples thought Jesus was the great deliverer Messiah which the rest of Israel was expecting.
2) Jesus rebuked Peter for objecting to Jesus' statement that he would suffer and die, and the rest of the book expands on this new identity of Jesus.

The author presents his whole intent by a continuous narrative from 1:14 to the end. As can be observed in the 'Constituent structure of Mark' (p. 28), some commentaries view this book as a string of episodes from beginning to end, without any particular structure. These many episodes could be listed as a series, but some are groups of things Jesus *did*, and others are groups of what Jesus *taught*. So, we cannot simply make a long list of episodes. On the other hand, Wallis considers this book as a complex of two simultaneous chiastic structures ascending from the beginning to a climax at 'Peter's confession of who Jesus is and Jesus' transfiguration', then descending from there to the end at 16:8. In this analysis, I recognize various groupings of episodes culminating in 'Peter's confession', and then a building up of Jesus' disciples' understanding of who Jesus really is up to his death and resurrection.

Each episode has a common introductory part (presenting the participants, location, time, what started the action), the action part, and sometimes a comment about the peoples' reactions to the events.

Above we mentioned some of the most important matters of motif, rhetorical prominence, and climax.

BOUNDARIES AND COHERENCE

Since here we are talking about the entire book, its boundaries are clearly marked by the obvious: no writing preceding the written account, and the sudden ending at 16:8, followed by no writing that can be attributed to the same author.

The closing boundary of Mark is open to much dispute. The oldest manuscripts end it at 16:8, but later manuscripts place various conclusions following that point. All these later manuscripts date from the third century C.E.

Therefore, we must take Mark 1:1 to 16:8 as an integrated whole for this analysis and presentation.

Just as the beginning of the book points out, all that follows is about Jesus the Messiah: what he did and taught.

The book is in two main parts: Jesus demonstrating to the people of Israel who he is, and then Jesus demonstrating to his disciples more clearly who he is by what he taught, and by dying and becoming alive from the dead.

PROMINENCE AND THEME

The book theme is taken from 1:1 and a summary of the parts of the book.

BOOK CONSTITUENT 1:1 (Book Title of 1:1—16:8)

Theme: This is the good message about Jesus the Messiah, the Son of God. It begins like this:	
RELATIONAL STRUCTURE	CONTENTS
NUCLEUS$_1$	1:1a *This is* the good message about Jesus the Messiah the Son of God {MNG: here the focal concepts are the man who is also God, and the man who will rule over all Israel} [ANT].[MET]
NUCLEUS$_2$	1:1b It begins *like this*:

INTENT AND RHETORICAL STRUCTURE

The first problem that arises in dealing with the Gospel of Mark is the relationship of v. 1 to the rest of the book. Is it a title? If so, is it the title of the whole book or of just one section? Or is it only a part of vv. 1–8? Some commentators list other possibilities and some never quite make clear which one they accept.

The main division, however, is between the view that verse one is a separate entity and the view that it is integrally connected to what follows.

The display shows v. 1 as the title to the whole book, following Cole who flatly states that this verse is the title (and do not feel it necessary to defend his position). Cranfield and Lane also opt for v. 1 being an independent unit, title or superscription, but only for vv. 2–13.

Guelich and Gundry take a position in the middle, uniting v. 1 to vv. 2–3, but they consider that whole section a superscription for what follows (vv. 4–15 for Guelich, 4–8 for Gundry).

Hendriksen (p. 33), on the other hand, interprets the verse as dependent on what follows and considers the meaning to be: "The good news about Jesus Christ, the Son of God, began with John the Baptist. It was John who, *as predicted,* prepared the way for Christ's coming." This interpretation seems to relegate the quote to a minor status. According to Lane (p. 39), verses 1–13 "supply the key to the entire Gospel by introducing the central figure of the account. In accordance with the prophetic word, Jesus appears in the wilderness of Judea, summoned by the call of John the Baptist." Thus the "prophetic word" (from Isaiah and Malachi) is crucial, not peripheral, as Hendriksen's words seem to imply.

The occurrence of καθώς, 'as', at the beginning of v. 2 seems to be the chief argument against an independent v. 1. The "joiners" say that it never occurs at the beginning of a sentence elsewhere in Mark or in other New Testament documents and so it can't start a sentence here either.

They also claim that when it occurs with γέγραπται it always refers to the preceding rather than to the succeeding material (see Guelich p. 7). But in one or two occurrences of this combination one could argue that it refers to what follows as well as to what precedes (cf. I Cor. 2:8–10; II Cor. 9:8–10). Therefore, one could use this to support the contention that in Mark 1:1 it does refer to what follows.

Since the combination, καθώς γέγραπται, only occurs with a quotation this one time in Mark, stating that something "always" or "never" occurs seems a weak basis for an argument. These statements do gain some strength from occurrences elsewhere; but can we state definitely that Mark could not have begun a sentence with καθώς just because no one else did? In fact it would seem impossible for Mark to have written his account any other way. He would have had to put v. 4 before vv. 2 and 3, which would have interrupted his description of the person and work of John.

In checking other occurrences of this quote formula in the N.T., I found that most seem to have the following structure, a+b+c where a is a statement or argument; b is the quote formula and c is the quotation itself which usually supports the statement or argument.

In three occurrences, Mt. 26:24, Mk. 9:13 and Mk. 14:20, 21, there is no quotation present. In Rom. 2:23, 24 the quotation precedes the quote formula (in the Greek, though not in many English versions).

Of the other 17 occurrences, 16 follow roughly the formula given above; that is, c supports a, though I see some differences in several. However, Mk. 1:1–2 does not, as it stands, follow that pattern. Here c, the quotation, supports the following verses rather than a, unless you postulate that something has dropped out or was clearly implied to the reader of that time.

Two other problems with tying the quotation to verse one is (1) that there is no direct mention of Jesus Christ in the quotation, though it is assumed that the 'you' refers to him. Also, (2) when you simply tie verses 2 and 3 to verse 1, there is then no overt indication that verse 4 is the fulfillment of the Old Testament predictions.

So, no matter what interpretation one chooses, there are problems to be resolved and choices to be made.

NOTES

1:1 *This is* This is a suggested addition wherever it is necessary to have a complete sentence for a title.

the good message Predating the Christian era the concept εὐαγγέλιον 'gospel' was important in both pagan and Jewish cultures. (For more information on this, see Lane pp. 42, 43.) It indicated a reward that was given for the bringing of good messages; but gradually it came to be used as a designation for the good message itself. And this is how Mark used it here (see Hendriksen).

about Jesus Christ This phrase translates the Greek genitive phrase Ἰησοῦ Χριστοῦ 'of Jesus Christ'. This phrase may mean either that the good news is 'about Jesus Christ' or 'from Jesus Christ'. Nearly all commentators and translations prefer the former, and this fits the message of the whole book much better.

There seems to be no problem in accepting 'Jesus' as a name. It was, in fact, quite a common name meaning " 'Yahweh is salvation', the name given to the divinely-appointed leader, sent to save God's people in their hour of need (Jos. 1:1–2)." (Cole, p. 105)

In contrast to this, there are differences of opinion regarding the status of 'Christ' here. A few commentators maintain that by the time Mark wrote his gospel, this had become accepted as merely a name. However, there are more who believe that here, at least, it is used as a title, 'the anointed one'. Whichever view you take, you are likely to find that, where there is an established church, the name 'Christ' will be known, and the people may insist on using it. For this reason the display shows both 'Christ' and 'the Messiah'.

the Son of God The phrase Son of God is a title for Jesus. This title indicates that Jesus has the same nature and character as God. It also indicates that the relationship between God the Father and Jesus, his Son, is similar to the relationship of human fathers and sons in that both the father and the son are equal in privileges and responsibilities, authority, honor and obedience from their subjects. God the Father does not have a physical body. He did not have a sexual relationship that resulted in Mary conceiving and giving birth to Jesus. The Son of God existed eternally as the Son with his Father.

One needs to consider carefully the target language rendering of "son of God". Much thought and thorough comprehension checking must be made in rendering 'son of Father God'. Within the context of the whole Bible, these familial terms comprehend the concepts of 1) the son is derived from his father, 2) the son has shared identity with his father, 3) the son is in intimate relationship with his father, and 4) the son has a unique status in relationship to his father. Therefore, the words chosen in any particular language must also have these concepts accessible, without being total overridden by some concept like 'biological procreation'.

Furthermore, we understand from cognitive science that a lexical item does not carry all possible concepts simultaneously, but are usually used in specific contexts choosing the appropriate focal concepts, thus increasing implicatory force. So, in this work, I will mention one or two focal concepts, as mentioned in commentaries.

The GNT has [υἱοῦ θεοῦ] 'son of God', where 'son' is used in an extended way, i.e. not the physical male offspring, careful comprehension checking must verify that 'physical male offspring' is not understood, but rather 'the man who was also God'. In some languages, the focal sense of 'Son of God' is 'male offspring of God', or the concept 'born as the result of physical union between male and female'.

In most western cultures at least, we are so accustomed to hearing this phrase that it has become almost meaningless, and we have no difficulty with it. In some other societies the phrase is taken only according to its central meaning. The result is that those people, on reading 'son of God', will immediately ask, "If Jesus was God's son, who was God's wife?"

And for such people it is not adequate to try and explain that it is only an extended use of the phrase.

A good analysis of this anthropomorphic use of 'son' would then suggest that the point of comparison would be "having the same attributes". To spell out this anthropomorphic use, we would have something like "Jesus is the one who has the attributes of God like a son has the attributes of his father".

It would be impossible to suggest what might be the rendering of "Son of God" for any specific translation. That would have to be decided by the intended recipients of the translation after careful consideration of the matters mentioned above. The meaning given in the display retains the divinity concept but avoids the sexual concept.

Another key question here is, should this phrase be included in the text at all in this location? It is given a {C} 'difficulty in deciding' rating by the UBS and included in the text in brackets, which indicates that it was difficult to decide whether to include it or not. Most of the translations include it (except The Message), and the commentators accept it with varying degrees of enthusiasm. One or two did not mention the controversy but seemed to accept its inclusion. Therefore, I have also included it.

{MNG: the focal concept here is the man who was also God} This meaning concept is included in the display to signal all the problems involved with the term 'son of God'. This does not suggest that 'son' may be rendered this way; it only suggests what concept should be carefully investigated with the target audience.

BOUNDARIES AND COHERENCE

This paragraph consists of only one verse. For the question of whether verse 2 begins a new paragraph, see the discussion under Intent and Rhetorical Structure above.

PROMINENCE AND THEME

The theme is taken from the whole of 1:1a–b.

BOOK CONSTITUENT 1:2–13 (Beginning of the Book 1:1—16:8)

THEME: The good message about Jesus the Messiah begins when John the Baptizer appeared to announce Jesus' arrival, and when God audibly said that Jesus was his beloved Son when John baptized him.

MACROSTRUCTURE	CONTENTS
CLAIM₁	1:2–8 The good message about Jesus the Messiah, the Son of God, began when John the Baptizer announced the coming of Jesus, just as it was prophesied.
CLAIM₂	1:9–13 After Jesus was baptized by John, God showed him to be His Son by the Holy Spirit descending upon him; by Himself, God the Father, declaring it; by Satan testing him; and by the angels taking care of him.

INTENT AND RHETORICAL STRUCTURE

This unit 1:2–13 is the introductory part where the author presents the protagonist of the entire book, starting with a prophecy from Isaiah (and Malachi), to its fulfillment by John the Baptizer, whose charge was to introduce God's promised Messiah to Israel.

Two paragraphs make up this Introduction. The first paragraph identifies John, who announces Jesus as the expected Messiah of Israel. The second paragraph tells how God audibly announced that Jesus was his loved Son. Both paragraphs are structurally of equal prominence.

The motif of Jesus' identity is central in the whole book. This motif is the unifying concept of this unit.

BOUNDARIES AND COHERENCE

The opening of the book was discussed under v. 1, here taken to be the title of the book. The start of v. 2 is the beginning boundary of this unit, vv. 2–13. The GNT starts v. 2 with 'just as was written', to develop the topic of John the Baptizer as fulfilling the mentioned prophecy by introducing Jesus as the longed-for Messiah of Israel. The closing boundary is marked by ending comments about John and the introduction of Jesus as the main character of the book.

This unit is bound by two paragraphs, where the first is a CLAIM that Jesus is God's promised one, and a second CLAIM that God himself declared that Jesus is 'my beloved one'.

PROMINENCE AND THEME

The CLAIM constituent of this first introductory part of the book has structural prominence. Therefore the theme statement is primarily derived from the CLAIM₁ but including a marked prominent item in CLAIM₂.

PART CONSTITUENT 1:2–8 (Declarative Paragraph of 1:2–13)

THEME: The good message about Jesus the Messiah, the Son of God, began when John the Baptizer announced the coming of Jesus, just as it was prophesied.

¶ PTRN RELATIONAL STRUCTURE	CONTENTS
description	1:2–3 Just as Isaiah foretold, [See expanded display on page 37.]
DECLARATION — 'John'	1:4–5 John appeared in a solitary place. [See expanded display on page 39.]
—description₁	1:6a Like the prophet Elijah had done, John wore rough clothes made from the hair of camels, and a leather belt,
—description₂	1:6b and he ate food which consisted of locusts and honey.
SIMULTANEOUS	1:7–8 John declared how great is the coming one. [See expanded display on page 40.]

INTENT AND RHETORICAL STRUCTURE

This unit (1:2–8) is the first in the introductory part of the book of Mark. It gives background and support for the teaching of the whole book; namely, that Jesus is the Messiah.

The foundational communication relation for this initial paragraph are a *standard* (vv. 2–3), and a CONGRUENCE (vv. 4–8).

There is a question as to Mark's intended effect on the reader at this point. He could be trying to affect the reader's *ideas* or his *feelings*. Since this is in the introductory part of the book, it seems best to assume that the intent is to affect the *feelings* of the readers. Therefore, this unit is probably an objective sub-type of descriptive paragraph consisting of a *description* (vv. 2–3) and a DECLARATION (vv. 4–8).

In this opening orientation part of the book, the author straightforwardly presents who Jesus really is. However, almost immediately, he hides the identity of this central character. This is according to Blum's contention that the Jewish view of the Messiah was hidden but revealed at the appropriate time. Both the motifs of Jesus as the Messiah and his hidden identity frequently appear throughout the writing.

In this paragraph Mark is giving support for the teaching of the whole book; namely, that Jesus is the Messiah.

NOTES

1:6a *like the prophet Elijah had done* The Greek merely states what John wore and ate. This would have been enough for the readers in those days to make a connection with Elijah (see 2 Kings 1:8). But present day readers would be less likely to understand why these descriptions are put here. At least 16 commentaries note the reference to Elijah here. Therefore it has been put in the display as implied information.

John wore *rough* clothes made *from* the hair of camels Since people in many parts of the world have no knowledge of camels, some description may be helpful for them to understand that this was the type of clothing worn by poor people.

1:6b *food which consisted of* This information is added lest this diet seem like a punishment or a magical rite. This was the kind of food found in the desert, and it was high in vitamin content.

EXPANSION OF THE DESCRIPTION 1:2–3 IN THE 1:2–8 DISPLAY

RELATIONAL STRUCTURE	CONTENTS
┌─orienter───────────────────────	1:2a The prophet Isaiah wrote *that God said to his son:*
│ ┌─NUCLEUS₁────────────────	1:2b "I will be sending my messenger ahead of you;
│ │ NUCLEUS₂────────────────	1:2c he will prepare people *to receive you.*
CONTENT─┤ ┌─orienter────────	1:3a He will call out *to the people who come to where he is* in the desert,
│ │ │ ┌─standard────	1:3b '*As people prepare* the road
│ │ CONTENT₁──CONGRUENCE────	1:3c and *as people straighten out pathways for an important official*,
│ NUCLEUS₃─┤	
│ CONTENT₂──CONGRUENCE────	1:3d prepare *yourselves to receive* the Lord;
│ └─standard────	1:3e make *yourselves* ready [MET, DOU]

NOTES

1:2–4 Once vs. 1 has been separated as an Introduction, then vv. 2–4 are one sentence grammatically and semantically, which can be summarized as "Just as Isaiah wrote…, John the Baptizer appeared…". To avoid having all of that in one sentence in the SSA display, it is broken up into several sentences, of which 2a is the first.

As with many words and phrases in this first section of Mark, there is more than one interpretation of how καθώς is used here. This depends especially on whether v. 1 is interpreted as a title or a partial sentence connected to v. 2.

Viewing v. 1 as a title leads to a conclusion like the one offered by Bratcher and Nida (p. 5): "καθώς begins a new sentence whose conclusion is v. 4, (the quotations from the O.T. in vv. 2–3 being parenthetical),: 'As it is written…John the Baptizer appeared…'."

On the other hand, Gundry (p. 31) believes that καθώς never begins a sentence and that v. 1, therefore, cannot be a title. So his view of καθώς is that it "defines 'beginning of the good news of Jesus Christ' as in accordance with O.T. quotations in vv. 2b–3, the phrase covers only those verses whose subject matter corresponds to the O.T. quotations, i.e. vv. 4–8, which tell how John the Baptizer's activities correspond to the quoted passages…".

I agree with the first interpretation in viewing καθώς as beginning a new sentence. However, to call vv. 2–3 parenthetical lessens the importance of these quotations which are important to Mark's presentation, establishing the authenticity of what he is going to claim.

the prophet Isaiah All modern editions of the Greek text have τῷ Ἠσαΐα τῷ προφήτῃ 'Isaiah the prophet' and, thus, many modern translations follow that well-attested text. In contrast, Textus Receptus has τοῖς προφήταις 'the prophets' which is followed by the King James and New King James versions.

However, it is more likely that the change made by some teacher of the Jewish laws was from τῷ Ἠσαΐα τῷ προφήτῃ, 'Isaiah the prophet' to τοῖς προφήταις than the other way around. Since the first O.T. passage Mark quoted is from Malachi, not Isaiah, this is seen by some to have been a 'correction' in order to include the other prophet.

the prophet Isaiah wrote In some translations it may be necessary for 'prophet' to say something like 'person who received messages directly from God' for those who do not understand the function of a prophet. It may also be useful to make clear that this had happened many years earlier. The wording in the display may be seen as clarifying the metonymy "in Isaiah".

that God said to his son This clarifies who the speaker was and to whom he said it in the following quotation; i.e., the referents of the pronouns 'I' and 'your' in the quotation.

1:2b I will be sending The Greek ἀποστέλλω 'I send' is in the present tense, but the sense is clearly future; and that is made clear in translations such is JB, NIV, TEV, and Beck.

1:2c The Greek word is ἰδού 'behold!', 'see!'; 'look!' But, since the readers were not being asked to look at anything, and since nearly all modern English versions do not render it at all, the display does not represent this word. The Greek expression is, according to Bratcher & Nida (p. 6), used here as "a demonstrative particle...calling attention to what follows". If one chooses to represent it, whatever is best in the vernacular for this function should be used, not necessarily 'listen'. In fact, a wording suggesting 'pay attention' would be better.

ahead of you The Greek is πρὸ προσώπου σου 'before your face'. The King James and the New King James versions translate this literally. Bratcher and Nida (p. 7) call this phrase a Semitism meaning 'in front of', and this is the interpretation that many modern translators use. But one certainly does not want to use a word or phrase that means 'face to face' or even 'right in front of you'.

1:3a He will call out In the display the third person pronoun, 'he' is substituted for 'a voice' because the latter might be interpreted by some readers as a disembodied voice or an evil spirit. It is, in fact, a figure of speech, synecdoche, a part being used to represent the whole, i.e., the voice represents the man who will do the calling.

to the people who come to where he is This clause is added to clarify to whom he was crying out his message. Without this, the readers might not understand how there would be anyone in a desert to listen to his message.

in the desert The Greek word here translated 'desert' is ἔρημος defined by BAGD as 'desert, grassland, wilderness' and the latter definition is often found in English translations. It refers to the very dry area west of the Jordan River along (or just off) the road which ran between Jerusalem and Galilee.

1:3b *As people prepare* the road Some modern readers might interpret the clause "Prepare the way of the Lord" as meaning that they should do some kind of road repair, especially in third world rural areas where villagers may make a habit of sweeping the local roads and clearing stones, etc. from them. In order to avoid that, the metaphor has been filled out in detail.

1:3c and, *as people straighten out pathways for an important official* The same problems could arise from a literal rendering of this second directive. Therefore, once again, the metaphor is filled out.

1:3d prepare *yourselves to receive* This continues the explication of the metaphor.

the Lord This is referring to the coming of Christ, the Messiah. TN is wrong in saying it refers to God; it was the 2nd member of the Trinity who came, not the 1st member.

1:3e make *yourselves* ready Continuing in the same vein, what is to be made ready has been made explicit. In the case of doublets which are quoted from O.T. poetic passages, we maintain the doublet.

EXPANSION OF CONGRUENCE 1:4–8 IN THE 1:2–8 DISPLAY

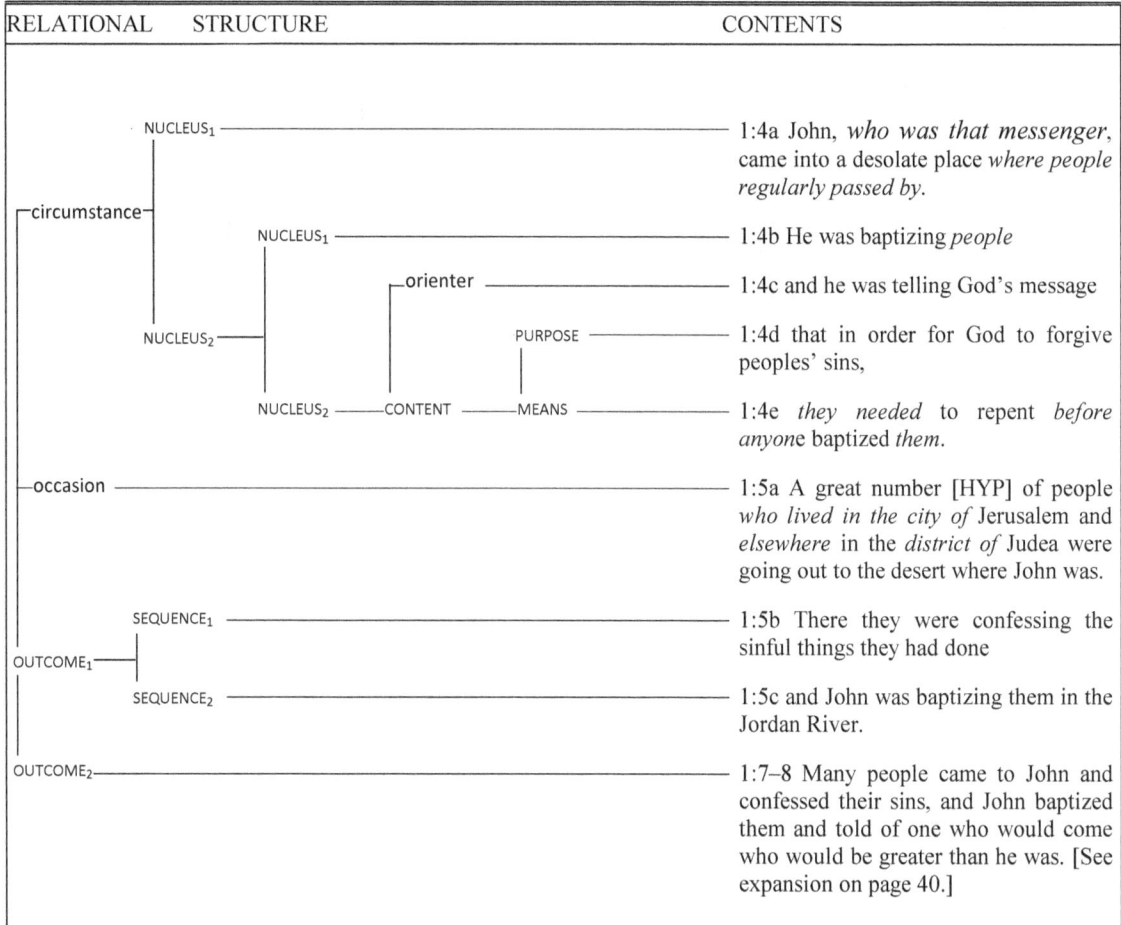

NOTES

1:4a *who was that messenger* This relative clause was added to make the connection clear between vv. 2–3 and v. 4; that is, that v. 4 states the fulfillment of the prophecy. In effect it spells out the force of Καθὼς γέγραπται... ἐγένετο Ἰωάννης 'as it was written...John appeared' in vv. 2–4.

came into a desolate place where people regularly passed by The word often translated as 'desert' or 'wilderness' refers to an area west of the Jordan River which was uninhabited and uncultivated, but where there was a common route used by people traveling between Galilee and Judea.

1:4b He was baptizing *people* The GNT text has Ἰωάννης βαπτίζων 'John baptizing' with a {C} rating. Some manuscripts have ὁ occurring before the participle which leads to the translation 'John the Baptizer'. Metzger believes that "In view of the predominant usage in the Synoptic Gospels of referring to John as 'the Baptist'..., it is easier to account for the addition than for the deletion of the definite article before 'Βαπτίζων'." (See Mark 6:14, Matt. 3:1, 14:8.) On the basis of Metzger's argument the display uses the participle as above.

1:4c and he was telling God's message Notice that this proposition is parallel to the one above which might be construed as supporting the argument made there. In some languages it may be necessary to add 'to them' to complete the case frame.

1:4d that, in order for God to forgive their sins This proposition and the one preceding spell out more thoroughly the meaning of "a baptism of repentance for forgiveness of sins"; making the abstract nouns into full clauses. In some languages it will be necessary to say 'forgive them for having sinned'.

1:4e *they needed* **to repent** *before anyone* **baptized** *them* The wording here avoids two abstract nouns and makes clear the relationship between those two events: 'baptism of repentance' implies that some who were coming to be baptized had not repented (cf. Matt. 3:7–8).

1:5a a great number of people The Greek text has a hyperbole here which, if translated literally as in some of the older versions, would be 'all the country of Judea' and 'all the people of Jerusalem'. It is here translated non-figuratively.

who lived in the city of **Jerusalem** *and elsewhere* **in** *the district of* **Judea** This continues the non-figurative explication of the hyperbole. The words 'city of' and 'district of' are included to make clear to what geographical (political?) entities they are related. The words 'elsewhere in' are supplied to make clear that Jerusalem is a city within the district of Judea. It is not clear why the Biblical writers often list Judea first when the two places are mentioned together. (e.g., Is. 2:1, 11:1, 13:9, Jer.4:5–6 Luke 6:17), but they (and all the English versions except TfT) never make clear that the one was a city inside the other, a district.

EXPANSION OF OUTCOME 2 IN THE 1:2–8 DISPLAY

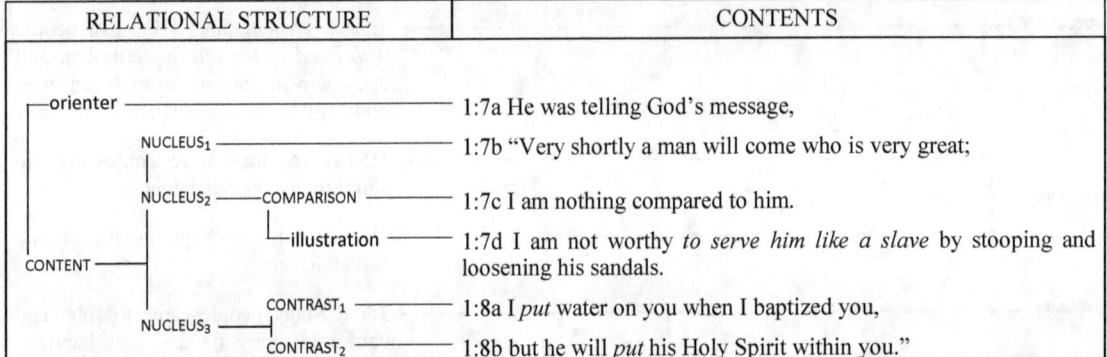

NOTES

1:7b–c Very shortly Several commentators note that the Greek ἔρχεται...ὀπίσω, 'is coming after me' signifies immediacy, not some vague future possibility. (See Vincent Taylor, C.S. Mann, and Hugh Anderson for examples; also NLT.)

who is very great; I am nothing compared to him. Since comparative structures are not used in many languages, an attempt is made here to convey the meaning of 'ἰσχυρότερός μου, 'greater than I', by this relative clause plus the following clause (7c).

1:7d *to serve him like a slave* This implied information spells out the implied connotation of 'loosen his sandals'; cf. NLT, and CEV footnote.

1:8a I *put* **water on you** Some Greek manuscripts supply the preposition ἐν, 'in'; but the GNT gives a {B} 'almost certain' rating to the version without it. Several important manuscripts do not have the preposition, and it is felt to be more likely that a scribe would add the preposition than delete it.

Unless there is an established transliteration of βαπτίζω, 'to baptize', in use, it may be wise to choose as neutral a term as possible so as not to seem to favor one type of baptism over another. Here we have used the same verb, 'put', for both the baptism John did and the kind Jesus was going to do, in order to strengthen the parallelism. Some expressions used for 'baptize with water' may not collocate with 'baptize with the Holy Spirit'. It is for this reason that the display avoids the word 'baptize'.

1:8b but he will *put* **his Holy Spirit within you** The GNT gives an 'A' 'certain' rating to the reading with the preposition ἐν, 'in' in this position. The overwhelming weight of Greek manuscript evidence supports the reading with ἐν. The addition of καὶ πυρι in several witnesses reflects the influence of the parallels in Mt 3.11 and Lk 3.16–17 it was undoubtedly added by some scribe familiar with those two passages.

As mentioned above, 'put', has been used for both 8a and 8b to show parallelism.

within you This phrase is used to avoid the idea of the Holy Spirit being only on the outside, as the water would be.

BOUNDARIES AND COHERENCE

The start of a new paragraph at v. 9 is marked by a switch from a discussion of John the Baptizer to the baptism of Jesus. Coherence within the paragraph is provided by three occurrences of the verb 'baptize' of the noun 'baptism', plus two occurrences of the word ἔρημος 'desert', plus the fact that the whole paragraph is about John the Baptizer.

PROMINENCE AND THEME

The structurally prominent units from both the *description* and the DECLARATION have been included in the theme statement.

PART CONSTITUENT 1:9–13 (Episode of 1:2–13)

THEME After Jesus was baptized by John, God showed him to be His Son by the Holy Spirit descending upon him; by Himself, God the Father, declaring it; by Satan testing him; and by the angels taking care of him.

¶PTRN RELATIONAL STRUCTURE	CONTENTS
occasion	1:9a During that time *when John was telling God's message*, Jesus went from Nazareth *town to where John was,* in Galilee *district*,
⎯step	1:9b and was baptized by John (OR, John baptized him) in the Jordan *River*.
⎯step₁	1:10a Immediately after *Jesus* came up out of the water,
⎯step₂	1:10b he saw *that God had* opened up heaven
⎯step₃	1:10c *and he saw* the Spirit *of God* as it was descending on him*self in the form of* a dove
⎯orienter	1:11a And God [MTY] spoke *to him* from heaven,
OUTCOME₁ ⎯ GOAL ⎯ GOAL ⎯ CONTENT	1:11b "You are my Son whom I love; I am very pleased with you."
⎯circumstance	1:12 Immediately the Spirit *of God* sent *Jesus* into the desert.
CONTRAST₁ ⎯ NUCLEUS₁	1:13a There he was tempted by Satan for forty days
NUCLEUS₂	1:13b and *at the same time* he was among wild animals.
OUTCOME₂ ⎯ CONTRAST₂	1:13c But angels took care of him.

INTENT AND RHETORICAL STRUCTURE

This is the final unit of the introductory part of the book, but it is transitional from the introduction to the body of the book which presents the things that Jesus did and said that demonstrated who he was.

This complex paragraph introduces Jesus and sets the stage for his ministry. It also adds two incidents which give credence to John's previous claims about the one who was to come after him.

First, there was the descent of the Spirit 'as a dove' upon Jesus followed by the voice from heaven declaring Jesus to be God's son. And, secondly, the Spirit drove him out into the desert where he was tempted by Satan for 40 days. Mark dealt with all of these only briefly in order that he might proceed to Jesus' ministry.

Since this unit has many temporal sequences, it is a narrative paragraph pattern of the causality type displaying an *occasion* (1:9a) with two *OUTCOMES* (1:9b–11, and 1:12–13).

NOTES

1:9a During that time This section begins with καὶ ἐγένετο ἐν ἐκείναις ταῖς ἡμέραις, 'and (became) in those days'. The word, ἐγένετο, is essentially untranslatable, though earlier translations have 'it came to pass'. Its main function is to mark progression in the narrative to a new episode or set of events.

when John was telling God's message This clause has been included to clarify to what 'that time' refers.

town, which is* in Galilee *district Since Nazareth and Galilee will be unfamiliar to many readers, geographical specifications have been supplied, as in v. 5.

1:9b Here the passive is retained as the first choice because the focus is on Jesus, not on John. But the active alternative is supplied for translation into languages that do not have passive constructions.

1:10a after *Jesus* came up out of the water The Greek verb is ἀναβαίνων 'coming up', a participial form. Some interpret it as a temporal participle and translate it 'as Jesus was coming up out of the water'. Either interpretation is possible.

The pronominal referent has been supplied since the previous person mentioned was John.

1:10b *that God had* opened up heaven The Greek verb form, σχιζομένους, is a present, middle participle from the verb σχίζω, 'open/unfold' (in middle voice). This is not a combination common in other languages; therefore the above adjustment has been made, supplying the agent of the action.

1:10c the Spirit *of God* The Greek text has only 'the Spirit'. Nearly all versions make some adjustment here; either the word, 'spirit' is capitalized or 'holy' is added (cf. LB, NCV, TEV) and both are capitalized.

descending on him*self* The question which arises here is the interpretation of the preposition, εἰς. It can have several nuances of meaning in this environment; 'on', 'to', or 'into' are the ones most in use. 'On/upon' seems to be the most popular choice among commentators, though several prefer 'into'. Of those commentators consulted, only Vincent Taylor prefers 'to'.

***in the form of* a dove** There have been several interpretations of this phrase: a) 'in the form of a dove', b) 'with the motion of a dove', and c). 'looking like a dove'. Translators most often retain 'like a dove'; but it may be necessary in some languages to specify in what way the Spirit was like a dove. Luke 3:22 reads specifically: καὶ καταβῆναι τὸ πνεῦμα τὸ ἅγιον σωματικῷ εἴδει ὡς περιστερὰν, 'and the Holy Spirit came down in a bodily form as a dove'.

For this reason and because the commentators are divided, the display follows Luke.

1:11a And God spoke The Greek text has φωνὴ, 'voice', which is metonymy for God. Also, the verb in Greek is γίνομαι, 'come', which does not collocate with 'come' as the subject. So 'spoke' is supplied as a more natural verb (cf. LB, NEB, CEV).

The GNT gives a {C} rating for the clause with the verb, 'come' as there are some manuscripts which omit the verb and a few which substitute 'heard' for it. Metzger says "The omission of the verb appears to be either accidental or in partial imitation of Matthew's καὶ ἰδοὺ φωνὴ ἐκ τῶν οὐρανῶν λέγουσα (Mt 3.17)." He takes the reading with 'heard' to be a deliberate change by a scribe.

to him This phrase is implied by the form of God's speech and added here for those languages which require it to complete the case frame.

1:11b my Son whom I love See note 1:1a.

1:12 the Spirit *of God* The text has merely 'the spirit', but all understand it to mean the Spirit of God (cf. CEV), or 'Holy Spirit' (as in NLT).

1:13b and *at the same time* It is possible to interpret this episode as describing three successive events; but there is nothing in the Greek to specify it, so the verse has been translated as if the temptations, the being with wild animals, and the care of the angels, all occurred over the same span of time. It seems semantically that the presence of Satan and the wild animals were two points of danger, and the presence of the angels was to protect Jesus from both. Therefore 13c begins with 'but' rather than 'and' (cf. TEV, CEV, and note especially JBP).

BOUNDARIES AND COHERENCE

The start of a new paragraph at v. 14 is indicated by a change of location from Judea to Galilee, and the beginning of the actual ministry of Jesus. Coherence is also provided by the whole paragraph being about the events surrounding Jesus' baptism by John.

PROMINENCE AND THEME

The theme is drawn from the most prominent proposition of the GOAL of the 1st *OUTCOME*, the 2nd CONTENT under that GOAL, and the most prominent proposition of the 2nd OUTCOME.

BOOK CONSTITUENT 1:14—8:30 (Part I of 1:1—16:8)

THEME: By Jesus claiming to have the authority to establish a new order over the religious rituals teaching and healing in and around Galilee district, he was leading his disciples to answer his question, 'Who do you say I am?'

MACROSTRUCTURE	CONTENTS
INTRODUCTION	1:14–15 After John was arrested, Jesus came and preached the good news which came from God.
ACT I	1:16—3:6 Jesus demonstrated his power and authority by summoning some followers, healing many sick people, and establishing a new order over the religious rituals fostered by the Pharisees which led to the religious authorities planning to kill Jesus.
ACT II	3:7—8:30 By Jesus appointing his disciples to teach and heal people in and around Galilee district, he was leading his disciples to answer his question, 'Who am I?'

INTENT AND RHETORICAL STRUCTURE

This unit is the second constituent of the book: it follows the *introductory* part and opens the main BODY of the writing. The BODY is in two halves, Part I and Part II. The climactic point that marks Part I from Part II is commonly referred to as 'Peter's confession of Jesus as God's chosen Messiah'.

The author intends that the reader understand that Jesus' disciples did not initially clearly understand who he was.

BOUNDARIES AND COHERENCE

The opening and closing boundaries coincide with those of the included episodes, and discussed at those points. This entire unit coheres by Jesus leading his disciples to understand who he was.

PROMINENCE AND THEME

The theme statement reflects a condensation of all the constituent units and their prominence.

PART CONSTITUENT 1:14–15 (Introductory Episode of 1:14—8:30)

THEME: After John was arrested, Jesus came and preached the good news which came from God.

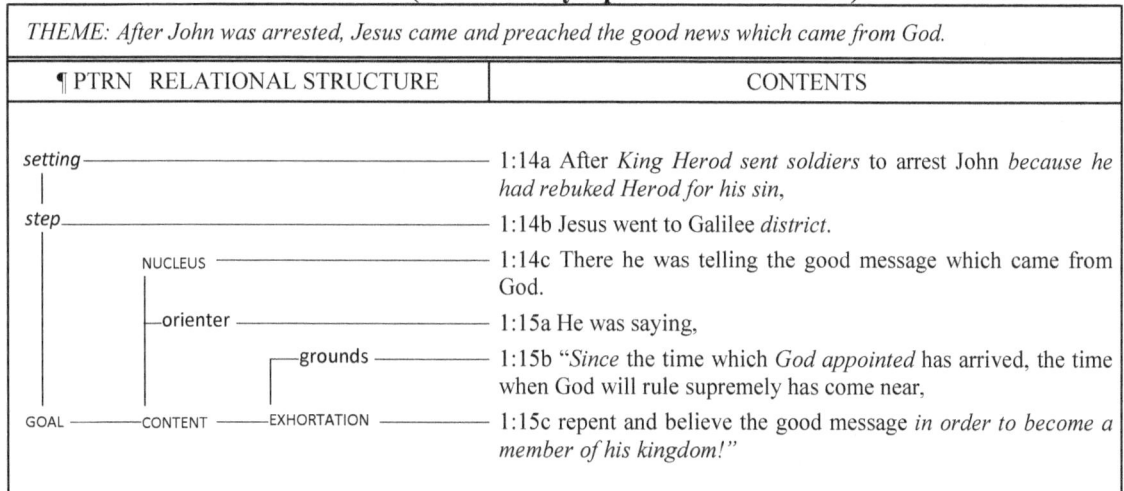

INTENT AND RHETORICAL STRUCTURE

This unit is the introductory episode of the first half of the book in which the author presents Jesus as Messiah to Israel.

This is a narrative paragraph of the objective type consisting of a *setting* (v. 14a), a *step* (v. 14b), and a GOAL (vv. 14c–15). Its intent is to introduce the main participant (Jesus), the location of his actions and teachings throughout this first half of the book, and a summary of the message he spoke to the people of Israel.

NOTES

1:14a After *King Herod sent soldiers to* arrest John The verb in Greek is a passive infinitive which could be difficult to translate. Thus, it has been made active and an actor supplied.

because he had rebuked Herod for his sin This implied information is given elsewhere in Mark (6:17–29), but it has been supplied here to avoid giving a wrong implication that John was imprisoned for some crime that he had committed.

1:14b to Galilee *district* In case there might be confusion as to whether Galilee were a town, district or some other entity, the information is supplied.

1:14c And then he was telling the good message which came from God Some manuscripts have τῆς βασιλείας, 'of the kingdom' following εὐαγγέλιον, 'gospel/good news'. However, UBS assigns the rating A, 'certain', to the reading without the addition, and Metzger feels it is obvious that copyists made the insertion to bring Mark's text into conformity with the frequently used fuller expression.

The last phrase is a translation of τὸ εὐαγγέλιον τοῦ θεοῦ, 'the gospel of God'. The genitive has been taken as indicating source.

1:15b the time which God *appointed* 'time' is a metonymy standing for a specific time. Therefore 'which God has appointed' spells out the metonymy.

when God will rule supremely Hiebert says that the primary meaning of 'kingdom' is the sovereign's actual rule, the reign itself. However, since many languages do not use verbal nouns, and the term 'kingdom' may not be familiar, the concept has been translated as a full clause with 'rule' as the verb and 'God' as subject.

1:15c repent and believe the good message *in order to become a member of his kingdom!* The statement in 15b that the 'time…has come near' is the basis for the appeal to repent and believe in 15c. But there is some implied relationship between 'kingdom being near' and the necessity to repent. Therefore the part in italics has been supplied to specify this relationship.

BOUNDARIES AND COHERENCE

A new paragraph at v. 16 is indicated by a switch from a generic statement about the beginning of Jesus' ministry to specific events at the start of his ministry. Coherence is seen in the paragraph consisting of the content of Jesus' proclamation.

PROMINENCE AND THEME

The theme is drawn from a condensation of the *setting* and the nuclear proposition of the GOAL.

PART CONSTITUENT 1:16—3:6 (Act I of Part I 1:14—8:30)

THEME: Jesus demonstrated his power and authority by summoning some followers, healing many sick people, and establishing a new order over the religious rituals fostered by the Pharisees which led to the religious authorities planning to kill Jesus.

MACROSTRUCTURE	CONTENTS
EPISODE	1:16–20 Jesus summoned four fishermen and they immediately went with him.
SCENE₁	1:21–45 Jesus demonstrated who he is by healing many sick people and people with evil spirits.
SCENE₂	2:1—3:6 Jesus had some sharp discussions with the religious authorities about his authority over religious practices, culminating in the authorities planning to kill him.

INTENT AND RHETORICAL STRUCTURE

In this first act of the story, the author introduces Jesus' support group, the actions Jesus does demonstrating who he (the unknown one) is, and his authority over revered religious practices.

The basic structure is three sequential units demonstrating it being a narrative. The choosing of a few disciples is a low-key action, but then the story moves on to several unusual miracles and healings, which then climax in Jesus clashing with the religious authorities over religious taboos and practices.

BOUNDARIES AND COHERENCE

This unit 1:16—3:6 is very closely related to the introductory statement of vv. 14–15.

Verse 14 opens with a δέ 'but' which is typical of a turning point, whereas v. 16 opens with a καί 'and'. The topic of vv. 14–15 present a generic description of what Jesus did in the rest of the first half of the book. At v. 16, however, the author begins relating details about what Jesus did and said.

PROMINENCE AND THEME

All the constituents of this first part of the body are of equal prominence. Therefore the theme statement is a synthesis of all the constituents.

ACT CONSTITUENT 1:16–20 (Episode of 1:16—3:6)

¶PTRN RELATIONAL STRUCTURE	CONTENTS
THEME: Jesus summoned four fishermen and they immediately went with him.	
occasion	1:16a While *Jesus* was walking along by Lake Galilee,
SEQUENCE₁ — NUCLEUS	1:16b he saw two men, Simon and Simon's *younger* brother, Andrew.
circumstance — RESULT	1:16c *They were* throwing their *fishing* nets into the lake,
reason	1:16d because they were men *who earned money by* catching *and selling* fish.
orienter	1:17a Jesus said to them,
OUTCOME₁ — SEQUENCE₂ — CONTENT — MEANS [proposal]	1:17b *"Just as you have been gathering fish,* come with me, and I will cause that you become men who will gather people
purpose	1:17c in order that they may become my disciples." [MET]
SEQUENCE₃ [acceptance]	1:18 Immediately they left *the work they were doing with* their nets, and they went with him.
circumstance	1:19a After they had gone on a little further,
SEQUENCE₁ — NUCLEUS	1:19b *Jesus* saw some other men, two of whom were James and James' *younger* brother John, who were the sons of Zebedee.
circumstance	1:19c *They were both* in a boat mending *their fishing* nets.
OUTCOME₂ — SEQUENCE₂	1:20a And immediately, he summoned them *to come with him*.
SEQUENCE₃	1:20b They left their father Zebedee, *who remained in the boat with the hired servants,* and they went away with *Jesus*.

INTENT AND RHETORICAL STRUCTURE

This unit is the first act in this part about what Jesus did that demonstrated who he was while he was in the Galilee area.

Here the author intends to affect the reader's knowledge by telling an account of how Jesus started gathering some disciples around him to learn from him and to assist him.

This is a narrative paragraph of the causality type consisting of an *occasion* (v. 16a), and two OUTCOMES (vv. 16b–18), and (vv. 19–20).

NOTES

1:16a *Jesus* Having changed the participial form of the verb to an active indicative, a subject for the verb was also supplied.

1:16b *Simon* At some time Jesus gave Simon a new name, Peter (see 3:16), by which he is most often referred to in the New Testament. Some translators may want to put that information in a footnote.

Simon's younger brother, Andrew Since many languages require the exact relationship to be specified, 'younger' has been supplied for them. "Because of the general practice among Jews of Biblical times to list the name of the older brother first, we may assume that Simon was older than Andrew..." (Bratcher & Nida, p. 40).

1:16c *They were throwing* Once again a participle has been changed to an indicative and the subject has been supplied.

fishing nets For cultures where this form of fishing is not known it may be helpful to include the function of the nets; also in 19c.

1:16d *they were men who earned money by catching and selling fish* It is often helpful to add the purpose of an action, especially where that action is not common in the culture. The implied words are included to make clear what the real goal of catching fish was.

1:17b *just as you have been gathering fish* The word 'fishers' in the Greek is a metaphor which may not be literally translatable. In cultures where there would be a collocational clash in the concept of fishing for men, an acceptable substitute must be found. 'Gather' is one possibility.

people The Greek says 'men' but they were to make disciples of both men and women; cf. CEV, NLT.

1:17c This proposition spells out the implied purpose of the 'gathering'; in other words, it spells out the topic of the metaphor.

1:18 *the work they were doing with* The point of this short phrase is not that they left their nets behind, but that they stopped their work in order to follow Jesus, so this implied information has been supplied. The word 'nets' could be considered a metonymy, the instrument standing for the work done with that instrument.

went with him The primary sense of the Greek word ἀκολουθέω means literally 'to follow', but here and elsewhere in the N.T. it means "follow someone as a disciple" (BAGD p. 31).

1:19b *Jesus* It may not be necessary to specify who saw the men mending their nets; but it is supplied for those who might require it.

1:19c *They were both* Having changed the verb from a participial form to an indicative, a subject is supplied.

1:20a *to come with him* Both the Greek verb, καλέω, and the English verb, summon, can mean 'call into one's presence'. If the receptor language has no equivalent for 'into one's presence', perhaps the phrase, 'with him' could be used.

1:20b *with Jesus* The Greek has 'after him', but a literal translation could give the wrong meaning; the display follows TEV and CEV.

BOUNDARIES AND COHERENCE

A new paragraph at v. 21 is indicated by a further change in location and Jesus' expelling a demon. Coherence is provided by three occurrences of δίκτυον 'nets', and two occurrences of πλοῖον 'boat'. Coherence is also provided by the paragraph consisting of the account of Jesus' calling his first four disciples.

PROMINENCE AND THEME

The theme is drawn from condensations of the most prominent propositions of the two OUTCOMES.

ACT CONSTITUENT 1:21–45 (Scene of 1:16—3:6)

THEME: *Jesus demonstrated who he is by healing many sick people and people with evil spirits.*	
MACROSTRUCTURE	CONTENTS
EPISODE₁	1:21–28 People were amazed at Jesus' teaching and also as a result of him expelling a demon.
EPISODE₂	1:29–31 Jesus healed Simon's mother-in-law.
EPISODE₃	1:32–34 Jesus healed many people and expelled many evil spirits.
EPISODE CLUSTER	1:35–45 Jesus continued his ministry by telling God's message, expelling evil spirits, and curing a leper.

INTENT AND RHETORICAL STRUCTURE

The author, through this first scene 1:21–45 of Act 1, intends to hint as to who Jesus is by his healing and expelling evil spirits from several people.

The three episodes and the episode cluster are presented in sequential order, giving evidence that this whole unit is a narrative.

Mark makes a point that Jesus did not want the evil spirits nor the healed people to publicize what he had done, in order to keep his identity hidden. Even so, he had to stay away from the towns, and people kept mobbing him, even in isolated places.

BOUNDARIES AND COHERENCE

The opening boundary was mentioned in the discussion of the previous episode. Here Mark uses a frequently occurring adverb εὐθύς 'immediately'. This word frequently is used to focus on a new turning event in the narrative, as it does here. The healing of the demoniac in the synagogue starts a series of healings, culminating in the cleansing of a leper.

PROMINENCE AND THEME

All the constituents of this second act are of equal prominence. Therefore the theme statement is a synthesis of all the constituents.

SCENE CONSTITUENT 1:21–28 (Episode of 1:21–45)

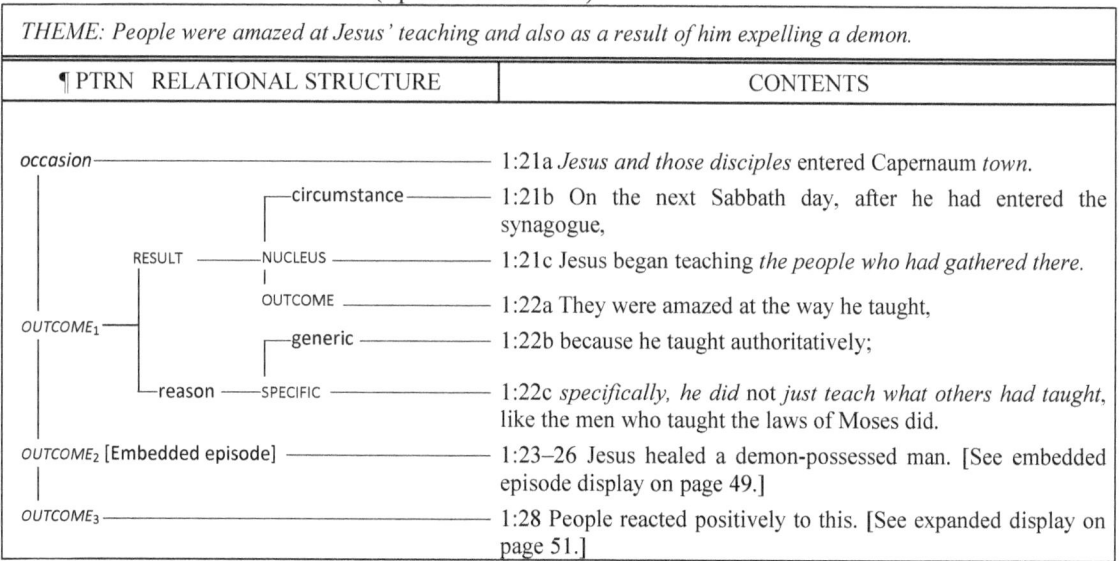

INTENT AND RHETORICAL STRUCTURE

This is the first of three healing episodes mentioned as Jesus started his ministry in the Galilee area.

The 1:21–28 episode details an incident in Capernaum. It is basically a narrative of the causality type, consisting of an *occasion* and three OUTCOMES.

NOTES

1:21a *Jesus and those disciples* The Greek text does not have an overt free subject. For clarity it may be helpful to spell out the referents. In some cases translators may want to say 'and those four disciples'.

Capernaum *town* This being the first mention of Capernaum, it may be necessary to identify it as a town. Peter and Andrew lived there, and Jesus had already made his headquarters there.

1:21b after he had entered the synagogue There are several textual variations for the last half of this verse. Most are concerned with the Greek word, εἰσελθών, 'entered'; it is not found in some manuscripts and is present in others. Where it does not occur, in some cases, the other words are arranged differently or another word is added. In spite of all that, UBS scholars have chosen to put it in with brackets and gave it a {C} 'difficulty in deciding' rating. Metzger reports: "In view of the balance of transcriptional probabilities, a majority of the Committee preferred to adopt the reading supported by the predominant weight of external evidence." (Metzger, pp. 74,75)

synagogue This was a Jewish gathering place; CEV has 'Jewish meeting place'.

1:21c teaching *the people who had gathered there* The verb 'teach' implies an audience. Thus, in case this needs to be specified, it has been supplied in the display to complete the case frame.

1:22b because he taught authoritatively The concept of authority may be hard to translate; therefore, a substitute may need to be found. Ideas like: 'with power' or 'like a big (important) man' or some other phrase could be used which applies to a person to whom others should listen and obey.

1:22c *specifically, he did not just teach what others had taught* This fills in the implied information in the Greek phrase, καὶ οὐχ ὡς οἱ γραμματεῖς, 'and not as the scribes'. Commentators have taken this phrase to apply to content, not to manner. The scribes were very self-assured and self-confident; they were dogmatic and intolerant, but they always spoke with borrowed authority. They only repeated what other men had said; they simply quoted 'authorities'. (See also Cole, Hiebert, Taylor).

men who taught the Laws of Moses This spells out the meaning of the word γραμματεύς 'scribes'. CEV similarly has 'teachers of the Law of Moses'.

SCENE CONSTITUENT 1:21–28

EMBEDDED EPISODE 1:23–27 (Episode within Episode 1:21–28)

THEME: *Jesus expelled an evil spirit, which caused the people to be amazed.*

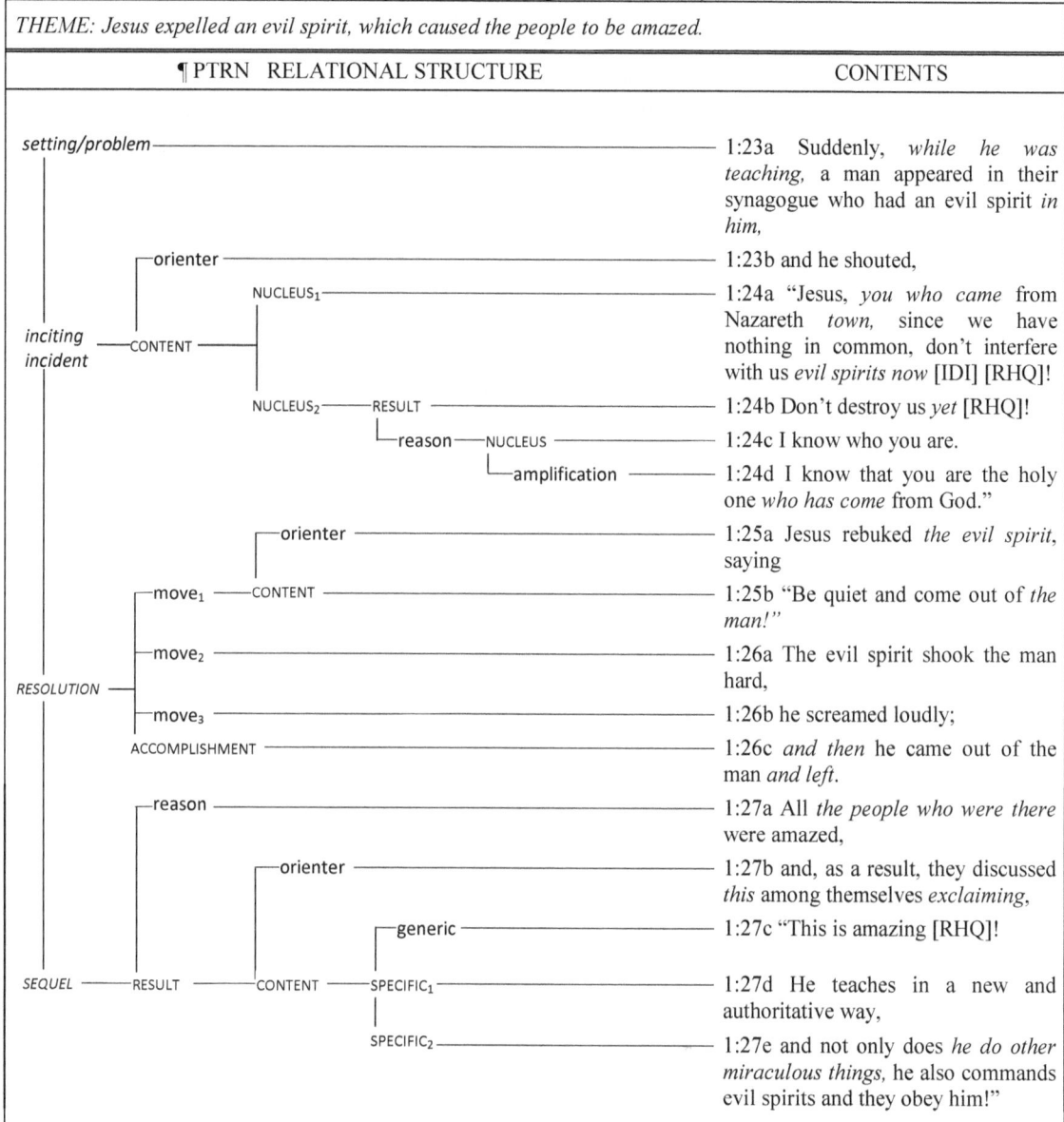

INTENT AND RHETORICAL STRUCTURE

This unit is the last act in this part about what Jesus did while he was in the Galilee district that demonstrated who he was.

Here the author intends to affect the reader's knowledge by telling an account of how Jesus started teaching and expelling evil spirits from people.

This is a narrative of sequential units, all of equal prominence.

NOTES

1:23a   Suddenly, *while he was teaching* Because there may be a sizeable gap between v. 21c and 23a, it may be necessary to fill in the time to which 'suddenly' refers.

a man appeared in their synagogue There are two opinions concerning this man. Some believe that this man had been in the synagogue all along and suddenly called out. Others believe that the 'suddenly' means that he had just come into the synagogue.

The UBS Handbook states that ἦν, 'was' "may be taken as equivalent to ἐγένετο, 'came', 'appeared'. The second is probably to be preferred, cf. Gould. An additional note states that a man with an unclean spirit would not normally be in attendance at the worship service in the synagogue (cf. also Anderson). None of the commentaries commented on this possible problem. Of the versions, CEV uses the word 'entered'; Phillips uses 'appeared'. The other versions use the traditional 'was'.

In consideration of the teaching and culture of the day and support from the UBS Handbook, the display shows 'appeared' as a kind of neutral stance as it could cover either the idea that the man had been there unnoticed (though unlikely) or that he had just come in.

who had an evil spirit *in him* The Greek ἐν πνεύματι ἀκαθάρτω, 'in/with (an) unclean spirit', literally seems to say that the man was 'in' the unclean spirit but most say the spirit was in the man or 'with' the man. However, if the latter could mean it was alongside the man, some adjustment should be made.

Few commentators discuss what this phrase means; but, those who do mention it, suggest 'possessed by' (Lane, Wessel, Gundry), 'controlled by' (cf. Hendriksen), or 'under spiritual influence of' (Swete). BAGD also suggests 'under the special influence'. Any of these are possible where 'in him' conveys the wrong information.

1:24a Jesus, *you who came* from Nazareth *town* This phrase is an expansion of the Greek Ἰησοῦ Ναζαρηνέ, 'Jesus Nazarene' since the latter is not the normal identification for most English speakers. If, however, it is common to identify a person by the name of his village, by all means be more literal.

since we have nothing in common The idiom, τί ἡμῖν καὶ σοί, 'what to us and to you' is clearly a rhetorical question with the sense of 'we have absolutely nothing in common'; but there is also an implied illocutionary force of 'so mind your own business!' Cf. NLT, "Why are you interfering with us?"

don't interfere with us *evil spirits now!* The idiom 'we have nothing in common' clearly implies some underlying plea from the demons. Because they had nothing in common with Jesus, something should happen/be done – or not happen or be done! Basically the implied plea is that Jesus should leave them alone. The whole quote is seen as coming from the demon who controls the man rather than from the man himself. And this 'we' means that he is speaking for all the demons, realizing that whatever Jesus will eventually do will affect them all. (See Gundry, Lane, Wessel). But he would like to, at least, delay that day. See also suggestions in TN.

1:24b Don't destroy us *yet* In the Greek this is a question, interpreted here as rhetorical. The display shows it as a strong plea. Most versions retain the question form, though The Message translates it as a statement, 'and you've come to destroy us!' following the demon's statement that he knew who Jesus was. Most of the commentators also translate it as a statement in connection with what he knows.

A command or plea seems to make the best sense in this context. Knowing who Jesus was implies the knowledge of his mission; perhaps, even, of the eventual outcome. Thus, the 'yet'.

1:24c I know who you are In this statement the demon switches from 1st person plural to 1st person singular. "The change from the plural, ἡμῖν us to the sing[ular] οἶδα I know, simply brings us back to the person speaking for himself, whereas in the ἡμῖν, the demon speaks for his class" (Gould).

Some commentators make no note on this switch except by implication. Wessel comments that this statement, especially with Jesus' name and title "may have been an attempt by the demon to get control over Jesus, 'since it was widely believed at that time that if you knew a person's identity and could utter his name, you could gain a magic power over him' (Nineham, p. 75)." (See also Cranfield, Anderson).

This, then, was an action by the one demon, not by the whole class of demons.

1:24d I know that you are the holy one *who has come* from God Genitive constructions are often difficult to translate, as in τοῦ Θεοῦ 'of God'. It may be necessary to specify in what way Jesus was 'of God'.

1:25a Jesus rebuked *the evil spirit* The Greek here has a pronoun, 'him' as the object of 'rebuke'. It may be necessary to specify to make it clear that it was not the man whom Jesus was rebuking.

1:25b come out of *the man!* The words 'the man' have been supplied to complete the case frame involving a verb of motion.

1:26a The evil spirit shook the man hard The Greek verb, σπαράσσω, means to tear apart, pull to and fro, convulse. This describes the kind of convulsions experienced by epileptics.

1:26c *and then* he came out of the man The preceding Greek verbs are aorist participles which can either be simultaneous with or antecedent to the finite verb. Of the versions consulted, most have interpreted at least one of the participles as antecedent to the main verb, 'came out'. (There are several interesting variations of relationships.) The display has chosen to interpret the participles as sequential and denoting actions antecedent to 'came out'. Thus, 'and then' has been added to clarify this.

and left The Greek merely says that the spirit came out of the man. No more mention is made of it, so it can be assumed that it left. In some languages it will be necessary to state this to avoid uncertainty.

1:27a All *the people who were there* were amazed The word 'All', specifically, 'all the people', were amazed who had been watching. It doesn't include anyone else, at least until those present went out and spread the word.

exclaiming The Greek verb is 'saying'; but 'exclaiming' is more appropriate to the content of what follows.

1:27c This is amazing The Greek is in the form of a rhetorical question. Thus it has been changed to a statement with a similar emotive meaning.

1:27d He teaches in a new and authoritative way The Greek for this section is διδαχὴ καινὴ κατ' ἐξουσίαν, 'a new teaching with authority'. There are a number of variant readings in the manuscripts for this section. Metzger writes that the "one preserved in ℵ B L 33 seems to account best for the rise of the others. Its abruptness invited modification, and more than one copyist accommodated the phraseology in one way or another to the parallel in Lk 4.36." Nevertheless, the UBS has given it a 'C', 'considerable doubt,' rating.

BOUNDARIES AND COHERENCE

A new paragraph at v. 28 is indicated by a new time and location and new participants. Coherence within the 21–28 paragraph is shown by three occurrences of the phrase 'evil spirit', and by the paragraph dealing with the expulsion of one such evil spirit.

PROMINENCE AND THEME

The theme is drawn from a condensation of the SEQUEL of OUTCOME₂.

EXPANSION OF OUTCOME₃ IN THE 1:21–28 DISPLAY

RELATIONAL STRUCTURE	CONTENT
COMMENT———————————————	1:28 The people immediately told *many others* throughout the whole district of Galilee *what Jesus had done*.

NOTES

1:28 The people immediately told *many others ... what Jesus had done* The text here literally is 'went forth the report of him'. It is unlikely that many languages handle this information in that form. The simplest way is to speak of people telling others of what Jesus had done. See also suggestions in TN.

BOUNDARIES AND COHERENCE

A new paragraph at v. 29 is indicated by a change in location and new topic, the healing of Peter's mother-in-law. Coherence in the 21–28 paragraph is provided by occurrences of συναγωγή 'synagogue', two occurrences of διδαχή 'teaching', and one of the cognate verb 'teach'. Coherence is also seen in the whole paragraph dealing with what happened in the synagogue on that day.

PROMINENCE AND THEME

The theme is drawn from condensations of the most naturally prominent propositions of the three OUTCOMES.

SCENE CONSTITUENT 1:29–31 (Episode of 1:21–45)

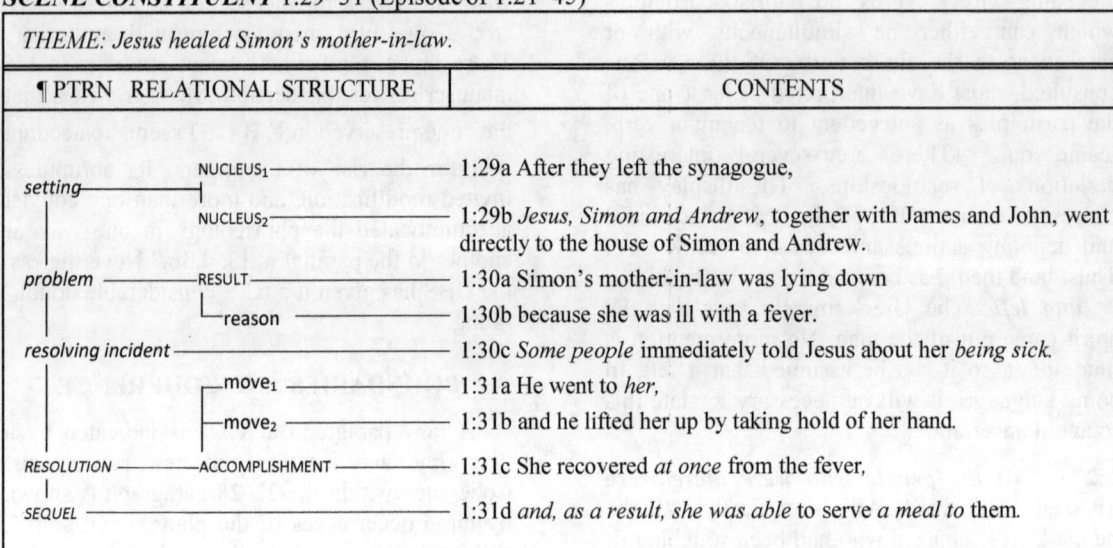

INTENT & PARAGRAPH PATTERN

This is the second of the three healing episodes in this scene, where Jesus demonstrated his power.

The intent of the 1:29–31 episode is to provide another example of Jesus performing a miracle. It is a narrative paragraph of the solutionality subtype consisting of a *setting*, a *problem*, a *resolving incident*, a RESOLUTION, and a SEQUEL.

NOTES

1:29b *Jesus, Simon and Andrew,* **together with James and John went directly** There are several variations in the order and in the verb forms (singular or plural) in this clause. UBS rates the text represented by C 'difficulty in deciding'. Metzger reports that most of the committee favored the plural because copyists would tend to change "the plural to the singular in order to (a) focus attention on Jesus, (b) conform the reading to the parallels in Mt 8:14 and Lk 4:38, and (c) provide a near antecedent for αὐτῷ 'him' of v. 30." There seems to be no good reason to go against the UBS decision.

In agreement with the plural form of the verbs the names of Jesus, Simon, and Andrew have been supplied as those who were meant by the third person plural form of the verbs.

1:30c *Some people* **immediately told Jesus** There being no overt subject in the Greek, one has been supplied. A translator might even want to add the words 'who were there' if that would be clearer.

about her *being sick* This can be considered either implied or assumed as being the content of what the people told Jesus (Cf. CEV).

1:31a He went to *her* The Greek verb προσελθών 'approaching' is a participle. Since it is here a finite verb, it needs a locative object. Thus, 'her' has been supplied.

1:31c She recovered *at once* **from the fever** This immediacy is implied by the fact that she then served them.

1:31d she *was able* **to serve** *a meal to* **them** The Greek is καὶ διηκόνει αὐτοῖς, 'and she served them'. No doubt everyone who read the Greek knew that a meal was implied in this setting; but, if it is not clear to current readers, it should be supplied.

BOUNDARIES AND COHERENCE

A new paragraph at v. 32 is indicated by a change in time and in topic (multiple healings and expulsion of demons). Coherence is provided by the word πυρέσσω 'fever' and the cognate verb πυρετός 'fever-stricken'.

PROMINENCE AND THEME

The theme is drawn from the most naturally prominent propositions of the *problem* and the RESOLUTION.

SCENE CONSTITUENT 1:32–34 (Episode of 1:21–45)

THEME: *Jesus healed many people and expelled many evil spirits.*

¶ PTRN RELATIONAL STRUCTURE	CONTENTS
occasion — NUCLEUS₁	1:32a In the evening, after the sun had gone down, *and restrictions on Jewish travel on the Sabbath day were ended,*
NUCLEUS₂	1:32b *some people* brought to Jesus many people who were sick and others who had evil spirits in them.
COMMENT	1:33 *It seemed as though everyone* [HYP] [MTY] *who lived in* the town was gathered at the doorway.
OUTCOME — NUCLEUS₁	1:34a Jesus healed many people who were ill with various diseases,
NUCLEUS₂ — NUCLEUS₁	1:34b he expelled many evil spirits *from people,*
NUCLEUS₂ — RESULT	1:34c but he did not allow the evil spirits to speak *about him,*
reason	1:34d because they knew he was *the Messiah.*

INTENT & PARAGRAPH PATTERN

This is the last of the three healing episodes in this scene, where Jesus demonstrated his power.

The author in this unit intends to affect the reader's knowledge about Jesus.

This is a narrative paragraph consisting of an *occasion* (vv. 32–33), and an *OUTCOME* (v. 34).

NOTES

1:32a *and restrictions on Jewish travel on the Sabbath day were ended, and then people were allowed to carry loads* As Bratcher and Nida point out (p. 58), "the expression 'that evening, at sundown', is not to be interpreted purely as tautological or meaningless repetition." They go on to state what has been included here in italics as implied information. Many commentators (e.g., Lane, Gundry, Marcus, Strauss, and see especially TN) make this point, but only TfT includes it in the translation. It is difficult to abbreviate this information:

- Carrying loads was considered work;
- work was prohibited on the Sabbath;
- but the Sabbath ended at sundown,
- after which carrying loads was permissible.

1:32b *some people* **brought** The Greek verb for 'bring' here does not have an overt subject. Therefore an indefinite subject has been supplied in the display.

1:33 *It seemed as though everyone who lived in the town was gathered at the doorway* Mark uses two figures of speech here. He writes that 'all the city' assembled at the door. 'The city', of course, is a metonymy which refers to the people who lived there. 'All' is considered hyperbole as it is unlikely that it could have been literally true.

1:34b *and he expelled many evil spirits from people* In the Greek there is no overt source expressed. Since many languages may require a source and because some people believe that evil spirits dwell in objects as well as people, the implied source is spelled out in this text.

1:34c *and he did not allow the evil spirits to speak about him* It is generally agreed in versions and commentaries that the speech which was not allowed was that referring to Jesus, so that has been filled in. It does not mean that the demons were never allowed to speak again.

1:34d *because they knew he was the Messiah* The versions translate this as 'they knew him' (literal) or as 'they knew who he was'. Neither of these seems an adequate reason for Jesus' actions; therefore, filling in the idea of his connection with God may help clarify the situation. (Cf. Bratcher & Nida, Evans, Hendriksen, and Lane.)

There are several variants of this information actually given in some manuscripts, mostly varying orders for the words meaning "him to be Christ". Metzger believes these to be scribal additions derived from the account in Luke 4:41. As he says: "If any one of the longer readings had been original in Mark, there is no reason why it should have been altered or eliminated entirely."

To some readers, it may seem strange that Jesus would prevent the demons from revealing his identity.

BOUNDARIES AND COHERENCE

A new paragraph at v. 35 is marked by an indication of time and a change in location, and a new topic: Jesus' ministry throughout Galilee. Coherence in the 32–34 paragraph is provided by two occurrences of the word δαιμόνιον 'demon' and one occurrence of the cognate verb δαιμονίζομαι 'demonized', πυρετός 'fever-stricken, and by the episode consisting only of the account of Jesus healing Peter's mother-in-law, and by the episode relating Jesus' healing ministry that evening.

PROMINENCE AND THEME

The theme is derived from the TWO NUCLEI of the OUTCOME which are the most prominent units.

SCENE CONSTITUENT 1:35–45 *(Episode Cluster of 1:21–45)*

THEME: Jesus continued his ministry by telling God's message, expelling evil spirits, and curing a leper.	
MACROSTRUCTURE	CONTENTS
occasion	1:35–39 Jesus traveled throughout Galilee, telling God's message and expelling evil spirits from people.
OUTCOME	1:40–45 After a leper pleaded with Jesus to cure him, Jesus cured him and arranged for him to be able to associate with people again.

INTENT & PARAGRAPH PATTERN

From this point on, the author focuses on what Jesus did in Galilee beyond his home region of Capernaum. This episode cluster of 1:35–45 occurs within the group of events in which Jesus heals many people. The unit consists of an *occasion* and an OUTCOME. Notice that the formerly leprous man proclaimed publicly what Jesus had done, even though Jesus had told him not to do so.

BOUNDARIES AND COHERENCE

The initial boundary was discussed as the closing boundary of unit 1:32–34. Here there is a new focus of Jesus expanding his actions and teaching to further places in Galilee. After v. 45 there is a shift from Jesus healing people to Jesus teaching that he has authority to regulate a new order of religious practices.

PROMINENCE AND THEME

The theme is derived from the *occasion* and from the OUTCOME.

EPISODE CLUSTER CONSTITUENT 1:35–39 (Episode of 1:35–45)

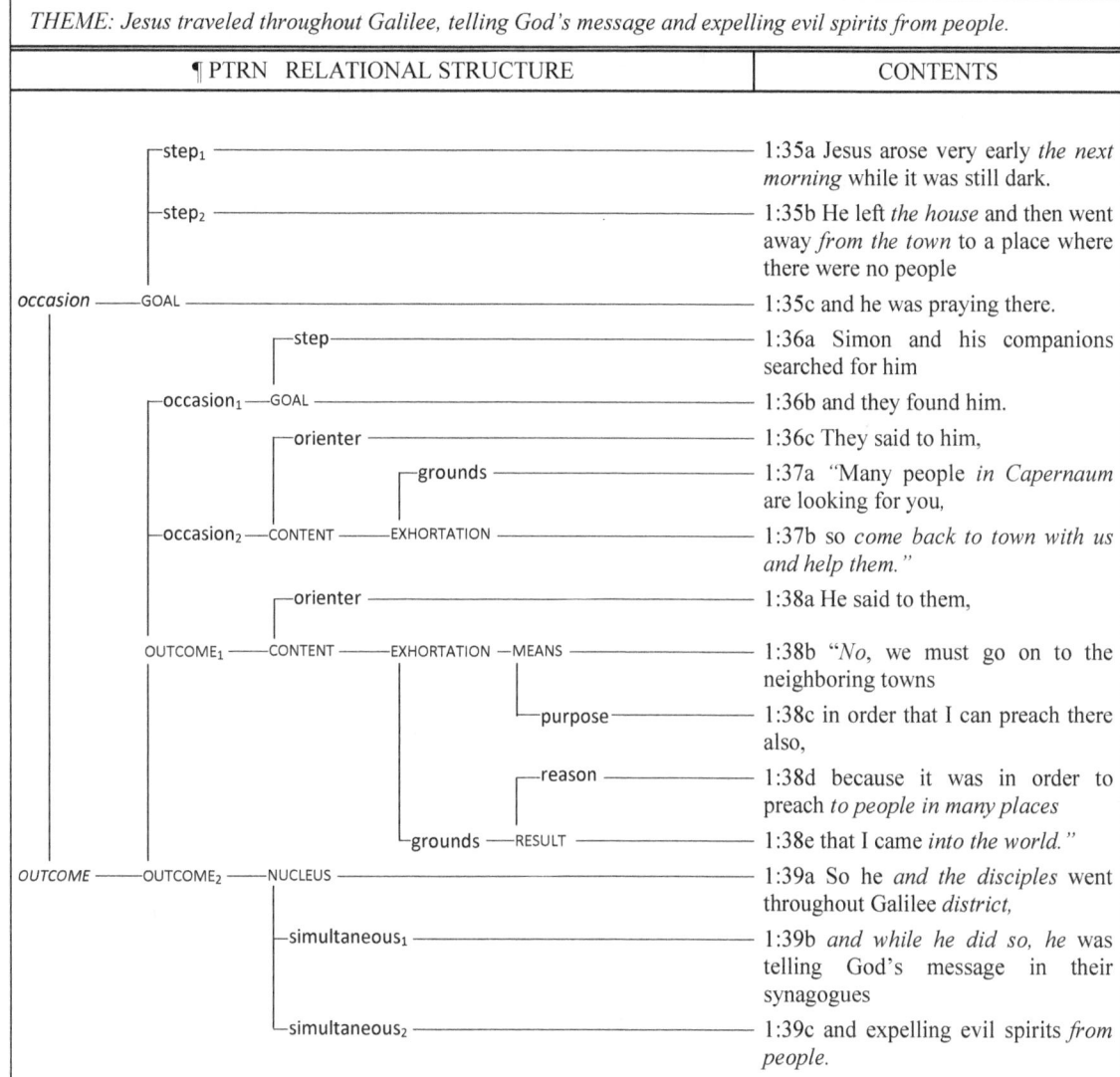

INTENT AND RHETORICAL STRUCTURE

This is one of two units that tell about Jesus and his disciples teaching and healing people in the greater area of Galilee.

The intent of this paragraph is narrative in form. It is of the causality type and consists of an *occasion* (v. 35) and an OUTCOME (vv. 36–39).

NOTES

1:35a Jesus arose very early *the next morning* The Greek here is πρωΐ ἔννυχα λίαν, 'very early at night'; but is usually translated as 'very early in the morning' or 'while it was still night'.

1:35b He left *the house* and then went away *from the town* Though it does not appear in the Greek, locative phrases for the verbs of motion have been supplied in the text to complete the case frame.

1:37 Many people *in Capernaum* are looking for you, *so come back to town with us and help them* The Greek words are ὅτι πάντες ζητοῦσίν σε 'all are seeking thee'. The 'all' here is hyperbolic and has been adjusted to make it clear that Peter really means 'come back to town with us and help them'.

Peter's statement can be looked at as disappointment that Jesus has left the city, or an implied request to return there to continue ministering to people; cf. Gundry, Hiebert, Lane, Hendriksen, Lenski, and Gould. Peter's statement seems pointless without this implicit information being understood.

1:38b ***No,*** **we must go on** The word 'No' is supplied to make clear that Jesus is rejecting Peter's suggestion. The words 'we must go' fit the context much better than 'Let's go'. Bratcher and Nida say "it is not as much a plea, a request, as an exhortation." Translations which have 'we must' include TEV, NLT, and CEV.

1:38d in order to preach *to many people in many places* The indirect object of the verb 'preach' has been supplied.

1:38e that I came *into the world* The Greek verb is ἐξῆλθον, 'go out/come out', with neither the place of origin or of goal mentioned. Therefore, the latter has been filled in; the former can probably remain implied. None of the versions examined (except TfT) supply locative phrases.

1:39 In this verse there are two places where texts vary. The first is right at the beginning, καὶ ἦλθεν, 'and he came' which introduces the sentence. Other manuscripts. have ἦν, 'he was'. The shorter form may have been introduced by copyists; but the UBS committee felt the longer one was needed to carry on the idea from the final verb in the previous verse which is ἐξῆθον, 'go out/come out'.

The second variant concerns the phrase εἰς τὰς συναγωγὰς αὐτῶν, 'in the synagogues of them'. Some manuscripts have ἐν, 'in' in place of εἰς. Metzger feels that this is a natural attempt to standardize the grammar for those who substituted εἰς for ἐν.

1:39a went...throughout Galilee *district* It is often helpful or necessary to add to place names such information as 'town, city, district', etc.

he and his disciples There are two reasons for including this information: first, to avoid the idea that Peter and the others were so disappointed that they refused to go further with Jesus; and second, this follows the Biblical pattern of mentioning only the most important individual in what was obviously a corporate action.

1:39c and expelling evil spirits *from people* See 1:34b.

BOUNDARIES AND COHERENCE

A new paragraph at v. 40 is indicated by the introduction of a new participant, a leper. Coherence in his brief paragraph is provided by two occurrences of the verb κηρύσσω 'preach'.

PROMINENCE AND THEME

The theme statement is taken from the two *simultaneous* propositions of the OUTCOME.

EPISODE CLUSTER CONSTITUENT 1:40–45 (Episode of 1:35–45)

THEME: After a leper pleaded with Jesus to cure him, Jesus cured him and arranged for him to be able to associate with people again.

¶PTRN RELATIONAL STRUCTURE	CONTENTS
setting/problem — GOAL — step₁	1:40a One day a leper came to Jesus.
step₂	1:40b He knelt down in front of Jesus.
CONTENT — orienter	1:40c He pleaded with him:
RESULT	1:40d "If you are willing *to cure me, please do so,*
reason	1:40e *since I know* you are able to do it."
occasion₁ — RESULT — reason	1:41a Because Jesus felt sorry for him,
RESULT	1:41b *ignoring taboos about touching lepers,* he reached out his hand and touched the leper
occasion₂ — CONTENT — orienter	1:41c and said to him,
reason	1:41d *"Since* I am willing *to cure you,*
RESULT	1:41e be cured!"
RESOLUTION₁ — OUTCOME	1:42 Immediately the man ceased to be a leper and was cured.
NUCLEUS	1:43 *Then in order that he would do the things necessary in order that people would associate with him again* Jesus spoke sternly to him before he sent him away.
CONTENT₁ — orienter	1:44a What Jesus said was:
CONTRAST₁	1:44b "Make sure that you do not tell anyone *about what happened.*
CONTRAST₂ — MEANS	1:44c Instead, go to the priest *in Jerusalem* and show yourself to him
purpose	1:44d *in order that he may examine you and verify that you are cured.*
RESOLUTION₂ — CONTENT₂ — MEANS	1:44e And take to him what Moses commanded *that a person who has been cured of leprosy should offer,*
purpose₁	1:44f *in order that he* may offer it *as a sacrifice to God,*
purpose₂	1:44g and in order that, *the local people* will know, *after the priest tells them,* that you have been cured."
SEQUEL — NUCLEUS — circumstance	1:45a However, after the man went *and saw the priest,*
NUCLEUS	1:45b he began to talk to many *people* about *how Jesus had cured him* [DOU].
CONTRAST₁ — RESULT	1:45c As a result, Jesus was no longer able to enter any town publicly,
reason	1:45d *because the crowds would surround him.*
OUTCOME — CONTRAST₂	1:45e Instead, he remained outside *the towns* in places where no people lived.
CONTRAST₃	1:45f But people kept coming to him from all over that region [HYP].

INTENT AND RHETORICAL STRUCTURE

This is the second of two units that tell about Jesus and his disciples teaching and healing people in the greater area of Galilee.

This is a narrative paragraph of the solutionality type and consists of a *problem* (v. 40), two RESOLUTIONS (vv. 41–44), a SEQUEL (v. 45a–b), and a COMMENT (v. 45c–f). The intent is to demonstrate Jesus' power to make a leper cured.

NOTES

1:40 There are some variations in texts in this verse. Some manuscripts omit καὶ γονυπετῶν 'and falling on his knees' and others have this phrase plus αὐτὸν 'him'. According to Metzger, the support for omission is strong; but the committee decided to retain the verb phrase in square brackets. This keeps the parallel with Matthew's and Luke's accounts which include the idea of the man kneeling before Jesus.

However, leaving this in violates the UBS' own principle that the reading that is most likely to account for the variants is the preferable one to choose. If the phrase had been there originally there would be no reason to omit it. If it were not there in the original, there are two good reasons for adding it: clarification and parallelism with the Matthew and Luke accounts. Following that principle, the phrase has been omitted in the display.

1:40d If you are willing *to cure me, please do so* Since, in many languages the verb, 'cleanse' refers only to getting rid of dirt it is suggested that 'cure' is more meaningful. This was not merely a statement of Jesus' ability, but a strong request for healing. NEB makes this clear with the wording 'begging his help'.

1:40e *since I know* **you are able to do it** This proposition is the grounds for the leper's plea that Jesus heal him. 'Since I know' is left unexpressed in the Greek text; but may be needed in some languages.

1:41a The latest edition of the GNT gives a B, 'almost certain,' rating to the reading σπλαγχνισθεὶς 'have pity or compassion'. A few manuscripts have ὀργισθείς, 'being angry'. There are internal reasons why either verb might be exchanged for the other one, but the external evidence for the first is overwhelming.

1:41b *ignoring taboos about touching lepers,* **he reached out his hand** There are several reasons for including this information. (1) Without these words, the mention of stretching out his hand seems superfluous. How could he touch the man without stretching out his hand? (2) It gives the rationale for the man's statement, "If you are willing…" and of Jesus' reply, "I am willing," explaining a possible unwillingness. (3) Most importantly, it conveys cultural information concerning lepers, which the original writer knew his audience would understand.

1:41d Since I am willing *to cure you* The Greek text is θέλω, καθαρίσθητι 'I am willing, be cleansed'. For the italicized part see the note on v. 40d. This proposition is the grounds for the exhortation which follows in v. 41e.

1:42 Immediately the man ceased to be a leper The wording of the text, 'the leprosy left him', is a personification which has been adjusted in the display.

1:43 *Then in order that he would do the things necessary so that people would associate with him again* **Jesus spoke sternly to him** The implied information has been included in the display to fill in the reason why the cured leper should do these things (in addition to the fact that the Mosaic law required to be done what Jesus mentioned specifically in v. 44).

A footnote in the NIV Study Bible says, "The sacrifices were to be evidence to the priests and the people that the cure was real and that Jesus respected the law. The healing was also a testimony to Jesus' divine power, since Jews believed that only God could cure leprosy (see 2 Ki 5:1–14)."

1:44b Make sure that you do not tell anyone *about what happened*. The italicized phrase is for those languages which need an object for the verb 'tell'. CEV has "about this". This was not an injunction that the man remain silent for the rest of his life.

1:44d *in order that he may examine you and verify that you are cured* This purpose clause is here to supply the purpose for which the man was to show himself to the priest. This information would have been understood by people in the original audience who were familiar with the O.T. regulations regarding leprosy (Lev. 13). CEV has "show the priest that you are well".

1:44f *in order that he* **may offer it** *as a sacrifice to God* Mark assumed complete understanding of the Jewish law in all of this instruction. (As Jesus probably did, too.) For readers today with little access to the Old Testament, it would be wise to supply this to make things clear. Thus it was included to avoid the wrong meaning that the man himself was to offer the sacrifice.

1:44g in order that, *the local people* **will know,** *after the priest tells them, that you have been cured* The GNT has only 'for a testimony to them'. The display spells out the meaning; CEV has "everyone will know that you have been healed". NLT's rendering is similar.

This is a further case where implied information has been supplied for clarity. It is an explication of the phrase εἰς μαρτύριον αὐτοῖς 'as a testimony to them', and states what is expressed five times in Lev. 13.

1:45a However, after the man went *and saw the priest* There is no mention in the text that the man actually saw the priest; but it is unlikely that anyone would have listened to him if he had not had 'clearance' from the priests. It can be considered as avoiding the wrong implication that the man did not see the priest (since it appears that he did disobey Jesus' other instruction).

1:45b he began to talk to many *people* The Greek text has a doublet here which has been reduced to one verb in the display.

about *how Jesus had cured him* The second part of the doublet, 'to spread the word' has variously been translated as 'the matter'; 'the news'; or 'what had happened to him'. The translation in the display makes explicit what the content of his talk was.

1:45d *because the crowds would surround him* This clause supplies the reason for the result in 1:45c.

1:45e he remained outside *the towns* The words in italics specify the object of the preposition 'outside'.

1:45f But people were coming to him from all over that region This has been listed as hyperbole and has often been translated as 'from everywhere', which would still be hyperbole. The Greek word is πάντοθεν 'from all directions' (BAGD) which need not be categorized as Hyperbole.

BOUNDARIES AND COHERENCE

A new paragraph at 2:1 is indicated by an indication of time and change in location, and a new topic: proof of Jesus authority to forgive sins. Coherence within the 40–45 paragraph is provided by the word λεπρός 'leper' and the cognate word λέπρα 'leprosy'. The very structure of the narrative having a *problem* and a RESOLUTION, in which Jesus heals and cleanses a leper, also shows that this is a coherent unit.

PROMINENCE AND THEME

The theme is taken from the most naturally prominent propositions of the *problem*, of the *two steps* in RESOLUTION$_1$, and an abbreviation of the first part of the NUCLEUS of RESOLUTION$_2$. The OUTCOME is not considered to be as thematic as the *problem* and RESOLUTIONS.

ACT CONSTITUENT 2:1—3:6 (Scene of 1:16—3:6)

THEME: Jesus had some sharp discussions with the religious authorities about his authority over religious practices, culminating in the authorities planning to kill him.

MACROSTRUCTURE	CONTENTS
background information	2:1–12 While Jesus was teaching in a crowded house, men brought a paralyzed man to be healed, and Jesus demonstrated his authority to forgive sins by healing the man.
buildup	2:13–17 Jesus invited Levi, a tax collector, to be his disciple, and refuted those who objected to his associating with such people.
central issue	2:18–22 John's disciples and others came to Jesus with a question about fasting and he answered them with parables.
final buildup	2:23–28 When the Pharisees complained about Jesus' disciples plucking grain on the Sabbath day, Jesus replied that he is able to determine what people should do on the Sabbath.
CLIMAX	3:1–6 After Jesus healed a man on the Sabbath, the Jewish leaders began to plan to kill him.

INTENT AND RHETORICAL STRUCTURE

The section from 2:1–3:6 consists of a series of five incidents which introduce the element of conflict with the Jewish religious authorities. The consensus of commentators is that these are not in chronological order or that they even occurred close to each other in time, but that Mark grouped them together. His intent seems either to group incidents with a common theme: i.e., controversy, or to illustrate the escalation of conflict from merely his opponents questioning in their hearts to their gathering together to plan how to get rid of Jesus.

Every episode has a *setting* and *occasion* or *problem*, which sets the stage for Jesus' teaching on subjects about the Jewish laws and traditions as opposed to his new order or system.

BOUNDARIES AND COHERENCE

There is a sharp contrast at this point from the previous scene by switching from Jesus healing people to Jesus setting up a new religious order of practices, thus clashing with the Jewish authorities. There is no grammatical conjunction, except asyndeton, at the beginning boundary, and similarly there is no conjunction at the closing boundary. However, the next unit has a change of location and a totally new direction of Jesus leading his disciples to realize who he is.

PROMINENCE AND THEME

This unit consists of five sub-units all dealing with the issue of religious rituals. The theme is a synthesis of the rhetorical build-up and climax.

SCENE CONSTITUENT 2:1–12 (Episode of 2:1—3:6)

THEME: *While Jesus was teaching in a crowded house, men brought a paralyzed man to be healed, and Jesus demonstrated his authority to forgive sins by healing the man.*

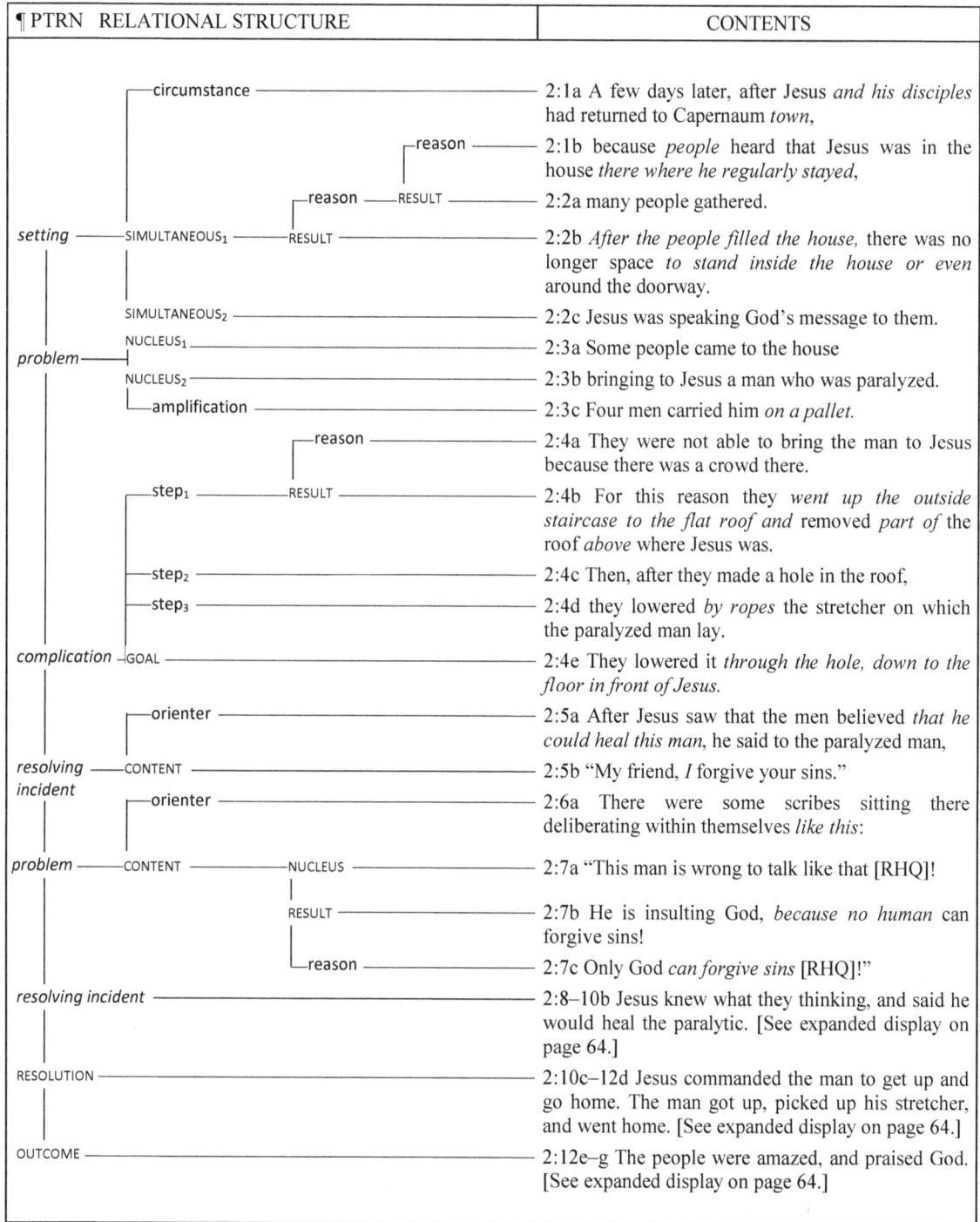

INTENT AND RHETORICAL STRUCTURE

The 2:1–12 episode is a narrative of the solutionality sub-type consisting of a *setting*, a *problem*, a *complication*, two *resolving incidents*, a RESOLUTION, and an OUTCOME. Here Mark continues his description of the initial phase of Jesus' Galilean ministry.

This episode, 2:1–12, is the first of five incidents of opposition between the Jewish authorities and Jesus. Here the opposition is covert, "some scribes sitting there deliberating within themselves".

This episode demonstrates that Jesus assumes the divine power to forgive sins. The healing of the paralytic was primarily to confirm Jesus' authority to forgive sins.

Two other important matters are mentioned here: 1) believing that Jesus could heal in v. 5, and 2) Jesus demonstrated to the scribes (and others) his authority to forgive sins when it was risky to do so.

There are two interesting repartee structures in this episode:

The first one is as follows:

1) There is the chain initiated by Jesus when he said to the paralytic that he forgives his sins,
2) the reaction of the religious authorities that Jesus was usurping God's authority,
3) Jesus refuting the authorities murmurings, and
4) Jesus commanding the paralytic to get up and walk.

The second repartee serves to bracket the episode by Jesus saying to the paralytic that he forgives his sins, and then he later says to him, "Get up and walk!"

NOTES

2:1b *people* **heard that Jesus was in the house** *there where he regularly stayed* The Greek for what the people heard is ὅτι ἐν οἴκῳ ἐστιν, 'that he is at home'. Since this may imply that he owned the house in some languages, which the Greek does not necessarily indicate, and since elsewhere Scripture reports that he did not have a home of his own, the display shows 'in the house where he regularly stayed'. This covers the concept of a place that people knew about because he habitually stayed there when he came to the town and also avoids implying that he owned the house.

2:2b *after the people filled the house*, **there was no longer space** *to stand inside the house* **or even around the doorway.** The Greek is μηκέτι χωρεῖν μηδὲ τὰ πρὸς τὴν θύραν, 'no longer to have room, not (or, 'not even') at the door'. As Bratcher and Nida say: "the meaning is that such a crowd was gathered in the house and overflowing into the street, that not even on the street, near the door, was there room for any more people."

2:3c **Four men carried him** *on a pallet.* Because some languages are very specific in regard to how a thing or person is carried, this information has been supplied from v. 4.

2:4 There are a couple of textual variations in verse 4, one of which is very minor and not mentioned in the GNT though Metzger mentions it briefly.

The verse begins with καὶ μὴ δυνάμενοι προσενέγκαι, 'and not being able to bring to', which is given a {B} rating by the committee, which felt that the absence of a direct object (αὐτόν) "may have led to the substitution of προσεγγίσαι ('to come near') or προσελθεῖν ('to come to')" (Metzger).

The following phrase, which is διὰ τὸν ὄχλον, 'because of the crowd', occurs in two or three manuscripts as ἀπὸ τοῦ ὄχλου, 'from the crowd'. This is thought by one of the committee to reflect a primitive Aramaic word and to be more in accord with Mark's style. However, it does not have enough support to appear in the textual apparatus.

2:4b **they** *went up the outside staircase to the flat roof* This clause has been added to clarify how they got up on the roof.

removed *part of* **the roof** *above* **where Jesus was** The Greek clause, ἀπεστέγασαν τὴν στέγην, 'They unroofed the roof', implies an intimate knowledge of the architecture and customs of the area at that time in history. That architecture is much the same today in that part of the world but quite foreign elsewhere, so some expansion may be needed lest the wrong information be transmitted. It seems apparent that they removed only enough of the roof to make room for the pallet to be lowered; but some people/languages may require the details for clarity.

For the location of the area where the roofing was removed the Greek is ὅπου ἦν, 'where he was'. Since the goal of the four men was to bring their friend to Jesus it is clear that the pronoun refers to him. But, for those languages which need to be specific, the name, Jesus, has been supplied.

2:4d **they lowered** *by ropes* **the stretcher.** The method by which the stretcher was lowered is filled in for those languages which will require the method to be specified.

2:4e They lowered it *through the hole, down to the floor in front of Jesus* This information is inferred by the previous information that the house was full, that the men wanted to take their friend to Jesus, and that Jesus, apparently, saw him immediately after the stretcher was lowered.

2:5a the men believed *that he could heal this man* The content of the men's belief has been supplied for clarity. This is a matter of filling out the case roles for the verb.

2:5b My friend The GNT has τέκνον which basically means 'child', but the primary sense is not intended here. Many versions have 'my son', but the literal sense of 'son' is not meant here, either. CEV also has "my friend".

***I* forgive your sins** The Greek for "forgive" in this sentence is passive and has been changed to active form in the display with the agent of the action supplied, that is, 'I' standing for Jesus. In v. 10 Jesus states that he has authority to forgive sins. There is a variation between present and perfect tenses. UBS gives the present tense, ἀφίενται, 'are forgiven' a B 'almost certain' rating. The perfect tense, ἀφέωνται 'have been forgiven', is felt to have been introduced by copyists from Luke's account. Metzger also notes: "Mark's use of the present tense (ἀφίενται) was followed by Matthew (Mt 9.2)."

2:6a *like this* This phrase is added to make it clear that the following quote is the content of what the scribes were thinking, and not speech coming from another source.

2:7a This man is wrong to talk like that The Greek for this quote is in the form of a rhetorical question. The scribes did not really want to know why Jesus was talking like that; but, rather, to condemn him for it.

2:7b *because no human* can forgive sins! This clause gives the implied contrast with the one that follows. TEV also has "No man can *forgive sins*".

2:7c Only God *can forgive sins!* The phrase in italics is repeated from 7b and it may not be needed here. In the Greek this clause is in the form of a rhetorical question, and many versions retain the form. Several of the more recent translations translate it as it appears here. (NCV, CEV, and The Message, for example.)

EXPANSION OF RESOLVING INCIDENT₂, RESOLUTION, AND OUTCOME 2:8–12 OF MARK 2:1–12 DISPLAY

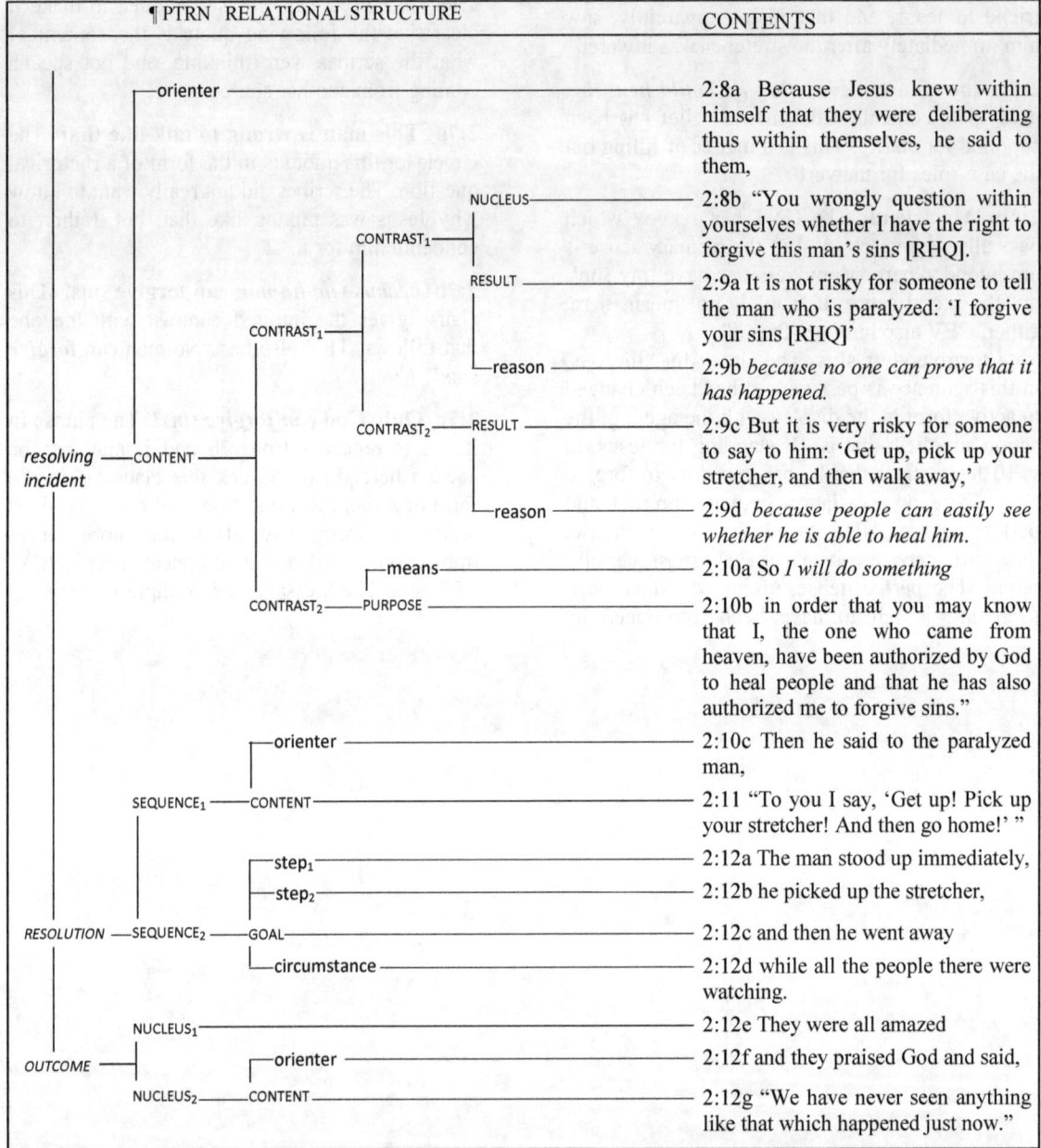

NOTES

2:8a Because Jesus immediately knew *within himself that they were deliberating thus within themselves* The verse begins in Greek with καὶ εὐθὺς ἐπιγνούς 'And immediately knowing' which could be awkward to translate. In order to avoid using the participle, the display shows 'Because' and the finite verb 'knew' to show the reason for Jesus' question which follows in 2:8b.

Reason is one relationship which can be communicated through the Greek participle.

The next phrase τῷ πνεύματι αὐτοῦ 'in his spirit' may also pose difficulties. The UBS Handbook states: "It is often difficult to use for *spirit* in this verse the same term which may be employed for *Holy Spirit*, and it is especially important to avoid a word for spirit which will imply a demon or a familiar spirit." To avoid this problem the display has 'within himself'. In many languages such a phrase may not be necessary; cf. TEV, JBP, NLT, and CEV.

Following this prepositional cluster a similar phrase occurs referring to the scribes. διαλογίζονται ἐν ἑαυτοῖς 'they questioned among themselves', has been translated in various ways. The New Living Translation has "they were discussing among themselves" but the others consulted imply by their translations that the scribes were thinking these things to themselves, not discussing it with each other. Several of the modern translations merely say that Jesus knew what they were thinking. Again the UBS Handbook points out a possible problem with the more literal translations. "In some languages one cannot 'question within oneself', for 'to question' means to ask another." They suggest using 'to think' or 'to wonder'. These things will also need to be considered in relation to the next portion of the verse.

2:8b *whether I have the right to forgive this man's sins.* This material has been supplied to fill in the meaning of the Greek ταῦτα 'these things', i.e., the things they were thinking.

2:9a **It is not risky for someone to tell the man** The Greek begins this verse with τί ἐστιν εὐκοπώτερον, 'What is easier?' followed by the quote. This rhetorical question is shown in the display as a statement.

Mark appears to be using the rhetorical question to get his audience to think about what he is about to say. The translator should use whatever device conveys this idea.

risky The Greek text presents questions of both interpretation and translatability. Comparisons are often difficult to translate except by complicated constructions, such as 'is easy... and is hard' or something similar. Translating in this way may skew the intended meaning, so some other construction may be better. In this case a statement such as the one used in the display may convey the meaning better.

Another problem might be of something being easier to say than another. The immediate answer might be that uttering the words is equally easy for both statements! So it is necessary to decide just what Jesus was implying here.

There are several interpretations in the commentaries: (1) He was implying that it is easier to say 'your sins are forgiven'; (2) He was implying that neither was easier than the other; (3) He was implying that it was easier to heal the man.

The first view is shown in the display, though the second is equally supported by commentaries. The third is a more minor view. This first view is shown in the display because of the implied information stated in 9b.

I forgive your sins The display has adjusted the passive construction to an active one, supplying 'I'. See v. 5 where the same adjustment was made.

2:9b *because no one can prove that it has happened.* This implied information has been supplied for those translators who need to state the reason it was not risky (i.e., easier to say). See The Living Bible, 1971 edition. (See also France, Strauss, TN, and many other commentators.)

2:9c **But** In adjusting the rhetorical question to a statement in such a form as that of the display, it is semantically appropriate to translate the Greek ἤ 'or' as 'but' to emphasize the contrast between the statements in 9a and 9c.

2:9d *because people can easily see whether he is able to heal him.* As in 9b, the implied information has been supplied.

2:10a *I will do something* This is clearly implied by the clause 'in order that you may know…'. That these words are implied is also shown by the fact that the subsequent sentence is unfinished, as shown by the dash which the editors have put in the Greek text. This clause has been supplied in the display for those languages that do not leave such information implied.

2:10b *I, the one who came from heaven* "I" has been supplied in the display lest readers think Jesus was talking about someone else.

The Greek ὁ υἱὸς τοῦ ἀνθρώπου 'the son of man' will probably be misinterpreted or have zero meaning if translated literally. In this writer's experience, a literal translation has always conveyed wrong meaning. L&N say "It is a title with Messianic implications that Jesus used concerning himself." The phrase occurs 93 times in Ezekiel, simply to mean 'human', but has a Messianic sense in Daniel 7:13. It is this sense that Jesus used it referring to himself. Thus the display shows 'the one who came from heaven' which supplies implied content (see "Son of Man" in *Key Biblical Terms*).

have been authorized *by God* The Greek is ἐξουσίαν ἔχει 'have authority'. This has been verbalized in the display and the agent, 'God', has been supplied since 'authority' implies authorization by someone. The passive voice has been retained in order to maintain the focus on Jesus.

Languages that do not have a passive voice may have to say something like 'God authorized me'. If there is another way to keep the focus on Jesus, by all means use it.

to heal people This information is implied by Jesus' actions which followed.

2:12d *there* This word may be helpful if the translator needs some limit to whom the 'all' refers.

BOUNDARIES AND COHERENCE

The start of a new paragraph at v. 13 is indicated by change in location and the introduction of a new participant (Levi).

Coherence is provided by three occurrences of the word παραλυτικός 'paralytic', four occurrences of ἀφίημι 'forgive', four occurrences of the word ἁμαρτία 'sins', and by the whole paragraph dealing with Jesus healing a paralyzed man.

PROMINENCE AND THEME

The theme is drawn from the two simultaneous propositions of the *setting* (to specify the place and participants), the two NUCLEI of *problem*$_1$, the NUCLEUS of *problem*$_2$, CONTRAST$_2$ of SEQUENCE$_4$, and SEQUENCES$_{3\&4}$ of the *RESOLUTION*.

SCENE CONSTITUENT 2:13–17 (Episode Cluster of 2:1—3:6)

THEME: Jesus invited Levi, a tax collector, to be his disciple, and refuted those who objected to his associating with such people.

RELATIONS	CONTENT
occasion	2:13–14 Jesus invited Levi to come with him as his disciple. [See expansion on page 67.]
OUTCOME	2:15–17 Theme: Jesus refuted those who objected to his associating with people like Levi. [See expansion on page 68.]

INTENT AND RHETORICAL STRUCTURE

The 2:13–17 episode cluster is a narrative of the causality sub-type consisting of an *occasion*, and an OUTCOME. Here Mark describes Jesus inviting Levi to be his disciple, and associates himself with these people who were unaccepted by the Jewish authorities.

This episode cluster, 2:13–17, is the second of five incidents of opposition between the Jewish authorities and Jesus. Here the opposition is directed to Jesus.

This episode demonstrates that Jesus has the authority to challenge what the Jewish religious leaders claimed to be correct behavior.

BOUNDARIES AND COHERENCE

A new paragraph at v. 18 is indicated by the first mention of Pharisees and a new topic, fasting. Coherence is provided by the topic of tax collectors and sinners and Jesus' association with them.

PROMINENCE AND THEME

The theme is drawn from the two SIMULTANEOUS propositions of the *setting* (to specify the place and participants), the two NUCLEI of *problem*$_1$, the NUCLEUS of *problem*$_2$, CONTRAST$_2$ of SEQUENCE$_4$, and SEQUENCES$_{3\&4}$ of the *RESOLUTION*.

EPISODE CLUSTER CONSTITUENT 2:13–14 (Episode of 2:13–17)

THEME: Jesus invited Levi to come with him as his disciple.	
¶ PTRN RELATIONAL STRUCTURE	CONTENTS
setting	2:13a Jesus left *the town of Capernaum* again and walked alongside Lake *Galilee*.
occasion — SEQUENCE₁	2:13b A large crowd came to him.
SEQUENCE₂	2:13d Then he taught them.
circumstance — SIMULTANEOUS₁	2:14a As he walked on further, he saw *a man named* Levi, who was the son of Alpheus.
SIMULTANEOUS₂	2:14b He was sitting in his office where he collected taxes *for those who ruled the country*.
OUTCOME — SEQUENCE₁	2:14c Jesus said to him, "Come with me *in order that you may be my disciple*."
SEQUENCE₂	2:14d He got up and went with Jesus.

INTENT AND RHETORICAL STRUCTURE

This unit is very different from other episodes in that its only purpose seems to be to introduce Levi and the subsequent growing conflict between Jesus and Jewish authorities.

The 2:13–14 paragraph is a narrative of the causality sub-type consisting of a *setting* followed by an *occasion* with an OUTCOME. This, along with the following paragraph, 2:15–17, is the description of the 2nd incident in the series of conflicts.

NOTES

2:13a *the town of Capernaum* This fills in the locative case role for the Greek 'went out' showing the name of the town he went out from. It may be that its previous mention in v. 1 will be too far from this verse for clarity.

Galilee The name of the lake has been supplied for those who will need it.

2:14a *a man named* It may be that 'Levi' will not be recognized as a man's name by some groups, so it has been supplied in the display.

2:14b *where he collected taxes for those who ruled the country* The Greek is καθήμενον ἐπὶ τὸ τελώνιον 'sitting in (*or* at, RSV) the custom house'. The people of Mark's day would have known what was involved in this work. The implied information has been supplied in the display.

2:14c *Come with me in order that you may be my disciple* The Greek is Ἀκολούθει μοι 'Follow me'. The implied information in this clause is that this refers to discipleship, not a physical going behind (THM). This implied information supplies the purpose for Levi to follow Jesus.

BOUNDARIES AND COHERENCE

A new paragraph at v. 18 is indicated by the first mention of Pharisees and a new topic, fasting. Coherence is provided by three occurrences of the word τελώνης 'tax-collectors' and one of the cognate word τελώνιον 'tax-collector's booth', and by the whole paragraph dealing with Levi: Jesus summoning Levi to be his disciple and then eating in Levi's house.

PROMINENCE AND THEME

The theme consists of SEQUENCE₁ of the OUTCOME.

EPISODE CLUSTER CONSTITUENT 2:15–17 (Episode of 2:13–17)

Theme: Jesus refuted those who objected to his associating with people like Levi.

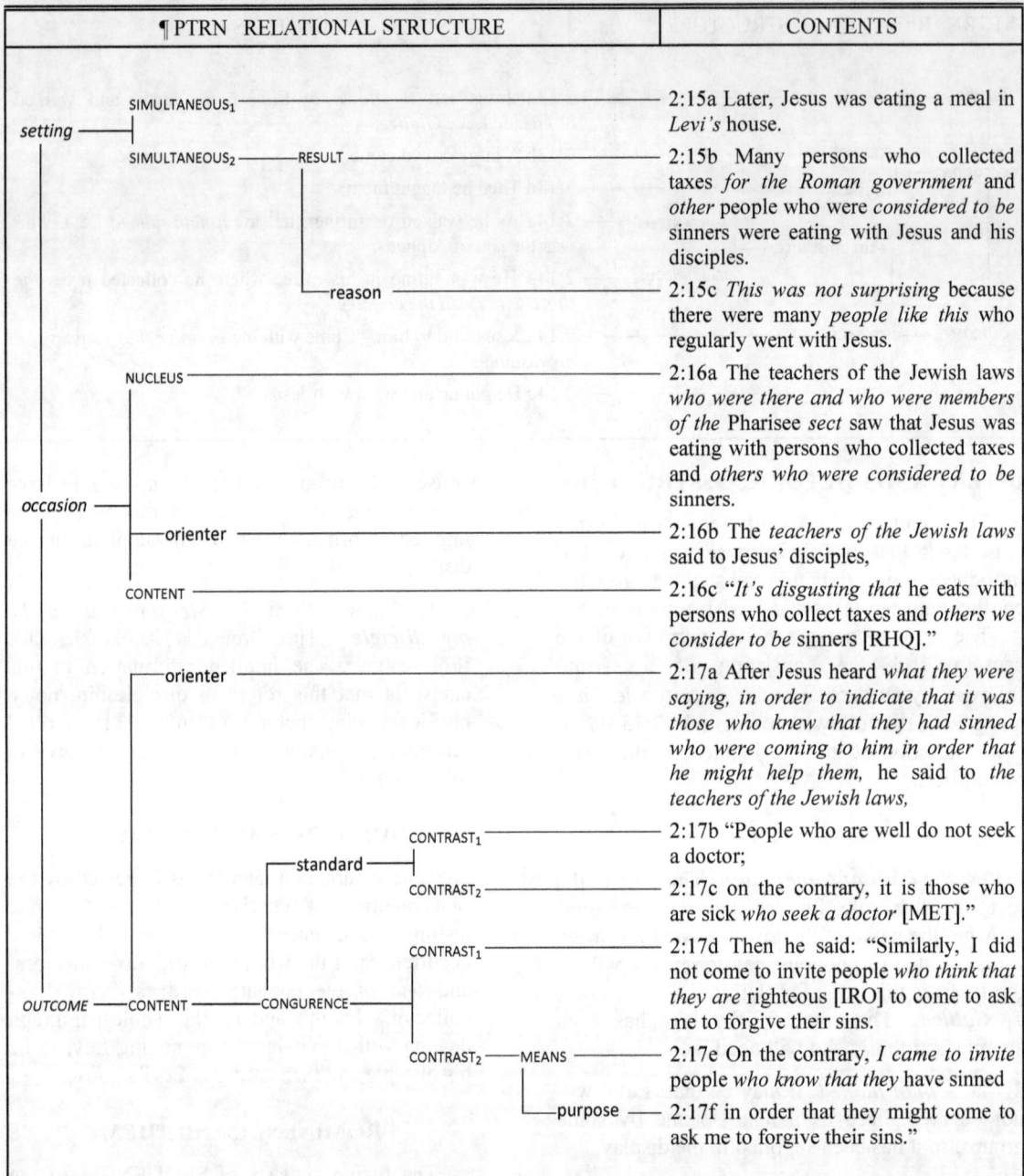

INTENT AND RHETORICAL STRUCTURE

The 2:15–17 episode is a narrative of the causality sub-type consisting of a *setting* followed by an *occasions* with an OUTCOME. This tells of the 2nd incident in the series of conflicts between Jesus and the Jewish authorities. In v. 16 the authorities pose a question to the disciples, but Jesus immediately replies in v. 17, thus binding this unit together by this repartee structure.

It would be unexpected to find such people eating with a religious teacher in that time and culture. So the explanation is given that there were many such people and they were accompanying Jesus.

NOTES

2:15c *This was not surprising* This has been supplied for clarification for those who accept the view that the Greek phrase, ἦσαν γὰρ πολλοί 'for there were many', refers to the 'tax-collectors and sinners'. In this view they were also the ones meant in the following proposition.

However, if the minority view is held that the many refers to the disciples (though there has been no previous mention of more than two or three disciples), 2:15c will need to be translated accordingly.

2:16a scribes It may be useful to spell out the meaning of this word, something like 'men who taught the laws of Moses'.

2:17a–c This sentence is in the form of a metaphor, for Jesus was not really talking about people who were physically sick. He was referring to their spiritual state.

who seek a doctor This phrase has been supplied to fill in the parallelism. If the language does not need it, don't use it!

2:17e *I came to invite* people *who know that they* have sinned. The display has filled in the implied identification of these 'sinners'. "These 'sinners' were people known for their failure to live by the religious law of Judaism, apparently in some matters" (Hurtado). "Jesus' call is to salvation; and, in order to be saved there must be a recognition of one's need" (Wessel).

2:17f *in order that they might come to ask me to forgive their sins* Implied information is supplied in the display as in 17d above.

BOUNDARIES AND COHERENCE

A new paragraph at v. 18 is indicated by a change in time and location, and new participants and a new topic: fasting. Coherence within the 2:15–17 paragraph is shown by two occurrences of ἀκολουθέω 'follow', two occurrences of τελῶναι καὶ ἁμαρτωλοί 'tax-collectors and sinners', and one occurrence of the cognate word τελώνιον 'tax-collecting booth'. Coherence is observed in that Jesus and teachers of the Jewish laws have a dialogue about eating with sinners.

PROMINENCE AND THEME

The theme is derived from a condensation of the *setting* (participants), *occasion* ("objected"), and OUTCOME ("refuted").

SCENE CONSTITUENT 2:18–22 (Episode of 2:1—3:6)

THEME: John's disciples and others came to Jesus with a question about fasting and he answered them with parables.

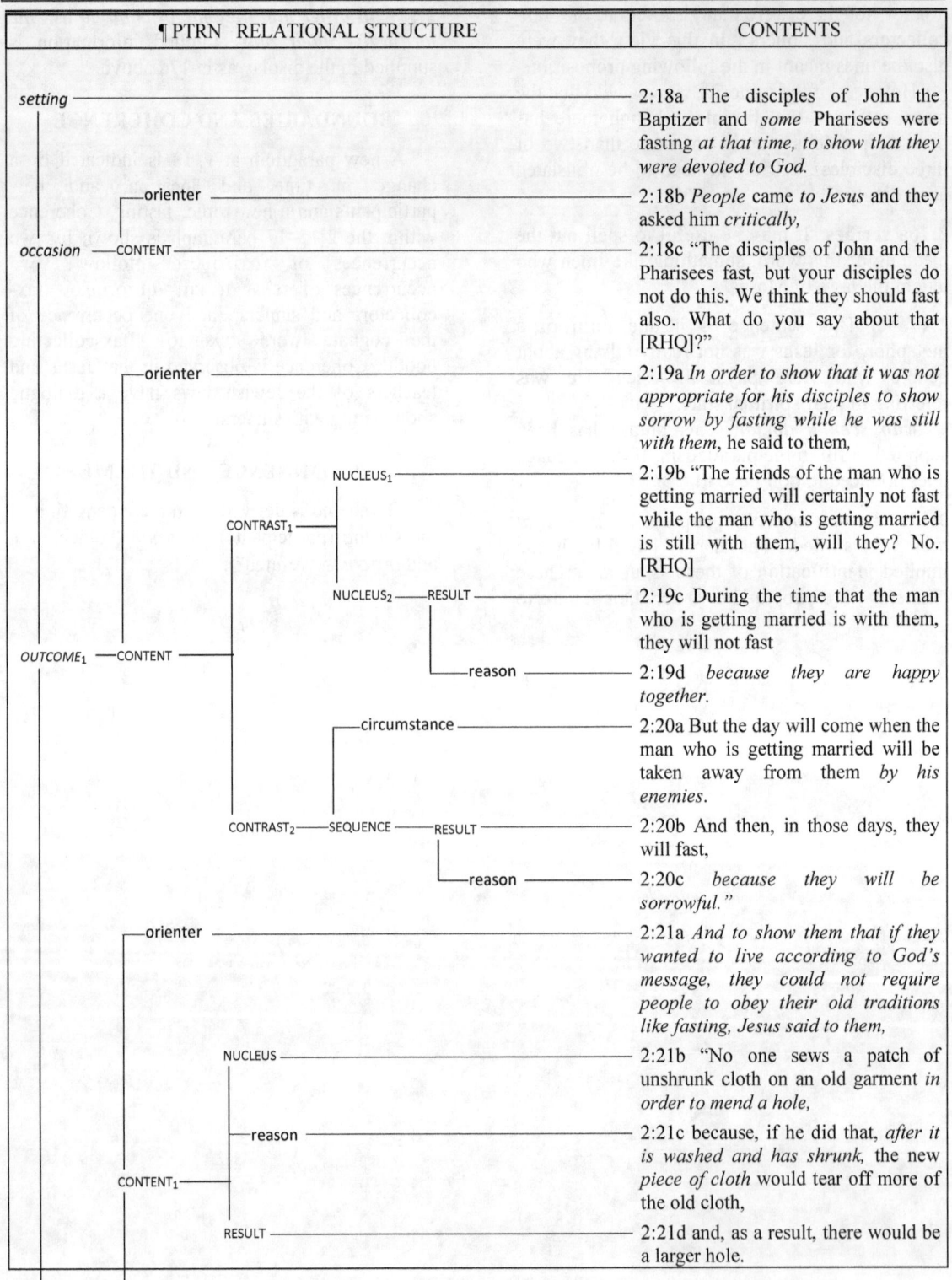

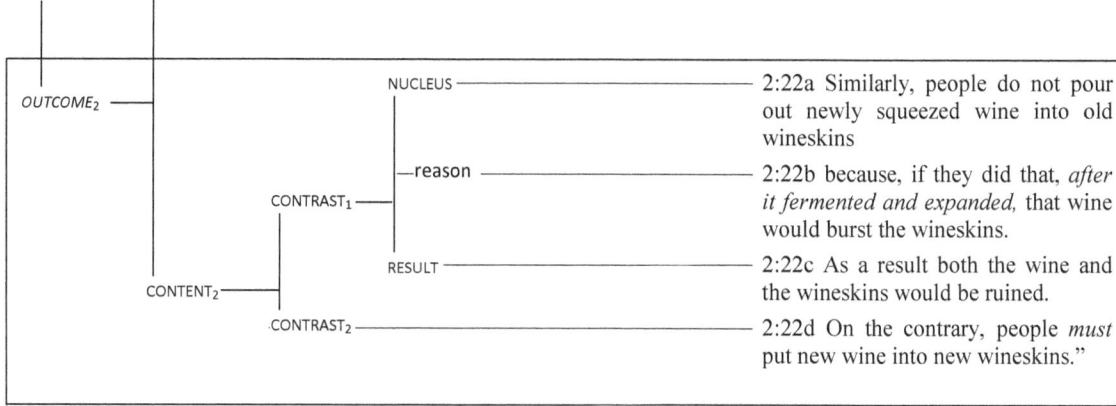

INTENT AND RHETORICAL STRUCTURE

The author's intent in this paragraph is to present some of Christ's teaching in response to the criticism of the Pharisees; it is the third of the five incidents of controversy. At this point a complaining question was posed directly to Jesus himself.

This is a narrative paragraph of the causality subtype. It consists of a *setting* (v. 18a), an *occasion* (v. 18b–c) and two OUTCOMES (vv. 19–20 and 21–22).

A dialogue structure binds this entire episode together by stating the critical question of the Jewish authorities in v. 18c, then Jesus answering their question in three units (vv. 19–20, 21, and 22). The criticizing question of the Jewish authorities is addressed to Jesus himself. Jesus answers this question by using three parables. In the new order that Jesus is establishing: 1) No one fasts during a wedding feast, 2) no one sews patches of new cloth over old garments, and 3) no one puts new wine in old wineskins.

NOTES

2:18a The disciples of John the Baptizer The text only has John's name; but for those less familiar with John than those who first read Mark's Gospel, it may be helpful to put this in for identification.

at that time This supplied information serves to indicate that a specific incident will be recounted.

to show that they were devoted to God Groups that do not make a practice of fasting may need a purpose filled in. There were various reasons for religious fasting at the time, so the display supplies a generic reason for fasting.

2:18b *critically* The question is rhetorical and implies this attitude.

2:19a *In order to show that it was not appropriate for his disciples to show sorrow by fasting while he was still with them* This is an explication of the topic of the metaphor, which Jesus used to answer their question.

2:19b will they? No This question was understood as rhetorical by the people of that day; everyone knew that that would not happen.

2:19d *because they are happy together.* This implied information supplies the logical explanation of why people would not fast in that situation, a point that is important in understanding the purpose of the metaphor.

2:20a *by his enemies* The case frame agent has been supplied in the display.

2:20c *because they will be sorrowful* Once again the logical explanation of why people would fast in this contrasting situation has been supplied.

2:21a *And to show them that if they wanted to live according to God's message, they could not require people to obey their old traditions like fasting* This implied information is the explication of the topic of Jesus' second metaphor. See Hendriksen, Strauss, Lane, Hiebert, and the suggested translation in TN.

2:21b *in order to mend a hole* The purpose someone might have for this action has been supplied. Actually you may find some cultures where this is done which may require some adjustment of wording.

2:21c *after it is washed and has shrunk* This cultural knowledge has been supplied for readers who will not know this qualification.

piece of cloth The display supplies this information for those languages which cannot have a "hanging" modifier.

2:22b *after it fermented and expanded* The display supplies this cultural knowledge that others may not have.

2:22c both the wine and the wineskins would be ruined The GNT accepts the reading: καὶ ὁ οἶνος ἀπόλλυται καὶ οἱ ἀσκοί 'the wine perishes and the wineskins'. It has been given a C 'difficulty in deciding' rating, though Metzger says that it best explains the origin of the others.

Some versions have followed manuscripts in which the additional verb, ἐκχέω 'to pour out, spill' is found. Thus, some translate that the wine is spilled out, not that it is ruined.

2:22d People *must* put new wine into new wineskins 'Must' is included as a possibility, though it does not come from the manuscripts which the GNT uses. The text the UBS committee chose has no verb and was given only a C rating. Many other manuscripts have βλητέον 'must be put'.

Metzger explains the UBS committee's choice as follows: "Not observing that εἰ ... ἀσκοί is parenthetical and therefore that the force of βάλλει carries over to the words after ἀλλά, copyists inserted βλητέον (from Lk 5.38) or βάλλουσιν (from Mt 9.17)."

BOUNDARIES AND COHERENCE

A new paragraph at 2:23 is marked by an indication of time and location, and a new topic: what is acceptable to do on the Sabbath. Cohesion is this paragraph is provided by three occurrences of the word νηστεύω 'fast', two occurrences of the word οἶνος 'wine' and two of ἀσκός 'wineskins. Coherence is also seen in that the whole paragraph deals with fasting.

PROMINENCE AND THEME

The theme of the 18–22 paragraph is drawn from most of the *setting*, a brief condensation of the CONTENT of the *occasion*, and a very brief summary of the second OUTCOME.

SCENE CONSTITUENT 2:23–28 (Episode of 2:1—3:6)

THEME: When the Pharisees complained about Jesus' disciples plucking grain on the Sabbath day, Jesus replied that he is able to determine what people should do on the Sabbath.

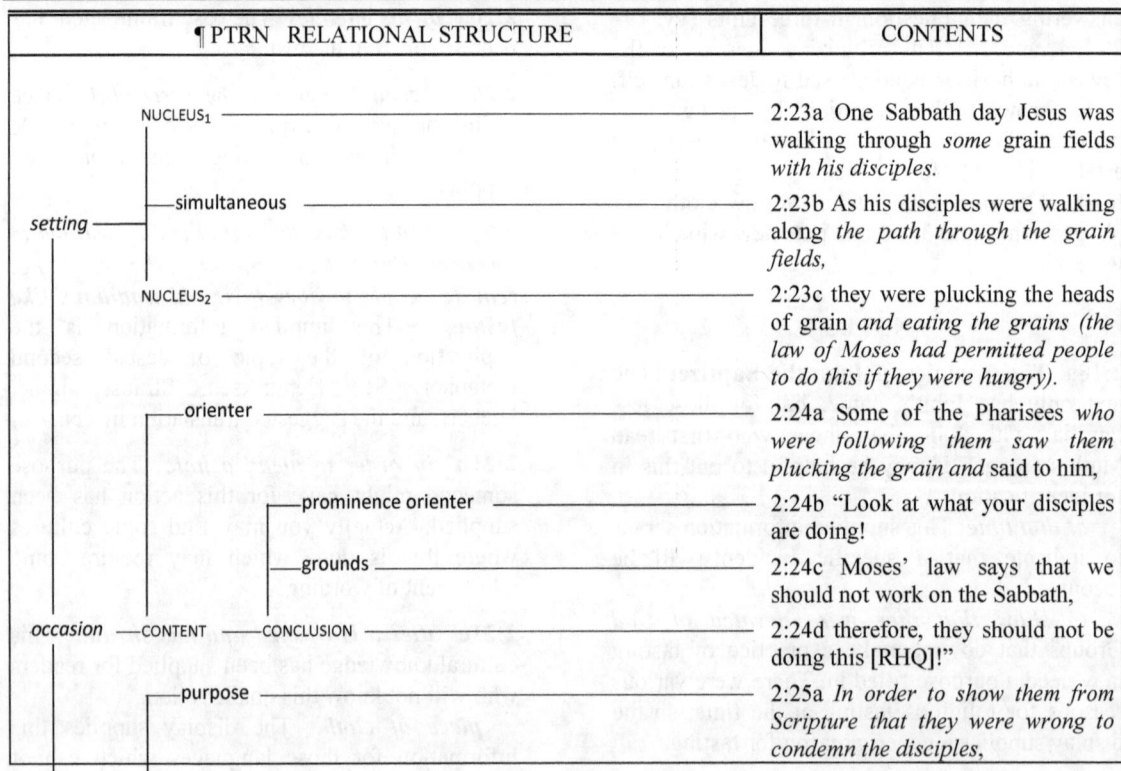

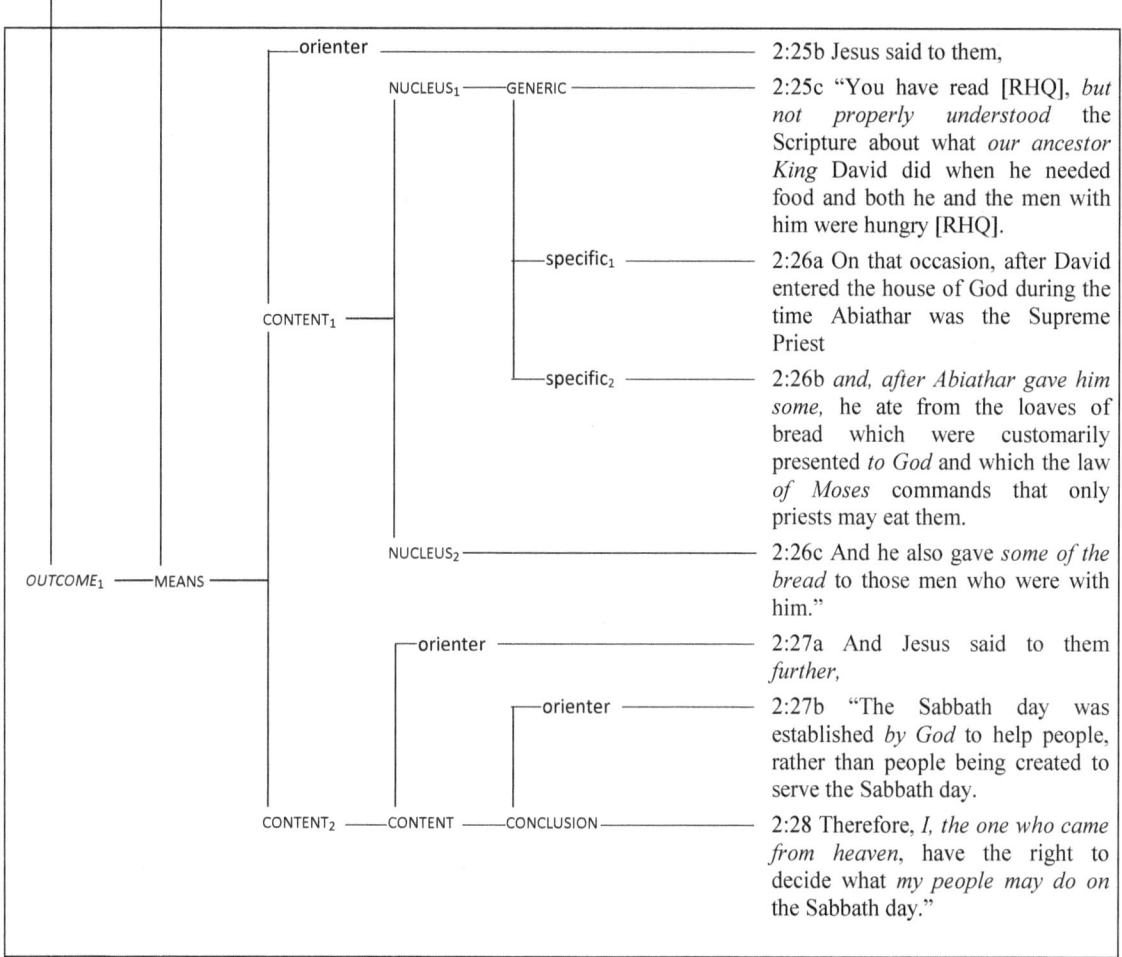

INTENT AND RHETORICAL STRUCTURE

The author here records the fourth controversy with the Pharisees in this chapter, with a fifth occurring in 3:1–6.

The paragraph pattern is of narrative *occasion* + OUTCOME subtype. This episode consists of a *setting* (v. 23), an *occasion* (v. 24), and an OUTCOME (vv. 25–28).

A dialogue structure binds this entire episode together by stating the critical question of the Jewish authorities in v. 24, and then Jesus answering their question in two units (vv. 25c–26, and 2728). The criticizing question of the Jewish authorities states that it was unlawful to work on the Sabbath day. Jesus answers this question by showing from Scripture that with God's approval David violated the law in order to show mercy to his companions, and that being merciful has priority over other law requirements regarding the Sabbath.

This episode demonstrates that Jesus assumes the divine power to establish the purpose of the Sabbath day. It is one of the revelations of his hidden identity motif in this part of the book.

NOTES

2:23a *with his disciples* The display has moved the first mention of the minor participants from the second clause in the Greek text to the first clause in the propositionalized text.

2:23b *the path through the grain fields* This phrase has been supplied for those who need to specify where they were walking. For some, what is said in 23a may be enough.

2:23c *and eating the grains (the law of Moses had permitted people to do this if they were hungry)* The display has supplied a cultural implicature here. Without this information, many readers will assume that the disciples were stealing it.

2:24a *who were following them* This is included to keep readers from asking, 'where did the Pharisees come from?'

saw them plucking the grain The display has filled out an ellipsis in the event sequence.

2:24b Look *at what your disciples are doing* The GNT has only ἴδε meaning literally 'Look'. It is true that this word is sometimes used just to draw attention to what follows, but in this context it has its literal meaning; the words in italics complete the case frame from the situational context.

Moses' law says that we should not work on the Sabbath The display here supplies the major premise of the syllogism implied by the Pharisees' rhetorical question: "Look, why are they doing what is not lawful on the Sabbath?" Verse 24c supplies the conclusion. Some languages may need to supply the missing background information of the pharisaical definition of work: 'they are working by plucking the heads of grain', since this action may not seem like work to the reader.

2:25a *In order to show them from Scripture that they were wrong to condemn the disciples* The display includes the communication intent of Jesus' answer.

2:25c *but not properly understood* The verb, 'read', implies understanding of what is read. The rhetorical question form is used as a rebuke to indicate that they did not understand or should have understood.

what *our ancestor,* **King** *David* The display fills in the implicature, identifying 'David'.

when he needed food and both he and the men with him were hungry This is a doublet (coordinated by 'and') since needing food and being hungry can be understood to have the same meaning. The doublet is even more obvious in the Greek text since the verbs are both singular, with the reference to 'those with him' following.

2:26a the Supreme Priest All versions have 'Supreme Priest', but 'high' is ambiguous; see comment in THM.

2:26b *and, after the Supreme Priest gave him some* In the Greek text, this event of the Supreme Priest giving David bread is not mentioned, so the display supplies this Old Testament information which members of the receptor culture willow to avoid wrong implications.

to God Here the case frame is filled out in the display, supplying the OT knowledge which the original readers would have had.

2:26c *some of the bread* Lest there be some misunderstanding, the display fills out the case frame, indicating what it was that David gave to his men.

2:27b The Sabbath day was established *by God* The display supplies the agent who established the Sabbath. With regard to supplying 'God' as the implied agent, see TN, Bratcher & Nida.

2:28 *I, the one who came from* **heaven** See note on v. 10.

have the right to decide what *my people may do* The GNT has 'is lord of', but the wording in the display expresses the meaning much more clearly; see TN.

BOUNDARIES AND COHERENCE

A new paragraph at 3:1 is indicated by a change in time and location, and a new topic (healing on the Sabbath). Cohesion in this paragraph is provided by four occurrences of the word σάββατον 'Sabbath', and occurrences of the word στάχυς 'grain' and σπόριμος 'grainfield'. Cohesion is also seen in the whole paragraph dealing with the topic of what is acceptable to do on the Sabbath.

PROMINENCE AND THEME

The theme consists of condensations of the *orienter* and the CONCLUSION of the *setting*, and the CONCLUSION of CONTENT$_2$ of the *OUTCOME*.

SCENE CONSTITUENT 3:1–6   75

SCENE CONSTITUENT 3:1–6 (Episode of 2:1—3:6)

¶ PTRN RELATIONAL STRUCTURE	CONTENTS
THEME After Jesus healed a man on the Sabbath, the Jewish leaders began to plan to kill him.	
setting ─┬─ SIMULTANEOUS₁	3:1a *On* another *Sabbath day*, Jesus entered the synagogue again.
└─ SIMULTANEOUS₂	3:1b There was a man there whose hand was shriveled/atrophied.
occasion ─┬─ MEANS	3:2a *Some Pharisees* watched Jesus carefully
├─ PURPOSE₁	3:2b in order to see whether he would heal the man on the Sabbath day.
└─ PURPOSE₂	3:2c *They were watching Jesus* in order that they might prosecute him for having disobeyed their religious laws, *which prohibited working on the Sabbath day.*
move₁ ─┬─ orienter	3:3a Jesus said to the man whose hand was shriveled/atrophied,
└─ CONTENT	3:3b "Stand up in front of everyone".
move₂	3:3c So the man stood up.
move₃ ─┬─ orienter	3:4a Then Jesus said to *the Pharisees,*
└─ CONTENT ─┬─ GENERIC	3:4b "Do *our religious* laws permit people to do good on the Sabbath day, or to do evil?
└─ specific	3:4c *Specifically, do those laws tell us* to heal *a person* or *do they tell us* to harm *someone by letting him* die?"
move₄	3:4d But the Pharisees did not reply.
ACCOMPLISHMENT ─┬─ move₁ ─┬─ RESULT	3:5a Jesus looked around at them angrily,
└─ reason	3:5b and because he was very distressed that they were not sensitive *to what the man needed,*
├─ move₂ ─┬─ orienter	3:5c he said to the man,
└─ CONTENT	3:5d "Reach out *your* hand!"
└─ ACCOMPLISHMENT ─┬─ circumstance	3:5e When the man reached out his hand,
OUTCOME ┘ └─ NUCLEUS	3:5f his hand became normal again.
SEQUEL ─┬─ step	3:6a After they left *the synagogue*, the Pharisees at once *met with some of* the Jews who supported *King Herod* Antipas, *who ruled Galilee district,*
└─ GOAL	3:6b and planned with them how they could kill Jesus.

INTENT AND RHETORICAL STRUCTURE

The author here records the fifth controversy with the Pharisees of unit 2:1—3:6. This episode culminates the series of five, an episode in which Jesus healed a sick person on the Sabbath, after which the authorities planned on how to kill him.

The paragraph pattern is of the narrative causality subtype. This episode consists of a *setting* (v. 1), an *occasion* (v. 2), and an OUTCOME (vv. 3–6).

NOTES

3:1 On another *Sabbath day* The Greek has πάλιν 'again' As is clear from the following verse, as well as the parallel passage in Luke 6:6, this was on another Sabbath day.

hand was shriveled/atrophied It means that his hand had withered and become paralyzed (Bock, NET).

3:2a *Some Pharisees* The Greek has no identification of 'they', but 'Pharisees' is made specific in CEV, also in v. 6.

3:2c *for having disobeyed their religious laws, because of working on the Sabbath day* This spells out the reason for their accusation. They considered that healing was work (cf. NLT), and the source of their objection was their interpretation of the Mosaic laws.

3:3c *the man stood up* In Scripture, a command is assumed to be obeyed unless it is stated otherwise, but this is not true in many languages.

3:4b *the laws God gave Moses* This specifies what laws Jesus was referring to; it does not mean governmental law (See Mann, THM).

3:4c *harm someone by letting him die* The Greek has only 'to save life or to kill'. The latter is really hyperbole. The sense is 'to let someone die by refusing to help him'.

3:5a *angrily* Hiebert says that Jesus was angry because of their refusal to admit the truth.

3:5b *not sensitive to what the man needed* The Greek τῇ πωρώσει τῆς καρδίας 'hardness of heart' is an idiom meaning stubbornness; cf. CEV, TEV.

3:5f *became normal again* This represents the Greek word meaning 'restored'; cf. GW, L&N.

3:6a *with some of the Jews who supported King Herod Antipas* The wording in the display gives the meaning of Ἡρῳδιανοί 'Herodians'; cf. NLT "supporters of Herod", but it also makes clear which Herod is being referred to.

BOUNDARIES AND COHERENCE

A new paragraph at v. 7 is indicated by a change in location and a new topic: teaching and healing. Coherence in the 1–6 paragraph is shown by two occurrences of the word σάββατον 'Sabbath' and four occurrences of the word χείρ 'hand', and by the whole paragraph dealing with Jesus healing a man with a shriveled hand on the Sabbath day.

PROMINENCE AND THEME

The theme consists of a condensation of the two propositions of the setting (to identify the participants), the GOAL of the OUTCOME, and part of the *step* and SEQUEL (to identify participants) and the GOAL of the SEQUEL.

PART CONSTITUENT 3:7—8:30 (Act II of Part I 1:14—8:30)

THEME: By Jesus appointing his disciples to teach and heal people in and around Galilee district, he was leading his disciples to answer his question, 'Who am I?'

MACROSTRUCTURE	CONTENTS
lay-out	3:7–12 Many people crowded around Jesus in order to touch him because he had healed many. Because of the crowd he got into a boat and taught from it.
buildup	3:13—6:29 Jesus appointed his twelve apostles and involved them in his ministry throughout Galilee, where he became so popular that even King Herod began questioning who Jesus was.
pressure	6:30—8:21 While Jesus was traveling outside of Galilee and Judea, he taught his disciples that he was powerful by what he did and by accepting persons whom the disciples considered unclean.
CLIMAX	8:22–30 The episode of Jesus healing a blind man in stages is an analogy of how Jesus' disciples understood in stages that he was as the promised Messiah.

INTENT AND RHETORICAL STRUCTURE

By presenting this act, Mark wants the reader to understand how Jesus led his disciples to answer his key question of, "Who do you say that I am?" The act is structured around leading up to the climactic question and the disciples' answer through Peter. Here the enigma of Jesus' hidden identity of his being God's Messiah expected by the people of Israel is partially disclosed.

BOUNDARIES AND COHERENCE

As mentioned above, the central cohesive topic is Jesus' identity and the disciples' declaration concerning it. As mentioned under the previous unit, there is no grammatical marking of a boundary, but there is a sharp contrast of location and topic. As for the closing boundary, only καί 'and' opens the next unit, which introduces the second half of the book.

PROMINENCE AND THEME

This unit consists of four sub-units, all narrating events which occurred in and around the district of Galilee. The theme is a synthesis of a build-up to the climax of all the sub-units.

ACT CONSTITUENT 3:7–12 (Episode of 3:7—8:30)

THEME: *Many people crowded around Jesus in order to touch him because he had healed many. Because of the crowd he got into a boat and taught from it.*

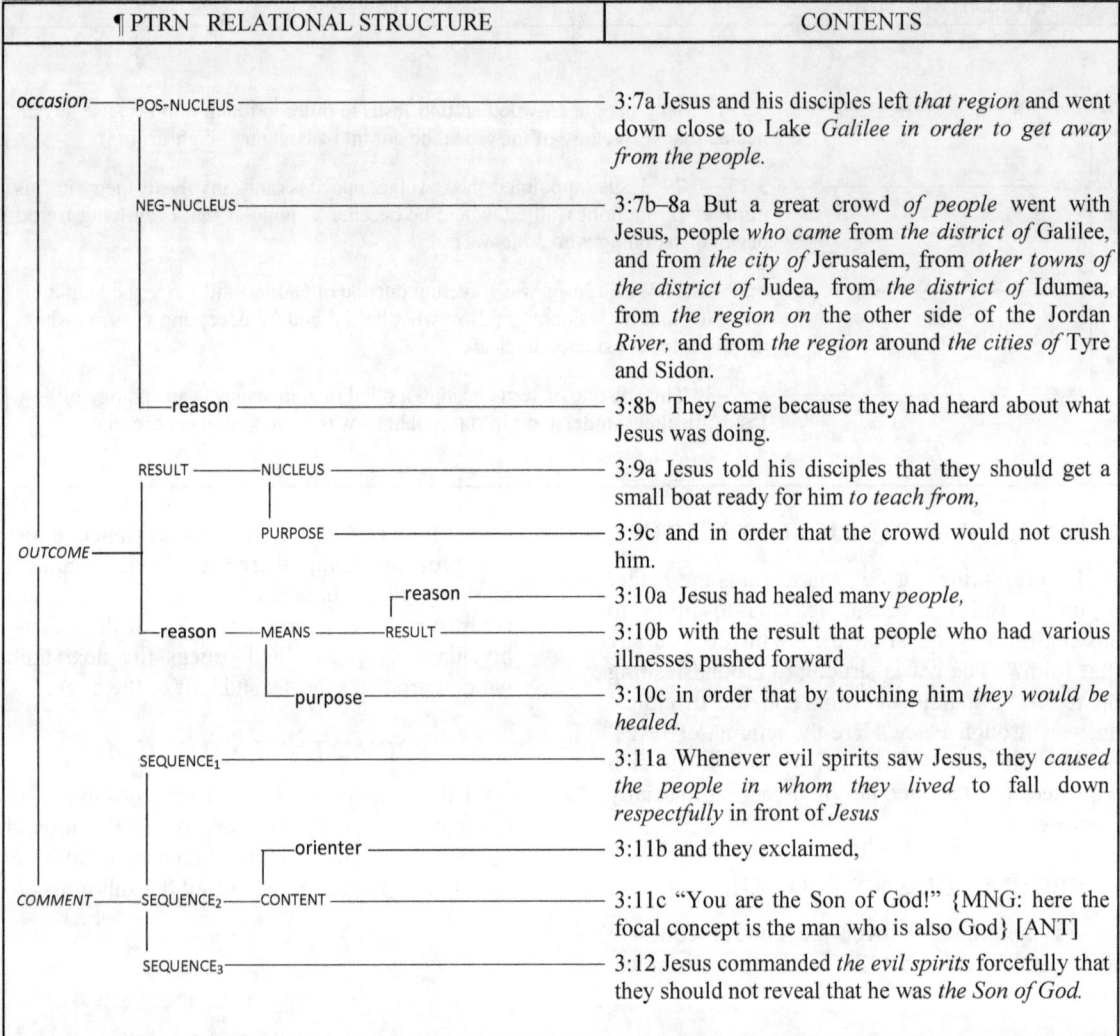

INTENT AND RHETORICAL STRUCTURE

This scene raises the question of Jesus' identity when the evil spirits identify Jesus as 'the Son of God'. Thus the author of this episode is giving evidence that Jesus is the Son of God.

The foundational communication relations for this episode are an OCCASION (3:7–8), an OUTCOME (3:9–10), and a COMMENT (3:11–12). From these relations we conclude that this is a narrative and that natural prominence is on the OUTCOME and the COMMENT.

NOTES

3:7a left *that region... in order to get away from the people* Commentators suggest several possible reasons for Jesus' action. Some suggest it was to avoid danger from his opponents, but a larger group suggest that it was primarily to get away from the crowds of people.

Lake *Galilee* The display specifies again which lake is meant.

3:7b But The Greek has καί 'and', but the context using the word ἀναχωρέω 'withdrew' seems to indicate that the crowds' action frustrated Jesus' hopes to 'get away' from people.

3:8a The wording in the display makes clear the nature of each of the places mentioned.

3:10a–c Translators will have to recognize that v. 10 is a flashback.

3:10 *they would be healed* The implied purpose of the touching is made specific. Cf. Lenski, Hiebert, Gould, and France.

3:9b *to get in it and teach from it* The purpose of getting a boat ready is made clear.

3:11–12 These verses break the chronological sequence of events but are crucial to the motif of Jesus concealing his identity.

3:11a they *caused the people in whom they lived* to *fall down* The display makes clear that it was not the evil spirits but their victims who fell down.

respectfully Stein notes that falling before someone was an action by an inferior individual in homage to a superior one.

3:11c Son of God See note on 1:1a. The Greek has only 'who he was' but it refers to his divine origin, not his name.

BOUNDARIES AND COHERENCE

A new paragraph at v. 13 is shown by a change in location and a new topic: the choosing of the twelve apostles. Cohesion in the 7–12 paragraph is maintained by the words θάλασσα 'lake and πλοιάριον boat', and by the mention of various geographical locations. Coherence is also seen by the topic of Jesus teaching from a boat.

PROMINENCE AND THEME

The theme consists of the three propositions of the *reason*, plus the NUCLEUS and 1st PURPOSE of the OUTCOME.

ACT CONSTITUENT 3:13—6:29 (Scene of 3:7—8:30)

THEME: Jesus appointed his twelve apostles and involved them in his ministry throughout Galilee, where he became so popular that even King Herod began questioning who Jesus was.

MACROSTRUCTURE	CONTENTS
lay-out	3:13–19 Jesus appointed twelve apostles.
buildup	3:20—4:34 Jesus taught about evil spirits and not speaking against the Holy Spirit, and several parables about how God's rule increases.
pressure	4:35—5:33 Jesus performed various miracles in the Galilee region, from calming a storm to bringing a young girl back to life.
CLIMAX	6:1–29 Jesus' identity is brought to the foreground. The people of Nazareth town were offended by what he was teaching, he also sent out his disciples two by two, and Herod thought that Jesus was John come to life, whom he had beheaded.

INTENT AND RHETORICAL STRUCTURE

At these high level groupings, it is somewhat difficult to determine which simultaneous structure is focal. There definitely is a progression of prominence from Jesus choosing his twelve disciples to where people are speculating as to who Jesus is. The author's intent here is to point out that Jesus became very popular in Galilee, to the extent that even King Herod was questioning who Jesus might be.

This matter of questioning Jesus' identity is basic throughout the book, and it is highly focused in this entire unit of 3:13—6:29.

This scene opens the question of Jesus' identity when the evil spirits identify Jesus as 'the Son of God'. This unit closes with Peter (speaking for the disciples) who identifies Jesus as 'the Son of God'.

The narrative roles for this episode are an *occasion* (3:7–8), an OUTCOME (3:9–10), and a COMMENT (3:11–12). From these roles we conclude that natural prominence is on the OUTCOME and the COMMENT.

BOUNDARIES AND COHERENCE

The boundaries are discussed under the included initial unit (3:13–19) and the concluding unit (6:1–29). This whole unit is bound together by the declaration that because of what Jesus did and said, many people went to him and wondered who he really was. Furthermore, the increasing intensity from appointing disciples to some people rejecting Jesus and everyone commenting on who he is, typically demonstrates a coherent structure.

PROMINENCE AND THEME

The theme statement is derived from the most prominent concepts of each sub-unit which lead up to the CLIMAX.

SCENE CONSTITUENT 3:13–19 (Episode of 3:13—6:29)

THEME: *Jesus appointed twelve apostles.*

¶PTRN RELATIONAL STRUCTURE	CONTENTS
occasion — SEQUENCE₁	3:13a *Later* Jesus went up into the hills.
move	3:13b After he summoned the *men* whom he wanted,
SEQUENCE₂ — ACCOMPLISHMENT	3:13c they came to him.
NUCLEUS₁	3:14a He appointed twelve *men*, whom he called apostles,
purpose₁	3:14b in order that they might accompany him,
OUTCOME — NUCLEUS — purpose₂ — PURPOSE	3:14c and in order that he might send them out to preach;
means — MEANS	3:15a and he gave them power
purpose	3:15b in order that they might expel evil spirits *from people*.
amplification — GENERIC	3:16a Specifically, he appointed these twelve *men*:
specifics₁₋₁₂	3:16b–19 (1) Simon, to whom he gave *an additional* name Peter;
	(2&3) James the *son* of Zebedee, and John the *younger* brother of James, *both* of whom he also called Boanerges, which means men *who act violently* like thunder;
	(4) Andrew;
	(5) Philip;
	(6) Bartholomew;
	(7) Matthew;
	(8) Thomas;
	(9) *another* James, the son of Alphaeus;
	(10) Thaddeus;
	(11) *another* Simon, who was a *member of the* Zealot *party, which advocated rebellion against the Roman government;*
	and (12) Judas Iscariot (OR, who was from *the town of* Kerioth) and who *later* betrayed *Jesus to his enemies.*

INTENT AND RHETORICAL STRUCTURE

This unit is part of the 3:13—6:29 Scene which starts out by Jesus appointing his twelve disciples in order for them to accompany him and in order to send them out to tell people God's message and heal.

The narrative roles for this episode are an *occasion* (3:13), and an OUTCOME (3:14–19). From these roles we conclude that the natural prominence is on the OUTCOME.

The author's purpose is to tell the readers whom Jesus chose to be his apostles.

NOTES

3:13a *Later* There is no time indicator in the text, but a lapse of time is implied; NLT has "Afterward".

3:14a whom he called apostles These words are not found in some manuscripts, but Metzger says "the external evidence is too strong in their favor to warrant their exclusion from the text." Their inclusion is given a C 'difficult to decide' rating.

3:16a he appointed these twelve *men* These words are also not in the Textus Receptus and so they are not in the KJV, but external and internal evidence favor their inclusion, which is given a C rating.

3:16b–19 The display includes information to make the meaning clear:

an additional **name** The display follows the suggestion by THM; an alternative would be 'new name' as in JBP.

younger **brother** The word 'younger' is supplied for languages which are required to make that distinction.

Andrew It is not known why Andrew is not listed immediately after Peter, or why it is not mentioned that the two were brothers, as Matthew and Luke do. In some languages it may be advisable to clarify and make specific those points.

men *who act violently like* **thunder** The Greek has 'sons of thunder' but 'sons of' is a Hebrew idiom which will certainly be misunderstood if translated literally. CEV has "thunderbolts" which is a bit better but still not clear; JBP has "thunderers"; TEV has 'Men of Thunder". Several commentators suggest the idiom refers to their fiery and vehement temperament. Since this is an idiom, the words 'like thunder' could probably be omitted.

another This word may be necessary to avoid confusion or misunderstanding.

Zealot *party, which advocated rebellion against the Roman government* The GNT has only 'Zealot' which will not mean much if translated literally. See Living Bible, TN, also the footnote in CEV.

from the town of **Kerioth** The alternate wording in the display makes clear the meaning of 'Iscariot'. Sixteen commentators state this, but of all versions consulted, only Beck translates the meaning of the word.

later **betrayed Jesus** *to his enem*ies The word 'later' is supplied to make the time frame clear; cf. CEV, NLT. For languages in which 'betray' is not a familiar concept, a wording such as 'enabled his enemies to seize him' would be suitable.

BOUNDARIES AND COHERENCE

The start of a new paragraph at v. 20 is indicated by a change in location and a new topic: expulsion of demons. Coherence in the 13–19 paragraph is provided by two occurrences of the word δώδεκα 'twelve' and a listing of twelve names.

PROMINENCE AND THEME

The theme consists of the 1st NUCLEUS of NUCLEUS$_1$ of the OUTCOME.

SCENE CONSTITUENT 3:20—4:34 (Episode Cluster of 3:13—6:29)

THEME: Although Jesus' family and/or others thought he had gone insane, Jesus taught about evil spirits and not speaking against the Holy Spirit, and several parables about how God's rule increases.

MACROSTRUCTURE	CONTENTS
occasion	3:20–35 Jesus told them that those who obey God are as dear to him as his close relatives.
OUTCOME	4:1–34 Jesus taught the crowds four parables about the various ways that people who hear his message react.

INTENT AND RHETORICAL STRUCTURE

Here the account begins to intensify since Jesus' family thinks he is deranged, and the Jewish religious authorities think he is out of his mind because of evil spirit influence. However, Jesus teaches serious truths showing that he is sane, and then he teaches about how God's rule increases.

BOUNDARIES AND COHERENCE

This unit 3:20—4:34 is bound together by Jesus teaching about evil spirits and how God's rule increases. The boundaries of this unit are defined under the first and the last episodes.

PROMINENCE AND THEME

Both units in this Episode Cluster Constituent are of equal prominence, so the theme is derived from a synthesis of both the nuclear units.

EPISODE CLUSTER CONSTITUENT 3:20–35 (Episode of 3:20—4:34)

THEME. *Jesus told them that those who obey God are as dear to him as his close relatives.*

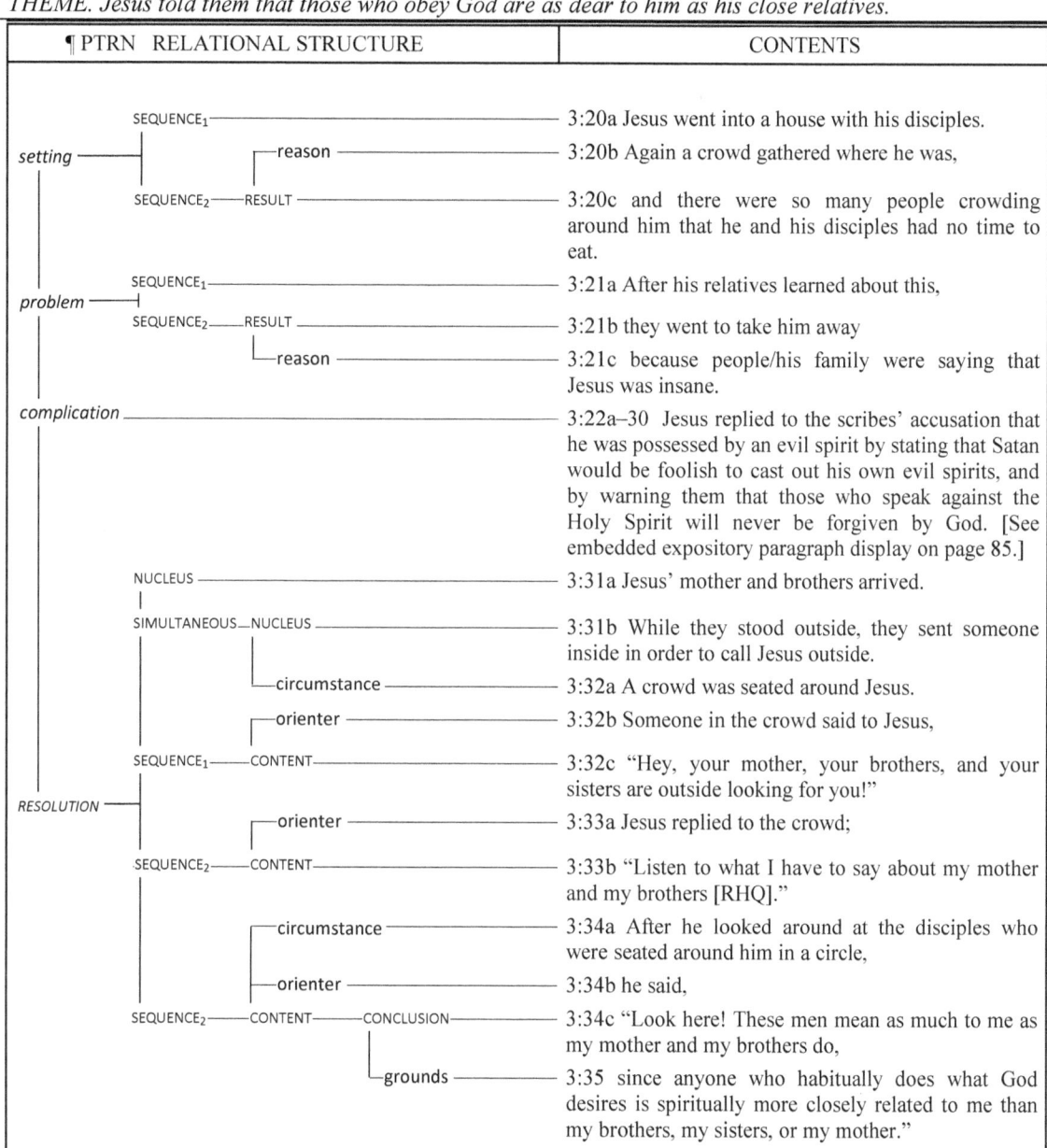

INTENT AND RHETORICAL STRUCTURE

This unit is the first of two units which concentrates on Jesus' teachings. The second one concentrates on a series of parables explaining how God's rule increases.

The foundational communication relations for this episode are a *circumstance* (3:20), and THREE SEQUENCES (3:21, 22–30, and 31–35). From these relations we conclude that this is a narrative and that natural prominence is on the *problem, complication,* and the RESOLUTION.

The author intends in this 3:20–35 unit to convey Jesus' teaching about the source of his power and about not speaking against the Holy Spirit.

The unit consists of an *occasion* (v. 20), an OUTCOME₁ (v. 21), an OUTCOME₂ (vv. 22–30), and an OUTCOME₃ (vv. 31–34).

The OUTCOME₁ where Jesus' family goes to apprehend Jesus, and OUTCOME₃ where Jesus' family arrive at the house where he is teaching, brackets the embedded OURCOME₂. There also seems to be an extended chiastic structure within OUTCOME₂ as follows:

A   Jesus is controlled by Beelzebub (v. 22)
   B   Jesus summons all the scribes (v. 23)
      C   Jesus demonstrates that infighting of the Beelzebub group would be self-destructive (vv. 23e–27)
   B'   Speaking against the Holy Spirit will never be forgiven (vv. 28–29)
A'   Jesus said all this because the scribes said that he was controlled by Beelzebub (v. 30)

The motif of Jesus expelling evil spirits is mentioned explicitly in v. 22b. In fact, this is the central topic of this entire discussion.

NOTES

3:20a *with his disciples* See note on 7:24.

3:20c *and there were so many people crowding around him* that *he and his disciples* **had no time** The italicized material gives the reason they had no time to do anything. See Hiebert, Lenski, France; also CEV.

3:21c **people/his family** It is not clear who is the subject of the verb 'were saying'. Most commentators say it was those who came to take him away, although RSV and NEB say the agent is 'people'. Both alternatives are given in the display.

EMBEDDED EXPOSITORY PARAGRAPH 3:22–30 (Episode embedded within the episode 3:20—4:34)

THEME: *Jesus explained why their claim that he was expelling evil spirits by Satan's power was ridiculous, and that such a claim was an unforgiveable sin.*

¶PTRN RELATIONAL STRUCTURE	CONTENTS
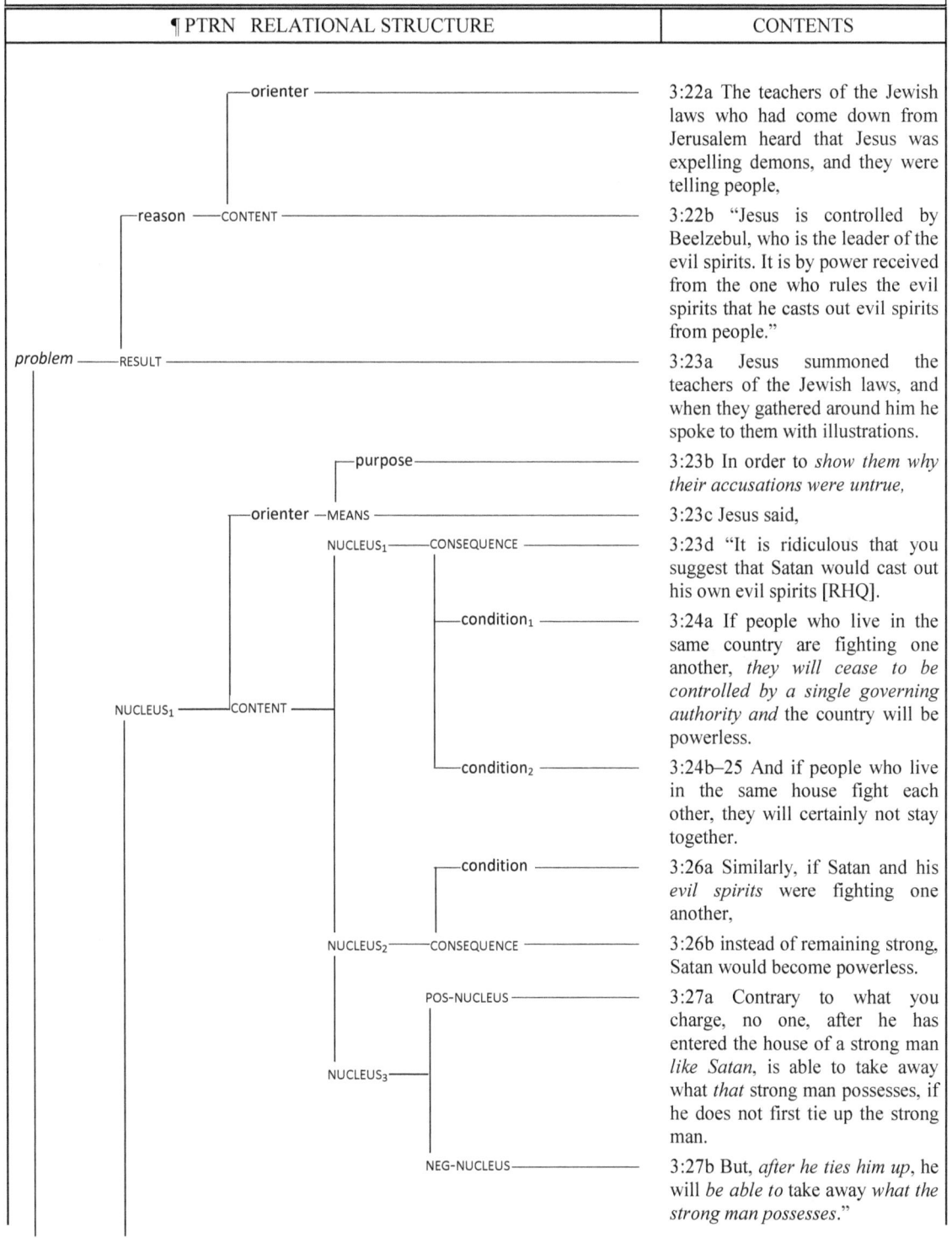	3:22a The teachers of the Jewish laws who had come down from Jerusalem heard that Jesus was expelling demons, and they were telling people,
	3:22b "Jesus is controlled by Beelzebul, who is the leader of the evil spirits. It is by power received from the one who rules the evil spirits that he casts out evil spirits from people."
	3:23a Jesus summoned the teachers of the Jewish laws, and when they gathered around him he spoke to them with illustrations.
	3:23b In order to *show them why their accusations were untrue,*
	3:23c Jesus said,
	3:23d "It is ridiculous that you suggest that Satan would cast out his own evil spirits [RHQ].
	3:24a If people who live in the same country are fighting one another, *they will cease to be controlled by a single governing authority and* the country will be powerless.
	3:24b–25 And if people who live in the same house fight each other, they will certainly not stay together.
	3:26a Similarly, if Satan and his *evil spirits* were fighting one another,
	3:26b instead of remaining strong, Satan would become powerless.
	3:27a Contrary to what you charge, no one, after he has entered the house of a strong man *like Satan*, is able to take away what *that* strong man possesses, if he does not first tie up the strong man.
	3:27b But, *after he ties him up*, he will *be able to* take away *what the strong man possesses*."

NUCLEUS₂	3:28–39 Jesus claimed that their saying he was expelling demons by Satan's power was an unforgivable sin. [See expansion on page 87.]
problem restated	3:30 Jesus said this because the teachers of the Jewish laws were saying: "As he casts out evil spirits, an evil spirit is controlling him, *not the Holy Spirit.*"

INTENT AND RHETORICAL STRUCTURE

This embedded unit presents Jesus' argument and teaching that his power to expel evil spirits does not come from Satan, and that those who say such are sinning against the Holy Spirit so will not be forgiven. Mark presents the *problem* (3:22–23a), while Jesus states the SOLUTION (3:23d–27) in two parts: the first (3:23d–27b) that Satan cannot remain strong if his dominion is divided against itself, and secondly that (3:28–39) the accusers are committing the unforgivable sin against the Holy Spirit.

NOTES

3:21c *people/his family* It is not clear who the agent of 'they were saying' is. Commentaries are divided. So the display supplies the two alternatives suggested.

3:22a *heard that Jesus was expelling demons* This proposition needs to be understood for the rest of the verses to make sense.

3:22b **Beelzebul,** *who is the leader of the evil spirits* The text, as is, does not make clear whether they were referring to one individual or two. CEV makes it clear with "Beelzebub, the ruler of demons".

3:22b **by** *power received from* **the one who rules the evil spirits** The words 'the one who' are considered a metonymy; the individual standing for the power possessed by that individual; cf. CEV, NLT.

3:23a **he spoke to them with illustrations** The text has 'in parables'. This clause provides a means proposition for the purpose clauses in 23b and 23c to relate to.

3:23b *in order to show them why their accusations were untrue* This is supplied to give the import of the illustration that follows.

3:23d *It is ridiculous that you suggest* There is a rhetorical question here, "How can Satan drive out Satan?", which doesn't make much sense. The question is not "How? but "Why?" Several commentators note that their comment was absurd, which supports the display wording, 'it is ridiculous'. This proposition supplies the topic of the two parables in vv. 24–25.

Satan would not oppose his own evil spirits As several commentators point out, the name of Satan here has two senses, the second of which refers to the demons who represented Satan.

3:24a **people** *who live in the same* **country** The word 'kingdom' is a metonymy, the place standing for the people who live there; cf. CEV.

will cease to be controlled by a single governing authority and **the country will be powerless** The Greek has only 'that kingdom cannot stand', which is obscure. The display supplies the reason that the kingdom will collapse. The word 'kingdom' here is considered a metonymy, the place standing for the power that its government has; see 22b.

3:24b *people who live in the same* **house** The word 'house' is another metonymy, the place standing for its occupants. Several translations use either the word 'family' or 'household' here.

3:26a **his** *evil spirits* **were fighting one another** See the second comment under v. 23a.

3:26b **instead of remaining strong** The Greek has 'he cannot stand', which is somewhat obscure.

he would become powerless The Greek has 'he has an end', which is very obscure. CEV has "that will be the end of him" which is clear but very idiomatic. Furthermore, 'his end has come' is hyperbole; hence 'would become powerless'.

3:27a strong man *like Satan* The words 'like Satan' are supplied to make clear the topic of this illustration. NLT does likewise.

if he does not This represents the Greek ἐὰν μὴ which is usually rendered by 'unless' in English. Some languages do not have an 'unless' construction, in which case it is necessary to render 'no A unless B' as 'only if B, A'.

3:27b after *he ties him up* This represents the single Greek word τότε 'then'.

3:29 sin The Textus Receptus has 'condemnation' but the wording 'sin' is given a B 'almost certain' rating.

3:30 *As he casts out evil spirits*, an evil spirit is controlling him, *not the Holy Spirit* The parts in italics simply repeat portions of the preceding context.

BOUNDARIES AND COHERENCE

A new paragraph at v. 31 is marked by a change in topic: Jesus' mother and brothers. Coherence within the 22–30 paragraph is provided by three occurrences of the name 'Satan', four occurrences of οἶκος 'house', and two occurrences of the verb βλασφημέω 'blaspheme' and one of the cognate noun 'blasphemies'. Coherence is also seen in the whole paragraph dealing with the subject of Jesus' expulsion of evil spirits.

PROMINENCE AND THEME

The theme is drawn from the CONSEQUENCE of the 1st NUCLEUS of the SOLUTION and 2nd CONTRAST of the 2nd NUCLEUS of the SOLUTION.

EXPANSION OF NUCLEUS₂ IN EXPANSION OF MARK 3:22–30 DISPLAY

¶ PTRN RELATIONAL STRUCTURE	CONTENTS
orienter	3:28a Jesus also said,
CONTRAST₁ — concession	3:28b I tell you sincerely that people may sin in many ways and they may say evil things about God,
CONTENT — CONTRAST₁ — CONTRAEXPECTATION	3:28c and those things, *God can forgive*.
CONTRAST₂ — condition	3:29a But, if anyone says evil things about the Holy Spirit,
CONTRAST₂ — CONSEQUENCE	3:29b God will never forgive those things ; that is, that person will be guilty of that sin forever."

NOTES

3:28b The Greek has 'sons of men' which is misleading. Most English translations have 'men' but the display carries the sense better with 'people', as does Beck.

say evil things about God Most versions do not define 'blasphemies' but the display attempts to spell out the meanings clearly. NCV has "things people say against God".

3:28c *God can forgive* The Greek has a passive construction 'will be forgiven'. The display supplies the implied agent of the action, but also has 'can forgive' because forgiveness depends on repentance; it is not automatic. See also CEV, NLT, JBP, TEV.

3:29b guilty of that sin forever The GNT has 'guilty of an eternal sin', but it is the guilt, not the sin, that lasts forever.

BOUNDARIES AND COHERENCE

A new paragraph at 4:1 is indicated by a new time and location, and topic: Jesus teaching by using various parables. Coherence in the embedded 20–30 paragraph is maintained by three occurrences of the word Σατανᾶς 'Satan, four occurrences of οἰκία 'house', and two occurrences of μερίζω 'divided'. Coherence is also seen in the paragraph dealing with the questions of whether or not Jesus was in complete control of his mind.

PROMINENCE AND THEME

The theme consists of the *orienter* and CONCLUSION of the 3rd OUTCOME.

EPISODE CLUSTER CONSTITUENT 4:1–34 (Episode of 3:20—4:34)

THEME: Jesus taught the crowds four parables about the various ways that people who hear his message react. He constantly used parables when he taught people.

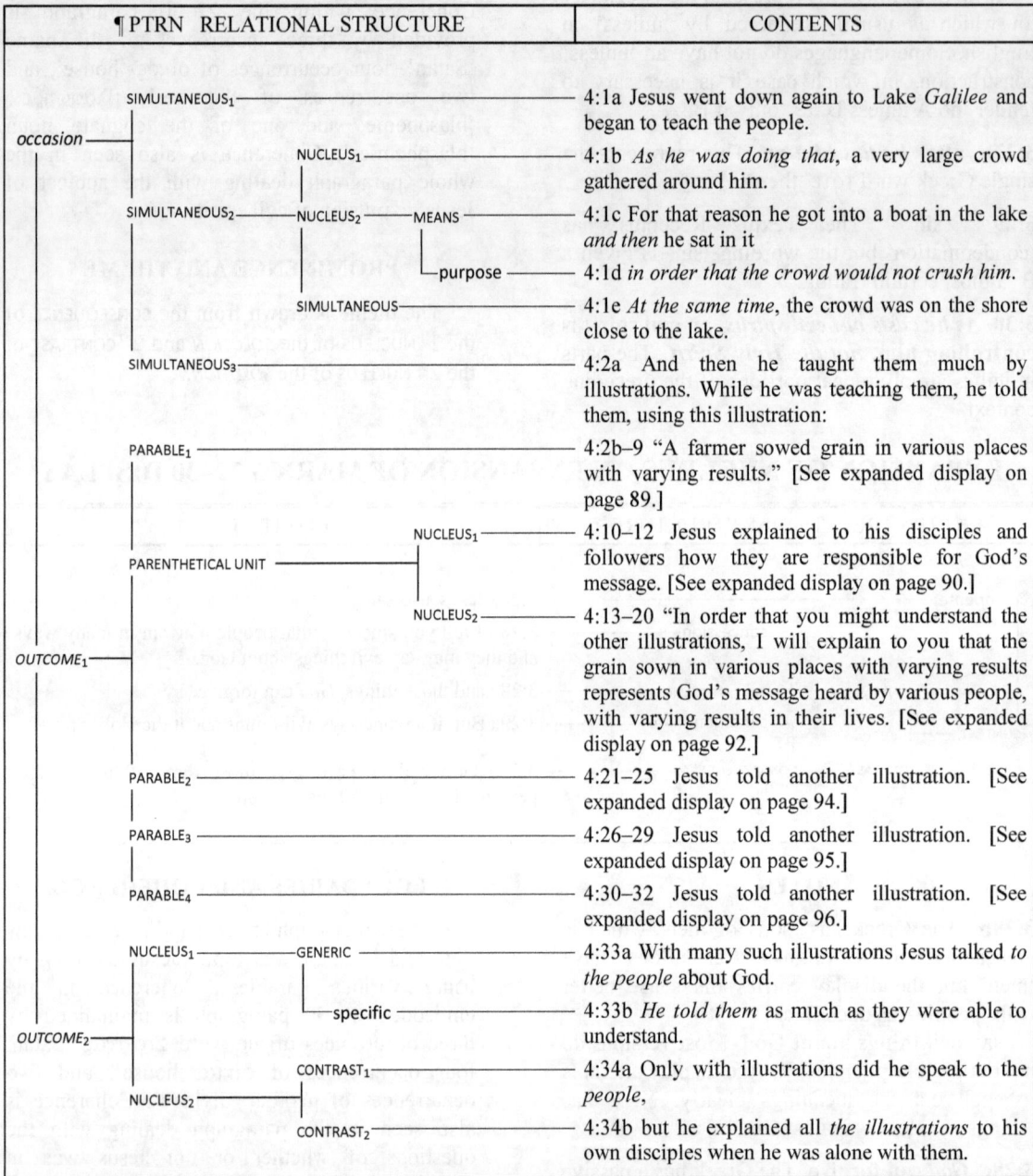

INTENT AND RHETORICAL STRUCTURE

This unit is the second of two units which concentrates on Jesus' teachings using a series of parables explaining how God's rule increases.

The author intends in this 4:1–34 unit to convey Jesus' teaching about how God's rule increases among people.

The unit consists of an *occasion*, and TWO OUTCOMES.

This OUTCOME$_2$ is crucial for the analysis of this unit, showing that the audience of the four parables was the people, and that the unit vv. 10–20 interrupts the series as a parenthetical unit demonstrating how Jesus explained all the parables to his disciples.

NOTES

4:1a lake *Galilee* See note on 2:13.

4:1d *in order that the crowd would not crush him* This supplies the reason for his getting into a boat; see TN.

EXPANSION OF PARABLE₁ 4:2b–9 IN THE MARK 4:1–34 DISPLAY

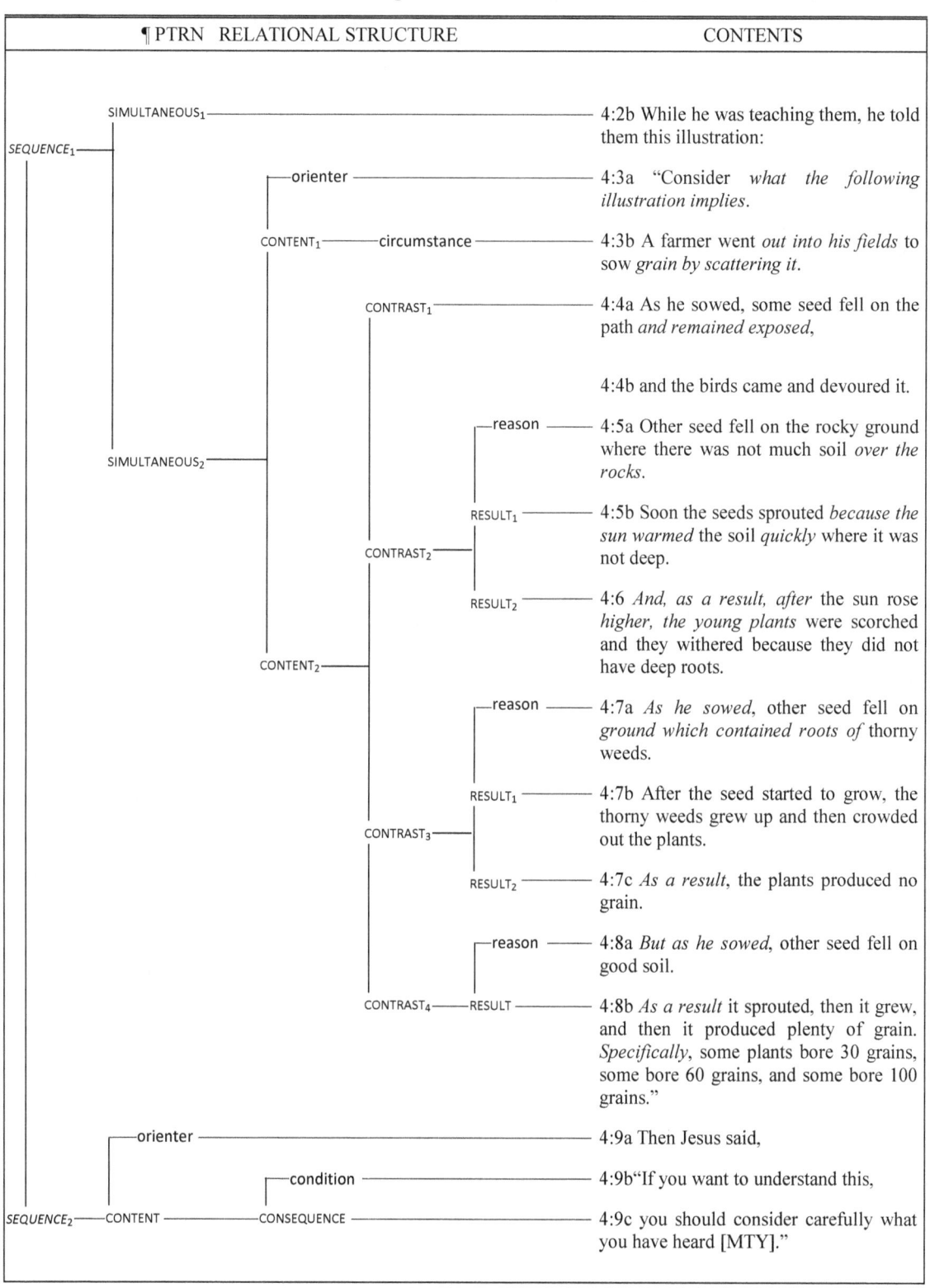

NOTES

4:3a Consider *what the following illustration implies* This is supplied as an orientation to the parable to make clearer what Jesus meant by 'Listen!'

4:3b *into his fields* These words specify where the farmer went. CEV has "in a field".

grain This is supplied as the contextual object of the verb 'sow'. NLT supplies "some seed", CEV has "seed".

4:4a *and remained exposed* These words are included to explain why the birds were able to devour it.

4:5a soil *over the rocks* TN says this "refers to ground that has solid rock underneath it."

4:5b *because the sun warmed* the soil The GNT has 'because the soil was shallow' but that does not explain the quick sprouting. The information in italics is supported by Hiebert, Lenski, THM, and Guelich.

4:6 *the young plants* were scorched The Greek has 'it was scorched', but the display makes clear it was the plants, not the seeds, that were scorched. See also TEV, NIV, and CEV.

4:7a *ground which contained roots of* thorny weeds The text says 'fell among thorns', but this suggests the farmer was stupid and does not make clear what the real situation was. The information in italics is made clear by Hiebert, Hendriksen, Lenski, Taylor, Swete, and THM.

4:9b–c If you want to understand this, you should consider carefully what you have heard The saying 'he who has ears to hear, let him hear' is idiomatic. NLT comes close to capturing the meaning with "Anyone who is willing to hear should listen and understand". TN is even closer, saying Jesus was urging "the crowd to give careful attention to the parable that they had just heard."

EXPANSION OF NUCLEUS₁ 4:10–12 OF THE PARENTHETICAL UNIT IN THE MARK 4:1–34 DISPLAY

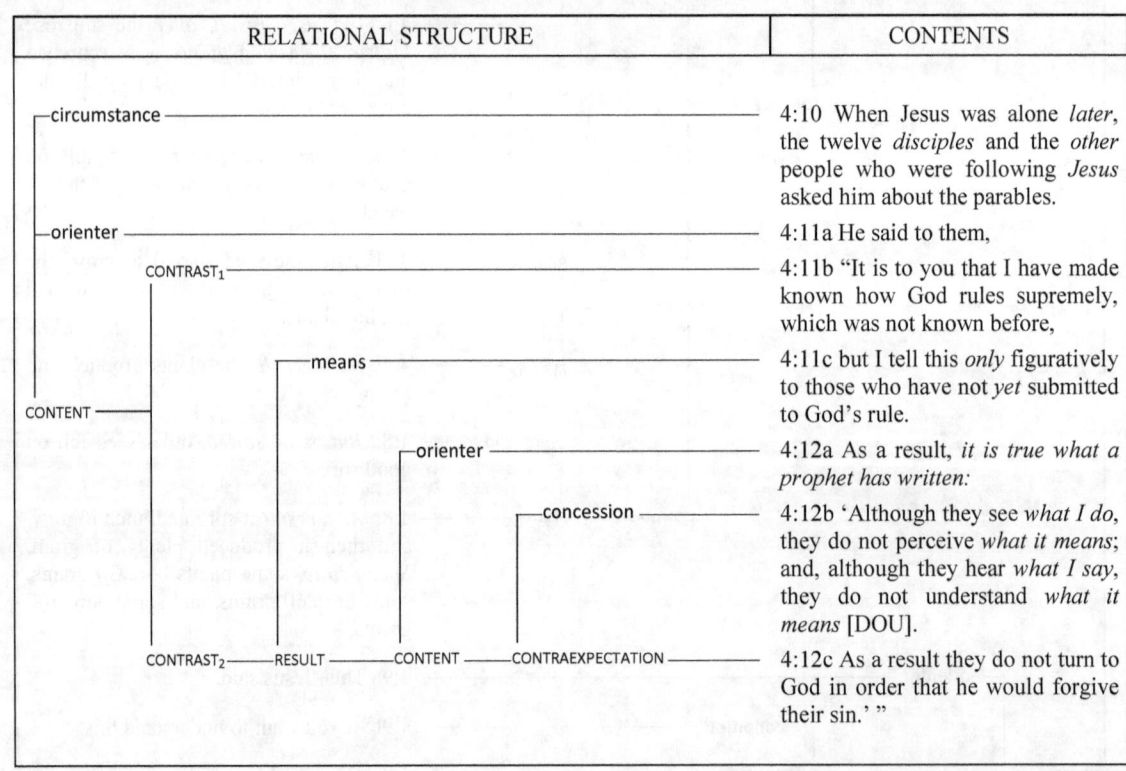

NOTES

4:10 *later* This is a situational implicature; cf. NLT.

the *other* people who were following *Jesus* This states more clearly the meaning of 'the ones around him'.

4:11b **how God rules supremely** The expression 'Kingdom of God' is considered to be a metonymy, the place standing for the event (ruling) that occurs there; cf. THM.

not known before The word μυστήριον often translated 'mystery' does not have the sense that 'mystery' does in current English; cf. THM "Knowledge which has not been known to people in general, but revealed to the initiated, i.e., to the believers."

4:11c **who have not *yet* submitted to God's rule** The word ἔξω 'outside' means 'those who are outside of God's kingdom (THM),' i.e. unbelievers.

4:12a *it is true what a prophet has written* This proposition makes clear that what follows is from Scripture (Is. 6:9–10, cited from the Septuagint).

4:12b **see *what I do* ... hear *what I say*** The verbs 'see' and 'hear' usually require an object; the display follows NLT which has "see what I do" and "hear my words" which suit the context very well.

understand *what it means* Similarly, 'understand' in many languages implies something which is understood. NLT has "perceive its meaning".

4:12c **turn to God** The primary meaning of the Greek verb is 'turn' but there is a secondary meaning here. CEV, TEV, and NEB also have "turn to God". THM says it is usually translated 'be converted' (also KJV).

EXPANSION OF NUCLEUS₂ 4:13–20 OF THE PARENTHETICAL UNIT OF MARK 4:1–34

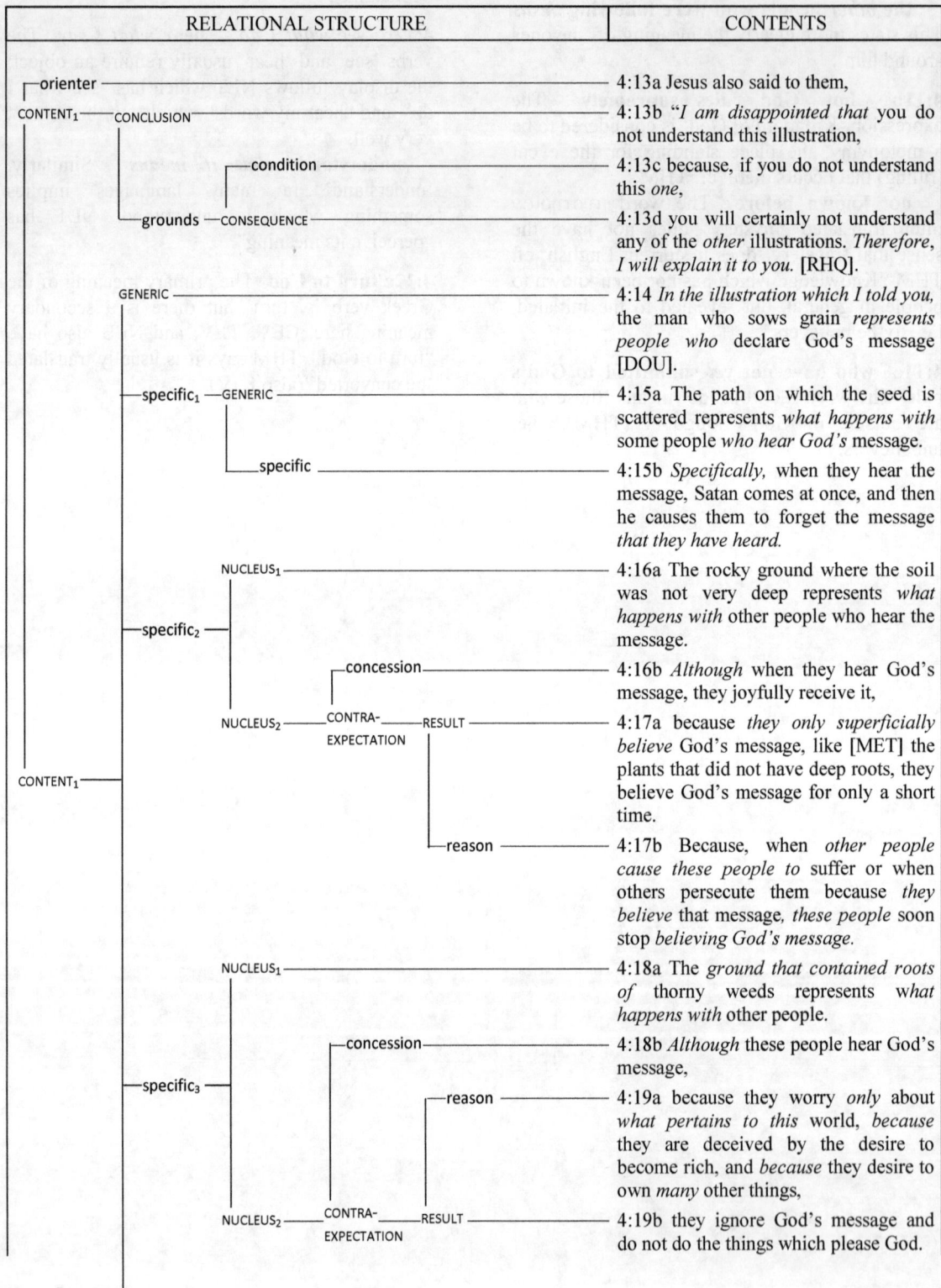

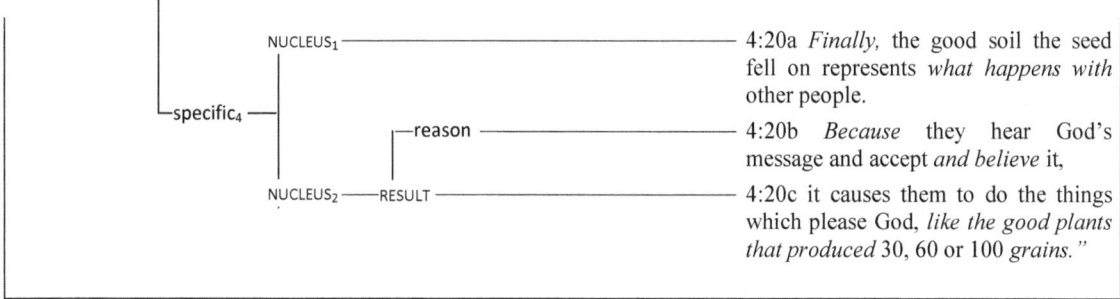

NOTES

4:13b *I am disappointed that* The GNT has 'Do you not know...?' which is a rhetorical question. At least seven commentators note that this clause is a rebuke by Jesus to his disciples for not understanding. This writer considers that it is also expressing disappointment, but commentators do not suggest that. Another solution followed by several versions (cf. CEV, NLT) is to make it a conditional clause and combine it with the next sentence: "If you do not understand...".

4:13d *you will certainly not* The Greek text has another rhetorical question, 'how will you understand...?' Semantically it functions as an emphatic negative statement as in the display. CEV and TfT are the only translations consulted that unskew the rhetorical question with "you won't understand".

other illustrations The word 'other' is contextually implied; cf. NLT, CEV, JBP.

Therefore, I will explain it to you What follows is Jesus' explanation of the parable. This clause in italics makes this specific; without such a clause, what follows seems abrupt and mysterious.

4:14 sows *grain represents people who declare God's* message Being a parable, this is also a metaphor. The wording in the display spells out the topic of the metaphor, indicating what the farmer sows (grain) and what message is being referred to (God's; cf. NLT). The CEV has "the message about the kingdom", which is probably too specific.

4:15a The path on which the seed is scattered represents *what happens with* some people The Greek text, which is literally translated as 'these are the ones along the path', is obscure. 'These' is represented in the display as 'some people' NIV also has "some people". The display, in vv. 15–20, attempts to make it clear especially that Jesus is comparing not four kinds of seeds but four kinds of soil (see Mann). All the modern translations (except TfT) suggest what is wrong; e.g., NIV "some people are like seed..."

4:15b causes them to forget The GNT has 'takes the word'. CEV has 'snatches it away' but this is still figurative. The wording in the display states what really happens; cf. also LB "to try to make them forget it".

4:16a The rocky ground *where the soil was not very deep* The word πετρώδης 'rocky places' is describing not soil which is full of rocks but as in v. 5 "shallow soil with underlying rock" (NLT).

4:17a *they only superficially believed* God's message, like This proposition spells out the topic of the metaphor. Nearly all English translations retain much of the metaphorical language: the GNT has 'they do not have roots in themselves', CEV "They don't have any roots". The translation closest to making the meaning clear is NCV, which has "They don't allow the teaching to go deep into their lives".

4:17b because *they believe* that message The Greek has only 'on account of the word' which implies some verbal connection between the preposition and the noun. The display supplies 'believe', as does NLT.

stop *believing God's message* The Greek word σκανδαλίζω means 'fall away', but here it means "cease believing" (Lenski); JBP has "give up their faith".

4:18a *roots of* thorny weeds See note on v. 7.

4:19a worry *only* about *what pertains to this* world The Greek has 'cares of the age'. But the word αἰών 'age' here means the activities of everyday life. Many versions have 'world'; but TEV, NLT, CEV and NIV have "this life" which is better.

deceived by the desire to become rich The literal rendering of the Greek wording is 'seduction of riches'. The display removes the abstract nouns. CEV's rendering "fooled by the desire to get rich" is excellent.

desire *to own many* other things This renders what is literally 'desires of other things' but supplies the verb 'to own'. CEV supplies "to have". Some versions have "evil desires" (REB, NCV), but "evil" is unwarranted.

4:19b ignore *God's* message The Greek has συμπνίγω 'choke the word' which mixes the figurative and non-figurative parts and also retains the personification.

4:20b and accept *and believe* it The words 'and believe' are included as implied. Lenski says the meaning is "to come to believe something to be true and then respond accordingly."

4:20c do the things which please God The word 'bear fruit' is a dead metaphor; no versions examined (except TfT) render this in a non-figurative way. LB comes closest with "produce a plentiful harvest for God". BAGD say the word here means "in a resolve to do what is right".

EXPANSION OF PARABLE₂ 4:21–25 OF THE MARK 4:1–34 DISPLAY

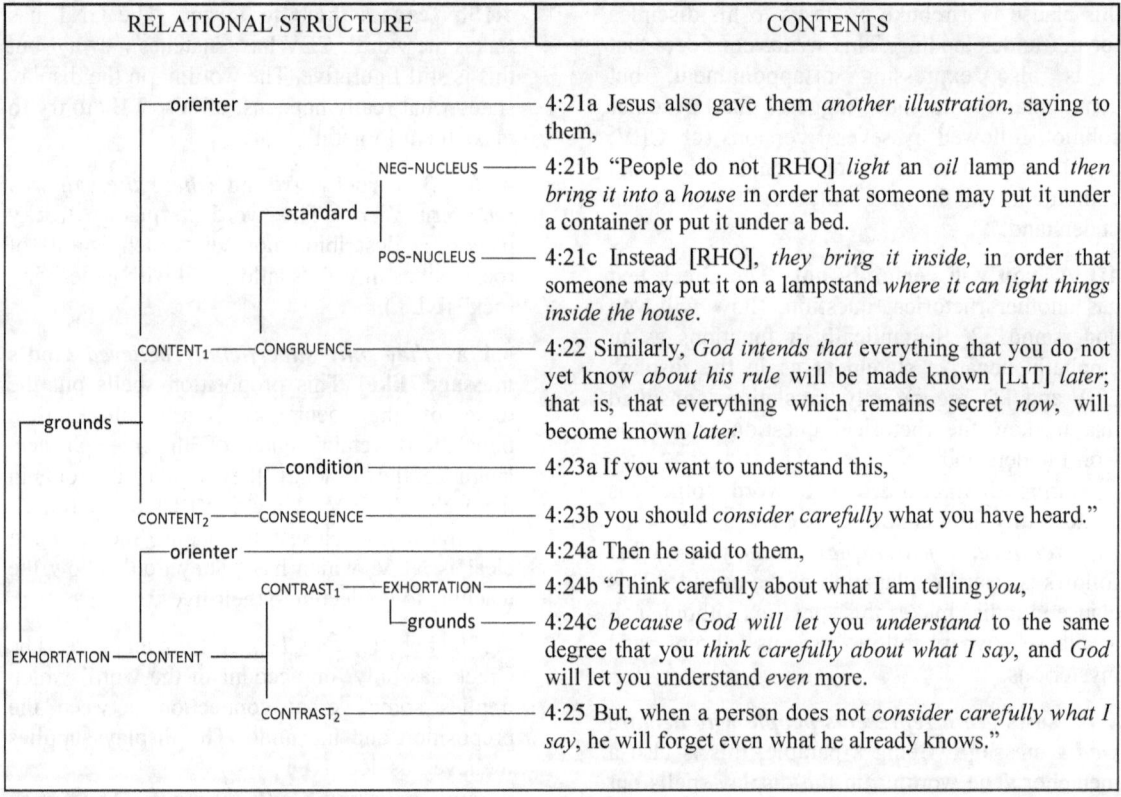

NOTES

4:21a *another illustration* This word is included to make clear that what follows is another parable.

4:21b *light* an *oil* lamp and *then bring* it into *the house* The bits in italics represent implied information on lamp-lighting in Biblical times. People then knew only olive oil, which was burned in lamps.

4:21c where it can light things inside the house This expresses the implied purpose of putting it on a lampstand. NCV has "where its light will shine".

4:22 *God intends that* The GNT has only a passive construction, 'it may be manifested'. Although it does not state who will make it known, it is clear that it is God's intention (cf. JBP; TN). Lenski says "God will see to it that all secret things are revealed".

which is not known The GNT has κρυπτός 'hidden', but as THM notes, it does not refer to things that were purposely hidden. Rather, it describes something that has not been able to be seen or known.

about his rule Commentators are almost unanimous in connecting this with the reference to the 'mystery of the kingdom of God' in v. 11.

4:23a–b See the note on 4:9.

4:24b what you hear *me say to you* The text has only 'what you hear' but Jesus is referring to what he has been telling them. Thirteen commentators support this. But the only translation to indicate this is TfT.

4:24c *because God will let* **you** *understand* The GNT has a very cryptic 'will be measured to you'. Twenty commentaries say this "refers to paying attention and responding to it" (Blight). Two commentators plus CEV and TEV say it refers to judging others, which is what the same expression means in Matt.7:2, but not here.

the same degree that you *consider carefully what I say* EGT has "the more a man thinks the more he will understand."

4:25 The GNT has only 'he who has' which is very cryptic. Commentators suggest the implied content of 'has' is "a knowledge of the word" (Cranfield) or an understanding of the kingdom (five commentators). NLT supplies 'understanding'. The display follows the rendering in the TfT.

when a person does not *consider carefully what I say* The GNT has only 'who has not'. The rendering here follows the translation in 24c. NLT has "those who are not listening".

even what he *already knows* The GNT has 'even what he has'. Several commentators point out that this is a hyperbole meaning 'the little that he has'. Marcus says it means "the little knowledge about the kingdom."

he will forget even what he already knows The GNT has 'will be taken away'. But who is the agent of 'take away'? One could argue that it is Satan, but commentators make no such suggestion. TN suggests the agent is God. The other alternative is, as in the display, to consider that it simply means 'he will forget'. CEV also avoids the transitive verb 'take away' and has "will lose what little they have".

EXPANSION OF PARABLE₃ 4:26–29 OF THE MARK 4:1–34 DISPLAY

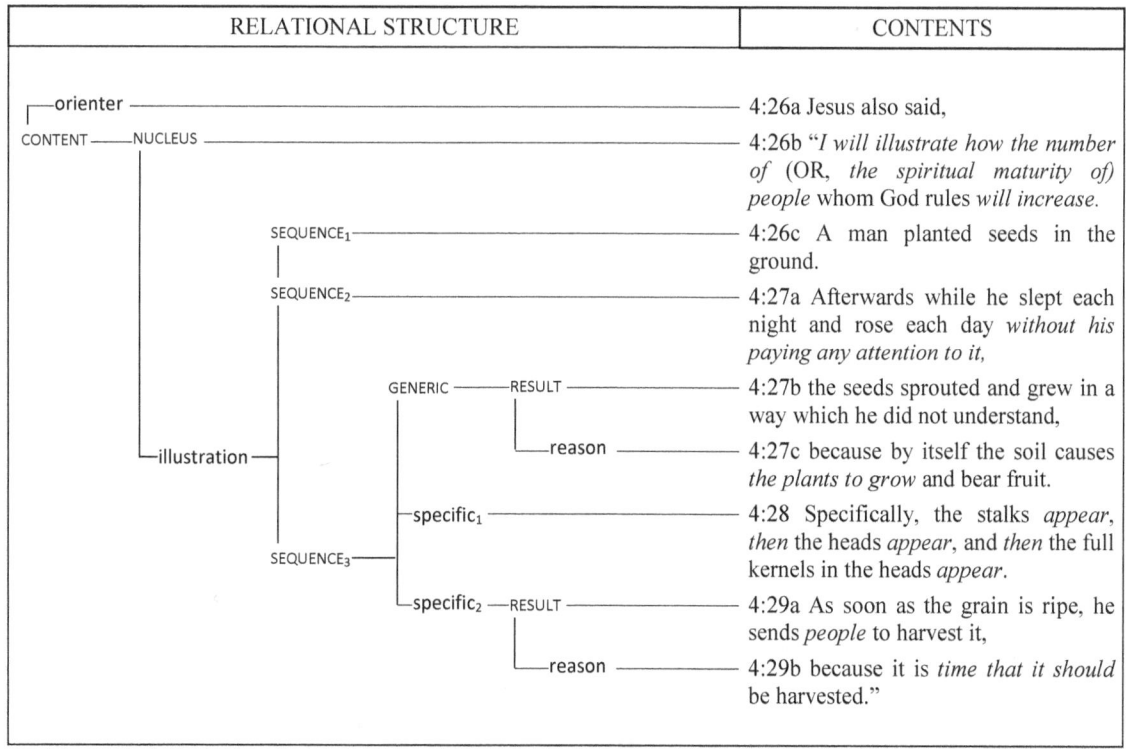

NOTES

4:26b *I will illustrate* The Greek has only 'this is the kingdom of God'. Several versions render this as "the kingdom of God is like this" which makes clear that what follows is an illustration; hence 'I will illustrate'.

how the number of people... will increase inconspicuously Commentators differ widely on the meaning of this parable (see Blight). Since vv. 27–29 all describe growth, it seems clear that growth is the point of comparison (so Hendriksen, Stein, Swete, and NLT footnote). So the question is, does it refer to growth in numbers or in spiritual maturity? The display supplies both alternatives.

4:27a *without his paying any attention to it* The question here is, what is the significance of 'night and day, when he sleeps and when he rises'? Strauss says "apart from human intervention."

4:27c *caused the plants to grow and bear fruit* The GNT says the soil 'bears fruit' but the intervening action of causing the plants to grow may need to be made specific.

4:28 *appear* The events listed here are the intervening ones between the plants starting to grow and producing the crops. There are no verbs in the Greek; the display supplies 'appear', as does TEV. CEV supplies "keep sprouting and growing".

4:29 *is ripe* The Greek has παραδοῖ 'permits', but nearly all translations say 'is ripe'.

sends people to harvest it The Greek has 'sends forth the sickle', which is a metonymy; what the farmer does is send forth workers with sickles, to harvest the grain (so JBP, Gould). Alternatively, it may just mean that the farmer harvests it himself (so NEB, NIV, TEV and most commentators). THM says the Greek could mean either possibility. The decision depends on whether the word ἀποστέλλω 'sends' is taken literally or figuratively. BAGD does not promote either option.

4:29b *time that it should be harvested* The Greek has 'the harvest has come'. Many versions also supply 'time' (e.g., NEB, TEV, JBP, Beck, and Williams).

EXPANSION OF PARABLE₄ 4:30–32 IN THE MARK 4:1–34 DISPLAY

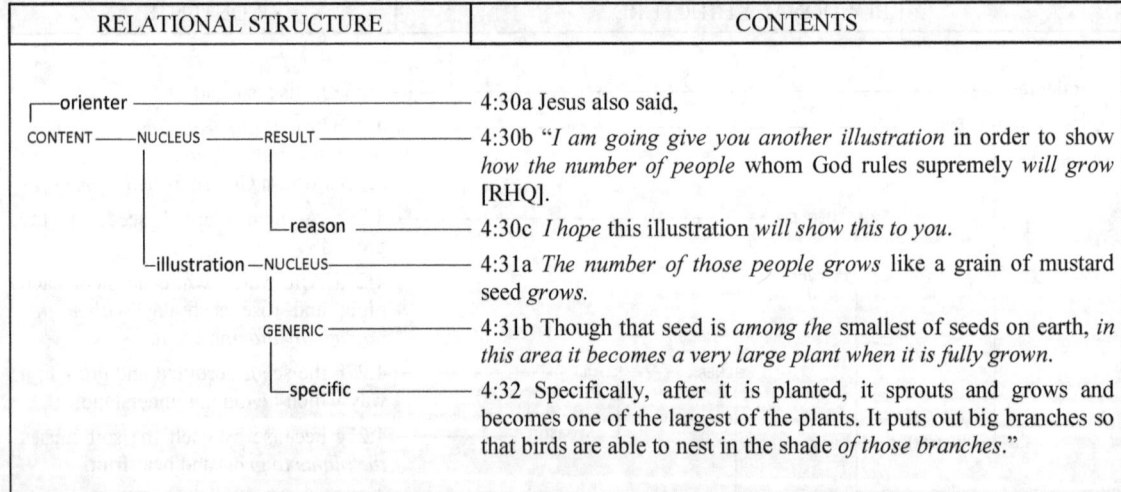

NOTES

4:30b *I am going to speak to you using another illustration* The GNT has a rhetorical question, 'How may we liken the kingdom of God?' See note on 4:21a. First of all, this is an 'editorial' we; it is rendered as 'I' by Williams, CEV, and NLT. Secondly, all translations examined (except TfT) retain the question, but it functions semantically as a statement and is so rendered in the display. Retaining the question form would indicate that Jesus did not know what to compare it with.

the number of people...will grow The point of comparison, here between a mustard seed and the kingdom of God, is again growth. Blight summarizes 17 commentators by saying "This parable contrasts the small and apparently insignificant beginning of the kingdom with its later glorious manifestation."

4:30c *I hope* **this illustration will show this to you** The GNT has another rhetorical question, 'By what shall we place a parable?' which is essentially a repetition of the first question. CEV reduces the two questions to one; Lenski says "Both questions mean the same thing."

4:31a *grows* This word conveys the point of comparison.

4:31b *among* **the smallest** Guelich states that there are smaller seeds, but the mustard seed was the smallest seed known to the people of Galilee; thus 'among the smallest'. NLT has "one of the smallest of seeds".

in this area it becomes a very large plant In many parts of the world, mustard grows only less than two feet tall. But this writer was shown a mustard tree on the top of Mt. Tabor that was at least 15 ft. tall (see also Stein, Hendriksen).

4:32 shade *of those branches* The GNT text has 'perch in its shade', but that would seem to indicate their being on the ground. Both CEV and NLT also supply 'branches' to make clear that the nests were not on the ground.

BOUNDARIES AND COHERENCE

The start of a new paragraph at 4:35 is indicated by a switch in location and a new topic: calming the sea. Coherence in the 1–34 unit is provided by a sandwich structure with the word παραβολή 'parable' in v. 2 and again in vv. 33 and 34 as well as in v. 30, and two occurrences of the clause 'he who has ears to hear, let him hear'. Coherence in this paragraph is also provided by its consisting of a set of parables by Jesus.

PROMINENCE AND THEME

The theme of the 4:1–34 paragraph is first a summary statement that v. 2–32 contain four parables (all indicated by expansions in the displays) and a brief summary of the topic of the four parables, plus a summary statement in vv. 33–34 about Jesus using parables.

SCENE CONSTITUENT 4:35—5:43 (Episode Cluster of 3:13—6:29)

THEME: *Jesus performed various miracles in the Galilee region, from calming a storm to bringing a young girl back to life.*	
MACROSTRUCTURE	CONTENTS
NUCLEUS₁	4:35–41 Jesus and his disciples crossed the sea in a boat and, while Jesus slept, a storm arose, so the disciples woke him, and he calmed the storm, causing the disciples to be awestruck.
NUCLEUS₂	5:1–20 Jesus expelled evil spirits from a Gerasene man and then allowed them to go into a herd of pigs which then ran down a hill and all drowned. As a result the local people asked Jesus to leave the area.
NUCLEUS₃	5:21–43 Jesus healed a woman who had been suffering from hemorrhaging, and caused Jairus' daughter to live again.

INTENT AND RHETORICAL STRUCTURE

This unit 4:35—5:43 consists of three episodes in which Jesus performs the miracles of calming a storm on Lake Galilee, expelling many evil spirits from a man, healing a woman, and raising a young girl from the dead. Mark intends that the reader understand that Jesus had God's power to control not only natural phenomena but even human life. This functions to cause the reader, Jesus disciples, as well as the story participants to wonder who this man might be.

The structure is three sequential episodes of successive increasing prominence.

BOUNDARIES AND COHERENCE

The opening and closing boundaries coincide with the first and last episodes of this unit, and they are discussed at those locations.

PROMINENCE AND THEME

This scene constituent consists of three nuclei. However, there is a progression of prominence from calming a storm on the lake to bringing a young girl back to life. The theme was derived from these considerations.

EPISODE CLUSTER CONSTITUENT 4:35–41 (Episode of 4:35—5:43)

THEME: Jesus and his disciples crossed the sea in a boat and, while Jesus slept, a storm arose, so the disciples woke him, and he calmed the storm, causing the disciples to be awestruck.

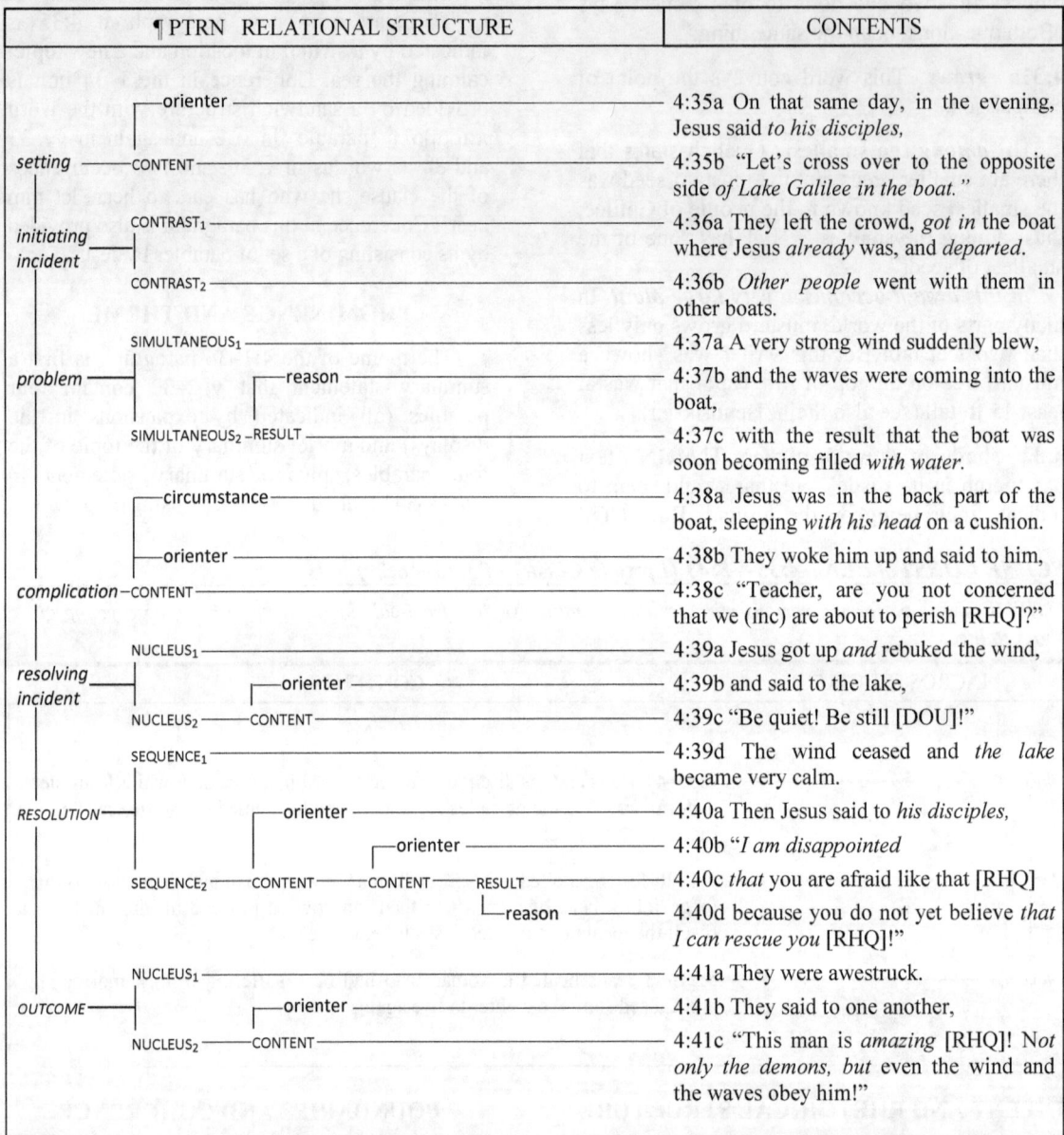

INTENT AND RHETORICAL STRUCTURE

This episode is the first of a series of miraculous actions that Jesus performed. The others involve evil spirits and bringing a young girl back to life. This was followed by the rejection of Jesus in Nazareth, his home town.

Here the author informs the reader about Jesus' power over natural phenomena, specifically, calming a storm over Lake Galilee. This account is presented with a complex narrative structure of the solution sub-type. The story opens with a typical *setting*, an *initiating incident*, a *problem*, a *complication*, a *resolving incident*, a RESOLUTION, and an OUTCOME.

NOTES

4:35a *to his disciples* The display clarifies who the pronoun 'they' refers to, as do CEV, NIV, TEV, and Beck.

4:35b opposite side *of Lake Galilee in the boat* The Greek has only 'the other side'. TEV, NEB, JBP, and NLT supply 'of the lake' without naming the lake, and no translations (except TfT) make clear they were to go by boat.

4:36a where Jesus *already* **was** The GNT has 'as he was', which is not clear. THM states that it means "his place, already in the boat". TEV and NLT also make this clear.

4:37c filled *with water* TEV and NLT also supply 'with water'.

4:38a sleeping *with his head* **on a cushion** The cushion was under his head, not his whole body. NLT, TEV, CEV, and JB make this clear; see also THM.

4:38c It is not clear whether 'Are you not concerned that we are about to perish?' is a real or a rhetorical question. The display treats it as real, but the sense is more fully 'You act as though you don't know that we are about to die, but we think you ought to be concerned'. Strauss agrees: "(It) is certainly a cry for help, but also carries an accusatory tone."

we For languages that have an inclusive/exclusive distinction in 1st person plural pronouns, the question is, did they think that they all would drown, or that the disciples would drown but not Jesus? TN says the inclusive is most likely meant; this incident occurred fairly early in Jesus' ministry, and they probably did not yet realize that Jesus could miraculously escape death – if indeed he would want to do that and allow them to drown.

4:39c Be quiet! Be still! Eight commentators (also most versions) follow the interpretation given here, i.e., that the two commands were addressed to the lake. But four commentators say the command "Be quiet!" was addressed to the wind, and "Be silenced!" was addressed to the waves. Either interpretation is possible.

4:40b *I am disappointed* Jesus asks another rhetorical question, expressing a rebuke: 'Why are you so afraid?' See 4:13. It is obvious why they were afraid. All versions except TfT retain the question.

4:40d not yet believe *that I can rescue you* The Greek has 'how have ye not faith?' which is another rhetorical question expressing a further rebuke. The great majority of commentators agree that the meaning is 'faith in me'. But none of them answer the question, 'faith that he could do what?' The display answers that question.

4:41c This man *is amazing!* The disciples respond with another rhetorical question (Stein, Gundry, Guelich) expressing amazement. Their question is literally 'Who is this man?' but they "were making a statement about Jesus' greatness, not wanting to know his name" (TRT).

Not only the demons, but **even the wind and the waves** The expression 'even the wind…' means 'not only diseases and demons…' (Gould, Swete).

BOUNDARIES AND COHERENCE

A new paragraph begins at 5:1, as evidenced by a change in location and a new topic: expelling a large group of evil spirits. Coherence in the 4:35–41 paragraph is provided by three occurrences of the word πλοῖον 'boat', two occurrences of διδάσκαλος 'disciples', and a chiastic structure involving three occurrences of the words 'wind' and 'waves'. Coherence is also seen in it being one episode concerning the storm on the lake.

PROMINENCE AND THEME

The theme is drawn from a condensation of the *initiating incident*, the 1st simultaneous proposition of the *problem*, the orienter of the *complication*, a condensation of the RESOLUTION, and NUCLEUS₁ of the OUTCOME.

EPISODE CLUSTER CONSTITUENT 5:1–20 (Episode of 4:35—5:43)

THEME: *Jesus expelled evil spirits from a Gerasene man and then allowed them to go into a herd of pigs which then ran down a hill and all drowned. As a result the local people asked Jesus to leave the area.*

¶PTRN RELATIONAL STRUCTURE	CONTENTS
setting	5:1 *Jesus and his disciples* arrived on the other side of Lake *Galilee* in the region where the people of the Gerasa area lived, and they disembarked.
problem	5:2–5 A man from that area who had an evil spirit came to meet Jesus. [See expanded display on page 101.]
RESOLUTION	5:6–13 Jesus expelled the evil spirits from the man, so they entered a herd of pigs [See expanded display on page 102.]
SEQUEL	5:14–20 The people asked Jesus to leave, but the healed man told everyone what had happened. [See expanded display on page 104.]

INTENT AND RHETORICAL STRUCTURE

This is the second unit of Jesus performing a miracle, this time by healing a man with many evil spirits.

The author intends that the reader understand how great God's power is over even a multitude of evil spirits.

This narrative is of the solutionality sub-type manifested by a simultaneous rhetorical paragraph pattern consisting of a *setting*, a *problem*, a RESOLUTION, and a SEQUEL.

In all other similar narratives where Jesus expels evil spirits who declare that Jesus is the Son of God, Jesus explicitly commanded them to be silent and not let his identity be known. Jesus also told the healed person to not tell anyone what he had done. However, in this unit in a territory outside of Judean Israel, the story is totally different: the man declared Jesus to be the Son of God, and in the sequel Jesus told him to go home and tell everyone what a great thing God had done for him. This is a very strange twist on the hidden identity motif of the book. Prof. Julia Blum suggests that the hidden identity concept applies only to Israel, but not to the non-Israeli people.

NOTES

5:1a ***Jesus and his disciples*** The display identifies who 'they' refers to, as does CEV.

Lake *Galilee* The lake is identified; see also TEV, CEV.

Gerasa area There is a textual problem here: should it be Gerasenes or Gadarenes? The latter is followed by the KJV, but the former has much better manuscript support, and is found in all the modern versions.

EXPANSION OF PROBLEM 5:2–5 IN THE MARK 5:1–20 DISPLAY

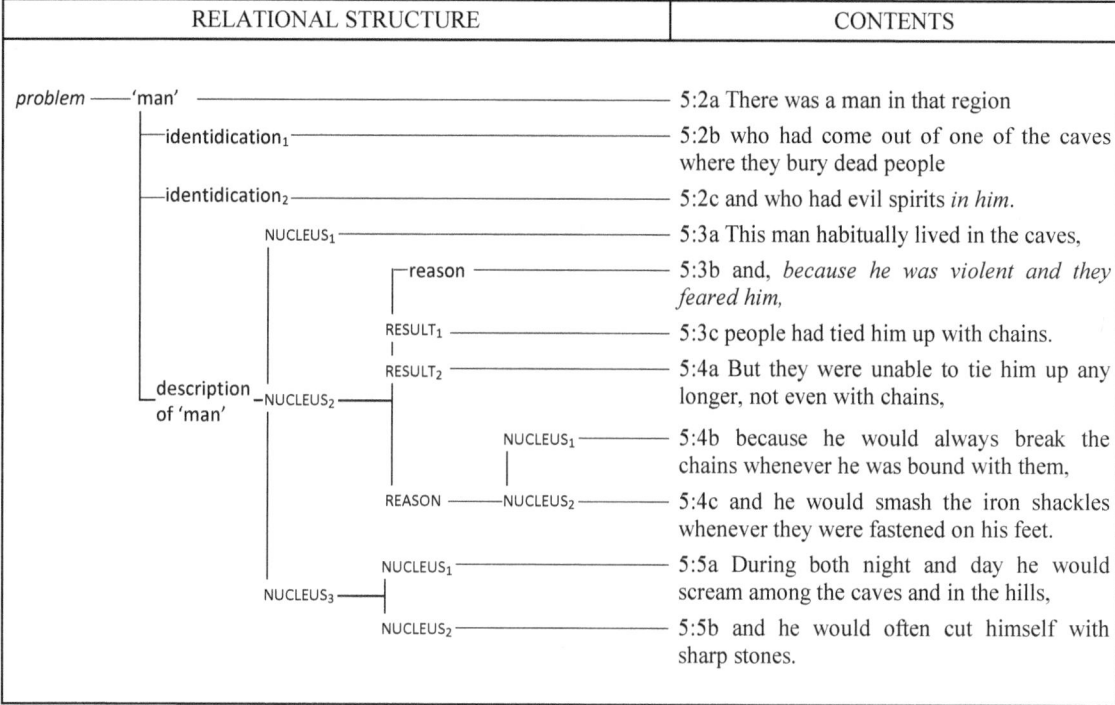

NOTES

5:2b The words 'met him' are conveyed in v. 6 "he ran to Jesus". The other reason they are omitted here is that they are part of the 'live action' of the episode which begins at v. 6. For many languages, in telling a narrative, it is essential to put all the background information at the beginning, before giving any of the events of the narrative.

5:3b *because he was violent and they feared him* This supplies the explanation for fastening him with chains (see Lane, Hendriksen).

5:4a But they were unable to tie him up any longer, not even with chains There is a chiastic structure in this verse:
    fetters
    and chains
    chains
    and fetters

The display puts 'chains' in 4a and 4b, and puts 'shackles' in 4c. TEV and NIV handles the chiasm by other means. NLT and CEV simply reverse the order of the 4 phrases to eliminate the chiasm.

EXPANSION OF RESOLUTION 5:6–13 IN THE MARK 5:1–20 DISPLAY

RELATIONAL STRUCTURE	CONTENTS
move₁ — SIMULTANEOUS₁	5:6a That man saw Jesus from a distance.
⎣ SIMULTANEOUS₂	5:6b He ran to Jesus,
move₂ — MEANS	5:6c and knelt before Jesus
⎣ purpose	5:6d in order to reverence him.
move₃ — orienter	5:7a The evil spirit cried out loudly,
⎣ CONTENT — EXHORTATION₁	5:7b "Jesus, Son of God, you who are truly great, leave me alone [RHQ]!
EXHORTATION₂	5:7c I implore you that you will not punish me.
EXHORTATION₃	5:7d Ask God to witness *what you promise*."
reason₁ — orienter	5:8a Jesus said to the evil spirit,
⎣ CONTENT	5:8b "You evil spirit, come out of this man!"
reason₂ — orienter	5:9a *Because the demon didn't leave quickly,* Jesus asked him,
⎣ CONTENT	5:9b "What is your name?"
move₄ — CONTENT₁ — orienter	5:9c He replied,
CONCLUSION	5:9d "My name is Crowd,
⎣ grounds	5:9e because there are many of us evil spirits in this man."
CONTENT₂ — ORIENTER	5:10a And *the evil spirits* fervently begged Jesus
⎣ CONTENT	5:10b that he not send them out of the region.
CIRCUMSTANCE	5:11 At the same time, a large herd of pigs was grazing nearby on the hillside.
move₅ — orienter	5:12a *The evil spirits* pleaded with Jesus,
CONTENT — MEANS	5:12b "Send us to the pigs
⎣ purpose	5:12c in order that we might enter them!"
ACCOMPLISHMENT — SEQUENCE₁	5:13a He permitted them to do that.
SEQUENCE₂ — SEQUENCE₁	5:13b The evil spirits left the man
⎣ SEQUENCE₂	5:13c and they entered the pigs.
OUTCOME — SEQUENCE₁	5:13d Then the herd, *which numbered* about 2,000, rushed over a cliff into the lake,
⎣ SEQUENCE₂	5:13e and they drowned in the lake.

NOTES

5:6d *in order to reverence him* This is included to make clear the purpose of the action; see THM.

5:7b leave me alone! The GNT has 'What to me and to you?' L&N say it means 'Why do you bother me?' NLT accordingly translates "Why are you bothering me?" Several translations have "What do you want with me?" but that fails to communicate the imperatival force of the question. Of the translations examined, other than TfT, only Beck uses an imperative: "let me alone!"

Son of God See note 1;1a.

5:7d Ask God to witness *what you promise* Although these seem strange words to come from demons, THM says this is what 'by God' means. A shorter rendering would be 'swear to God' (NIV).

5:7–8 Since the verb elegh 'xx' 'was saying' indicates an action which preceded the action in v. 7, the order could be reversed to put the events in chronological order (cf. L&N). LB does likewise.

5:9a *Because the demon didn't leave quickly* The question here is, why did Jesus ask the demon what his name was, especially when he had already told the demon to leave? Hendriksen offers several possible explanations, none very satisfactory. Several commentators reject the notion that it was "Jesus' attempt to gain mastery over the demon by learning its secret name" (Strauss). But Marcus disagrees and says "knowing the name of a demon grants power over it." Those who disagree with Marcus have no better explanation, and in this writer's opinion, show they have had no experience trying to deal with demons. The display does not provide Marcus' explanation, but some translators may feel it necessary to be included. However, that still leaves unanswered the question, why did Jesus delay asking this question? No commentators mention it. The words in italics supply what seems to be a reasonable explanation.

5:9d Crowd The GNT has 'legion' which will be unknown to modern readers. Suggestions are "Mob" (TEV), "Lots" (CEV), crowd, multitude, army. A legion at full strength has 6000 soldiers.

5:10a the *evil spirits* The question here is, who is the subject of the singular form of the verb 'kept imploring'? The majority of commentators say 'the man' but in view of what was said, that doesn't make any sense. France suggests it was the man speaking for the demons, but that too is not very satisfactory. The best solution is simply to follow Marcus and NLT and render it, as in the display, as 'the evil spirits'.

5:12a *The evil spirits* The display identifies the referents of the pronoun 'they', as do NEB, JB, NIV, TEV, JBP and others.

5:13d *which numbered* The GNT has only 'about 2000'. Several versions indicate this was the approximate number of pigs; cf. NIV, TEV, NEB and others.

EXPANSION OF SEQUEL 5:14–20 IN THE MARK 5:1–20 DISPLAY

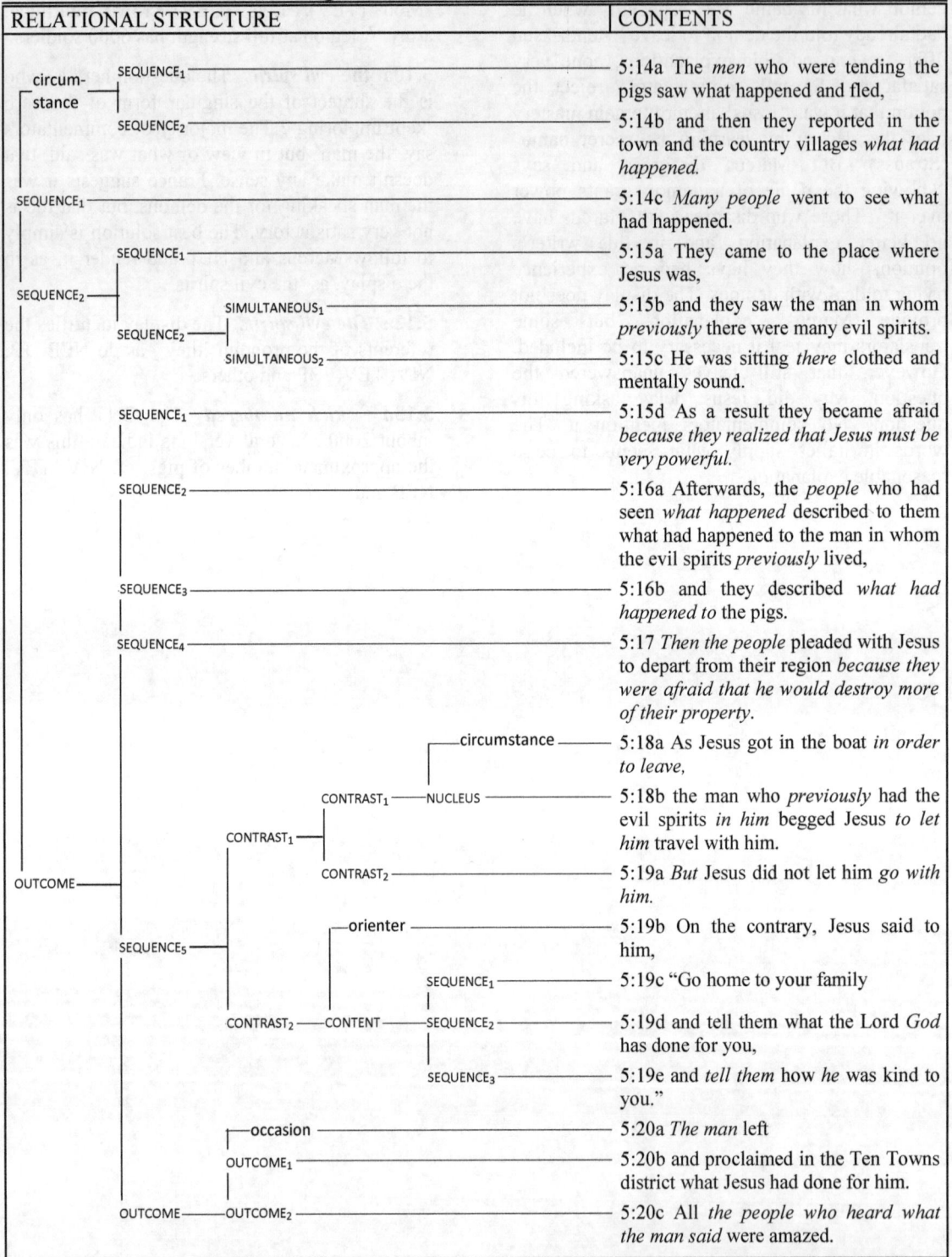

NOTES

5:14b reported...*what had happened* The GNT has only 'reported' but all versions examined supply some object for the verb.

5:14c *Many people* went The GNT has only 'they'; the display supplies a better identification of who went. NLT supplies "everyone" but that is hyperbole.

5:15b *previously* The GNT has 'the demon-possessed man' which sounds as though he still had the demons; thus the display supplies 'previously'. Other translations use a passive past perfect tense 'had been possessed' or supply a word such as "once" (CEV) or "used to" (TEV).

5:15c *mentally sound* The word in the GNT means "to be of a sound mind " (BAGD). L&N say it means 'able to reason and think properly".

5:15d *because they realized that Jesus must be very powerful* Without understanding this implicit information, readers may not understand why the people would be frightened. See Bruce, Lenski, and Anderson.

5:16b *what had happened to the pigs* The GNT has only 'about the pigs'. The wording here is clearer; cf. NLT, JBP, JB.

5:17 *because they were afraid that he would destroy more of their property* Since Jesus had cured the demoniac, why did the people want Jesus to leave? Four commentators say it was because they were upset by the loss of the pigs, but the only people who would have been upset would have been the owners of the pigs. Eight commentators say it was because they feared to have someone with such great power in their midst. That may be true, but that is not satisfactory: Jesus used his power for good. Guelich supports the interpretation given here.

5:18a *in order to leave* This makes clear that Jesus was acceding to their request.

5:18b *previously* See note on 15b.

5:19d *the Lord God* The question here is, to whom does 'Lord' refer? Four commentators say Jesus was referring to himself, but eighteen say he was referring to God. Since the parallel passage in Luke 8:39 says 'God', that is the interpretation followed here.

5:20b *Ten Towns district* This wording makes clear the meaning of 'Decapolis'. Several versions say 'Ten Towns' but only NLT (and TfT) make clear that 'Ten Towns' was the name of a region.

5:20c *All the people who heard what the man said* TEV and CEV also make clear who is meant by 'all'.

BOUNDARIES AND COHERENCE

A new paragraph at v. 21 is marked by a change in location and a new topic: the healing of Jairus' daughter. Coherence within the 1–20 paragraph is provided by three occurrences of πνεύματι ἀκαθάρτῳ 'evil spirit', two of δαιμονίζομαι 'demonized', and two occurrences of χοῖρος 'pigs'. Coherence is seen in this paragraph as being one episode regarding Jesus' dealing with a man plagued by a crowd of demons.

PROMINENCE AND THEME

The theme is taken from brief portions of the *setting* (to identify the participants) and the *problem*, plus the NUCLEUS of the GOAL of the RESOLUTION and a condensation of $step_2$ and that same GOAL.

EPISODE CLUSTER CONSTITUENT 5:21–43 (Episode of 4:35—5:43)

THEME: *Jesus healed a woman who had been suffering from hemorrhaging, and caused Jairus' daughter to live again.*

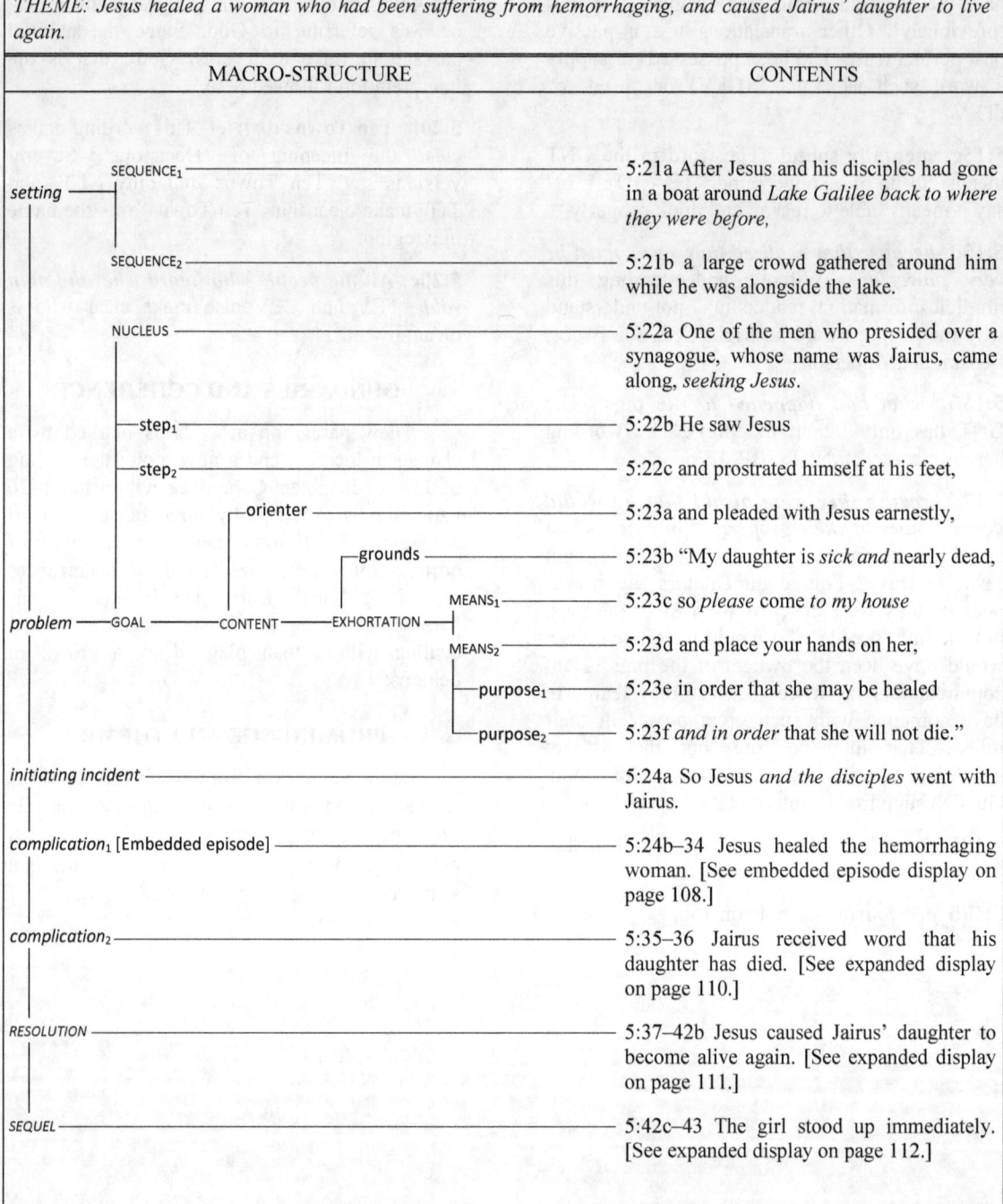

INTENT AND RHETORICAL STRUCTURE

This is the third unit of Jesus performing miracles, this time by healing a hemorrhaging woman and bringing a young girl back to life. This narrative is complex in that there is a primary story line with an embedded story within it.

The author intends that the reader understand how God has great power over a severe illness and even death.

This narrative is of the solutionality sub-type manifest by a simultaneous rhetorical paragraph pattern consisting of a *setting*, a *problem*, an *initiating incident*, a *first complication* of an

EMBEDDED NARRATIVE, a *second complication*, a RESOLUTION, and a SEQUEL.

NOTES

5:21a *and his disciples* Mark follows the usual Biblical pattern of mentioning only the central figure in the narrative.

had gone in a boat around Lake Galilee back to where they were before Some Greek manuscripts omit the words 'in a boat' but the matter is irrelevant; it is clearly implied anyway. Several versions include 'the lake'. None make clear that they returned to where they had started from. And none make clear that 'crossing' means 'skirting around, staying not far from shore'. That was true then and is still true for sailboats.

5:22a who presided over a synagogue This spells out the word ἀρχισυνάγωγος 'synagogue-chief'.

seeking Jesus This seems to be implied; cf. TN.

5:23b *sick and* **nearly dead** The GNT is 'has an end' which Louw and Nida say means "so very sick that death is imminent".

5:23c come *to my house* No versions examined (except TfT) supply the implied destination of the verb 'come'.

EMBEDDED EPISODE 5:24b–34 (Episode within the Episode 5:21–43)

THEME: *Jesus cured a woman who had been suffering from hemorrhaging for twelve years, and assured her that the illness would never return.*

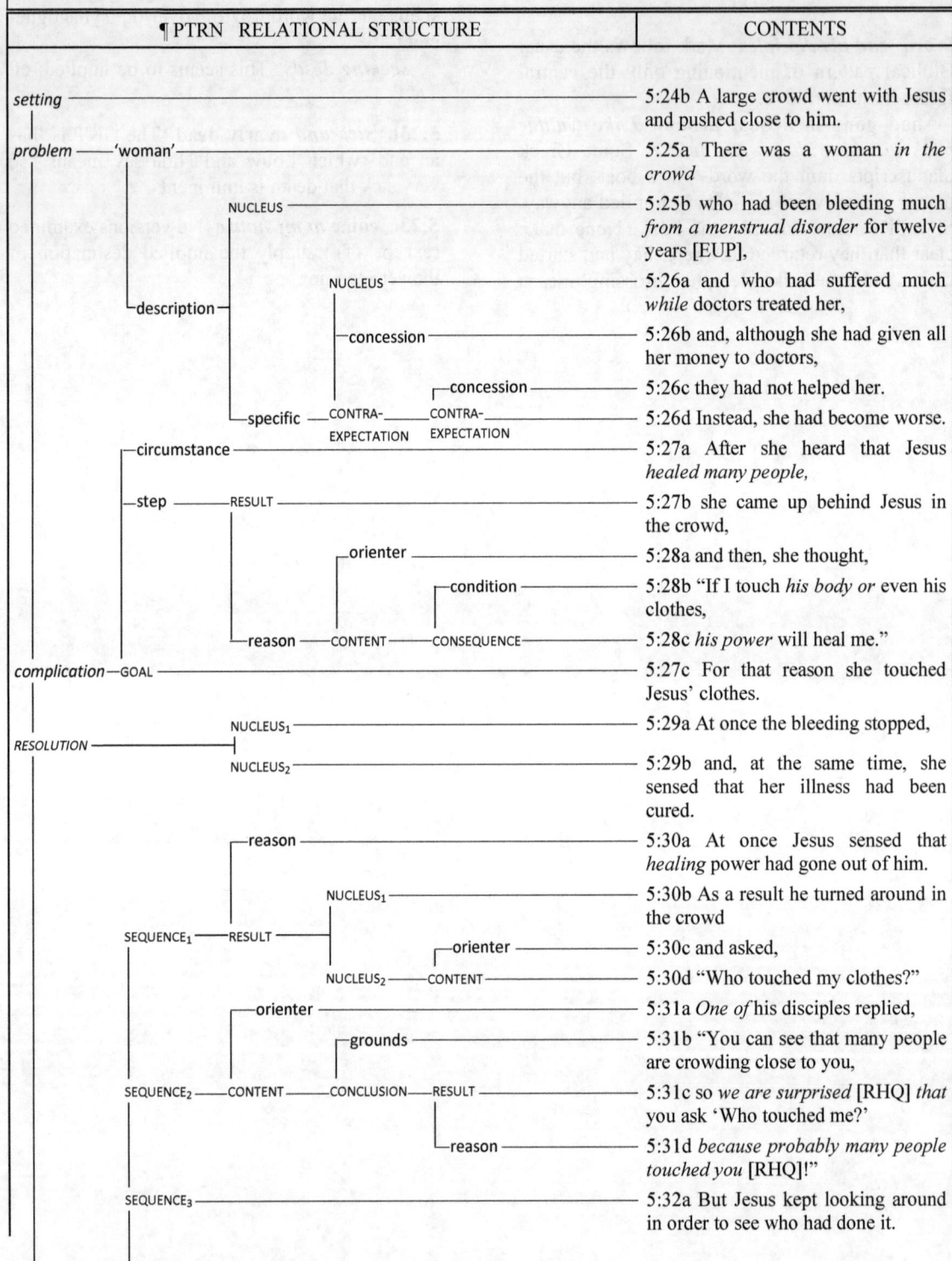

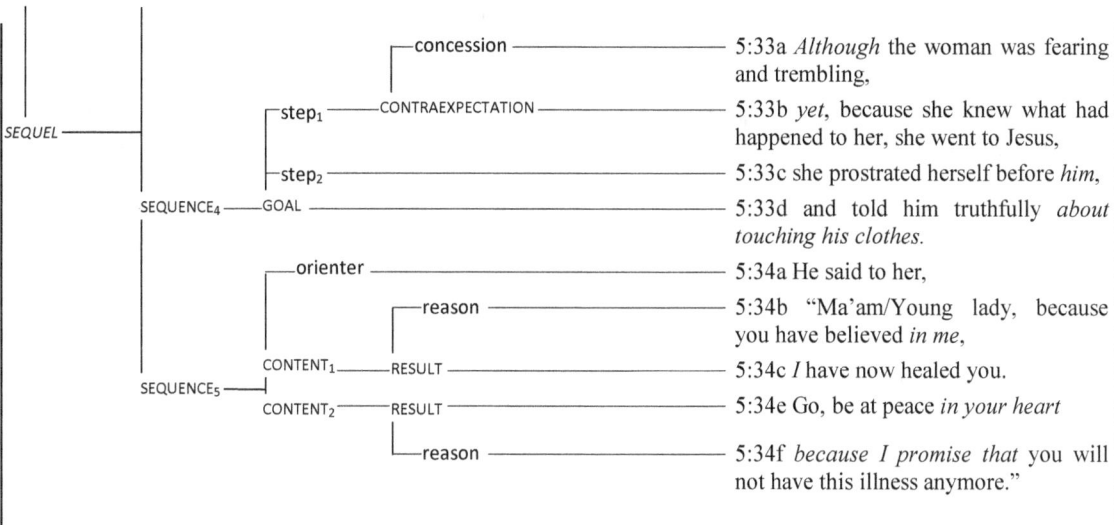

INTENT AND RHETORICAL STRUCTURE

This embedded episode has the same rhetorical function as the inclusive episode; i.e., the author intends that the reader understand how great God's power is over severe illnesses. The structure is a solutionality type narrative consisting of a *setting*, an *initiating event*, two *complications*, a RESOLUTION, and a SEQUEL.

Besides the main author intent mentioned above, he also intends by what he says in the SEQUEL that the reader understand that Jesus wanted to keep his identity hidden in Israel.

NOTES

5:25b bleeding much *from a menstrual disorder* How translators handle this euphemism depends on what is culturally acceptable. English translations say 'bleeding' or 'hemorrhaging' but do not state where the bleeding was. In some cultures the opposite is acceptable: one can state that the problem was in connection with a monthly feminine disorder, but not mention the word 'blood'.

5:27a heard that Jesus *healed many people* The GNT has only 'heard the things about Jesus'. Of translations examined, only LB states what she heard about Jesus: "all about the wonderful miracles Jesus did". The display is more specific.

5:28a she thought The wording of the Greek is 'she said' but she obviously did not speak vocally. Hence 'she thought' (also NIV). Alternatively, one can follow TEV, JB, NEB with 'said to herself'.

5:28b *his body* or even his clothes The GNT has 'even his garments'; the word 'even' implies that something more likely is implied; in this case, his body. No translation examined (except TfT) makes this clear.

5:28c *his power* will heal me The GNT has a passive 'I will be healed'. The display is just a bit more specific regarding the source of the healing.

5:30a *healing* power The word 'healing' is added to help avoid the impression that afterward he had less power than before.

5:31a *One of* his disciples They did not all reply in unison.

5:31c *so we are surprised that* This expresses the force of the rhetorical question, "You say…?" Several versions render it as "How can you ask…?" which is better than a literal translation, but still does not capture clearly the notion of surprise at Jesus' question.

5:31d *because probably many people touched you* This supplies the situational implicature of why they were surprised at Jesus' question.

5:33a fearing and trembling Commentators are very divided, suggesting at least five reasons for the woman's reaction. The display does not choose one of them. But the one that makes the most sense is that she feared that Jesus would be angry because of her action – touching someone who was hemorrhaging – would make him ceremonially unclean until evening.

5:33b what had happened to her A more specific alternative would be 'that she had been healed'.

5:34b Ma'am/Young lady The GNT has 'daughter' which BAGD say is used figuratively as a friendly greeting to girls and women.

believed *in me* The GNT has 'your faith has healed you', which is a personification, which is retained by all translations examined except TfT. A good alternative is 'because you believed that I could heal you'.

5:34e peace *in your heart* The Greek text has 'go in peace' Many commentators note that this was a standard Jewish farewell that basically meant 'May things go well with you'. See also TN.

5:34f *because I promise that* you will not have this illness anymore The Greek has 'be whole from your plague'. This seems to be a very strange thing to command. TN says that Jesus spoke these words "to assure her that she would remain healed", and that is what the display conveys. CEV has "May God give you peace".

BOUNDARIES AND COHERENCE

V. 35 marks the continuation of the episode regarding Jairus' daughter. Coherence within the 24b–34 unit is provided by occurrences of γυνή 'woman' in vv. 25 and 33 and the phrases ἥψατο τοῦ ἱματίου flow of blood' (v. 25) and 'fountain of blood' (v. 29), and the whole paragraph dealing with Jesus healing the woman.

PROMINENCE AND THEME

The theme is drawn from the NUCLEUS of the description of the *problem* and the GOAL of the RESOLUTION.

EXPANSION OF COMPLICATION₂ 5:35–36 IN THE MARK 5:21–43 DISPLAY

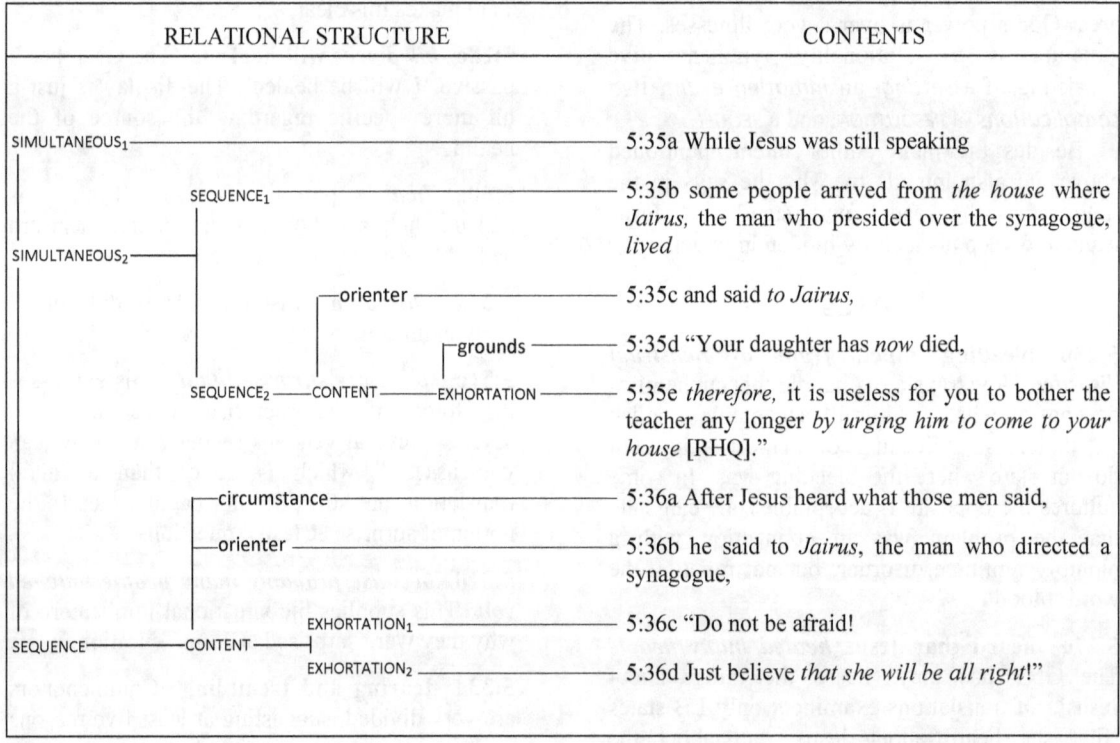

NOTES

5:35b See note on 21a.

Jairus His name is repeated from 22a. See also NIV, TEV, CEV, NLT.

5:35c said *to Jairus* This makes clear to whom they were addressing their remark, as does TEV.

5:35e it is useless The rhetorical question 'Why bother...?' is rendered as a statement that expresses the force of the question; NLT and NCV translate similarly.

by urging him to come to your house This conveys the import of the word σκύλλω 'bother'. See Hiebert, TRT.

EXPANSION OF RESOLUTION 5:37–42b IN THE MARK 5:21–43 DISPLAY

RELATIONAL STRUCTURE	CONTENTS
step₁	5:37 He allowed only Peter, James, and John, who was the *younger* brother of James, to go with him.
step₂ — SEQUENCE₁	5:38a Then, after they arrived at the house where Jairus lived,
SEQUENCE₂	5:38b Jesus saw that the people there were in turmoil and were weeping and wailing loudly [DOU].
SEQUENCE₃	5:39a He entered the house,
SEQUENCE₄ — orienter	5:39b and said to them metaphorically, knowing that *he was going to restore her to life*,
CONTENT — EXHORTATION	5:39c "Don't be in such a turmoil and stop crying [RHQ],
grounds — NUCLEUS	5:39d because the child is not dead;
CONTRASTIVE NUCLEUS	5:39e on the contrary, she is sleeping."
SEQUENCE₅ — RESULT	5:40a But the people only laughed at him,
reason	5:40b *because they knew she was dead.*
step₃ — SEQUENCE₁	5:40c After he sent all the other people outside the house,
SEQUENCE₂	5:40d he took the child's father and mother and *the three disciples* who were with him.
SEQUENCE₃	5:40e They entered *the room* where the child was lying.
GOAL — SEQUENCE₁	5:41a He took hold of the child's hand
SEQUENCE₂ — orienter	5:41b and said to her *in the Aramaic language*,
CONTENT — EQUIVALENT₁	5:41c "Talitha Koum,"
EQUIVALENT₂	5:41d which means, "Little girl, I tell you, get up!"
OUTCOME — SEQUENCE₁	5:42a At once the girl, who was twelve years old, got up
SEQUENCE₂	5:42b and started to walk around.

NOTES

5:36b *Jairus* The GNT does not repeat his name, but some versions do – e.g., CEV, NLT.

5:36d *believe that she will be all right* The GNT has only "just believe'. The concept 'believe' requires some content of the cognitive process to be understood. Here, it is that Jesus would heal his daughter so that she would live; cf. Marcus, Cranfield, Hiebert, and Lane. TN suggests as a translation, "that I can save your daughter", which is excellent.

5:37 *younger brother* The word 'younger' is supplied for translation into those languages in which that distinction is necessary.

5:39b *knowing that he was going to restore her to life* The words that Jesus spoke to them, 'The child is not dead, just sleeping', without the above implicit information being supplied in some way, will leave the impression that Jesus was either ignorant or being silly. TN suggests as a footnote, "he said that she was sleeping because he knew that he would soon make her live again", which is almost the same wording as in the display.

5:40b *because they knew she was dead* This clause supplies the reason they laughed. See TN.

5:40d *the three disciples* The GNT has only 'those with him' but several versions make 'the three disciples explicit; cf. NLT, CEV, and TEV.

5:41b *in the Aramaic language* Jesus' words to the girl, 'Talitha koum', which are Aramaic, will seem very strange if not explained in some way. TN says "They are probably from the language that Jesus and the little girl spoke as their mother tongue".

EXPANSION OF THE SEQUEL 5:42c–43d IN THE MARK 5:21–43 DISPLAY

RELATIONAL STRUCTURE	CONTENTS
SEQUENCE₁	5:42c When this happened, *all who were present* were very astonished.
⎯orienter	5:43a Jesus ordered them strictly
SEQUENCE₂ ⎯ CONTENT	5:43b that they should not tell anyone *about what he had done,*
⎯orienter	5:43c and then he told *her parents*
SEQUENCE₃ ⎯ CONTENT	5:43d that they should bring her something to eat.

NOTES

5:42c **When this happened** This phrase represents the word εὐθύς 'immediately', which is missing in many manuscripts. Its inclusion is given a D 'impossible to decide' rating, but it is probably implied anyway.

all who were present This wording makes clear who the 'they' in the Greek refers to.

5:43b *about what he had done* The Greek has only 'this'; CEV and NLT have 'what had happened'. An alternative would be 'that he had healed the girl'.

BOUNDARIES AND COHERENCE

A new unit at 6:1 is indicated by a change in location and a new topic: Jesus' ministry in his home town. Coherence in the 5:21–43 unit is provided by the same participants (Jesus, his disciples, and Jairus), and a movement toward Jairus' house, during a single time span. There is, however, an embedded episode of Jesus healing a hemorrhaging woman which occurs as the first complication in the inclusive episode. Coherence can also be observed by occurrences of the name Jairus in vv. 22 and 35, two occurrences of ἀρχισυνάγωγος 'synagogue ruler', and occurrences of θυγάτριον 'little daughter' (v. 23) and θυγάτηρ 'daughter' (v. 35). Coherence is also seen in the paragraph dealing just with the restoring of Jairus' daughter to life (v. 35). Coherence of the embedded episode is by occurrences of ῥύσει αἵματος 'hemorrhage', γυνή 'woman', ἥψατο τοῦ ἱματίου αὐτοῦ 'touch robe', and σῴζω 'heal'.

PROMINENCE AND THEME

The theme is drawn from the NUCLEUS of the *problem*, and NUCLEUS₁ of the *RESOLUTION* of the embedded episode, plus a rephrasing/condensation of the GOAL of the *RESOLUTION* of the main episode.

SCENE CONSTITUENT 6:1–29 (Episode Cluster of 3:13—6:29)

THEME: *Jesus' identity is brought to the foreground. The people of Nazareth town were offended by what he was teaching, he also sent out his disciples two by two, and Herod thought that Jesus was John come to life, whom he had beheaded.*	
MACROSTRUCTURE	CONTENTS
NUCLEUS₁	6:1–6b Jesus taught in the synagogue, and the people who heard him were astonished and offended
NUCLEUS₂	6:6b–13 Jesus began to send out his disciples two-by-two and gave them power and instructions.
NUCLEUS₃	6:14–29 King Herod heard about Jesus and mistakenly thought that John the Baptizer had come back to life after he had had John executed due to the insistence of his wife, Herodias.

INTENT AND RHETORICAL STRUCTURE

This Scene Constituent 6:1–29 is part of the scene that presents Jesus' ministry in the Galilean area. Jesus commences his ministry by choosing his twelve apostles, and concludes by him sending them out in pairs to teach and heal in Galilee. This unit is climactic in the scene by focusing on Jesus' rejection by his own people in Nazareth (6:1–6b), his sending his twelve into all the towns in Galilee (6:b–13), and even Herod wondering who Jesus is (6:14–39). The last episode also mentions that Herod had John the Baptizer beheaded, making it pivotal and transitional between Jesus' ministry in Galilee and Jesus' ministry into the neighboring gentile area, which lay outside of the Jewish authority and Herod's authority area. Internally, this unit has three sequential episodes of equal prominence.

BOUNDARIES AND COHERENCE

The initial and closing boundaries are marked and described in the discussion of the first and last episodes of this unit. After this unit, Jesus' ministry is to non-Jewish people, leading up to the climax of this first part of the book.

PROMINENCE AND THEME

The theme is derived from a consideration of the three nuclei of this unit, and a mention that the disciples and other people were wondering who Jesus really was.

EPISODE CLUSTER CONSTITUENT 6:1–6a (Episode of 6:1–29)

THEME: *Jesus taught in the synagogue, and the people who heard him were astonished and offended.*

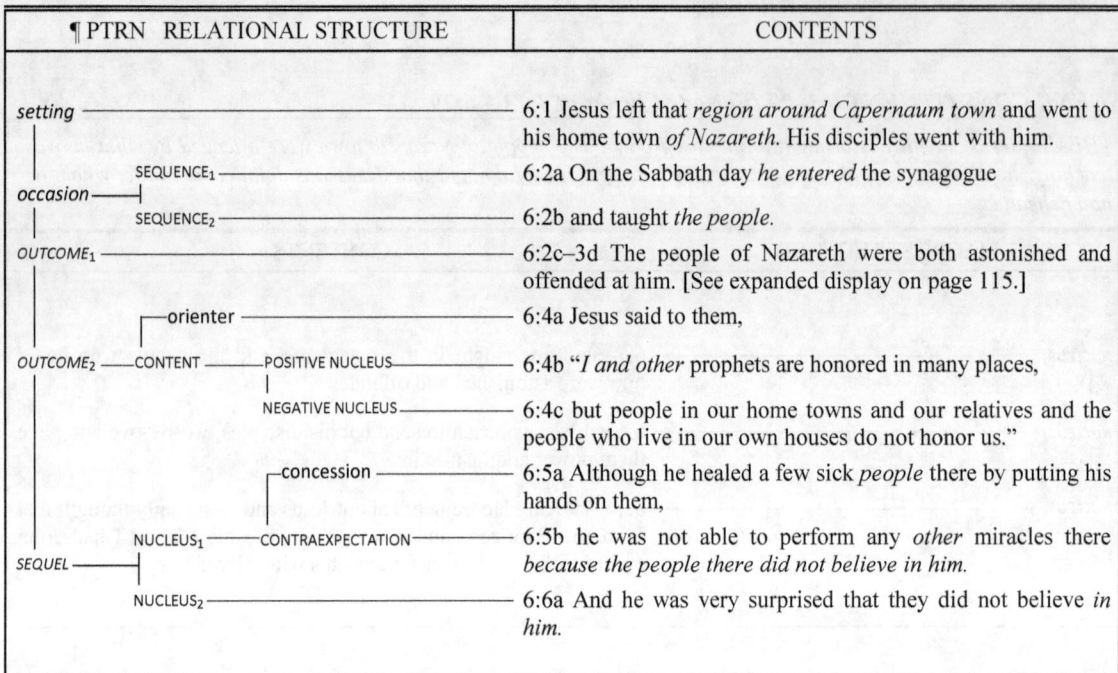

INTENT AND RHETORICAL STRUCTURE

The author's intent is to tell how the people of his home town rejected and were offended by his claims. The narrative is a causality type narrative consisting of a *setting*, and *occasion*, two OUTCOMES, and an author COMMENT about the narrative.

NOTES

6:1 that region *around Capernaum* The Greek has only 'from there'; the display specifies what that region was; see 2:1, 5:21. This is supported by eight commentaries.

home town *of Nazareth* Only NLT gives the name of the town.

6:4b *I and other* prophets Several commentators say that by making this statement, Jesus was accepting the designation 'prophet' for himself. No version (except TfT) makes this clear.

6:5b any *other* miracles Healing a few sick people was performing miracles; hence 'other' here.

because the people there did not believe in him NIV Study Bible footnote says "Jesus had the power to perform miracles at Nazareth, but he chose not to heal in such a climate of unbelief." The word 'believe' requires some content of what is believed; the display supplies one of the possible contents.

EXPANDED DISPLAY OF OUTCOME₁ 6:2c–6:6 OF EPISODE₃ OF MARK 6:1–6a

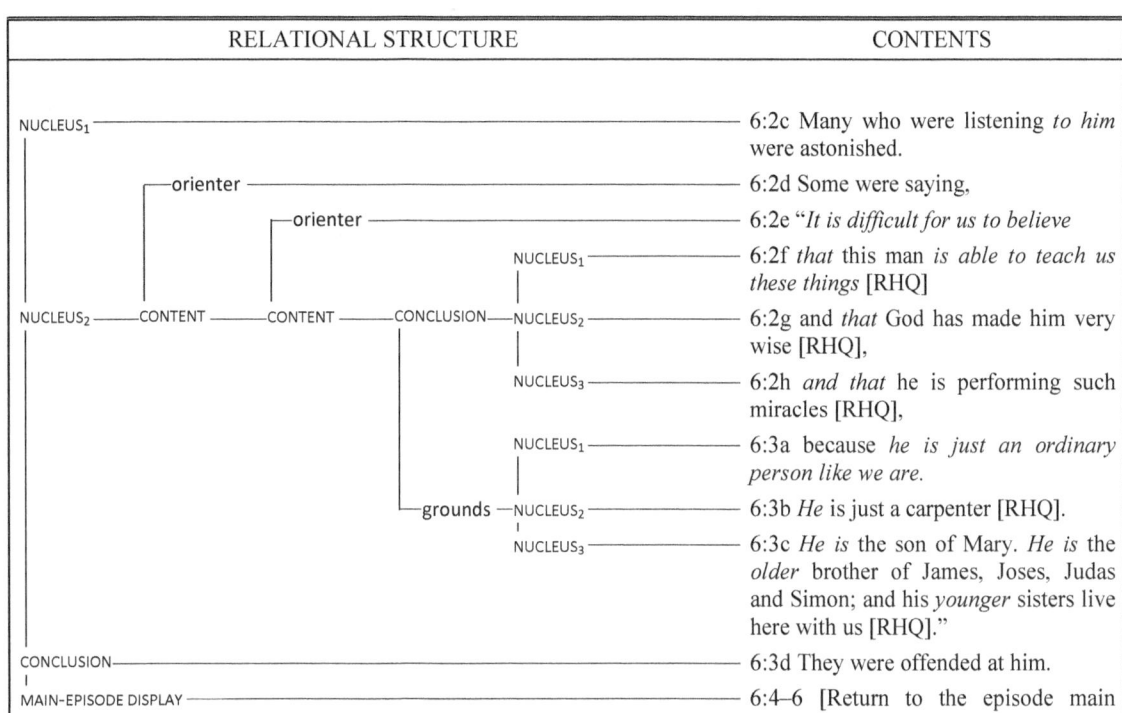

NOTES

6:2e shocked/astonished In this context the word ἀναχωρέω has a negative connotation. It does not mean 'amazed' (NIV, TEV)

It is difficult for us to believe The GNT has 'whence to this man these things?' but it is not a real question seeking information (cf. THM); it is just giving expression to their astonishment (also Lane). TN suggests as a translation "It is unbelievable that this man has learned all these things!"

6:2g made him very wise The wording here replaces the abstract noun 'wisdom' with the adjective 'wise'.

6:2h *and that* The word 'that' which is found in the KJV is from much later Greek manuscripts.

6:3b *just a* carpenter The rhetorical question, 'Isn't he a carpenter?' is in effect a derogatory statement of belittlement; JBP has "only", NLT has "just".

6:3c *older* brother of ....*younger* sisters See note on 5:37.

BOUNDARIES AND COHERENCE

A new paragraph at v. 6b is indicated by a change in location and a new topic: sending out the disciples. Coherence within the 2–6a paragraph is indicated by two occurrences of δύναμις 'miracle' and several kinship terms: son, brother, sister, and relatives, and also because of the paragraph consisting of events in Nazareth.

PROMINENCE AND THEME

The theme is drawn from both propositions of the *occasion* plus the 1ˢᵗ NUCLEUS of OUTCOME₁ and the SEQUEL.

EPISODE CLUSTER CONSTITUENT 6:6b–13 (Episode of 6:1–29)

THEME: Jesus began to send out his disciples two-by-two and gave them power and instructions.

¶ PTRN RELATIONAL STRUCTURE	CONTENTS
setting	6:6b Then Jesus went from town to town *in that region* teaching *the people.*
move₁ — NUCLEUS₁	6:7a *While he was doing that,* he summoned the twelve *disciples*
NUCLEUS₂	6:7b and prepared to send them out two-by-two *to various towns.*
move₂ — CONTRACTION — NUCLEUS₁	6:7c *He* gave them the power to cast out evil spirits *from people.*
NUCLEUS₂	6:8a He told them to take along only a walking stick when they were traveling.
amplification — CONTRAST₁ — RESULT	6:8b *He told them* not to take food, nor a bag *in which travelers carry supplies,* nor any money,
reason	6:8c since *the people to whom they were to minister were to supply what they needed.*
CONTRAST₂ — CONTRAST₁	6:9a He allowed them to wear sandals,
CONTRAST₂	6:9b but *he did* not *allow them* to take extra clothes.
orienter	6:10a *Also,* he said to them:
move₃ — CONTENT — CONTRAST₁ — NUCLEUS₁	6:10b "*After you enter a town and someone has invited you to stay in his house,* when you enter the home,
NUCLEUS₂	6:10c stay in that same *home* until you leave *that town, so that the person who owns the house will not be offended.*
CONTRAST₂ — NUCLEUS	6:11 Wherever *the people* do not welcome you and *wherever the people* do not listen to you, shake off the dust from your feet as you leave *that place,*
purpose	6:11b in order to signal to them *that their guilt remains with them like the dust from their feet remains in their town.*"
ACCOMPLISH-MENT — NUCLEUS₁	6:12 After *the disciples* went out *to the various towns,* they were saying that *people* should repent;
NUCLEUS₂	6:13a they were expelling many demons *from people;*
NUCLEUS₃	6:13b and they were anointing many sick people with *olive* oil and healing them.

INTENT AND RHETORICAL STRUCTURE

The purpose of this unit (6:6b–13) is to tell about selecting his 'apostles'.

This is an objective type narrative consisting of a *setting*, three *moves*, and an *ACCOMPLISHMENT*.

NOTES

6:6b *in that region* These words are included to specify what towns Mark was referring to. CEV has "neighboring villages", TEV has "villages around there".

6:7a the twelve *disciples* The GNT has only 'the twelve' but TEV and NLT have "twelve disciples" while CEV has "twelve apostles".

6:7b *to various towns* These words are included to make clear where Jesus was sending them.

6:8b food The Greek has 'bread' but this was a synecdoche, just a way of indicating food (cf. CEV, NLT.)

bag *in which travelers carry supplies* This is one of the meanings of the word πήρα 'bag'. NLT has "traveler's bag", CEV "traveling bag", JB has "haversack", JBP has "satchel", NEB has "pack". Eight commentators consulted say this is the meaning.

Seven commentators (also TEV) say it means beggar's bag. But Jesus and the disciples never traveled as beggars.

6:8c *since the people to whom they were to minister were to supply what they needed* The question here is, how were they to survive if they carried no food or money with them? Four commentators and footnotes in two versions support the explanation given here.

6:9b take extra clothes The GNT has 'do not wear two tunics', but four commentators say this means they were not to take along an extra tunic (also CEV, GW, NCV, NLT). The display is more generic in the prohibition, having 'clothes' instead of 'tunic' (cf. CEV "change of clothes").

6:10b *After you enter a town and someone has invited you to stay in his house* This material supplies the intervening actions which must take place before that of 10c.

6:10c *so that the person who owns the house will not be offended* The question is, why were they to stay in only one house? Several commentators say they were not to seek better accommodations elsewhere, but even if true, that does not answer the question. Four commentators say they were to remain grateful to the one offering the first invitation, which is a more positive way of expressing what is in the display.

6:11b signal to them *that their guilt remains with them like the dust from their feet remains in their town* Several explanations of this symbolic act are offered, but Guelich's seems quite good: He suggests it probably symbolized three things: (1) the place was declared to be pagan, (2) there would be no further contact with the place, and (3) the messengers had done their job and now washed their hands of any further responsibility for the people living there. Hendriksen's comment points in the direction of the display: "a heavy load of guilt rests on such a place."

The TR has a long additional bit about Sodom and Gomorrah, in which the sentence mentioning those two places is so poorly attested that it is not even mentioned in the 4th edition of the GNT.

6:12 *to the various towns* See note on 6:7b.

6:13b *olive* **oil** The type of oil is specified; as in NLT, CEV.

BOUNDARIES AND COHERENCE

The start of a new paragraph at v. 14 is indicated by the introduction of a new participant (King Herod) and a new topic (the death of John the Baptizer). Coherence within the 6b–13 paragraph is shown by the occurrence of πνεῦμα ὁ ἀκάθαρτος 'evil spirits' in v. 7 and δαιμόνιον 'demons' in v. 13, and a set of instructions to the disciples.

PROMINENCE AND THEME

The theme consists of NUCLEUS$_2$ of *step*$_1$ and a summary of the propositions of step$_2$.

EPISODE CLUSTER CONSTITUENT 6:14–29 (Expository Paragraph of 6:1–29)

THEME: *King Herod heard about Jesus and mistakenly thought that John the Baptizer had come back to life after he had had John executed due to the insistence of his wife, Herodias.*

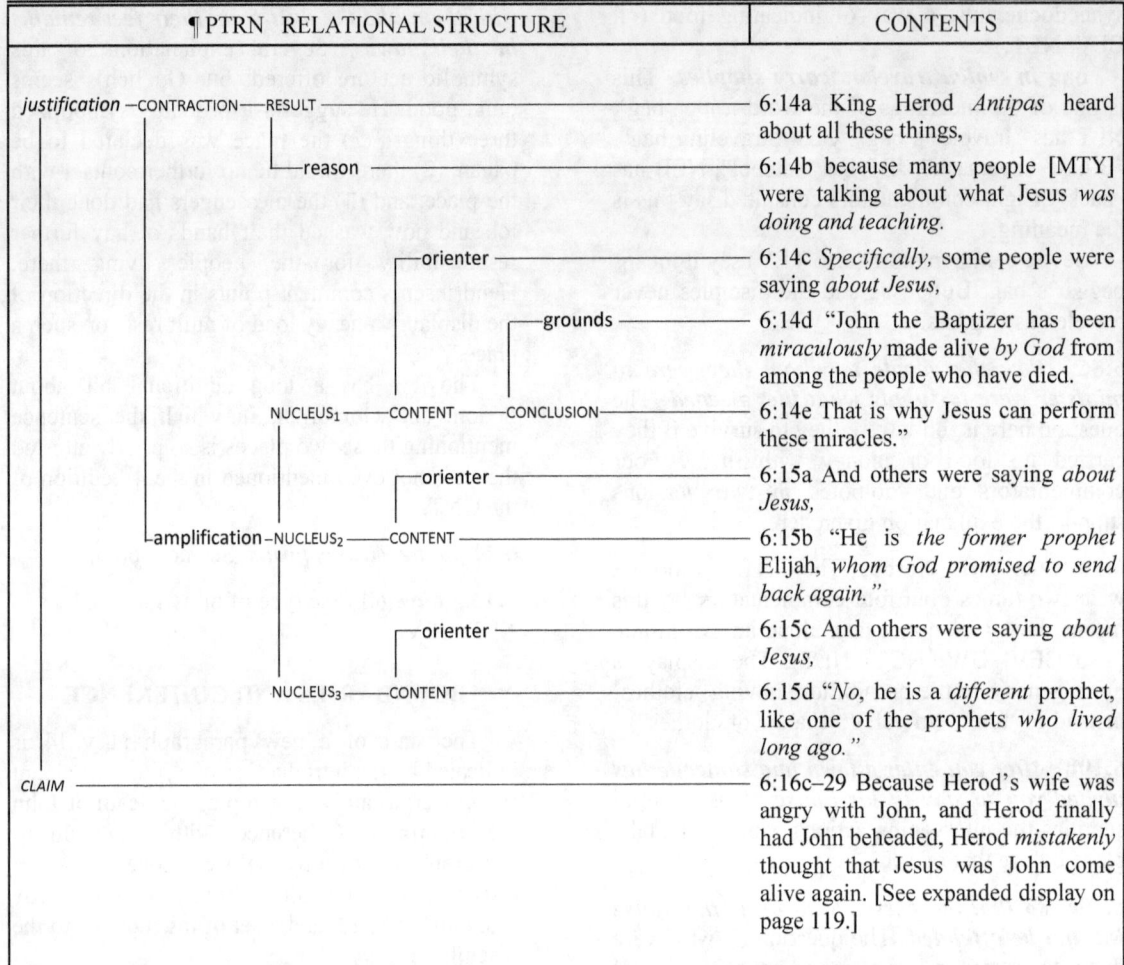

INTENT AND RHETORICAL STRUCTURE

The author here intends to close the initial scene in the book about Jesus starting to make himself known to the people of Israel.

This unit 6:14–29 is a complex expository aragraph with an embedded narrative providing the *reason* for Herod CONCLUDING that John had come back to life.

This unit is an objective expository paragraph consisting of a *justification*, and a CLAIM.

Within the CLAIM there is an embedded narrative (vv. 17b–29) telling how and why John was treacherously killed by the plotting of Herod's wife, Herodias.

Even the story plot is tightly bound together: Herodias wanted someone to execute John (v. 19 *occasion*) and could not do so (v. 20), but an opportunity came (v. 21) and she bought it up (v. 27–28 OUTCOME).

NOTES

6:14a Herod *Antipas* His other name is supplied because there were several Herods.

6:14b Jesus *was doing and teaching* The GNT has 'his name had become known'. This is a double metonymy: name stands for the person, Jesus, and Jesus stands for what he had been doing.

6:14c some people were saying The best manuscripts have the plural 'they were saying', and this is given a B 'almost certain' rating. The singular 'he was saying' is found in some manuscripts, and in the KJV.

6:14d *miraculously* **made alive** *by God* The display makes clear that this was a miracle, and that God was the agent.

6:15b *the former prophet* **Elijah,** *whom God promised to send back again.* The text has only 'he is Elijah'. The material in italics is crucial implicit information which the Jews would have known from Malachi 4:5. NLT has "the ancient prophet;" LB has a bit more: "The ancient prophet, now returned to life again".

6:15d *No,* **he is a** *different* **prophet**. The 'No' makes clear that others were refuting the 'He is Elijah' claim. The word 'different' is included to make clear that Elijah was a prophet. CEV has "some other prophet".

EXPANSION OF CLAIM 6:16–29 IN THE MARK 6:14–29 DISPLAY

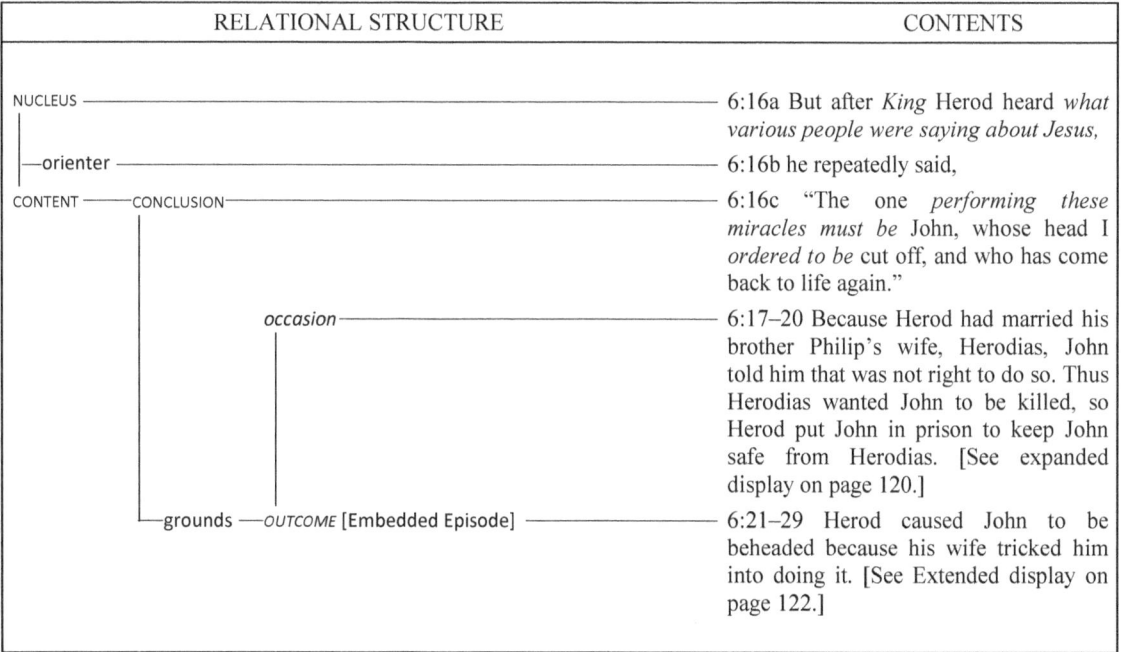

NOTES

6:16a **heard** *what various people were saying about Jesus* The GNT has only 'heard'. Some versions have 'heard about Jesus', but in the context, it is stating that Herod's thoughts about Jesus were different from what others were saying about him.

6:16c **The one** *performing these miracles* CEV has 'this' but the wording in the display makes clear who 'this' refers to.

I *ordered to be* **cut off** The GNT has 'I beheaded' but Herod only gave the orders. CEV has "I had his head cut off".

EXPANSION OF OCCASION 6:17b–20 IN THE MARK 6:16–29 EXPANSION DISPLAY

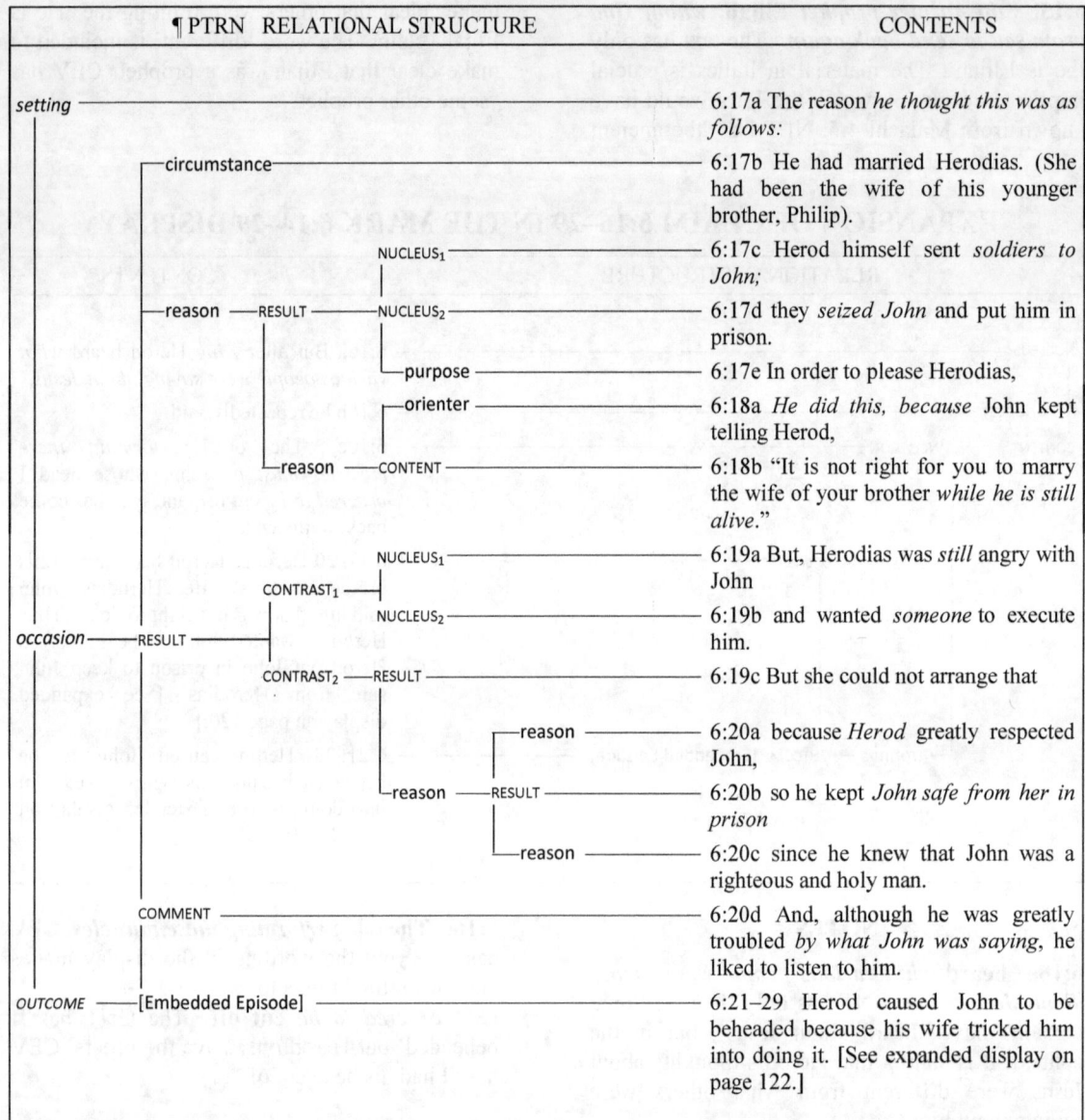

NOTES

6:17a *The reason King Herod concluded this is as follows* What follows in vv. 17–29 is a flashback stating the events which provided the reason for the conclusion drawn about John. It is introduced in the Greek simply by γάρ 'for'.

6:17–19 These verses are well known for not conveying chronological order. CEV combines vv. 17–18, as does LB.

6:17b *Sometime before this* The flashback is indicated in the Greek and in almost all the versions simply by a past perfect tense. CEV makes the time sequence clear by including the word 'earlier'.

younger **brother** See note on 1:16. But it is very difficult to know whether Philip was younger or older. Commentators give no help. Herod the Great had a succession of five wives. The two brothers had the same father but different mothers. THM says Philip was younger; TN says he was older.

6:18b *while he is still alive* This is implicit; there would have been no restriction if Philip had already died.

6:17c–d sent *soldiers to John; they* seized *John* The GNT has only 'having sent seized'. NLT is very clear with "sent solders to arrest and imprison John".

6:19a *still* angry The point is that imprisonment of John did not satisfy Herodias. TN suggests "continued to feel anger…" See Hendriksen.

6:19c Yet The Greek conjunction is καί 'and' but all versions examined give it an adversative sense and render it as 'But'.

could not *arrange that* The GNT has only 'she was not able'. NLT adds "without Herod's approval". A complete formulation of the events would be:

she wanted him executed
    but she couldn't *arrange that*
        without Herod's approval,
    but that was not possible
because Herod kept him safe.

6:20b safe *from her in prison*. The GNT has 'kept him safe', which means that keeping John in prison, he prevented Herodias from harming John.

6:20d greatly troubled *by what John was saying* TN says "Herod was uncertain about what he should do in response to John's teaching". There is a textual problem here; many Greek manuscripts have 'he did many things', which doesn't make much sense. The wording in the display has excellent manuscript support and follows Mark's use of 'many' as an adverb, not a noun.

EXPANSION DISPLAY OF OUTCOME [EMBEDDED EPISODE 6:21–29 (EPISODE WITHIN THE EXPOSITION OF 6:16–29)]

THEME: *Because of Herod's foolish promise, he had to order John the Baptizer to be executed.*

¶ PTRN RELATIONAL STRUCTURE	CONTENTS
setting — NUCLEUS₁	6:21a But a day came when Herodias was able to cause someone to execute John.
setting — NUCLEUS₂	6:21b When it was Herod's birthday, he invited the main government officials, the main army leaders and the most important men in Galilee district in order that they might eat and celebrate with him.
problem — circumstance	6:22a While they were eating, Herodias' daughter came into the room and, by dancing, she pleased King Herod and his guests.
NUCLEUS₁ — orienter	6:22b The king said to her,
NUCLEUS₁ — CONTENT	6:22c "Ask me for whatever you desire and I will give it to you."
NUCLEUS₂ — orienter	6:23a He also said to her,
NUCLEUS₂ — CONTENT	6:23b "May God punish me if I do not do what I have promised, which is that, whatever you ask for I will give it to you. I will give you up to half of what I rule over, if you ask for it."
resolving incident — SEQUENCE₁ — orienter	6:24a The girl left the room, went to her mother, told her what Herod had said, and asked her:
SEQUENCE₁ — CONTENT	6:24b "What do you want me to ask for?"
SEQUENCE₂ — orienter	6:24c In order to force Herod to have John executed, she replied,
SEQUENCE₂ — CONTENT	6:24d "Ask King Herod to give you the head of John the Baptizer on a platter so I can know he has been executed."
resolving incident — orienter	6:25a The girl quickly reentered the room where the king was, went to him and said,
CONTENT	6:25b "I want you to cut off and give me at once on a tray the head of John the Baptizer."
complication — RESULT	6:26a When King Herod heard what she asked for he became very sorry about what he had promised, but he could not refuse what she requested
reason	6:26b because he had promised that he would give her anything she asked for, and because he had promised that while his guests were present.
move₁	6:27a So the king at once ordered the man who executes *prisoners* to *go and cut off John's* head and bring it to him.
move₂	6:27b That man went and cut off John's head in the prison.
move₃	6:28a He brought it back, put it on a serving dish and gave it to the girl.
RESOLUTION — ACCOMPLISHMENT	6:28b The girl gave it to her mother.
SEQUEL — SEQUENCE₁	6:29a After John's disciples heard what had happened,
SEQUENCE₂	6:29b they went and took John's body and put it in a tomb.

INTENT AND RHETORICAL STRUCTURE

This embedded episode (6:21–29) explains why Herod thought that Jesus was John come back to life. This is a typical solutionality type narrative consisting of *setting*, a *problem*, two *resolving incidents*, a RESOLUTION and a SEQUEL.

Mark tells how Herodias managed to have John the Baptizer executed.

NOTES

6:21a day *when Herodias was able to cause someone to execute John* The Greek has 'coming a suitable day'. NLT and CEV have 'chance' but no versions examined (except TfT) explicate 'chance to do what?'

6:21b birthday In cultures where birthdays are not celebrated, it may be necessary to say 'the day when they celebrated the anniversary of the day on which he had been born' (cf. TN).

6:22a *While they were eating* This supplies the time of the girl's dancing.

6:23b There are textual uncertainties here. Some manuscripts have a word which means either 'many times' or 'solemnly'. Of versions consulted, only NRSV and TEV translate it.

May God punish me if I do not do what I have promised The Greek has ὀμνύω 'he swore' and the wording in the display conveys the meaning of the word clearly; cf. THM.

half of what I rule over The king said 'half of my kingdom', and for languages which do not know about kingdoms, the wording in the display will convey the meaning well.

6:24a left *the room, went to* her mother, *told her what Herod had said,* and asked her The material in italics supplies the intervening actions.

6:24c *In order to force Herod to have John executed* This clause supplies the implied purpose: she didn't really want his head; she wanted him dead.

6:24d *Ask King Herod to give you* The wording in the display forms a complete sentence.

so that I can know he has been executed This may be crucial information in many languages. See TN's suggestion for a footnote. When this writer was checking one translation of this passage and asked 'Why did she want John's head?' the answer immediately was, "It says right there she wanted it on a plate!"

6:25b *cut off and* give me The verb in italics supplies the necessary intervening action (cf. Hiebert).

6:26 sorry *about what he had promised* Commentators (e.g., Hiebert, Lenski) and CEV also make clear what he was sorry about.

6:27a go and cut off John's head and bring it The display supplies the intervening actions.

BOUNDARIES AND COHERENCE

The start of a new unit at v. 30 is marked by a return to the ministry of the apostles, and then a change in location. Coherence within the 14–29 paragraph is shown by five occurrences of the name 'Herod', two occurrences of θυγάτηρ 'girl', and four occurrences of βασιλεύς 'king'. Coherence is seen by the topic of Herod thinking Jesus was John come back to life.

PROMINENCE AND THEME

The theme of this expository paragraph is basically taken from the NUCLEUS and CONTENT of the CLAIM.

ACT CONSTITUENT 6:30—8:21 (Scene of 3:7—8:30)

THEME: While Jesus was traveling outside of Galilee and Judea, he taught his disciples that he was powerful by what he did and by accepting persons whom the disciples considered unclean.

MACROSTRUCTURE	CONTENTS
circumstance	6:30–34 The apostles returned to Jesus to report what they had done. Then they all went off to a lonely place, but many people followed them.
occasion	6:35—8:10 By Jesus performing miracles and teaching about what is or is not acceptable to God, he taught his disciples that the non-Jewish people were also to hear the good news about God's rule.
OUTCOME	8:11–21 After the Jewish authorities demanded that Jesus perform a sign that would prove that God had sent him, and he refused to do so, Jesus taught his disciples to not imitate the authorities' bad influence of questioning what God was doing.

INTENT AND RHETORICAL STRUCTURE

Following the account of Herod ordering the execution of John the Baptizer, Jesus avoids the Judean area under Herod's authority. The following episodes take place mainly in gentile areas like the Tyre and Sidon region, and the Decapolis region. At first Jesus remained in the Galilean area, until after the incident of Jesus arguing with the Pharisees and teachers of the Jewish law about the question of clean and unclean. This episode probably took place in the Capernaum area. It seems to be written here to teach that the Good News is also for those who are considered unclean. This unit consists of a *setting*, an *occasion*, and an OUTCOME.

BOUNDARIES AND COHERENCE

The initial and closing boundaries are marked and described in the discussion of the first and last episodes of this unit. This entire unit is held together by Jesus ministering to people who are considered by his Jewish disciples as outside of God ruling over them.

PROMINENCE AND THEME

The theme of this unit consists of a condensation of each of the structural items, preserving the natural prominence of the structure.

SCENE CONSTITUENT 6:30–34 (Episode of 6:30—8:21)

THEME: The apostles returned to Jesus to report what they had done. Then they all went off to a lonely place, but many people followed them. When they arrived, there was a crowd, and Jesus pitied them and began to teach them.

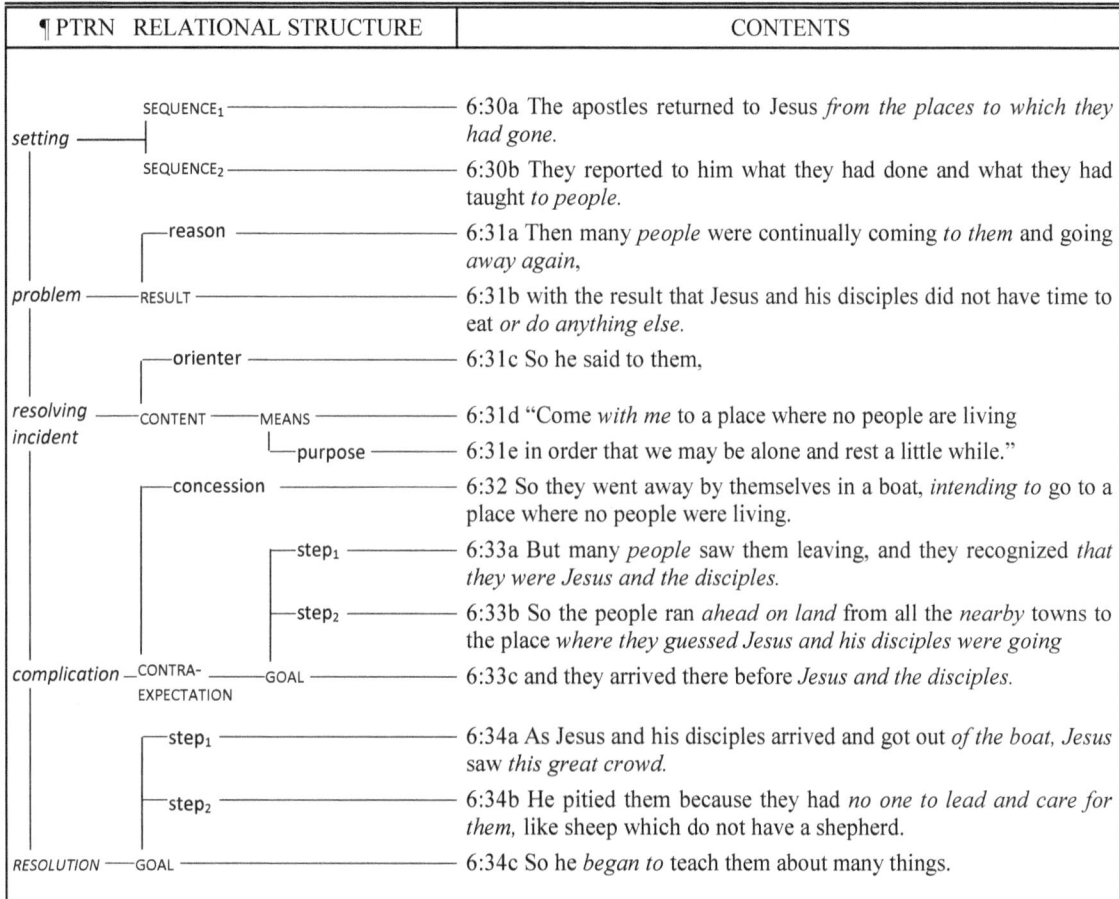

INTENT AND RHETORICAL STRUCTURE

Mark intends to inform the reader that Jesus and his disciples could not escape the crowds, so Jesus continued to teach and heal the sick. This episode is a solutionality type of narrative consisting of a *setting*, a *problem*, a *resolving incident*, a *complication*, and a RESOLUTION.

NOTES

6:30a returned ...*from the places to which they had gone* The Greek has only 'assembled'. It refers to 6:12–13. NLT has "returned…from their ministry tour" which is very good.

6:31b with the result that The Greek conjunction καί which usually means 'and', but here it introduces a result.

to eat *or do anything else* Almost all the versions have 'even to eat'. There is no word in the Greek that signals 'even' but it is implied. The meaning is not that they had time to do many other things but not to eat; it means they had no time to do anything by themselves, not even to eat.

6:31d Come *with me* The Greek says 'come yourselves' but the sense is that they were to go with Jesus.

6:32 *intending to* go to a place where no people were living The Greek says 'to a solitary place'. But that was only their intention; they were unsuccessful. The CEV indicates this with "where they could be alone".

6:33a recognized *that they were Jesus and the disciples* The Greek has only 'many knew'.

TEV has "knew at once who they were". Most other versions have 'recognized'.

6:33b ran ahead on land The Greek has 'on foot' which is somewhat idiomatic.

to the place *where they guessed Jesus and his disciples were going* The Greek has only 'there'; the display spells out what 'there' means. JB has a similar rendering: "many could guess where". CEV has "figured out where they were going".

The KJV, following the Textus Receptus, adds the words 'came together unto him'. But manuscript evidence and internal factors favor their omission (which is given a B 'almost certain' rating).

6:34b *no one to lead and care for them* The question here is, what is the point of similarity in the simile, 'like sheep without a shepherd'? The display follows the suggestion in TN. Lenski suggests the former (lead them), THM and France suggest the latter (care for them).

BOUNDARIES AND COHERENCE

A new unit at v. 35 is marked by a change in time and a new topic: the miraculous feeding of the 5000. Coherence within the 30–34 paragraph is provided by references to travel by boat and on foot.

PROMINENCE AND THEME

The theme of this unit is drawn from SEQUENCE$_1$ of the *setting*, the CONCESSION of the *complication*, a condensation of *steps$_1$*, the *setting*, a *problem*, a *resolving incident* and two of the CONTRAEXPECTATION, and the GOAL of the RESOLUTION.

SCENE CONSTITUENT 6:35—8:10 (Episode Cluster of 6:30—8:21)

THEME: *By Jesus performing miracles and teaching about what is or is not acceptable to God, he taught his disciples that the non-Jewish people were also to hear the good news about God's rule.*	
MACROSTRUCTURE	CONTENTS
CONJOINED$_1$	6:35–56 By Jesus performing three miracles, he showed to his disciples how powerful he was: he miraculously fed 5,000, he walked on the surface of the lake, and he healed many sick people.
CONJOINED$_2$	7:1–23 Jesus' first confrontation with the Jewish authorities was over the matter of ritual cleanness and uncleanness. Jesus answered extensively.
CONJOINED$_3$	7:24—8:10 By Jesus performing three miracles that benefited the non-Jewish people, he taught his disciples that the good news is also for those who are considered unclean.

INTENT AND RHETORICAL STRUCTURE

Although this episode cluster consists of three equally prominent episodes, the chiastic structure of [A, B, A'] places focus on the middle unit. Mark intends that the reader understand that Jesus was teaching that his disciples should not consider the 'unclean gentiles' outside of God's rule.

BOUNDARIES AND COHERENCE

The initial and closing boundaries are marked and described in the discussion of the first and last episodes of this unit. The unique topic of this unit is that the gentiles are also acceptable to God.

PROMINENCE AND THEME

The theme statement consists of a synthesis of the three included units, paying special attention to the prominence placed by the chiastic structure of the unit.

EPISODE CLUSTER CONSTITUENT 6:35–56 (Episode Sub-Cluster of 6:35—8:10)

THEME: By Jesus performing three miracles, he showed to his disciples how powerful he was: he miraculously fed 5,000, he walked on the surface of the lake, and he healed many sick people.

MACROSTRUCTURE	CONTENTS
CONJOINED₁	6:35–44 When it became late in the afternoon, the people became hungry, and there was no place to obtain food, so Jesus miraculously multiplied bread and fish for them, and everyone had plenty to eat.
CONJOINED₂	6:45–52 Jesus sent his disciples ahead of him to Bethsaida by boat while he stayed to pray. Later he saw that they were having a difficult time due to a wind blowing against them, so he went to them, walking on the water.
CONJOINED₃	6:53–56 As soon as Jesus and his disciples reached land and got out of the boat, people began to come to Jesus, bringing sick people in order that he might heal them; and he healed all who touched him.

INTENT AND RHETORICAL STRUCTURE

A small problem arises in this cluster of episodes in that the location of the first episodes is in some uninhabited area (near Capernaum?). Apparently, this group of episodes are a transitioning of Jesus and his disciples from their usual Galilean area before they went to the surrounding gentile area.

Mark intends that the reader understand that Jesus had power to miraculously provide food for a multitude of people, to calm the winds and the waves on the lake, and to heal many people who only touched his clothes.

These three episodes are of equal prominence not demonstrating any particular rhetorical structure.

This is the first episode cluster constituent of the unit 6:35—8:10, consisting of three equally prominent episodes about Jesus performing miracles in the area just outside of Galilee. Mark intends that the reader understand how powerful he was to sustain life, to even walk on water, and to heal sick people. He also intends that his disciples realize that Jesus is powerful even beyond his home area of Galilee.

BOUNDARIES AND COHERENCE

The initial and closing boundaries are marked and described in the discussion of the first and last episodes of this unit. The unique topics of this unit are Jesus' power to help people, his walking on water, and healing many sick..

PROMINENCE AND THEME

The theme is taken from a condensation of the three conjoined units, which all point to Jesus power to perform miracles.

EPISODE SUB-CLUSTER CONSTITUENT 6:35–44 (Episode of 6:35–56)

THEME: When it became late in the afternoon, the people became hungry, and there was no place to obtain food, so Jesus miraculously multiplied bread and fish for them, and everyone had plenty to eat.

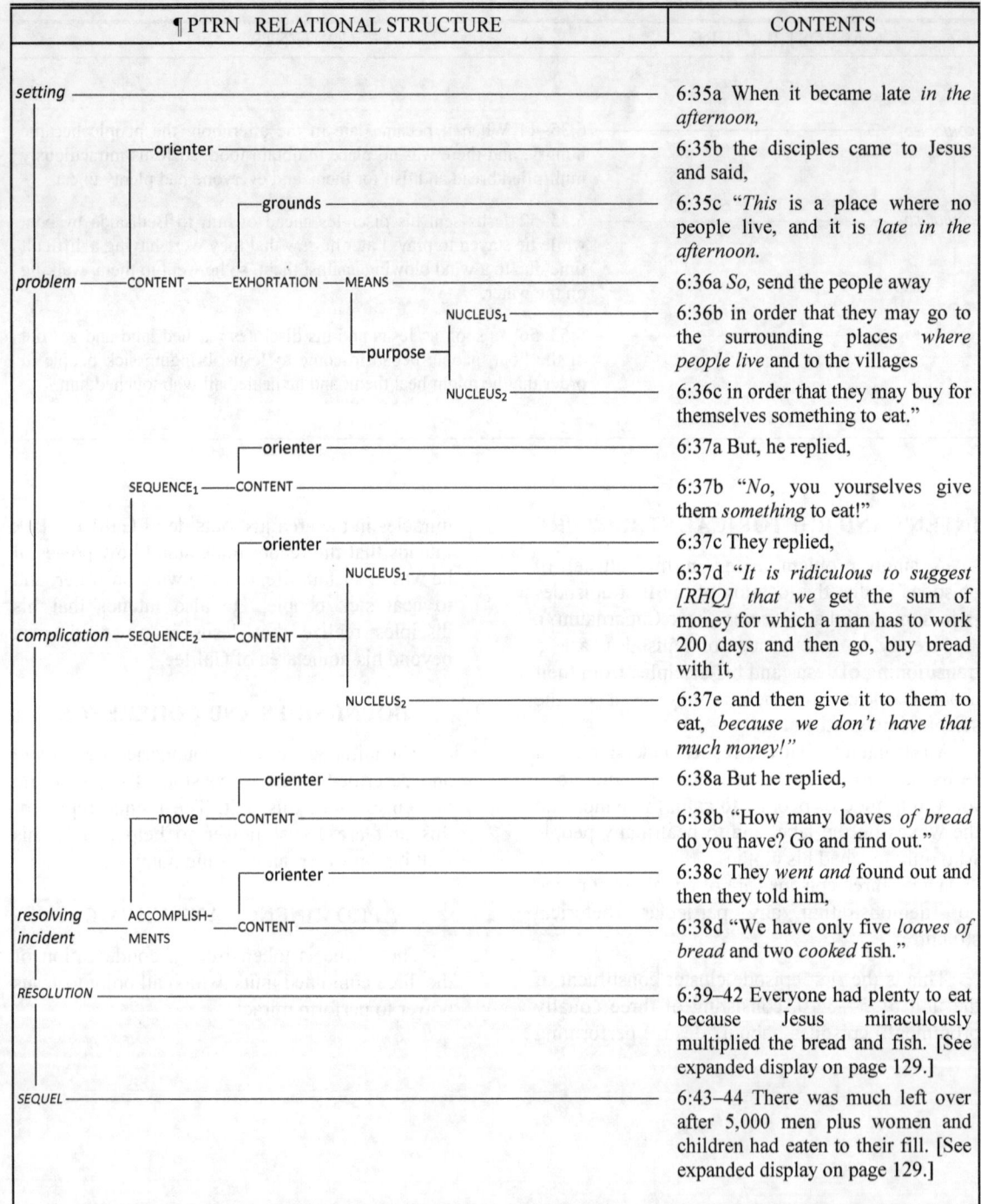

INTENT AND RHETORICAL STRUCTURE

This unit is a solutionality type narrative consisting of a *setting*, a *problem*, a *complication*, a *resolving incident*, a RESOLUTION, and a SEQUEL. Mark intends that the reader understand that Jesus had power to feed five thousand people in an uninhabited area.

NOTES

6:35a late *in the afternoon* The Greek expression 'became a much later hour' means the latter part of the afternoon. NLT has the same wording as the display, and eight commentators agree.

6:36a *So* There is no conjunction in the Greek, but v. 36 is the conclusion to the disciples' comment. JB also includes 'so'.

6:37b *No* This is included to signify that Jesus' reply is a rejection of their proposal.

6:37d *It is ridiculous to suggest* The disciples' answer is in the form of a rhetorical question. Several commentators say it suggests something impossible to accomplish, which was true, but Marcus is nearer the mark by saying they considered the suggestion "is clearly absurd."

for which a man has to work 200 days The text has '200 denarii' which will mean nothing if translated literally. It is not recommended that it be converted to some other currency, as is done by TEV, JBP, NEB, and Williams. NIV is very good with "eight months of a man's wages" (also Hiebert and Lane). NLT is rather idiomatic (and hyperbolic) with "a fortune".

6:37e *because we don't have that much money anyway* This provides the reason why they thought the idea was ridiculous. NLT suggests the same with its rendering "With what?"

6:38b **loaves** *of bread* The Greek has only 'loaves'. Some translations simply say 'bread'. NLT has "food". 'Surprisingly, no translations examined (except NLT and TfT) have 'loaves of bread'. The loaves were much smaller than the loaves we are used to; they were small, flat barley loaves, and one person could easily eat two or more in one meal.

6:38d **two** *cooked* **fish** The fish were not fresh; they were "cooked or pickled" (THM, Marcus), "could have been dried, smoked, salted or pickled" (TRT), "cooked, pickled, or smoked" (Anderson).

EXPANSION OF RESOLUTION & SEQUEL 6:39–44 IN THE MARK 6:35–44 DISPLAY

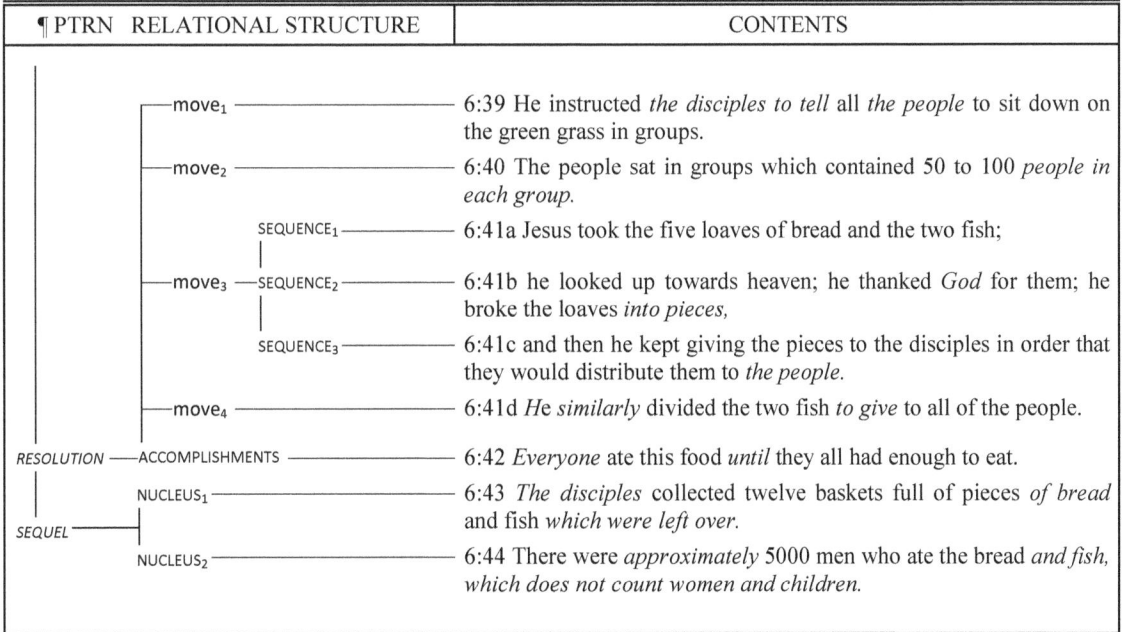

NOTES

6:39 **instructed** *the disciples to tell all the people* **to sit down** Commentators are divided as to whether 'instructed them to recline' means that Jesus commanded the people directly (four commentators and four versions) or whether it means he gave the instructions to the disciples to pass on (nine commentators and eight versions). The display goes with the majority because

Biblical narratives often omit intervening actions.

6:41c kept giving them The imperfect tense on the verb indicates a repetitive action. It seems that the disciples kept returning to Jesus for more bread to distribute.

6:41d The question arises, did Jesus distribute all the bread before starting to distribute the fish? No answer is given in the commentaries.

6:43 pieces *of bread* and fish *which were left over* The GNT has 'twelve baskets of fragments and from the fishes'. Most commentators say that it means that the pieces of fish were in the baskets along with the bread. JBP has "that were left over;" see also TEV, NLT, and CEV.

6:44 *approximately* LB, with "about", is the only version besides TfT that indicates that 5000 was an approximation.

bread *and fish* The GNT has 'the loaves' which seems to suggest they ate no fish. NIV leaves it ambiguous with "had eaten". LB has "that meal". Some manuscripts do not have the words 'the bread' (cf. NIV) but they are implied anyway.

which does not count women and children Thirteen commentators state that there were women and children who also ate. Only France suggests that maybe this was an all-male gathering. But the parallel passage (Matt. 5:21) makes clear there were women and children there also.

BOUNDARIES AND COHERENCE

The start of a new paragraph at v. 45 is indicated by a change in time and a new topic: Jesus walking on the water. Coherence within the 35–44 paragraph is provided by three occurrences of the verb ἐσθίω 'to eat' and several references to bread and fish. Coherence is also seen by the topic of Jesus feeding 5000 men plus women and children.

PROMINENCE AND THEME

The theme is drawn from the *setting*, a modification of the *problem*, and a condensation of the RESOLUTION.

EPISODE SUB-CLUSTER CONSTITUENT 6:45–52 (Episode of 6:35–56)

THEME: Jesus sent his disciples ahead of him to Bethsaida by boat while he stayed to pray. Later he saw that they were having a difficult time due to a wind blowing against them, so he went to them, walking on the water.

¶ PTRN RELATIONAL STRUCTURE	CONTENTS
setting — SEQUENCE₁ — SIMULTANEOUS₁	6:45a At once Jesus ordered his disciples to get into the boat and then go ahead of him to Bethsaida town, which was on the other side of Lake Galilee,
SIMULTANEOUS₂	6:45b while he would stay and dismiss the many people who were there.
SEQUENCE₂	6:46 Later, after the disciples departed and after he had dismissed the people, he went into the hills in order to pray.
problem — NUCLEUS₁ — SIMULTANEOUS₁	6:47a When it was evening, the disciples' boat was in the middle of the lake,
SIMULTANEOUS₂	6:47b and Jesus was by himself on land.
NUCLEUS₂ — RESULT	6:48a He saw that as the disciples rowed they were having a very difficult time,
reason	6:48b because the wind was blowing against them.
RESOLUTION — CONTRAST₁ — MEANS	6:48c He approached them early in the morning, when it was still dark, by walking on the water.
purpose	6:48d He intended to walk by them.
CONTRAST₂ — SEQUENCE₁ — RESULT	6:49a But when they saw that someone was walking on the water,
reason	6:49b they thought that he was a ghost.
reason — RESULT₁	6:49c As a result they screamed
RESULT₂	6:50a because they all saw him and were terrified.
orienter	6:50b But right away Jesus said to them,
move₁ — CONTENT	6:50c "Be calm! Don't be afraid, *because it is I*."
move₂	6:51a He got into the boat where they were
SEQUENCE₂ — ACCOMPLISHMENTS	6:51b and the wind stopped.
SEQUEL — CONCLUSION	6:51c The disciples were completely amazed
grounds₁	6:52a because, *although they had seen Jesus greatly increase* the amount of loaves *of bread and the fish*, they did not understand *how powerful Jesus was*,
grounds₂	6:52b because they were not able to think clearly about it.

INTENT AND RHETORICAL STRUCTURE

This is the second of the three episodes of this cluster of episodes in which Jesus does miracles.

This unit is a solutionality type narrative consisting of a *setting*, a *problem*, a RESOLUTION, and SEQUEL.

NOTES

6:45a other side *of Lake Galilee* There is a textual problem here. The great majority of manuscripts have 'to the other side', and nearly all versions follow suit. There are a few manuscripts which have 'ahead of him' and they are followed by NIV and REB.

The display specifies what other side is being referred to; TEV and JBP have "the other side of the lake". NLT has ""across the lake" which is misleading because the place from which they departed and Bethsaida are both on the north end of the lake.

6:46 *After the disciples departed* This is implied; in the Scriptures, a command is assumed to be carried out unless stated otherwise.

dismissed *the people* The Greek has 'farewelled them' without specifying whom 'them' refers to. TEV supplies 'the disciples' which is incorrect. NLT correctly has "the people".

6:48c early in the morning, when it was still dark The Greek has 'about the fourth watch of the night' which will not be clear in most cultures. The fourth watch was between 3 AM and 6 A.M.; NEB translates accordingly. CEV has "not long before morning", Williams has "a while before daybreak".

6:49a saw that someone The GNT has 'seeing him', but 'him' would imply that they knew who it was; therefore the display has 'someone'.

6:50c Be calm This is the meaning of the Greek word; CEV has "Don't worry", THM suggests "cheer up".

6:51c completely amazed The KJV adds 'and wondered', which was probably added by copyists who remembered a similar wording in Acts 2:7. The omission is given a C 'difficulty in deciding' rating.

6:52a *although they had seen Jesus greatly increase the amount of loaves of bread and the fish* The GNT has 'they did not understand about the loaves' which is a very truncated way of expressing what is in the display. NLT is excellent with "they still didn't understand the significance of the miracle of the multiplied loaves".

did not understand *how powerful Jesus was* The verb 'understand' requires some semantic content of what is understood. The wording in the display is one of the alternatives suggested in TN.

6:52b not able to think clearly about it The GNT has an idiom 'their hearts were hardened'. TEV says "their minds could not grasp it"; CEV has "Their minds were closed"; Hiebert says it means they were spiritually imperceptive.

BOUNDARIES AND COHERENCE

A new paragraph at v. 53 is marked by a change in location and a new topic: Jesus' further healing ministry. Coherence within the 45–52 paragraph is provided by two occurrences of πλοῖον 'boat', two occurrences of ἄνεμος 'wind' and two of θάλασσα 'lake'. Coherence is also seen by the topic of Jesus walking on the water and calming the storm

PROMINENCE AND THEME

The theme consists of the two SIMULTANEOUS propositions of the *setting*, the two propositions of the *problem*, and the NUCLEUS of CONTRAST$_1$ of the *RESOLUTION*.

EPISODE SUB-CLUSTER CONSTITUENT 6:53–56 (Episode of 6:35–56)

THEME: *As soon as Jesus and his disciples reached land and got out of the boat, people began to come to Jesus, bringing sick people in order that he might heal them; and he healed all who touched him.*

¶PTRN RELATIONAL STRUCTURE	CONTENTS
occasion	6:53 After they went across *Lake Galilee in a boat,* they came to the shore at Gennesaret *town* and tied up *the boat there.*
⎡ SEQUENCE₁	6:54 As soon as they got out of the boat, *the people there* recognized Jesus.
OUTCOME₁ ⎯ SEQUENCE₂	6:55a So they ran throughout the whole district *in order to tell others that Jesus was there,*
⎣ SEQUENCE₃ ⎯ SEQUENCE₁	6:55b and the people *placed* on stretchers *those* who were sick
⎣ SEQUENCE₂	6:55c and carried them to any place where they heard *people say* that Jesus was.
⎡ SEQUENCE₁	6:56a In whatever village, town, or other place where he entered, people would bring to the marketplaces those who were sick.
OUTCOME₂ ⎯ SEQUENCE₂ ⎯ MEANS	6:56b The *sick* people would beg Jesus *to let* them touch *him or* even the edge of his clothes
⎣ purpose	6:56c *in order that Jesus might heal them.*
OUTCOME₃	6:56d All those who touched *him or* his garment were healed.

INTENT AND RHETORICAL STRUCTURE

This episode 6:53–56 is the last episode in the cluster. It is another causative type narrative consisting of an *occasion*, and three OUTCOMES.

NOTES

6:53 further across *Lake Galilee in a boat* The display supplies bits of situational information. It also says 'further around' instead of 'across'; to this day, sailboats or rowboats do not cross the lake; they skirt around fairly close to the shore.

tied up *the boat there* THM says the Greek word could mean moored, anchored, or tied up. CEV translates generically "brought the boat to shore".

6:54 *the people there* The Greek 'knowing him' without specifying the agent. NLT has "the people standing there" which is excellent.

6:55a *in order to tell others that Jesus was there* This proposition states more generically their purpose of running through the countryside.

6:56c *in order that Jesus might heal them* See note on 3:10.

BOUNDARIES AND COHERENCE

A new paragraph at 7:1 is marked by a reintroduction of the Pharisees and a new topic: acceptable and unacceptable food. Coherence within the 6:53–56 paragraph is provided by occurrences of κακῶς 'sick' and ἀσθενέω 'having illnesses'.

PROMINENCE AND THEME

The theme consists of a condensation of the *occasion*, the two SEQUENCES of SEQUENCE₃ of OUTCOME₁, and the author COMMENT about the episode.

EPISODE CLUSTER CONSTITUENT 7:1–23 (Episode of 6:35—8:10)

THEME: Jesus' first confrontation with the Jewish authorities was over the matter of ritual cleanness and uncleanness. Jesus answered extensively. Jesus also explained the matter to his disciples.

RELATIONAL STRUCTURE	CONTENTS
CLAIM Sub-Episode	7:1–16 Jesus talked to the Pharisees about their ideas on "clean and unclean". [See expanded display on page 135.]
justification Sub-Episode	7:17–23 Because his disciples asked him about this, Jesus explained to them that all that is really evil and that defiles a person originates within that person. [See expanded display on page 139.]

INTENT AND RHETORICAL STRUCTURE

The foundational communication relations for this unit are TWO EPISODES (7:1–16, and 17–23). From these relations we conclude that this is a narrative unit consisting of a CLAIM and a *justification* with the CLAIM being the most prominent episode.

This unit is cast in a surface narrative form, but it is semantically an expository discourse in which Jesus explains to the Pharisees and teachers of the Jewish law that uncleanness, as far as God is concerned, is not a matter of external touching but of internal thought and attitudes.

These two episodes seem to present that Jesus is preparing his disciples to accept the non-Jewish people as clean before God.

BOUNDARIES AND COHERENCE

This 7:1–23 unit begins with a totally different set of participants than the previous episode. The opening of the next episode is introduced with a δέ 'and', and a new location, time, and participants. This unit presents Jesus' teaching about what it really meant to be 'acceptable' and 'unacceptable' to God.

PROMINENCE AND THEME

The theme statement consists of the CLAIM and the *justification* of the expositional paragraph, which is presented as two episodes.

EXPANSION OF EPISODE₁ 7:1–16 IN THE MARK 7:1–23 DISPLAY

¶ PTRN RELATIONAL STRUCTURE	CONTENTS
─circumstance────────	7:1 *Some* Pharasees and some of the teachers of the Jewish laws who had come from Jerusalem gathered around him.
┌contraction ─SEQUENCE─ 'defiled'────	7:2a They saw that some of Jesus' disciples *were eating food* with defiled hands,
│ └description ───	7:2b that is, they had not *ceremoniously* washed them.
SEQUENCE₁─AMPLIFICATION───── GENERIC	7:3a The Pharisees and all *the other Jews* do not eat,
├specific₁ ─CONGRUENCE─────	7:3b. unless they wash *their* hands in a special way
│ └standard───────	7:3c holding *strictly* to the tradition of the elders.
├specific₂────────────	7:4a *For example: after buying food* in the market place, they will not eat *it* unless they first sprinkle *it*
└specific₃ ─GENERIC─────	7:4b And there are many other *teachings they hold to*
├specific₁────────────	7:4c such as washing cups *in a special way*
└specific₂────────────	7:4d and washing *other* utensils and bronze *bowls*.
evidence── ┌orienter────────	7:5a The Pharisees and the teachers of the Jewish laws questioned him,
│ ┌concession─────	7:5b "Why do your disciples not adhere to the traditions of the elders
SEQUENCE₂──CONTENT──CONTRAEXPECTATION───	7:5c but instead, they eat food in a way that makes them unacceptable *to God*?"
evidence₁────────────────	7:6–8 Jesus said, "You Pharisees prefer to obey your traditions instead of obeying what God said, just like Isaiah prophesied." [See expansion on page 136.]
INFERENCE──INFERENCE──────	7:9–13 Jesus then gave an example that showed how they fulfilled the prophecy. [See expansion on page 137.]
evidence₂────────────────	7:14–16 Jesus told the crowd that what comes out from inside a person's mind is what defiles that person. [See expansion on page 138.]

NOTES

7:2a with defiled hands The text has only the word ἀκάθαρτος 'unclean'. It means 'ritually impure' which in turn means 'caused them to be unacceptable to God'. But that wasn't really true; it was only what the Jewish leaders thought was true.

7:2b *ceremoniously* washed them The text has only 'unwashed', but this refers to a special ceremonial washing. NT has "as required by their ancient traditions".

7:3a *the other Jews* The text has 'all the Jews' but Pharisees were Jews, so 'other' is implied (cf. TEV, CEV). Another good way of expressing the meaning is 'most of the Jews, especially the Pharisees'. The phrase 'all the Jews' can be considered a hyperbole.

7:3b in a special way The Greek has 'with a fist'; commentators are very divided as to what that means, but the rendering of the KJV ("oft") is certainly not correct. The display follows NCV by using a very generic phrase.

7:4a *For example* These words make explicit that what follows is an example of what he has just accused them about. Cf. TfT.

***buying food in* the marketplace** The text has only 'from the marketplace' but 'buying food' must be understood to make clear that the washing mentioned later in the verse refers to the food, not to the buyers. See CEV, NLT.

If the readers do not understand why things needed to be sprinkled, it may be necessary to add something like: 'they mistakenly think that if they didn't do that, it would make them unacceptable to God, because some person or thing unacceptable to God had touched it'.

7:4d It is very difficult to know if the words 'and beds' were in the original text. Nearly all modern versions omit them; TEV is an exception.

7:5b The text is possibly a rhetorical question introduced by 'why'. It functions as a rebuke, claiming that his disciples had sinned by eating with 'unwashed' hands (cf. Hiebert, Lane).

EXPANSION OF EVIDENCE₁ 7:6–8 IN THE MARK 7:1–23 DISPLAY

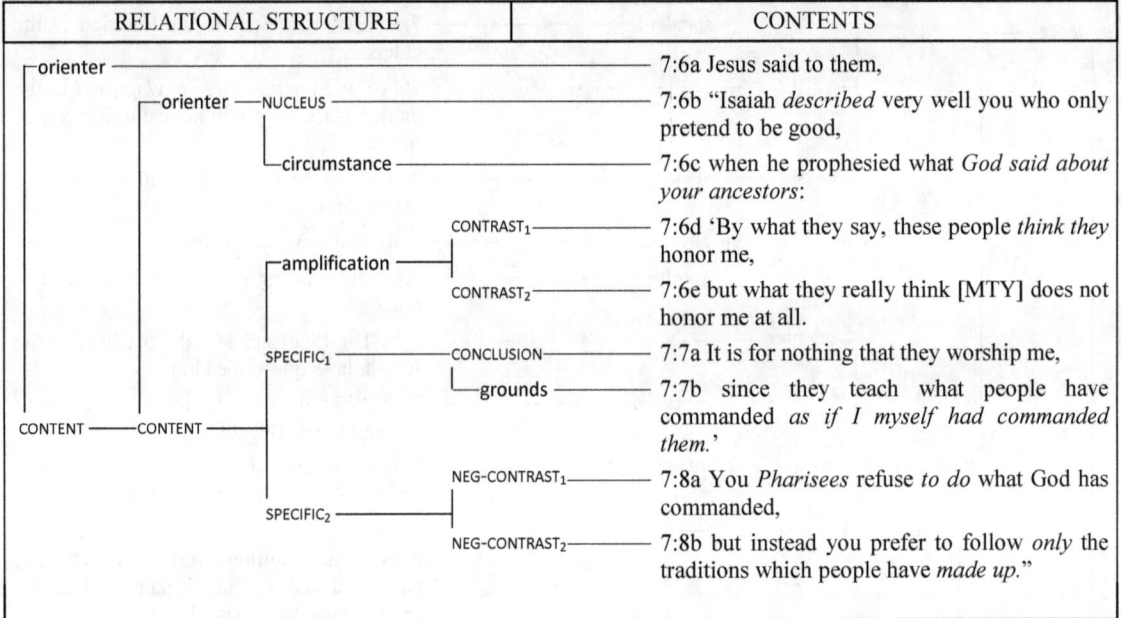

NOTES

7:6b *described* **very well** The text says that Isaiah prophesied well about them, but Isaiah was not predicting about them. The sense is that Isaiah's words (cited from Is. 29:13 in the Septuagint) very accurately described those who were criticizing Jesus' disciples (cf. Hiebert, Lenski, France, Hendrikson, Swete).

7:6d *think they* **honor me** The text is 'with their lips honor me'; 'with their lips' is forefronted, which gives it emphasis. The words representing that phrase are also forefronted in the display. The phrase has two figures of speech. First, 'lips' is a metonymy, standing for speech. TEV has "with their words"; see also CEV. Secondly, they were not really honoring God by what they said; they only thought they were.

7:6e what they really think does not honor me at all The text has 'their hearts are far from me', which is another figure of speech. 'Heart' refers to a person's "mind, emotions, will" (TN). The rendering here, "what they really think [MTY] does not honor me at all", CEV translates as "You never really think about me".

7:7a it is for nothing The Greek word meaning 'in vain' is also forefronted, giving it emphasis, represented in the display by a cleft construction.

7:7b *as if I myself had commanded them* This second half of the sentence is implied. Cf. TEV "as though they were God's rules"; also see NLT. The KJV has a long extra bit about various kinds of washings, repeated from v. 4. It does not occur in the oldest and best manuscripts.

7:8a You *Pharisees* refuse *to do* what God has commanded This replaces the participial form 'leaving the commandment of God' with a finite verb and makes 'commandment' plural, as do NLT, CEV, 20th Century.

7:8b which people have *made up* The Greek has 'of men', but 'men' refers to people in general (cf. CEV "humans") The display also replaces the genitive construction by supplying the verb 'taught'; CEV also has "made up".

EXPANSION OF INFERENCE 7:9–13 IN THE MARK 7:1–23 DISPLAY

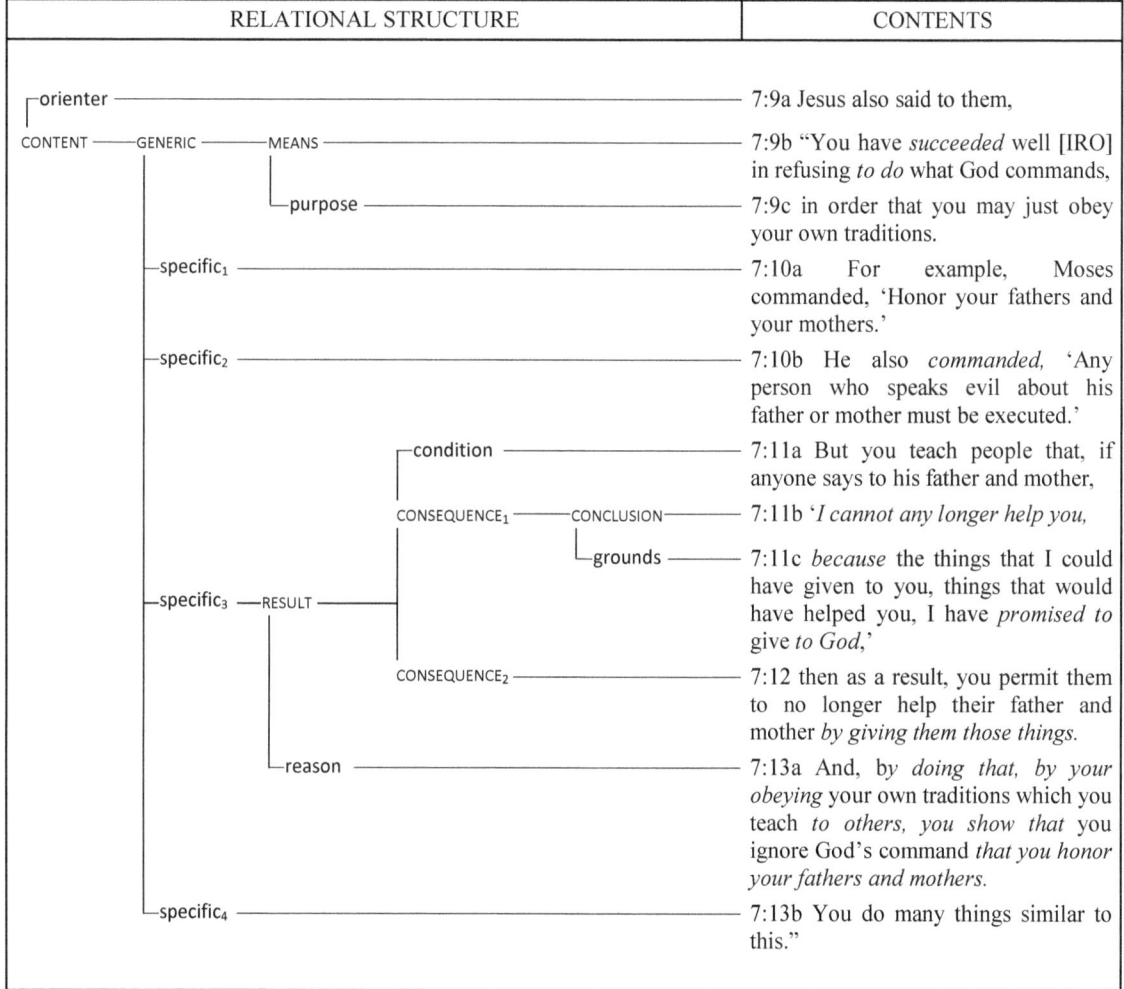

NOTES

7:9b *succeeded* well The Greek text 'you have a fine way' is irony (BAGD); several translations make this clear (e.g., JB "How ingeniously", TEV "you have a clever way of". An alternative would be 'you think that you are smart…'

7:9c obey This represents the word τηρήσητε 'you may keep' but scholars are very uncertain whether the reading should be this or ἵστημι 'establish'. Most versions choose the former.

7:10a For example The Geek conjunction γάρ here does not signal reason, but introduces an example. NLT has "For instance". The commandment referred to is found in Ex. 20:12.

7:11b–c *I cannot any longer help you, because* This is the implied conclusion of stating that something was 'Corban'. Cf. NLT, "Sorry, I can't help you," CEV "without helping their parents".

7:10b *must be executed* A literal translation of the Greek is 'dying he shall die'; the display gives the correct sense. Williams, TEV and NLT have "must be put to death".

7:11c I have *promised to* give *to God* This translated the word 'Corban' which means 'set aside as a gift for God'.

7:12 *by giving them those things* This phrase explains in what way they could no longer help their parents.

7:13a command *that you honor your fathers and mothers* This states, repeating from v. 10, what command he was referring to.

by your obeying your own traditions The Greek has 'by your tradition'; the display supplies the implied verb 'obeying'. CEV has 'follow'.

EXPANSION OF EVIDENCE₂ 7:14–15 IN THE MARK 7:1–23 DISPLAY

RELATIONAL STRUCTURE	CONTENTS
┌─circumstance───────────────────	7:14a Then Jesus summoned the crowd; and, *after they came near*
├─orienter───────────────────────	7:14b he said to them,
│ ┌─orienter────────────────────	7:14c "All of you people, listen to me! *Try to* understand *this:*
│ │ ┌─concession──────────────	7:15a Nothing which enters a person from outside *of himself* can cause *God to regard* this person *to be* unacceptable to him.
CONTENT─CONTENT─CONTRAEXPECTATION─	7:15b On the contrary, it is what comes from inside a person which defiles a person."

NOTES

7:14c *Try to* understand The text has an imperative 'understand' but one cannot easily command understanding. CEV and NLT both have "try to".

7:15a cause *God to regard* this person *to be* unacceptable to him. See note on 7:4b–c.

7:16 Some early Greek manuscripts have 'if anyone has ears to hear, let him hear'. Its omission is given an A 'certain' rating in the GNT. It is included in KJV and supported by Mann, but is omitted in all other modern translations. If someone desires to include it, see note on 4:9.

EXPANSION OF EPISODE₂ 7:17–23 IN THE MARK 7:1–23 DISPLAY

¶ PTRN RELATIONAL STRUCTURE	CONTENTS
occasion — NUCLEUS — circumstance	7:17a After *Jesus and his disciples left the crowd and* entered a house,
	7:17b his disciples questioned him about the parable that *he had just spoken about what defiled a person*.
INFERENCE — CONTENT — NUCLEUS₁ — orienter	7:18a He replied,:
	7:18b "*I am disappointed that* [RHQ] you also do not understand *what it means*.
NUCLEUS₂ — RESULT	7:18c You ought to understand [RHQ] that nothing which *enters a person from* outside of him can cause *God to regard* this person *to be unacceptable to him*
reason	7:19a because no food enters a person's mind; instead it goes into his stomach and afterwards it passes *out of his body*."
COMMENT	7:19b *By saying this*, Jesus declared that God *considers that* all kinds of food are acceptable for us to eat.
OUTCOME — evidence — CONTENT — orienter	7:20a He also said,
CONCLUSION₁	7:20b "It is that which comes from within people which causes them *to be defiled*.
grounds₁	7:21–22 Specifically, what comes from within people *causes them* to think evil, to act immorally, to steal *things*, to murder *people*, to commit adultery, to be greedy, to act maliciously, to deceive *people*, to act indecently, to envy *people*, to speak evil against *God*, to be proud, and to act foolishly.
grounds₂	7:23a The desire to commit evil actions *like* those originates within people,
CONCLUSION₂	7:23b and those are what cause *God to consider* people *to be unacceptable to him*."

NOTES

7:17a *and the disciples* This is implied by what immediately follows. CEV also has for the subject of this sentence "Jesus and his disciples".

7:17b parable that *he had just spoken about what defiled a person* The GNT has only 'this parable'. NLT has "the statement he had made". The display makes it even clearer.

7:18b *I am disappointed that* The text has a rhetorical question (TN, Blight), 'Are you also undiscerning?' functioning as a rebuke expressing disappointment (see 4:13). It is translated by a statement in TEV.

7:18c You ought to understand that This is representing another rhetorical question, 'Do you not understand that...?' CEV has "You surely know that..."

7:19a his mind The Greek has 'his heart' which is figurative; see note on 7:6e.

passes *out of his body* The Greek has ' goes out into the latrine'. The wording in the display is somewhat euphemistic, following TEV and NIV. A good alternative would be to be more literal and render as 'goes into the toilet'.

7:19b By saying this There is no indication in the text that the rest of this verse is a comment by Mark, not by Jesus, but most versions take it to be a comment by Mark.

***God considers* that all kinds of food are acceptable for us to eat** The text has 'purging all foods'. NLT has "every kind of food is acceptable", but this is not clear. CEV has "fit to be eaten", but this too is not clear. It may be necessary in some cases to state it negatively: no food can cause God to regard a person who eats it to be unacceptable to him.

7:21–22 Specifically This verse is introduced by γάρ, which here is not signaling reason, but introducing "a phrase that explains 7:20" (TN). CEV has no conjunction. For the rest of these two verses, the display conveys a long list of abstract nouns with verb phrases for each one.

7:23a actions *like* those The display represents more clearly the Greek word οὗτος 'things'.

BOUNDARIES AND COHERENCE

A new paragraph at v. 24 is indicated by a change in location and a new topic: the expulsion of a demon from a gentile woman's daughter. Coherence in the 1–23 unit is provided by six occurrences of the word ἀκάθαρτος 'unclean', two occurrences of ἔξωθεν 'from outside', and two occurrences of the phrase τὸ ἔξωθεν εἰσπορευόμενον εἰς τὸν ἄνθρωπον 'what comes out of a man'. Coherence is also seen in the whole paragraph dealing with what causes a person to become unacceptable to God, and what does not.

PROMINENCE AND THEME

The theme consists of the 1–23 unit is taken from a portion of the RESULT proposition of the *grounds* of the *evidence, the evidence* of the INFERENCE, and a brief a summary of the INFERENCE.

EPISODE CLUSTER CONSTITUENT 7:24—8:10 (Episode Sub-Cluster of 6:35—8:10)

THEME: By Jesus performing three miracles that benefited the non-Jewish people, he taught his disciples that the good news is also for those who are considered unclean.

MACROSTRUCTURE	CONTENTS
CONJOINED₁	7:24–30 Jesus went to the region around Tyre to be away from people, but they learned of it, and a gentile woman there came to ask Jesus to expel an evil spirit from her daughter, which Jesus did, after testing her faith.
CONJOINED₂	7:31–37 Jesus went back to Lake Galilee, and some people brought a deaf-mute man to Jesus and asked him to heal the man, which he did.
CONJOINED₃	8:1–10 Again a great crowd gathered to hear Jesus, and after two days had no more food to eat, so Jesus miraculously provided food for them.

INTENT AND RHETORICAL STRUCTURE

This episode cluster (7:24—8:10) is the third constituent of the scene (6:35—8:10) in which Jesus teaches his disciples that the 'unclean' gentiles should also benefit from their ministry. In this episode cluster Jesus performs three miracles: expelling an evil spirit from a young girl living in the area of Tyre, healing a deaf and mute man living in the Decapolis area, and feeding four thousand men plus women and children in the same area. This unit consists of three conjoined narrative episodes of equal prominence in sequential order.

BOUNDARIES AND COHERENCE

The boundaries are marked and described in the discussion of the first and last episodes of this unit. This unit presents three miracles that Jesus performed in the gentile area outside of the Galilee area.

PROMINENCE AND THEME

The theme consists of a summary of the three units and includes the purpose statement from the inclusive scene.

EPISODE SUB-CLUSTER CONSTITUENT 7:24–30 (Episode of 7:24—8:10)

THEME: *Jesus went to the region around Tyre to be away from people, but they learned of it, and a gentile woman there came to ask Jesus to expel an evil spirit from her daughter, which Jesus did, after testing her faith.*

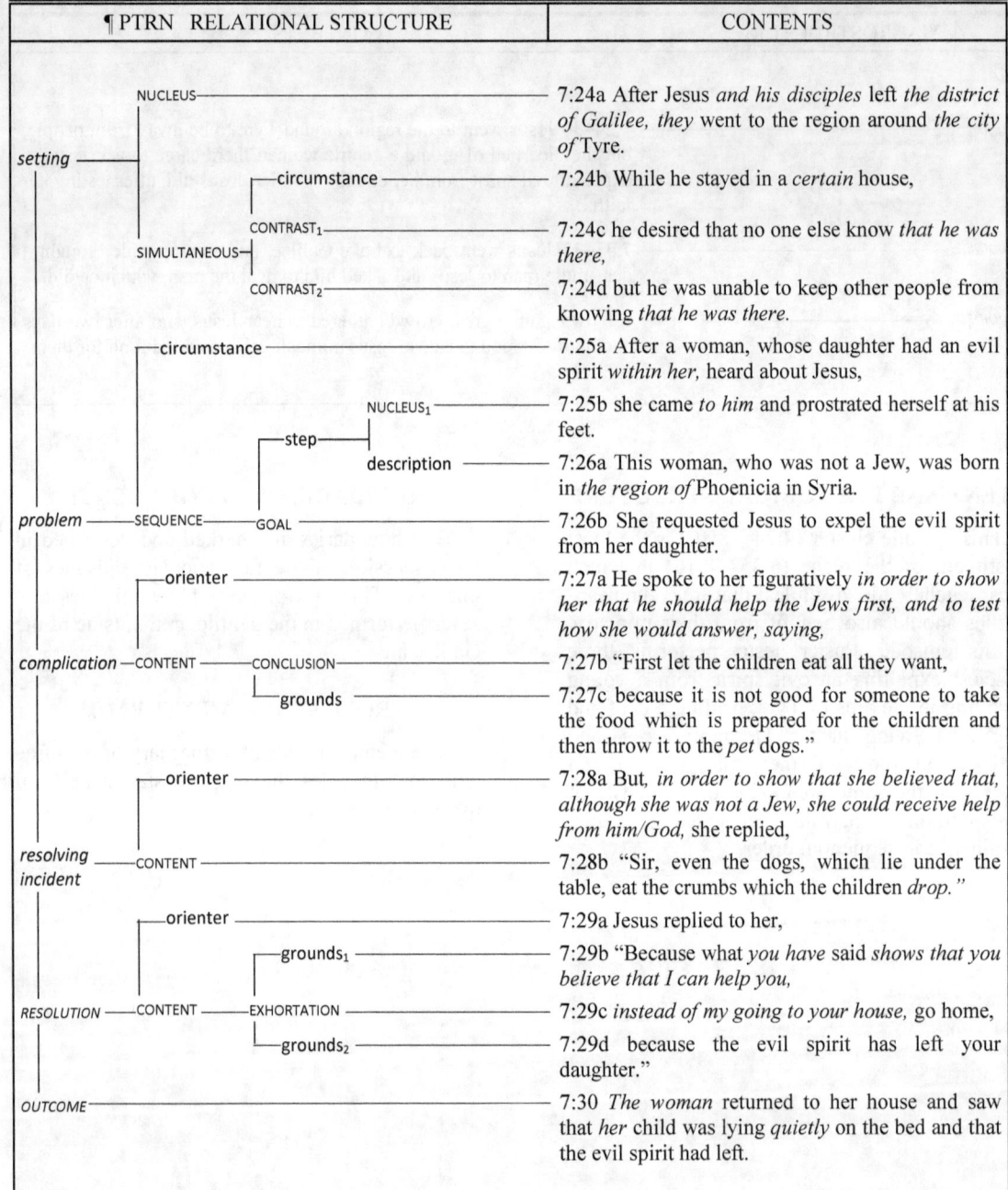

INTENT AND RHETORICAL STRUCTURE

This unit is a narrative. Mark intends that the reader understand that Jesus was teaching his disciples that even those considered to be ritually unclean should benefit from God's rule.

This unit consists of a *setting*, a *problem*, a *complication*, a *resolving incident*, a RESOLUTION, and an OUTCOME.

NOTES

7:24a Jesus *and his disciples* The text mentions only Jesus, but in the parallel passage starting at Matt. 15:21, it is clear that the disciples were with him.

district of...city of These are geographical implicatures. CEV has "city of Tyre". Some manuscripts include the words 'and Sidon', probably due to the wording in v. 31 and in Matt. 15:21. Of the versions, only KJV includes them.

7:24c know *that he was there* The text has only 'not know'. CEV, JB, and TEV have "know he was there," NLT and Williams have "that he was there".

7:25a evil spirit *within her* The text has 'had an unclean spirit' which is not clear. CEV, 20th Century and TEV have "in her", NIV has 'possessed by".

7:26a not a Jew The text has 'Greek', but commentaries say the word was commonly used by Jews to refer to any Gentile (Gould, Lenski, Meyer, Hendriksen, Taylor, and Guelich). NEB and NLT have "Gentile".

born in *the region of* **Phoenicia in** *Syria* The GNT has 'Syrophenician by race'. CEV's rendering, "in the part of Syria known as Phoenicia", is excellent. TN suggests "a part of the province of Syria called Phoenicia" is even better.

7:27a *in order to show her that he should help the Jews first, and to test how she would answer* Jesus' reply to the woman is in the form of a parable (Lenski, France, TN). The display spells out the topic of the figure, in the form of a purpose clause. NLT96 has in its text "First I should feed the children – my own family, the Jews". However, it is wisest to put the explanation of metaphors contained in conversation in the words of the author, not the original speaker. Further-more, at least five commentators say Jesus' purpose was to test the woman's faith. So this is also included in the display. This purpose is given in footnotes in two versions.

7:27c *pet* **dogs** The majority of commentators say that the diminutive ending on the word κυνάριον 'dogs' is significant, referring to little house dogs or pets. JB has "house dogs". Two commentators clearly disagree. But the woman's reply referring to the 'dogs under the table' supports the wording in the display.

7:28a *in order to show that she believed that, although she was not a Jew, she could receive help from him/God,* **she replied** The woman's reply was also in the form of a parable. Therefore the display handles this one just as in 27a.

7:28b There is a textual problem here. Some Greek manuscripts have the word 'Yes' and some do not. The GNT favors the omission, with a B 'almost certain' rating. It seems clear that some copyists inserted it because of its occurrence in the parallel passage, Matt. 15:27.

the children *drop* The GNT has only 'the children's crumbs'. CEV has "children drop from the table".

7:29b **what** *you have* **said** *shows that you believe that I can help you* The text has only 'because of this word'. Williams and Beck have "because you have said this". But what was it in her answer that motivated Jesus to say (29d) that her daughter was healed? The answer is that he had tested her faith in him, and her answer showed that she had passed the test. This is supported by twelve commentators. But no versions (except TfT) point this out.

7:29c *instead of my going to your house* The woman was wanting Jesus to go to her home to heal her daughter. Jesus is saying 'that will not be necessary'.

7:30 **lying** *quietly* The world 'quietly' is implied by the verb and is included in NLT and JBP.

BOUNDARIES AND COHERENCE

The start of a new paragraph at v. 31 is marked by a change in location and a new topic: the healing of a deaf and dumb man. Coherence in the 24–30 paragraph is provided by one occurrence of the phrase πνεῦμα ἀκάθαρτον 'evil spirit' and two of the word δαιμόνιον 'demon', plus one occurrence of θυγάτριον 'little daughter'; and two of θυγάτηρ 'daughter'. It is also seen in the paragraph just dealing with Jesus expelling a demon from a gentile woman's daughter.

PROMINENCE AND THEME

The theme is drawn from the SEQUENCE of the *problem*, the GOAL of the *problem*, and a summary plus a contraction of the *orienter* of the *complication* and a rephrasing of the two propositions of the CONTENT of the RESOLUTION. The *setting* is not considered thematic.

EPISODE SUB-CLUSTER CONSTITUENT 7:31–37 (Episode of 7:24—8:10)

THEME: *Jesus went back to Lake Galilee, and some people brought a deaf-mute man to Jesus and asked him to heal the man, which he did.*

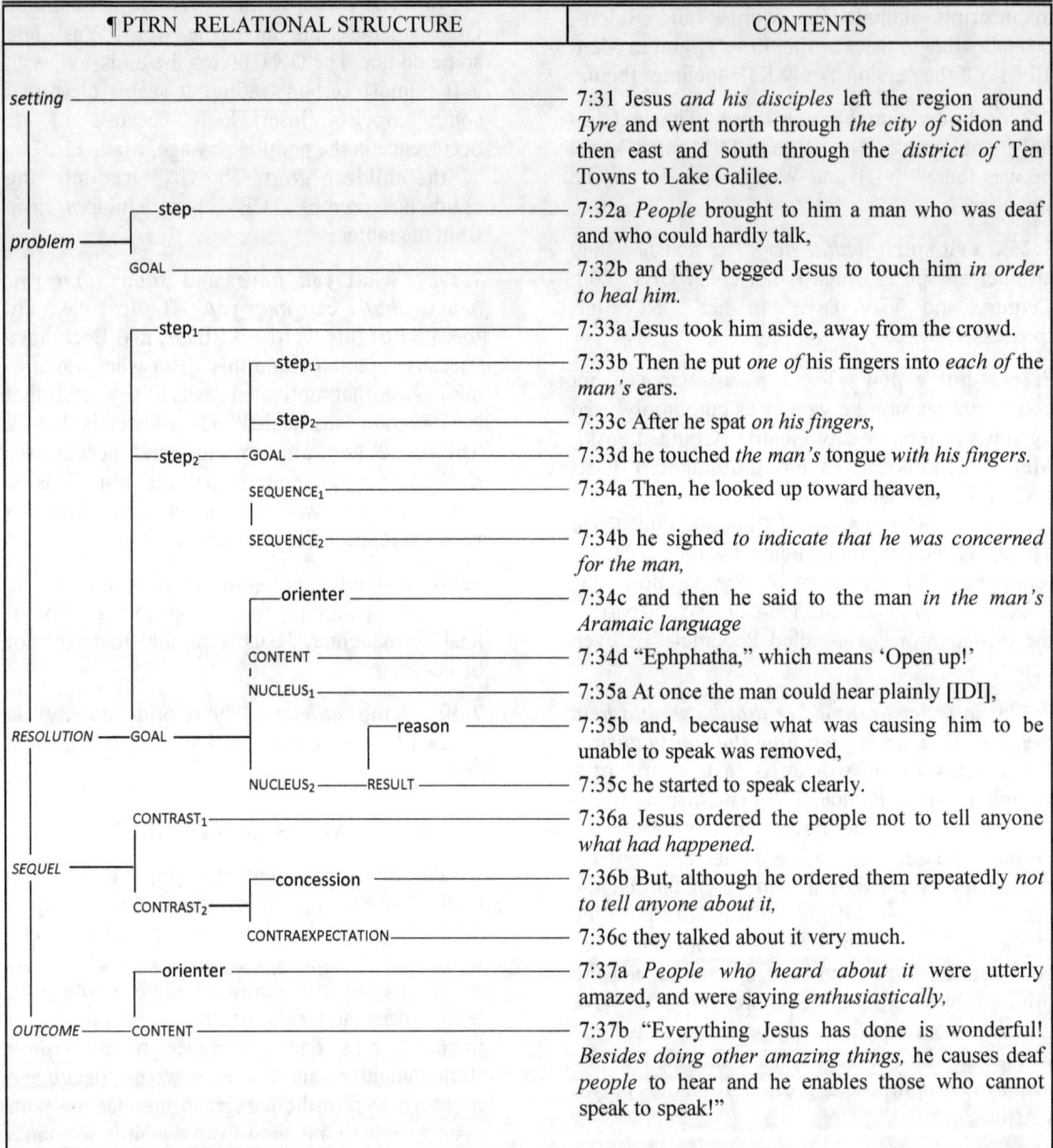

INTENT AND RHETORICAL STRUCTURE

This unit is a narrative in which Mark intends that the reader understand that Jesus does not hesitate to heal a gentile man. This unit starts with a *setting*, a *problem*, a RESOLUTION, a SEQUEL, and an OUTCOME.

NOTES

7:31 Jesus *and his disciples* See note on 7:24.

district of Ten Towns The Greek text has 'Decapolis' which means 'ten cities'. TEV and NEB have "territory of the Ten Towns". NLT has "region of the Ten Towns".

north.... east and south Commentators are somewhat divided on the route they took. From Tyre to Sidon is almost straight north. Then they must have turned east, crossed the Jordan River, then went south through the Ten Towns area and then west to Lake Galilee. This view is supported by Hiebert, France, and Lane.

7:32b *in order to heal him* See note on 3:10.

7:33b *one of* **his fingers into** *each of* **the** *man's* **ears** The Greek text has 'put his fingers into his ears', which is not very clear. The wording in the display follows Bruce.

7:33c–d **after he spat** *on his fingers,* **he touched** *the man's* **tongue** *with his fingers* The Greek text has 'having spat , he touched his tongue' which again is not very clear. Nine commentators support the wording in the display; see also NLT, REB, and NASB.

7:34b **sighed** *to indicate that he was concerned for the man* This indication of the purpose of the sigh is supported by Lenski, Meyer, Hiebert, Gould, Hendriksen, and Taylor.

7:34c *in the man's Aramaic language* See note on 5:41.

7:35a **could hear plainly** The Greek text has 'his ears were opened', which is an idiom (TN, Blight); see NLT, CEV, GW.

7:35b **what was causing him to be unable to speak was removed** The Greek has 'the bond of his tongue was loosened'. This is also considered to be an idiom. TN suggests "His speech defect was removed". NLT shortens the verse nicely by saying, "the man could hear perfectly and speak plainly".

7:37a *People who heard about it* The GNT has only 'they (were astounded)'. The display follows TEV's "All who heard".

7:37b *Besides doing other amazing things* The italicized swords convey the sense of 'even'. See TN: "in addition to other spectacular things/miracles Jesus has done, he…"

BOUNDARIES AND COHERENCE

A new episode beginning at 8:11 is marked by another instance of Jesus interacting with Pharisees. Coherence in the 1–10 paragraph is provided by three occurrence of ἄρτος 'bread'. Coherence is also seen in the paragraph dealing solely with Jesus healing a deaf and dumb man.

PROMINENCE AND THEME

The theme is drawn from a condensation of the *circumstance*, the two NUCLEI of the *problem*, and a very brief summary of the RESOLUTION. The *setting* is not considered thematic.

EPISODE SUB-CLUSTER CONSTITUENT 8:1–10 (Episode of 7:24—8:10)

> THEME: *Again a great crowd gathered to hear Jesus, and after two days had no more food to eat, so Jesus miraculously provided food for them.*

¶PTRN RELATIONAL STRUCTURE	CONTENTS
setting — SEQUENCE₁	8:1a At that time a large crowd *of people* gathered again,
SEQUENCE₂	8:1b and *after they had been there a couple days*, they had no more food to eat.
problem — orienter	8:1c Jesus summoned the disciples and, hinting that they should do something about the problem, said to them,
CONTENT — CONCLUSION	8:2a "I feel very sorry for these people
grounds₁	8:2b because they have been with me for three days and now they have nothing *left* to eat,
grounds₂ — RESULT	8:3a and *because*, if I send them home *while they are still hungry, some of* them will faint *while they are going* along the road.
reason	8:3b Some of them have come from far away."
complication — orienter	8:4a *One of* Jesus' disciples replied,
CONTENT	8:4b "It is impossible [RHQ] *for us*, here in this place where no people live, to find food which we can give *to satisfy this crowd*."
resolving incident — SEQUENCE₁	8:5a Jesus asked his disciples: "How many loaves *of bread* do you have?"
SEQUENCE₂	8:5c They replied, "Seven."
move₁	8:6a Jesus told the crowd, "Sit down on the ground!"
move₂	8:6c *After they sat down, Jesus* took the seven loaves, thanked *God for them,* broke *the loaves,* and then gave them to his disciples for them to distribute them.
move₃	8:6d So they distributed *the bread* to the crowd.
move₄ — orienter	8:7a They also had a few small *cooked* fish. So after Jesus thanked God for them, he told *his disciples,*
CONTENT	8:7b "Distribute these also."
move	8:7c After *they distributed the fish to the crowd,*
RESOLUTION — ACHIEVEMENT — ACCOMPLISHMENT	8:8a *the people* ate *this food* and they had enough to eat.
OUTCOME₁ — NUCLEUS	8:8b The *disciples* collected the left-over pieces; there were enough pieces to *fill* seven *large* baskets full *of those pieces.*
comment	8:9 They estimated that there were about 4000 people *who ate on that day.*
OUTCOME₂	8:10 Then Jesus sent the people *home.* Immediately after that, he got into the boat along with his disciples, and they went *across Lake Galilee* to the district of Dalmanutha.

INTENT AND RHETORICAL STRUCTURE

This unit is a solutionality type narrative consisting of a *setting*, a *problem*, a *complication*, a *resolving incident*, a RESOLUTION, and two OUTCOMES.

NOTES

8:1b *after they had been there a couple days* The Greek text has 'having nothing to eat', but this does not mean they brought along no food; it means that after a couple days (v. 2) "when they had nothing left to eat" (TEV); see also Hiebert, Lenski, Lane, Hendriksen, Swete, THM.

8:1c hinting that they should do something about the problem The question here is, what is the purpose of Jesus' statement here? Is he just saying what he feels about the situation at hand, or is he suggesting that they all needed to take the problem seriously? TN says Jesus is implying "that he wanted to feed the crowd before he sent them home". Several commentators agree. Hendriksen for example says Jesus is saying "It is *our own* probem. *We must do something about it.*"

8:3a *while they are still hungry* Another way of expressing it is, "without feeding them" (NLT, NIV).

8:4b *It is impossible* The disciples' reply is a rhetorical question, "Where in this remote place...?" It is an objection expressing an impossibility (TN).

8:6c *After they sat down* As noted previously (3:3), in Scripture an order is assumed to be carried out (and thus not expressed) unless indicated otherwise.

8:7a *cooked* fish See note on 6:38.

8:7c–8a *After they distributed the fish to the crowd, the people* ate *this food* The display supplies the intervening actions.

8:8b *large* baskets A number of commentators note that this is a different word σπυρίς for 'basket' than occurred in 6:43 κόφινος, denoting a larger basket. This is also specified in Williams, NLT and CEV.

full *of those pieces* It is implied that the pieces were of both bread and fish (TN).

8:9 *They estimated that there were* See the note at 6:44. This was an approximation, not an exact count.

8:10 went *across Lake Galilee* The display supplies the route; but see note on 6:53.

district of Dalmanutha Commentators agree that no one really knows where Dalmanutha was, but they all pretty well agree that it was on the western side of the lake.

BOUNDARIES AND COHERENCE

A start of a new paragraph at v. 11 is indicated by a change in location in v. 13 and a new topic, the evil influence of the Pharisees and of King Herod. Coherence in the 1–10 paragraph is seen from several references to bread, loaves, and fish. It is also seen in the paragraph being one episode of Jesus miraculously feeding 4000 men.

PROMINENCE AND THEME

The theme is taken from SEQUENCES 1 and 2 of the *setting*, and a restatement of the ACHIEVEMENT of the RESOLUTION.

SCENE CONSTITUENT 8:11–21 (Episode Cluster of 6:30—8:21)

THEME: After the Jewish authorities demanded that Jesus perform a sign that would prove that God had sent him, and he refused to do so, Jesus taught his disciples to not imitate the authorities' bad influence of questioning what God was doing.	
MACROSTRUCTURE	CONTENTS
occasion	8:11–12 Some Pharisees demanded that Jesus perform something that would demonstrate that God sent him. Jesus refused to do so.
OUTCOME	8:13–21 Jesus warned the disciples of the evil influence of the Pharisees and King Herod, and rebuked them when they worried about not having enough food with them.

INTENT AND RHETORICAL STRUCTURE

This episode cluster (8:11–21) is the final unit of scene 6:30—8:21 in which Jesus ministered in the area around Galilee preparing his disciples for his climactic question, "And who do you say that I am?"

The structure of this unit consists of an *occasion* and an OUTCOME, demonstrating it is narrative. Mark intends that the reader understand together with the disciples that Jesus' teachings and miracles were enough proof that God had sent him.

BOUNDARIES AND COHERENCE

The opening and closing boundaries coincide with those of the included episodes, and discussed at that point. Here Mark presents the final necessary evidence that demonstrates who Jesus is.

PROMINENCE AND THEME

The theme consists of the *occasion* and the OUTCOME considering its structural prominence.

EPISODE CLUSTER CONSTITUENT 8:11–12 (Episode of 8:11–21)

THEME: *Some Pharisees demanded that Jesus perform something that would demonstrate that God sent him. Jesus refused to do so.*

¶ PTRN RELATIONAL STRUCTURE	CONTENTS
occasion — RESULT	8:11a *Some* Pharisees came to Jesus and started to argue with him
— reason	8:11b because they hoped that, after asking him *to perform* a miracle *which would show that* God *had sent him*, he would *do/say something which would enable them to* discredit him.
— orienter	8:12a After he sighed deeply, he said,
OUTCOME — CONTENT — CONTRAST₁	8:12b "I am disgusted that [RHQ] you people, who have observed the things I have done, keep asking me to perform miracles.
— CONTRAST₂	8:12c I tell you that I will certainly not perform a miracle *just* for you people."

INTENT AND RHETORICAL STRUCTURE

The episode consists of an *occasion* and an OUTCOME. The natural prominence is on the OUTCOME.

The author intends in this episode that the reader understand that Jesus had done enough miracles to show that God had sent him.

NOTES

8:11b asking him *to perform* a miracle *which would show that* God *had sent him* The Greek text has 'asking him for a sign from heaven'. 'Sign' means 'miracle' (thus TEV); 'heaven' is a metonymy meaning 'God' (TN, TEV, NCV, and fourteen commentators.)

***he would do/say something which would enable them* to discredit him** The GNT has 'tempting him' but here it means "an attempt to cause someone to make a mistake, often by tricking him" (TN). TEV has "to trap him".

8:12a sighed deeply Hiebert says this sighing "shows his distress over the moral perversity of those Jewish leaders."

8:12b I am disgusted that The Greek has a rhetorical question, "Why…?" Lane supports the rendering in the display saying Jesus' comment "expressed his exasperation".

you people, who have observed the things I have done The GNT has 'this generation'. Commentators agree that the expression refers to the people among whom Jesus lived, but here Jesus could be expressing his disgust only with those who had already seen or heard about him performing many miracles – and still wanted another one.

8:12c *just* for you people Jesus did continue to perform miracles (e.g., 9:14–29, 10:46–52) but not just for them. An alternative to that in the display would be to follow Hendriksen, "no sign such as you are demanding."

BOUNDARIES AND COHERENCE

A new paragraph at the beginning of v. 13 is marked by a change in location and new topic, miracles. Coherence in the 11–12 unit is provided by three occurrences of the word σημεῖον 'miracle'. It is also provided by it dealing just with Jesus rebuking the Pharisees for wanting another miracle.

PROMINENCE AND THEME

The theme is taken from parts of the RESULT and *reason* propositions of the *occasion*, plus a condensation of CONTRAST₂ of the OUTCOME.

EPISODE CLUSTER CONSTITUENT 8:13–21 (Episode of 8:11–21)

Theme: *Jesus warned the disciples of the evil influence of the Pharisees and King Herod, and rebuked them when they worried about not having enough food with them.*

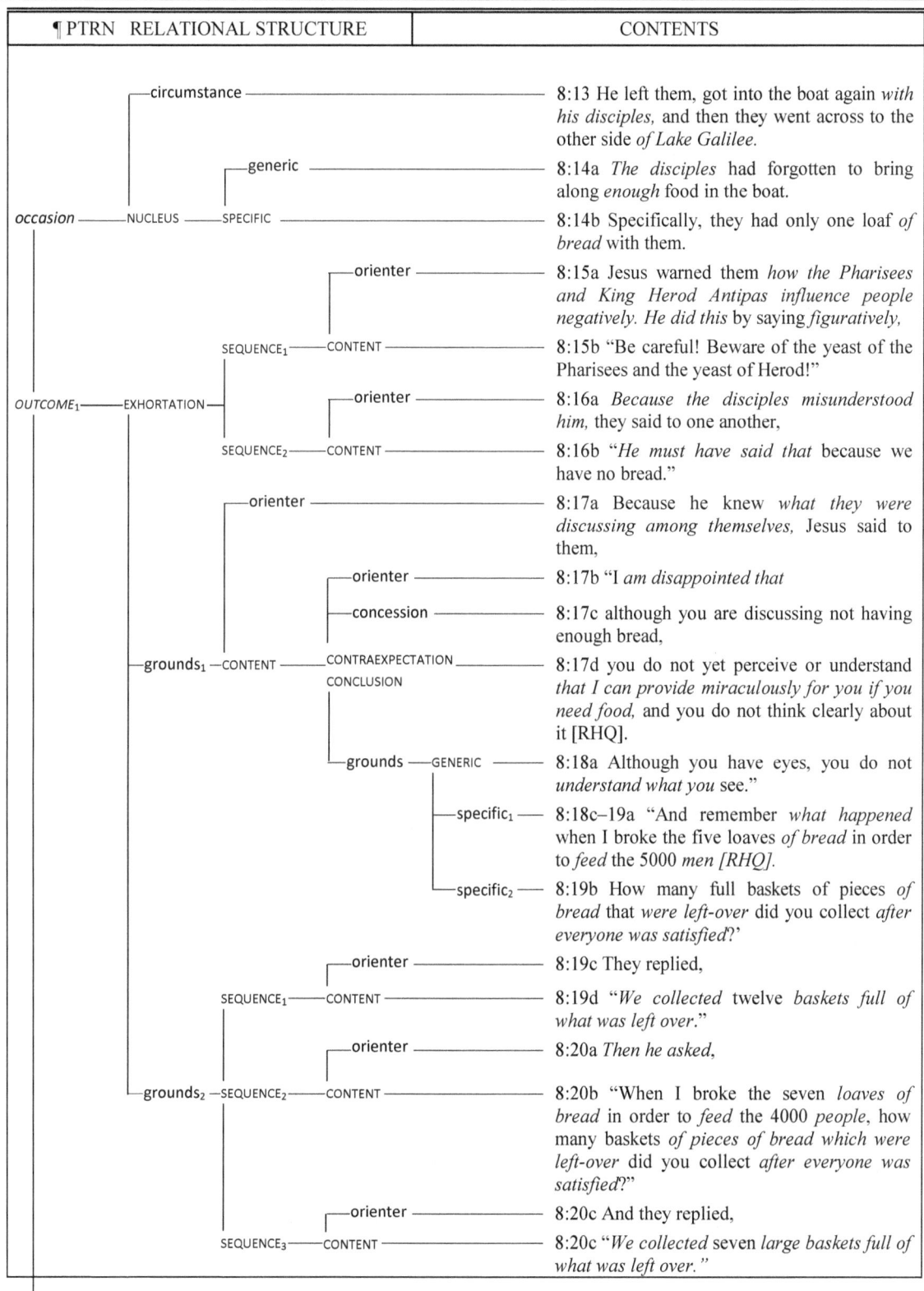

```
              ┌─orienter ─────────────────────── 8:21a Then he said to them,
              │
OUTCOME₂──CONTENT──┬─CONCLUSION ─────────────── 8:21b "I am disappointed that [RHQ]
                   │
                   └─grounds ──────────────────── 8:21c you do not understand yet that you
                                                       should not worry that you do not have enough
                                                       food."
```

INTENT AND RHETORICAL STRUCTURE

In this episode, Jesus taught his disciples to not adopt the evil practices of the Jewish authorities, nor be concerned about not having enough food with them.

Mark intends that the reader understand that Jesus taught his disciples by telling this short story. This episode consists of an *occasion*, and TWO OUTCOMES.

NOTES

8:13 *with his disciples* See note on 5:21.

other side of Lake Galilee See other note on 5:21.

8:14a *enough food* The Greek text says 'they had forgotten to take bread, except…'. In many languages there is no way to say 'no X, except Y'; one has to say 'only Y, no other X'. The disciples had brought food; it just wasn't enough. TEV says "any extra bread".

8:15a **warned them** *how the Pharisees and King Herod Antipas influence people negatively.* **He did this** *by saying figuratively* Jesus' remark was another parable. As was done previously (7:27), to make the meaning clear, the topic of the metaphor is given, but in the editor's words, not in Jesus' words. For Antipas, see note on 6:14.

8:16a *Because the disciples misunderstood him* This clause is a situational implicature, explaining why the disciples replied as they did (16b).

8:16b *He must have said* **that** The Greek text has an incomplete sentence beginning with 'because'. The display follows versions such as TEV, NLT, and CEV in making a complete sentence.

8:17a **knew** *what they were discussing among themselves* The Greek has only 'knowing'. Versions which supply a similar content of 'knowing' to that include the NEB, NLT, CEV, TEV, and NIV.

8:17b *I am disappointed that* This is another rhetorical question indicating rebuke (TN) introduced by 'Why?' See 2:16, 4:40, 8:12.

8:17d **understand** There are two words in the Greek; some commentators say they have almost the same meaning (TN), but some say they involve two steps—perception and judgment (L&N).

that I can provide miraculously for you if you need food The Greek has only 'understand'. But cognitive events need a content. The wording in the display is a situational implicature.

8:18a **not** *understand what you* **see** The Greek has only 'do you not see?' The word 'see' obviously has a non-literal meaning. See a similar rendering for a similar wording in 4:12.

8:18c **remember** The words 'do you not remember' are considered to be a rhetorical question.

8:19b *pieces of bread* **that** *were left-over* The GNT has only 'baskets full of fragments'. The display makes specific what fragments were meant.

after everyone was satisfied This is a crucial part of what Jesus was saying; the point is not now many baskets did they collect, but there were that many leftovers after everyone had eaten all they wanted. Similarly in v. 20b.

8:21b *I am disappointed that* This is another rhetorical question (here a yes/no question) that functions as a rebuke showing disappointment.

8:21c *that you should not worry that you do not have enough food* The great majority of commentators say that this question ('Do you not yet understand?') expresses the same rebuke that was given in v. 17. They should have remembered how abundantly he had provided for them previously, and that therefore their concern about food was completely unjustified.

BOUNDARIES AND COHERENCE

A new paragraph that begins at v. 22 is marked by a change in location and a new topic, the healing of a blind man. Coherence in the 13–21 paragraph is provided by several references to bread and loaves and two occurrences of σπυρίς 'basketfuls'. It is also seen in that it just deals with Jesus rebuking the disciples for worrying about not having enough bread.

PROMINENCE AND THEME

The theme is drawn from a rephrasing of SEQUENCE$_2$ of OUTCOME$_1$ and a summary restatement of the propositions of OUTCOME$_2$.

ACT CONSTITUENT 8:22–30 (Scene of 3:7—8:30)

THEME: *The episode of Jesus healing a blind man in stages is an analogy of how Jesus' disciples understood in stages that he was as the promised Messiah.*	
RELATIONAL STRUCTURE	CONTENTS
occasion	8:22–26 Jesus healed a blind man – in stages.
OUTCOME	8:27–30 Jesus asked his disciples what people were saying about him and, then, what the disciples thought about him

INTENT AND RHETORICAL STRUCTURE

This scene (8:22–30) is the final one within ACT II of the first part of the book, where Jesus leads his disciples to answer his key question of "who do you say that I am?" Here, Mark intends that the reader understand as the disciples did that Jesus is God's promised Messiah. In fact, even the disciples slowly understood who Jesus was.

The unit consists of an *occasion* and *OTUCOME*. The *occasion* is the only episode in all the Gospels in which Jesus heals a blind man by stages. Blindness and sight are closely associated with understanding, so that this episode is an analogy of how Jesus' disciples understood in stages who Jesus was. This being the climax of this part of the book, we can expect unusual and unique twists in the story development, as is evident here.

BOUNDARIES AND COHERENCE

The opening and closing boundaries coincide with those of the included episodes, and discussed at that point. This unit partially unravels the suspense of the book as to Jesus' identity.

PROMINENCE AND THEME

The theme is drawn from the units preserving the natural structural prominence.

SCENE CONSTITUENT 8:22–26 (Episode of 8:22–30)

THEME: *Jesus healed a blind man – in stages.*

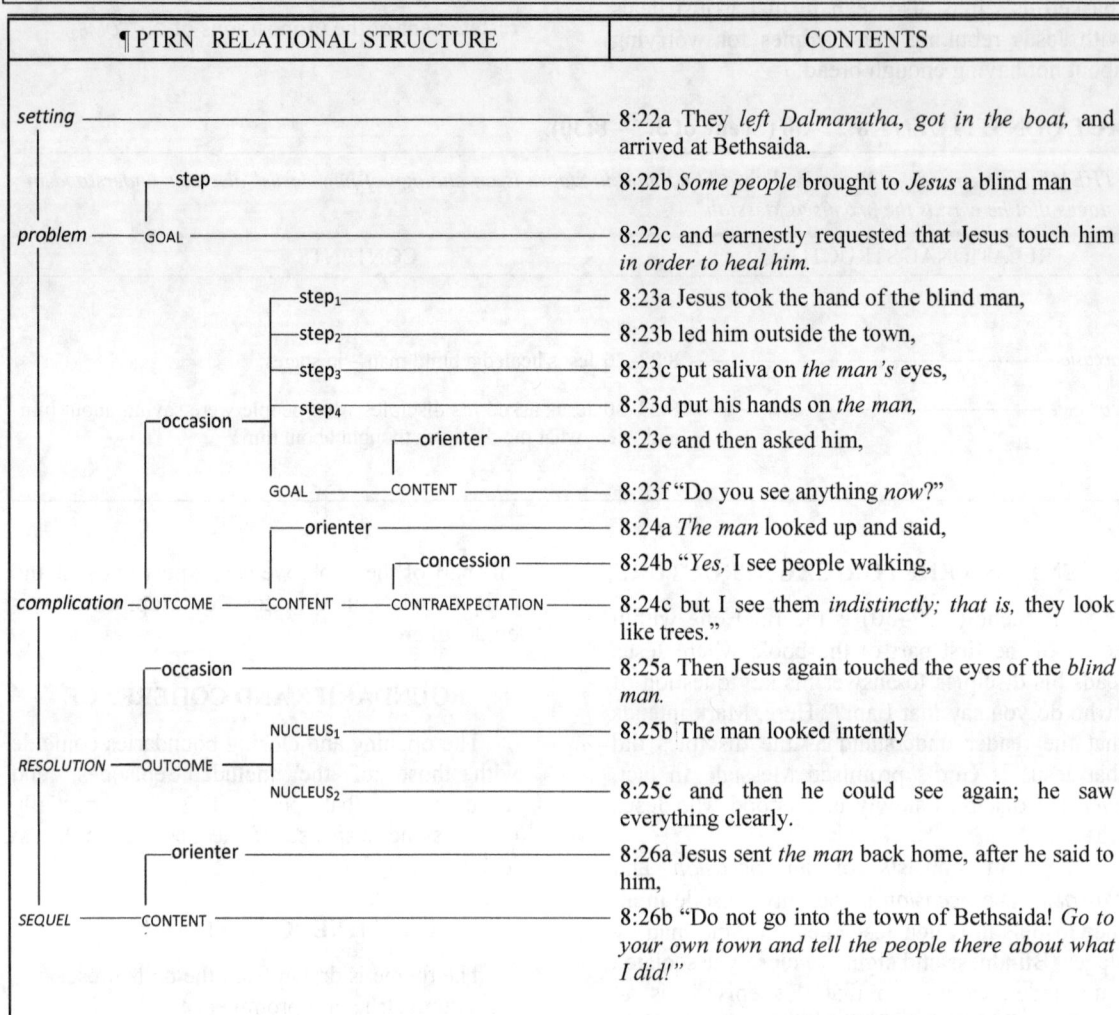

INTENT AND RHETORICAL STRUCTURE

Mark here intends that the hearer understand that this episode is about Jesus healing a blind man in stages.

This unit is a complex solutionality type narrative consisting of a *setting*, a *problem*, a RESOLUTION, a SECOND RESOLUTION, and a SEQUEL.

NOTES

8:22a left Dalmanutha, *got in the boat, and arrived* The display makes clear their movements leading up to their arrival back at Bethsaida.

8:22c *in order to heal him* See note on 3:10.

8:23f Do you see anything *now*? The word 'now' is a situational implicature; it is conveyed in NLT.

8:24b–c people walking, but I see them *indistinctly; that is,* they look like trees The text is confusing; it says 'I see people, but they look like trees walking'. Most trees don't walk; the display clarifies the meaning. Cf. JB.

8:26b *Go to your own town and tell the people there about what I did* Hiebert and THM suggest that Jesus did not want the news of this healing to cause crowds of people to come to him from Bethsaida. It is clear that the man was from another place.

BOUNDARIES AND COHERENCE

The start of a new paragraph at v. 27 is marked by a change in location and a new topic: Jesus' true identity. Coherence in the 22–26 paragraph is seen in one occurrence of τυφλός 'blind man', and two of ὄμμα 'eyes'. Coherence is also seen in it being one episode about Jesus healing a blind man in stages.

PROMINENCE AND THEME

The theme of this paragraph is basically taken from the *occasion* and OUTCOME of RESOLUTION$_2$.

SCENE CONSTITUENT 8:27–30 (Episode of 8:22–30)

THEME: *Jesus asked his disciples what people were saying about him and, then, what the disciples thought about him, and Peter replied that Jesus was the Messiah.*

¶ PTRN RELATIONAL STRUCTURE	CONTENTS
setting	8:27a Jesus and the disciples left Bethsaida and went *north* to the villages *near* Caesarea Philippi *city*.
┌─orienter	8:27b On the way, he asked his disciples,
problem$_1$──CONTENT	8:27c "Who do people say that I am?"
┌─orienter	8:28a They replied,
│ NUCLEUS$_1$	8:28b "Some people say that *you are* John the Baptizer *who has come back to life.*
RESOLUTION$_1$──CONTENT──NUCLEUS$_2$	8:28c And others *say that you are* Elijah, *the prophet whom God promised to send again before the Messiah.*
│ NUCLEUS$_3$	8:28d And others say that you are one of the *other* prophets *who lived long ago."*
┌─orienter	8:29a He asked them,
problem$_2$──CONTENT	8:29b "Who do you yourselves say that I am?"
┌─orienter	8:29c Peter replied,
RESOLUTION$_2$──CONTENT	8:29d "You are the Messiah."
OUTCOME	8:30 Then Jesus ordered that they should not say *that* about him to anyone *yet*.

INTENT AND RHETORICAL STRUCTURE

This unit is a complex solutionality type narrative consisting of a *setting*, a *problem*$_1$, a RESOLUTION to that problem, a further *problem*$_2$, a RESOLUTION to the second *problem*, and an OUTCOME.

NOTES

8:27a went *north* The word 'north' is included for those languages requiring such indicators of direction. See Swete, Strauss.

villages *near* Caesarea Philippi Hiebert and Hendriksen say the phrase 'villages of Caesarea Philippi' refers to the villages or towns around the city of Caesarea Philippi. Some commentators say the phrase also refers to the region of the same name, but that, if true, is irrelevant for translators.

8:28b *Some people say* that The GNT text has only 'John the Baptist'. The display makes it a full sentence, as do CEV, NLT, TEV, and NEB.

who has come back to life The death of John has been described in chapter 6.

8:28c *the prophet whom God promised to send before the Messiah* This is information that would come to mind to every Jew on the mention of Elijah (Mal. 4:5). See suggested footnote in TN.

8:28d the *other* prophets 'Other' is needed to be understood to make clear they thought Jesus was also a prophet. It is included in NLT.

who lived long ago This is included to make clear what prophets were being referred to.

8:29d the Messiah The word 'Christ' here is not a name; it is a title that means 'Messiah'. TEV, NEB, CEV, NLT, and Beck translate it correctly. For those not familiar with the word 'Messiah', it may be necessary to translate something like "The King and Savior whom God promised to send" (TN).

8:30 yet A literal translation would easily imply that Jesus did not think he was the Messiah. Jesus knew that such a proclamation at that time would do more harm than good.

BOUNDARIES AND COHERENCE

The start of a new paragraph at v. 31 is marked by a new topic: the first mention of Jesus' future suffering and death. Coherence in the 27–30 episode is shown by references to several prophets, and by it being one exchange between Jesus and his disciples regarding Jesus' identity.

PROMINENCE AND THEME

The theme is taken from the *orienters* and CONTENTS of PROBLEMS 1 and 2, and the *orienter* and CONTENT of RESOLUTION$_2$.

BOOK CONSTITUENT 8:31—16:8 (Part II of 1:1—16:8)

THEME: Jesus taught his disciples that he would go to Jerusalem to suffer and die, but his disciples thought all along that he would go to Jerusalem to reign as the Messiah king, liberating them from Roman rule.

MACROSTRUCTURE	CONTENTS
grounding: introduction	8:31—9:39 Jesus instructs his disciples about his death and resurrection, and their need to suffer for him in order to see his glorious rule.
intensify: ACT I	9:30—10:45 On their way to Jerusalem, Jesus taught his disciples that he must die and become alive again; but even so, they thought he was going to be the ruling king in Jerusalem.
knotting up: ACT II	11:1—13:37 When Jesus entered Jerusalem as Israel's king, he had a final conflict with the Jewish authorities. Then, he foretold what would happen to Jerusalem before he returned later.
CLIMAX: ACT III	14:1—16:8 The Jewish authorities and the Roman authorities executed Jesus. He suffered, died, and came back to life again, just as he said he would.

INTENT AND RHETORICAL STRUCTURE

We are now at the beginning of the second part of Mark. Jesus leads his disciples to understand that he is the suffering savior of Israel and all humans, and not the political deliverer from Roman rule. This unit consists of an *introduction*, and THREE ACTS, of which the last is the CLIMAX of the entire book. There is a definite progression of intensifying prominence leading up to the final climax.

BOUNDARIES AND COHERENCE

The opening and closing boundaries coincide with those of the included episodes, and are discussed at those points. This unit consistently tells that Jesus will suffer, die, and rise up again, and that his followers must be faithful to him even if it means dying for him.

PROMINENCE AND THEME

The theme is taken from a condensation of the four included units, maintaining the structural prominence displayed.

Not the Kingly Messia

Mark 1:14—8:30

---

[1] Images on these pages by Clarice Turney, used by permission. The first picture represents the disciples like the blind man who could not see clearly who Jesus was, thinking him to be the kingly Messiah (very blurred understanding). BUT, the second picture, both the disciples and the blind man could see clearly that Jesus was the suffering Messiah. The book of MARK is clearly split at Mark 8:31, depicting the two images of Jesus.

But, the suffering Messiah
Mark 8:31—16:8

PART CONSTITUENT 8:31—9:29 (Act I of Part II 8:31—16:8)

THEME: Jesus instructs his disciples about his death and resurrection, and their need to suffer for him in order to see his glorious rule.

MACROSTRUCTURE	CONTENTS
CONJOINED$_1$	8:31–33 Jesus rebuked Peter for objecting when Jesus spoke plainly to his disciples about his coming death and resurrection.
CONJOINED$_2$	8:34—9:1 Jesus explained to the crowd and his disciples what is required of someone who wants to be Jesus' disciple.
CONJOINED$_3$	9:2–29 Jesus took three disciples to a high mountain to show them his glory, and later told them that he must be evilly treated. He also showed them that evil spirits can only be expelled through much prayer.

INTENT AND RHETORICAL STRUCTURE

This introductory unit (8:31—9:29) is the initiating unit of the second half of Mark (8:31—16:8). Mark tries to make clear that Jesus must die and come back to life. Mark also impresses his readers that Jesus' followers must also suffer for Jesus' sake. The unit consists of three conjoined episodes of equal prominence.

BOUNDARIES AND COHERENCE

The opening and closing boundaries coincide with those of the included episodes, and are discussed at those points. As just mentioned, this unit presents that Jesus must suffer, die, and rise again, and that his disciples must be willing to suffer for him.

PROMINENCE AND THEME

The theme consists of a summary of the three conjoined units which make up this unit.

ACT CONSTITUENT 8:31–33 (Episode of Act I 8:31—9:39)

THEME: Jesus rebuked Peter for objecting when Jesus spoke plainly to his disciples about his coming death and resurrection.

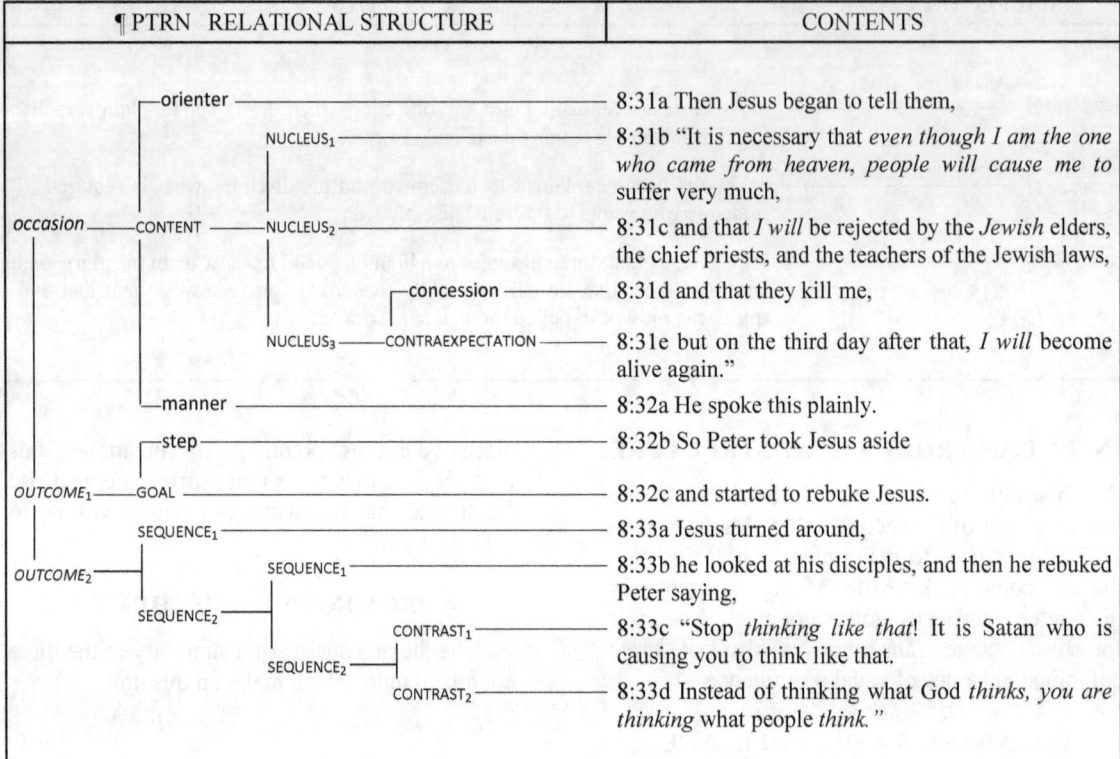

INTENT AND RHETORICAL STRUCTURE

Mark here intends that the hearer understand that Jesus rebuked Peter for rebuking Jesus for talking about dying.

This narrative is of the causality type consisting of an *occasion*, a first OUTCOME, and a second OUTCOME

NOTES

8:31b ***I, the one who came from heaven*** See note on 2:10. In decades of translation consultant work, this writer has found that a literal translation of 'Son of Man' always conveyed wrong meaning.

8:31c ***Jewish*** **elders** The word 'Jewish' is supplied for clarification. CEV has "the nation's leaders".

teachers of the Jewish laws For this rendering of 'scribes', see note on 1:22.

8:32b So The Greek has the conjunction καί 'and' here, but what follows is the outcome to Jesus' statement in the form of a strong objection by Peter; thus 'so' (cf. TEV).

8:32c started to rebuke Jesus If it is not clear why Peter rebuked Jesus, something like that expressed by Lane may be necessary: "A rejected Messiah was unthinkable to Jewish convictions and hopes".

8:33c Stop *thinking like that*! The text is literally 'go behind me', which is considered an idiom meaning 'leave and get out of my sight' (see NIV).

It is Satan *who is causing you to think like that* The text is literally 'Satan'. But Jesus is talking to Peter, not Satan. The ESV footnote is very good here: "It was only Peter's thoughts, not Peter personally, that Jesus rejected as being satanic."

8:33d God *thinks*... people *think* The GNT has only 'things of God...things of men'. NEB's wording is almost the same as that in the display: "you think as men think, not as God thinks".

BOUNDARIES AND COHERENCE

A new paragraph at v. 34 is marked by a switch from the disciples to a crowd, and a new topic: the saving of one's soul. Coherence in the 31–33 paragraph is provided by mention of various events that will occur at the end of Jesus' life, and two mentions of Peter. It is also provided by the paragraph being the first interchange between Jesus and the disciples about his coming death and resurrection.

PROMINENCE AND THEME

The theme is taken from the *orienter* and both the *concession* and CONTRAEXPECTATION of NUCLEUS$_3$, plus the *means* proposition.

ACT CONSTITUENT 8:34—9:1 (Episode of Act I 8:31—9:39)

THEME: Jesus explained to the crowd and his disciples what is required of someone who wants to be Jesus' disciple.

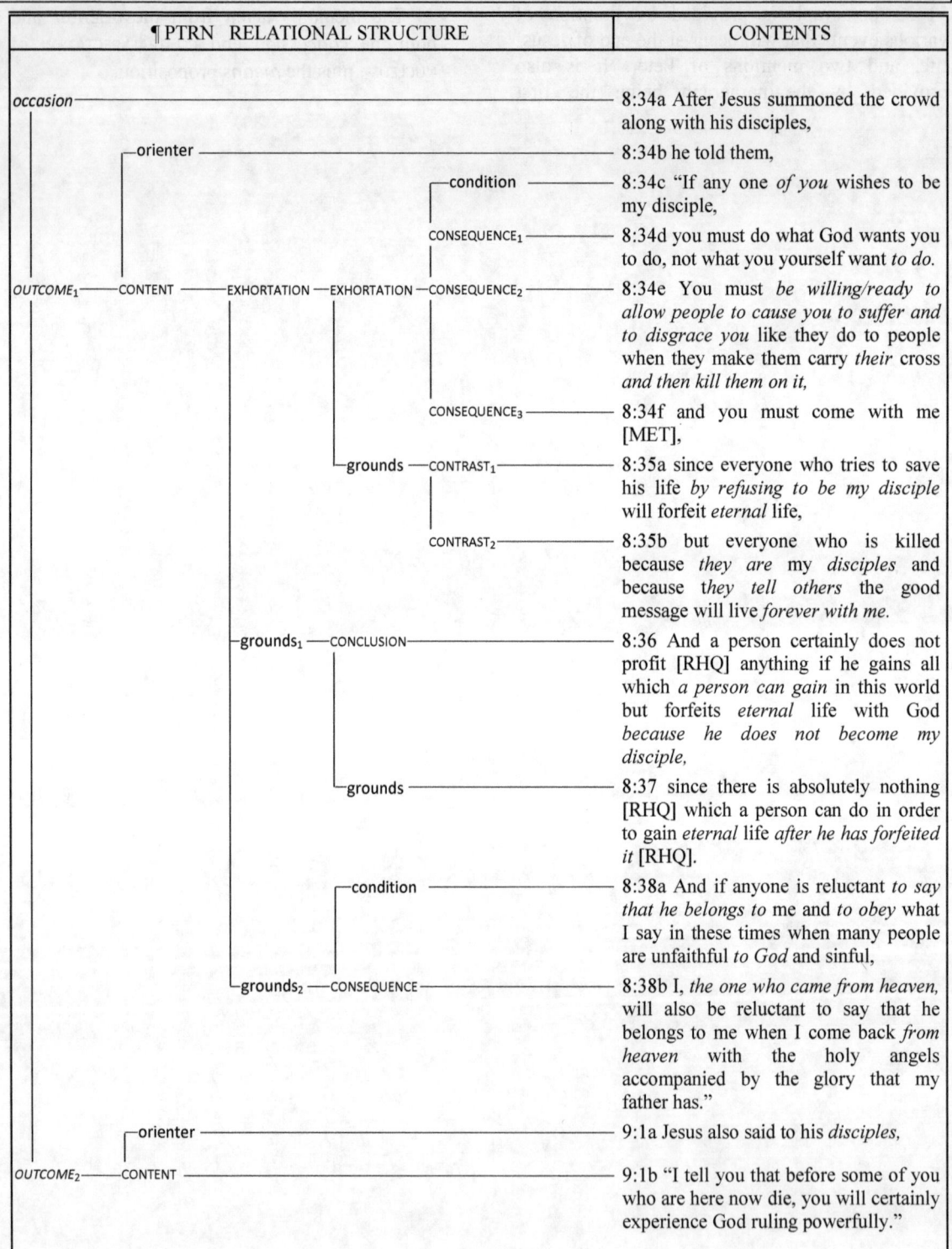

INTENT AND RHETORICAL STRUCTURE

Mark intends that the reader understand that from here on, he tells about totally different matters about Jesus.

This causality narrative consists of an *occasion*, a first OUTCOME, and a second OUTCOME.

As mentioned before, this is the first mention of the 'total commitment to him for discipleship' motif in this second part of the book. This creates rhetorical prominence to both the episode and this motif.

NOTES

8:34c to be my disciple The text literally has 'come after me', which is almost an idiom. NLT and CEV have "be my follower", but that is using a secondary sense of 'follow'. Williams also has "be my disciple".

8:34d not what you yourself want *to do* The Greek phrase 'deny himself' means "to refuse to think about what one wants for oneself" (L&N).

8:34e *be willing/ready to allow people to make you suffer and to disgrace you* like they do to people when they make them carry *their* cross and then kill them on it The words 'take up his cross' are a metaphor (Gundry, Lane). Its meaning, referring to the way Romans executed criminals, would have been very familiar to the people of that time. THM says that it denotes pain, shame, and execution, all of which are conveyed in the display.

8:34f come with me The Greek has 'follow me'; see note on 1:18.

8:35a *by refusing to be my disciple* The text has 'wants to save his life' but the context is talking about the cost of being a disciple of Jesus (see Cranfield, Gould, and Lenski). No versions examined (except TfT) make this clear.

forfeit **eternal life** At least twelve commentators make clear that 'lose his life' means to forfeit eternal life.

8:35b whom they kill The clause 'who loses his life' means "who dies or is killed" (TN). NLT and CEV have "give up your life".

they are **my** *disciples* The text has 'for 'my sake' which is somewhat nebulous. An alternative would be 'because of his faith in me'.

because t*hey tell others* the good message The words 'for the sake of the gospel' again are not very clear. TN says it means "because he tells other people about the gospel."

live *forever with me* The text has 'will save it'; TN suggests "it refers to a person's eternal life with God".

8:36 certainly does not profit This translates the rhetorical question, 'What does it profit...?' which semantically functions as an emphatic negative statement; cf. NCV.

because he does not become my disciple This supplies the reason, from the immediately preceding context, for forfeiting eternal life.

8:37 absolutely nothing This conveys another rhetorical question which expresses an emphatic negative statement. TEV also has a statement.

after he has forfeited it This is implied in the argument. Wessel says, "Once a man forfeits his share in eternal life, there is no way to get it back." TEV has "to regain his life".

8:38a reluctant *to say that he belongs to* me The text is literally 'ashamed of me' but as THM says, the sense is "ashamed to confess me publicly/to acknowledge his relation to me."

to obey **what I say** 'ashamed of my words' again means 'reluctant', which then requires some verb. The display follows the suggestion of TN in supplying 'obey'.

in these times when many people are 'This generation' refers to "the Lord's own generation" (Swete).

unfaithful *to God* Jesus calls the people 'adulterous', and commentators are unanimous in saying it means 'unfaithful to God'; it is considered a metaphor.

8:38b with the glory The text has 'in the glory' but BAGD says the meaning of the preposition here is 'accompanied by', which makes much more sense. THM agrees; so does NCV.

9:1a A number of versions, e.g., CEV, NLT, RSV, 20th Century, Williams, make clear that 9:1 belongs to the preceding episode. Verse 2 starts with a new time and a new location.

9:1b experience God ruling powerfully The text has 'see the Kingdom of God coming with power'. One problem is, how does a kingdom 'come', and how does anyone see it coming? As before (see note on 1:15), it is treated as a metaphor, and rendered as 'God's rule'. And 'see' is rendered as 'experience' (see suggestion in TN).

Another question is, what is Jesus talking about? The great majority of commentators say it refers to Jesus' transfiguration. Four say it refers to the establishing of the church as a spiritual kingdom. So the display does not attempt to make specific what Jesus was referring to.

BOUNDARIES AND COHERENCE

A new unit at 9:2 is indicated by a change in time and location, and a new topic: Jesus' changed appearance. Coherence in the 8:34–9:1 paragraph is provided by four occurrences of ψυχή 'life/soul'. It is also provided by it being a brief message by Jesus regarding the necessity of enduring persecution.

PROMINENCE AND THEME

The theme of the 8:34–9:1 paragraph is taken from the orienter and a very brief summary of OUTCOME$_1$. OUTCOME$_2$, not being developed, is not considered as thematic.

ACT CONSTITUENT 9:2–29 (Scene to Act I: 8:31—9:39)

THEME: Jesus took three disciples to a high mountain to show them his glory, and later told them that he must be evilly treated. He also showed them that evil spirits can only be expelled through much prayer.

MACROSTRUCTURE	CONTENTS
CONJOINED$_1$	9:2–8 Jesus took Peter, James and John up a high mountain where his appearance became different, and Moses and Elijah appeared and talked to Jesus.
CONJOINED$_2$	9:9–13 Jesus told them that the one like Elijah had come and had been evilly treated, and that the Messiah would also be evilly treated.
CONJOINED$_3$	9:14–29 When Jesus and the three disciples returned to the other disciples, they saw a large crowd and some teachers of the Jewish laws arguing with them. A man spoke out that he had brought his son to be healed but the disciples were not able to do it; Jesus expelled the evil spirit and later explained to the disciples why they had failed to do so.

INTENT AND RHETORICAL STRUCTURE

This episode cluster is still within the introductory scene of Jesus revealing to his disciples who he really is. Here, he revealed both his glory as well as his forthcoming suffering on behalf of all humankind.

The unit consists of three CONJOINED episodes, all of equal prominence.

BOUNDARIES AND COHERENCE

Both the initial and the closing boundaries coincide with the boundaries of the first and final included episodes. The unit is held together by its structure and its unique subject matter of Jesus' transfiguration, and his explanation that Elijah had already come but had been killed just like he would be killed.

PROMINENCE AND THEME

The theme consists of summaries of the three CONJOINED episodes.

SCENE CONSTITUENT 9:2–8 (Episode of 9:2–29)

THEME: *Jesus took Peter, James and John up a high mountain where his appearance became different, and Moses and Elijah appeared and talked to Jesus.*

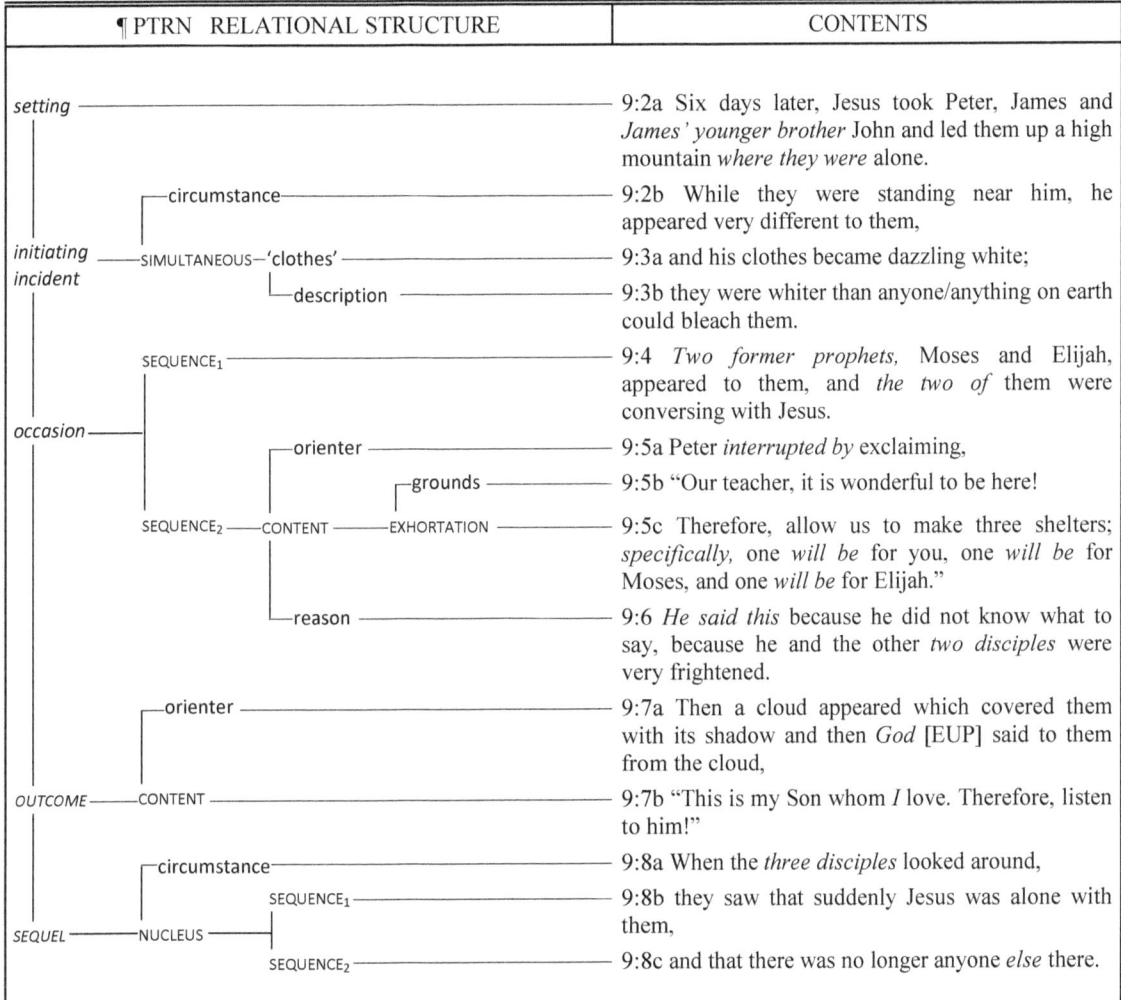

INTENT AND RHETORICAL STRUCTURE

When we observe the paragraph pattern, we observe how Mark wants to affect the reader's understanding about how great Jesus is. This causality type narrative has a *setting*, an *initiating incident*, an *occasion*, an OUTCOME, and a SEQUEL.

NOTES

9:2a *younger brother* **John** The words in italics are supplied for inclusion in translations where such information is needed. Following the Biblical principle that the older brother is named first, John is the younger brother.

9:2b appeared very different The Greek word means 'transfigured' which means that his appearance was changed; cf. JBP, NLT, Williams.

9:4 *Two former prophets* These words are supplied for identification where needed; see suggestion in TN.

9:5a *interrupted by* **exclaiming** The GNT has 'answering said', but Peter was replying to the situation, not to anything said to him. NLT has 'exclaimed'. The word 'interrupted' is a situational implicature.

9:7a God said to them The GNT has 'a voice came to them' which is considered a euphemism to avoid using the name of God; see TN.

9:7b Son whom I love See note 1:1a.

9:8c there was no longer anyone *else* there
The GNT has 'they saw no one except Jesus', but this could imply that the disciples could not see Moses and Elijah, but that they were still there. The wording is reordered to avoid using 'except' because some languages do not have an 'except'.

BOUNDARIES AND COHERENCE

A new paragraph at v. 9 is marked by a change in location and a discussion about Elijah. Coherence within the 2–8 paragraph is provided by two occurrences of the names Moses and Elijah, the adjective 'white' and the cognate verb λευκαίνω 'whiten, and two occurrences of νεφέλη 'cloud'. Coherence is also seen in this paragraph being one episode regarding Jesus' changed appearance while talking with Moses and Elijah.

PROMINENCE AND THEME

The theme is drawn from the *setting*, the circumstance of the *initiating incident*, and SEQUENCE$_1$ of the *occasion*.

SCENE CONSTITUENT 9:9–13 (Episode of 9:2–29)

Theme: Jesus told them that the one like Elijah had come and had been evilly treated, and that the Messiah would also be evilly treated.

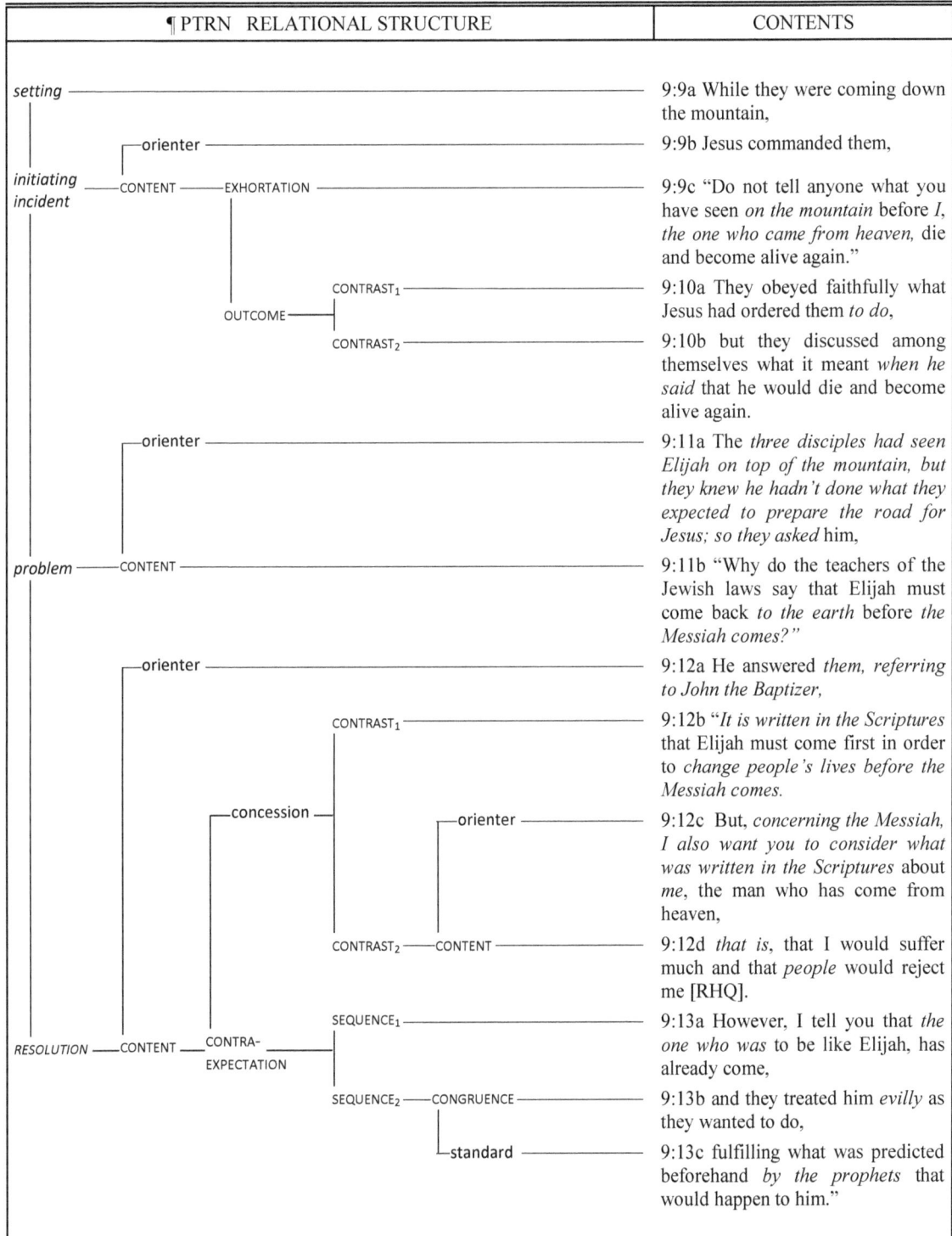

INTENT AND RHETORICAL STRUCTURE

In this episode Jesus reveals that he must suffer and die as John the Baptizer did.

This solutionality type narrative has a *setting*, an *initiating incident*, a *problem*, and a RESOLUTION.

NOTES

9:9c seen *on the mountain* The text has 'what they saw', but it was referring to the events on the mountaintop; see TN.

I, *the one who came from heaven* See note on 2:28.

9:11a The *three disciples had seen Elijah on top of the mountain, but they knew he hadn't done what they expected to prepare the road for Jesus* See Marcus, Gould, Swete, and TRT. This implicit information explains the disciples' question which follows.

9:11b before *the Messiah comes* The text has 'first'; NLT's rendering is the same as in the display; CEV's rendering, "before the Messiah does", is close to that in the display.

9:12a *referring to John the Baptizer* Although Mark does not mention John's name here (but see the parallel passage in Matt. 17:13), all commentators agree that Jesus' comments (especially v. 13) mean that Elijah had come in the person of John the Baptizer.

9:12b *It is written in the Scriptures* It is important that readers know where this information about Elijah came from (Mal. 4:5).

change people's lives There is much discussion by commentators as to what Jesus meant by 'to restore all things'. They all agree that it is referring to the ministry of John. The great majority say it refers to his ministry that had already occurred. A few say it refers to a ministry of Elijah still to come. But all agree that 'restore' is referring to a spiritual restoration; hence 'change people's lives'.

9:12c *But, concerning the Messiah* At this point, Jesus switches from a discussion about John as the forerunner of the Messiah to a discussion about himself as the Messiah. The display indicates this switch.

I also want you to consider what was written The text has 'how has it been written…?' which is a rhetorical question intended to cause the disciples to think carefully about what was written in the Scriptures. Several versions begin this clause with 'Why?' but 'why' questions often imply a negative evaluation, which is not meant here.

9:13a *the one who was to be like* Elijah The GNT says 'Elijah has already come' which was not literally true in referring to John the Baptizer. See suggestions in TN.

9:13c *fulfilling what was predicted* The text has 'just as was written'; the wording in the display is more precise and follows NLT.

BOUNDARIES AND COHERENCE

A new paragraph at v. 14 is signaled by a change in location and a new topic: expulsion of an evil spirit from a boy. Coherence within the 9–13 paragraph is seen in two occurrences of the phrase 'from the dead' and three occurrences of the name 'Elijah'. It is also seen in its being an interchange between Jesus and his disciples regarding Elijah.

PROMINENCE AND THEME

The theme is taken from SEQUENCE$_1$ of the RESOLUTION and CONTRAST$_2$ of the *concession*.

SCENE CONSTITUENT 9:14–29 (Episode of 9:2–29)

THEME: When Jesus and the three disciples returned to the other disciples, they saw a large crowd and some teachers of the Jewish laws arguing with them. A man spoke out that he had brought his son to be healed but the disciples were not able to do it; Jesus expelled the evil spirit and later explained to the disciples why they had failed to do so.

¶PTRN RELATIONAL STRUCTURE	CONTENTS
setting — circumstance	9:14 Jesus and the three disciples returned to w*here* the *other* disciples *were,* and they saw a large crowd around the other disciples and some teachers of the Jewish laws arguing with them.
SEQUENCE₁	9:15a As soon as the crowd saw Jesus, they were greatly surprised *at his sudden appearance,*
SEQUENCE₂	9:15b and they ran to him, and greeted him.
problem	9:16–19 The father of the boy who had been possessed by an evil spirit since he was a child told Jesus that his disciples were not able to heal the boy. [See expanded display on page 168.]
resolving incident	9:19 Jesus said, "Bring the boy to me!" [See expanded display on page 168.]
occasion	9:20–24 People brought the boy to Jesus, who talked to the boy's father. [See expanded display on page 169.]
RESOLUTION — OUTCOME	9:25–27 Jesus expelled the evil spirit from the boy. [See expanded display on page 170.]
SEQUEL	9:28–29 Later his disciples asked him how come they were unable to expel the evil spirit. [See expanded display on page 170.]

INTENT AND RHETORICAL STRUCTURE

In this paragraph Mark wants to affect the reader's understanding about how Jesus was able to cast out an evil spirit when his disciples had failed to do so. This solutionality type narrative has a *setting*, a *problem*, a *resolving incident*, a RESOLUTION, and a final SEQUEL.

NOTES

9:15a surprised *at his sudden appearance* A host of commentators say this was the reason for their surprise.

EXPANSION OF THE PROBLEM 9:16–18 FROM THE MARK 9:14–29 DISPLAY

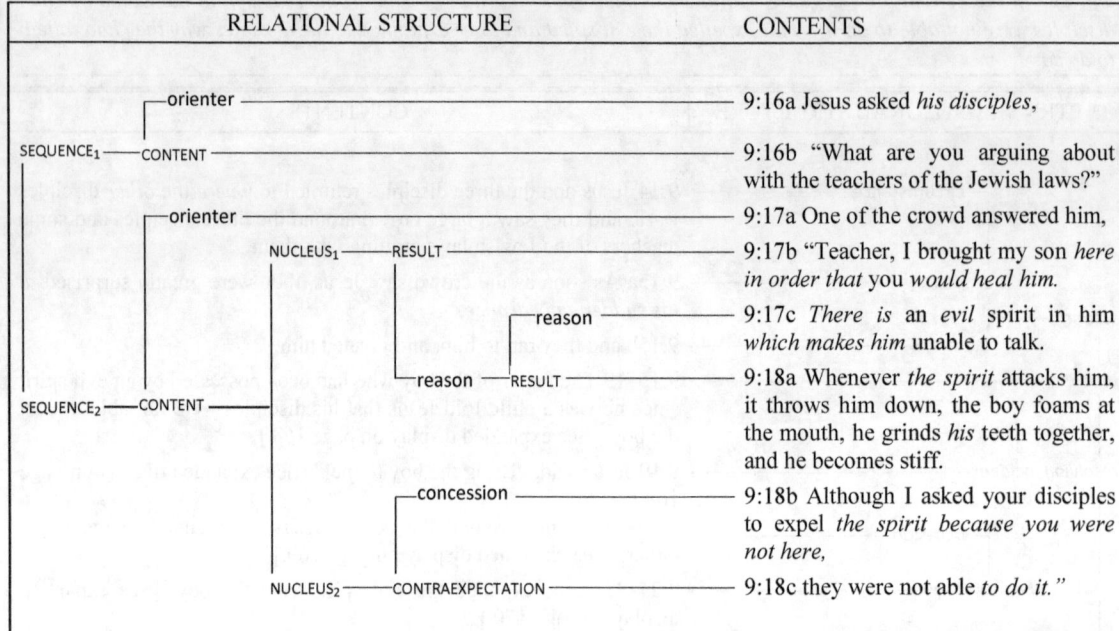

NOTES

9:16a asked *his disciples* The GNT just has 'them'.

9:17b brought my son *here in order that* you *would heal him* The text has 'I brought you my son'. NLT also adds "for you to heal him".

9:17c *which makes him* unable to talk The text has 'dumb spirit' which is very misleading in English. Most modern English versions make the meaning clear.

9:18b *because you were not here* These words supply the reason he asked the disciples; the man had brought his son to be healed by Jesus.

EXPANSION OF THE RESOLVING INCIDENT 9:19 FROM THE MARK 9:14–29 DISPLAY

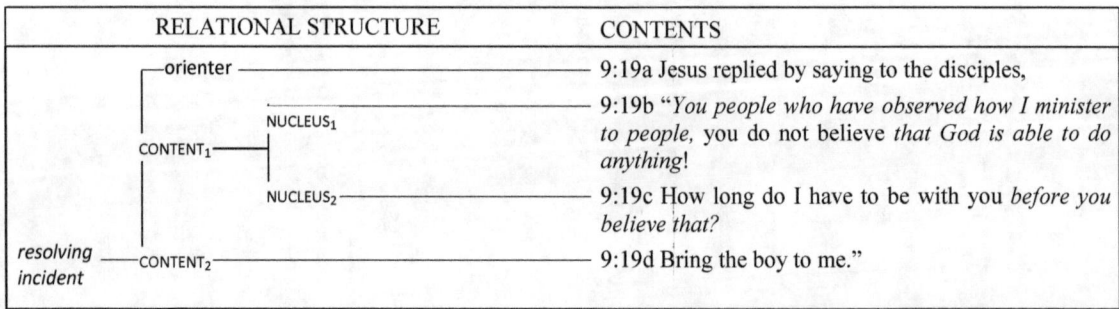

NOTES

9:19b *You people who have observed how I minister to people* Jesus again referred to 'this generation'. See note on 8:12. In this situation, Jesus meant something much more specific than 'the people who were alive at that time'. There is a lot of discussion by commentators as to whom Jesus was addressing as 'unbelieving generation', but the great majority think the words "were expressly directed at the nine disciples who had failed to cast out the evil spirit due to their lack of faith" (Blight).

believe *that God is able to do anything* The text has the adjective 'unbelieving'. But what did they not believe? The display supplies one possible content that fits the context; an alternative would be 'in God's power'.

EXPANSION OF THE RESOLUTION STEP 9:20–24 FROM THE MARK 9:14–29 DISPLAY

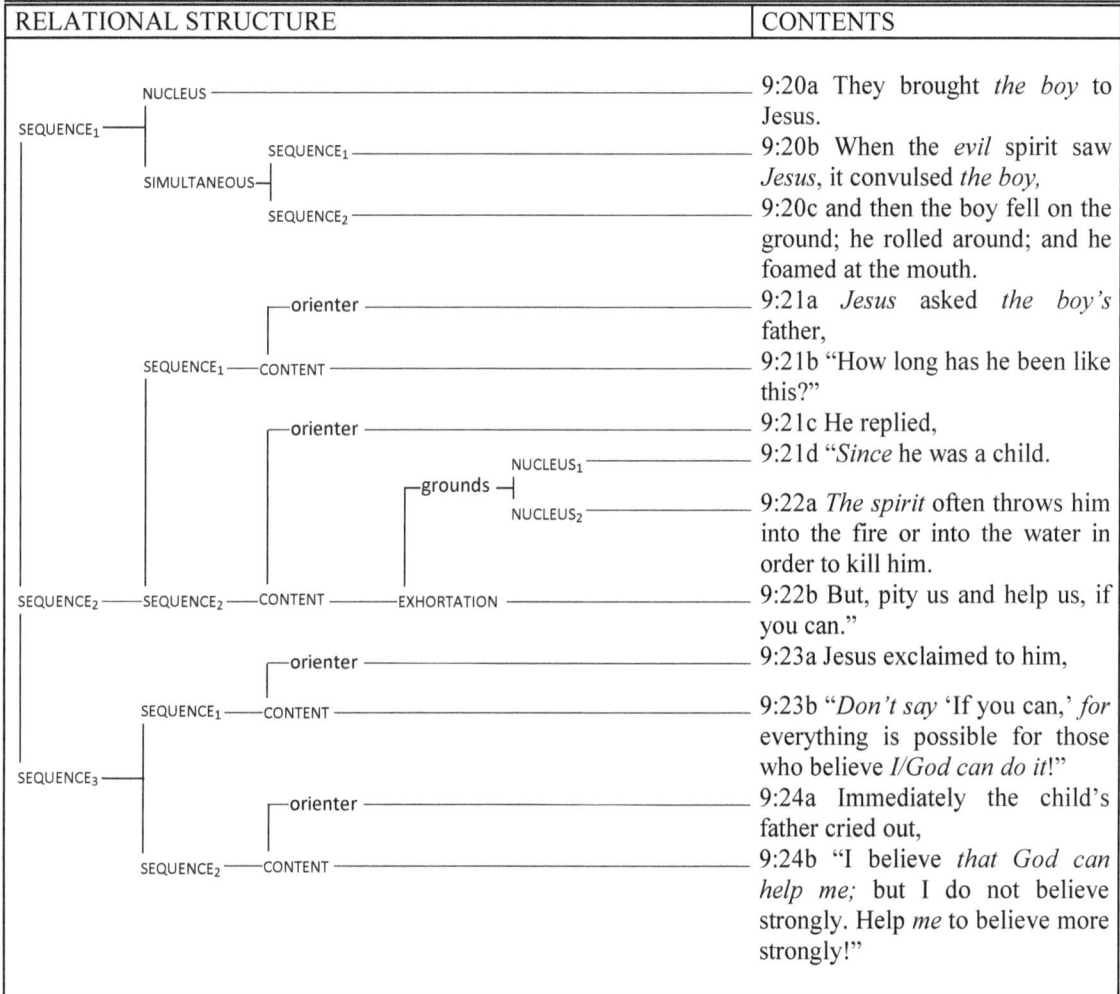

NOTES

9:23b *Don't say* **'If you can'** The Greek has 'if you can' which is a repetition of the man's words, but is also a mild rebuke (TN; also CEV "Why do you say 'If you can?' ".) The wording in the display tries to convey the rebuke.

A number of manuscripts add the word 'believe' (cf. KJV), but it is poorly attested.

those who believe *I/God can do it* The Greek has 'the one who believes' but the sense is generic; hence 'those who'. The word 'believe' semantically requires a content of what is believed; the words 'that I/God can do it' fit the context.

9:24b not believe *strongly* The man speaks of his 'unbelief', but since he has just said that he does believe, the sense is that his faith is weak. JB has "my little faith".

Help *me to believe more strongly* This sense of 'help my unbelief' is supported by a host of commentators.

EXPANSION OF RESOLUTION 9:25–27 FROM THE MARK 9:14–29 DISPLAY

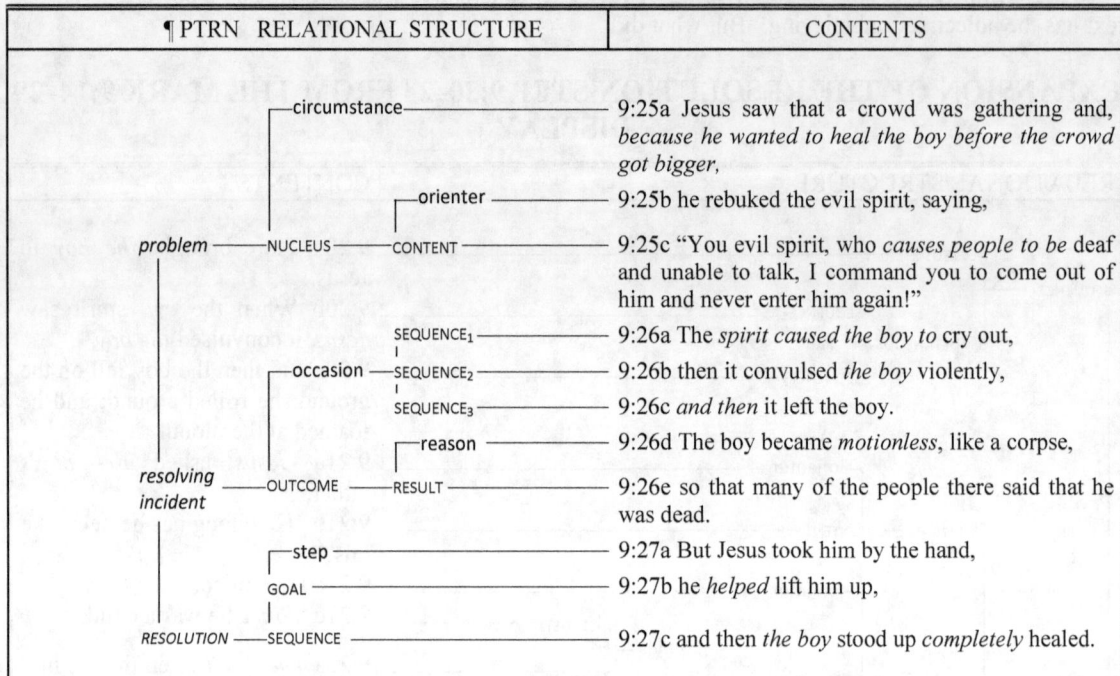

NOTES

9:25a *because he wanted to heal the boy before the crowd got bigger* This is the implicature of 'seeing that a crowd was gathering'. Gould says, "He did not wish to attract a larger crowd by prolonging the scene."

9:25c *who causes people to be* **deaf and unable to talk** This is the sense of 'dumb and deaf spirit'; cf. CEV.

9:26d *motionless* This word supplies the point of comparison in the simile 'like a corpse'. NLT also has "motionless".

EXPANSION OF SEQUEL 9:28–29 FROM THE MARK 9:14–29 DISPLAY

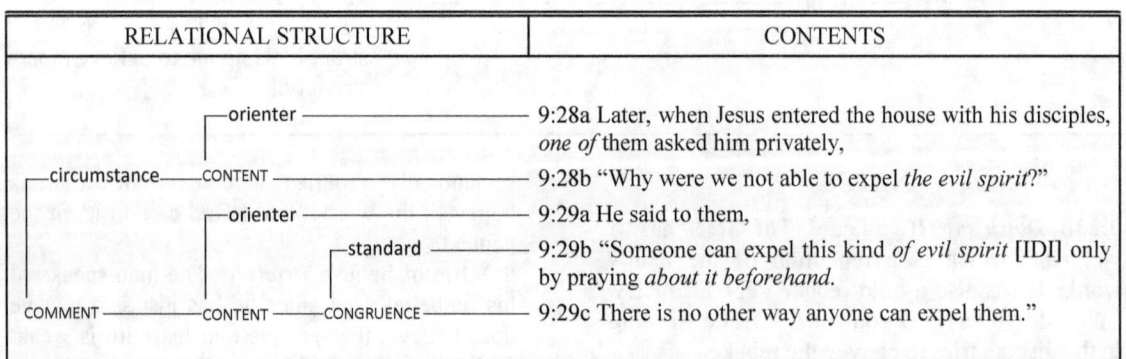

NOTES

9:29b **praying** *about it beforehand* Jesus said 'by prayer'. There is no evidence that he prayed right at that time; but he did expel the demon, so perhaps he prayed before commanding the demon to leave.

The KJV adds 'and fasting', but those words are not found in the best manuscripts. They were undoubtedly added because of the emphasis on fasting in the early church.

BOUNDARIES AND COHERENCE

A new paragraph at v. 30 is marked by a change in location and a new topic: a repetition of his prediction regarding his death and resurrection. Coherence within the 14–29 paragraph is shown by five occurrences of πνεῦμα 'spirit', two of συζητέω 'argue', and two of ἀφρίζω 'foams'. Coherence is also provided by it being one episode of Jesus healing a demon-possessed boy.

PROMINENCE AND THEME

The theme is drawn from the *setting*, the *problem*, the RESOLUTION, and the SEQUEL.

PART CONSTITUENT 9:30—10:52 (Act II of Part II 8:31—16:8)

THEME: On their way to Jerusalem, Jesus taught his disciples that he must die and become alive again; but even so, they thought he was going to be the ruling king in Jerusalem. So, James and John asked Jesus that they might be the most important in his kingdom.

MACROSTRUCTURE	CONTENTS
occasion	9:30–10:31 Jesus taught his disciples various matters about living peaceably under his rule, but primarily that he must suffer, die and become alive again, and that they must be totally committed to him.
OUTCOME	10:32–52 Jesus told them what was going to happen to him in Jerusalem. However, James and John asked to be the most important in his ruling kingdom.

INTENT AND RHETORICAL STRUCTURE

This ACT II (9:30—10:52) is the second unit of the second part of Mark (8:31—16:18). Mark here presents that even though Jesus explicitly taught his disciples that he must die in Jerusalem, they, even so, were vying for primary positions in his kingly rule over Israel from Jerusalem.

The paragraph structure consists of an *occasion* and an *OUTCOME*. Jesus continues to demonstrate to his disciples who he really is.

BOUNDARIES AND COHERENCE

Both the initial and the closing boundaries coincide with the boundaries of the first and final included episodes. The scope of this unit is that Jesus teaches his disciples that he will die, but even so the disciples thought he would be the political liberator from Roman domination.

PROMINENCE AND THEME

The theme consists of a summary of the two structural units, maintaining structural prominence.

ACT CONSTITUENT 9:30–10:31 (Scene to Act II 9:30—10:52)

THEME: Jesus taught his disciples various matters about living peaceably under his rule, but primarily that he must suffer, die and become alive again, and that they must be totally committed to him.

MACROSTRUCTURE	CONTENTS
DECLARATIONS	9:30–32 Jesus was teaching his disciples that he would be handed over to other men, killed and become alive again; but they did not understand what he was saying.
description₁	9:33–37 Jesus asked his disciples what they had talked about while they were traveling, they were ashamed to answer. So Jesus taught them by illustration about what kind of person God considers important. He also taught them about who is for them and who against them.
description₂	9:38–50 Jesus taught his disciples to not reject those who were performing miracles even if they were not accompanying him, to allow fellow believers who are in other groups to function without hindrance, to not cause fellow believers to sin, and to live peaceably with each other
description₃	10:1–12 Some Pharisees asked Jesus if the law permitted a man to divorce his wife. Jesus answered and supported his answer from scripture.
description₄	10:13–16 Jesus became indignant when he saw his disciples scolding people for bringing children for him to bless, because it is people who trust like children who will be part of God's rule.
description₅	10:17–31 A rich man ran to Jesus to ask what he should do in order to live eternally; After questioning the man, Jesus told him to sell all his possessions, which he refused to do, and the disciples were astonished that Jesus said that the rich had no advantage to be under God's rule.

INTENT AND RHETORICAL STRUCTURE

This is the first cluster of episodes in ACT II in which Jesus clearly tells his disciples that he must suffer and die, and that they too must suffer for his sake. In this cluster of episodes, Mark intends that the reader understand that Jesus taught his disciples about many specific matters for them to observe as people under his rule. The structure of this unit consists of an initial DECLARATION and five *descriptions*. In all of the included episodes his disciples were involved, and in most episodes Jesus spoke directly to his disciples.

BOUNDARIES AND COHERENCE

Both the initial and the closing boundaries coincide with the boundaries of the first and final included episodes. This unit is bound together by a series of specific teachings about how his disciples should act under Jesus' rule.

PROMINENCE AND THEME

The theme is a summary of the included episodes reflecting the paragraph pattern prominence structure.

SCENE CONSTITUENT 9:30–32 (Episode of 9:30–10:31)

THEME: Jesus was teaching his disciples that he would be handed over to other men, killed and become alive again; but they did not understand what he was saying.

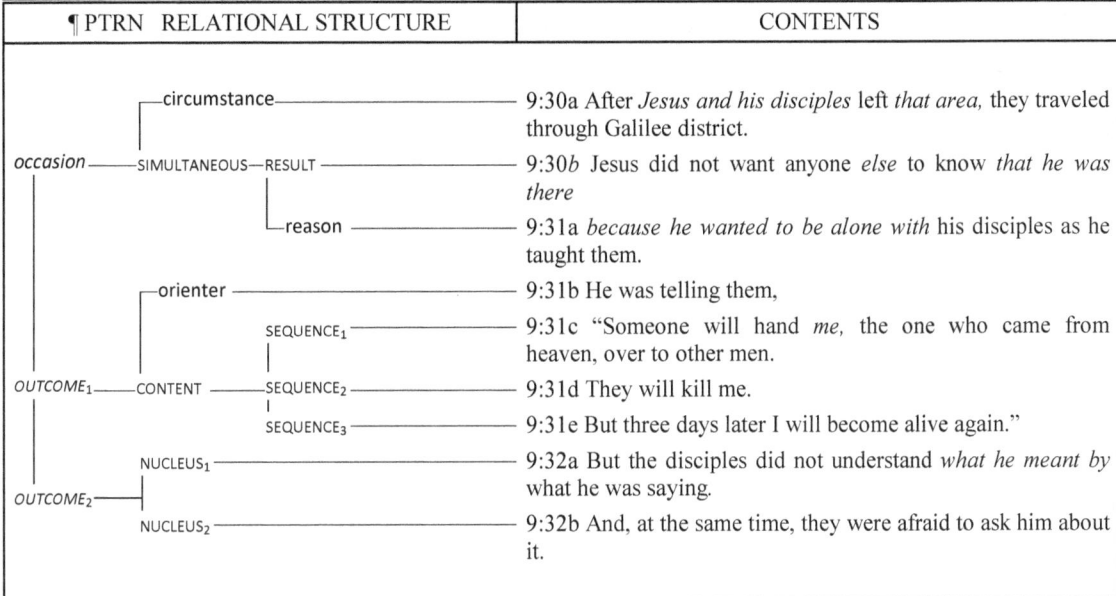

¶PTRN RELATIONAL STRUCTURE	CONTENTS
	9:30a After *Jesus and his disciples* left *that area,* they traveled through Galilee district.
	9:30b Jesus did not want anyone *else* to know *that he was there*
	9:31a *because he wanted to be alone with* his disciples as he taught them.
	9:31b He was telling them,
	9:31c "Someone will hand *me,* the one who came from heaven, over to other men.
	9:31d They will kill me.
	9:31e But three days later I will become alive again."
	9:32a But the disciples did not understand *what he meant by what he was saying.*
	9:32b And, at the same time, they were afraid to ask him about it.

INTENT AND RHETORICAL STRUCTURE

Mark here intends to inform the reader of how Jesus kept telling his disciples of his upcoming rejection, suffering, and return to life, but they just could not understand it. As a causality type narrative it consists of an *occasion,* an OUTCOME, and another OUTCOME.

NOTES

9:30a *Jesus and his disciples* The GNT text has only 'they'; the display identifies the participants (as does CEV).

9:30b **know** *that he was there* The text has only 'know'; 'know' semantically requires a content; cf. TEV, CEV.

9:31a *he wanted to be alone with* **his disciples** The GNT has only 'because he was teaching his disciples', but the point was that he wanted to maintain secrecy about what he was about to tell them; see Bruce, Gould, and Guelich.

9:31c *me,* the one who came from heaven See note on 2:10.

9:31e **But** There is no conjunction in the Greek, but many versions supply 'but'.

9:32a **understand** *what he meant by what he was saying* The Greek has 'understand the word' but several versions supply 'what he meant' (e.g., TEV, NIV, CEV, Williams).

BOUNDARIES AND COHERENCE

A new paragraph at v. 33 is marked by a change in location and a new topic: whom God considers important. Coherence in the 30–32 paragraph is shown by the word διδάσκω 'teaching' and the content of what Jesus was teaching his disciples.

PROMINENCE AND THEME

The theme is taken from the *orienter* and three SEQUENCES of OUTCOME₁, plus NUCLEUS₁ of OUTCOME₂.

SCENE CONSTITUENT 9:33–37 (Episode of 9:30–10:31)

THEME: When Jesus asked his disciples what they had talked about while they were traveling, they were ashamed to answer. So Jesus taught them by illustration about what kind of person God considers important. He also taught them about who is for them and who against them.

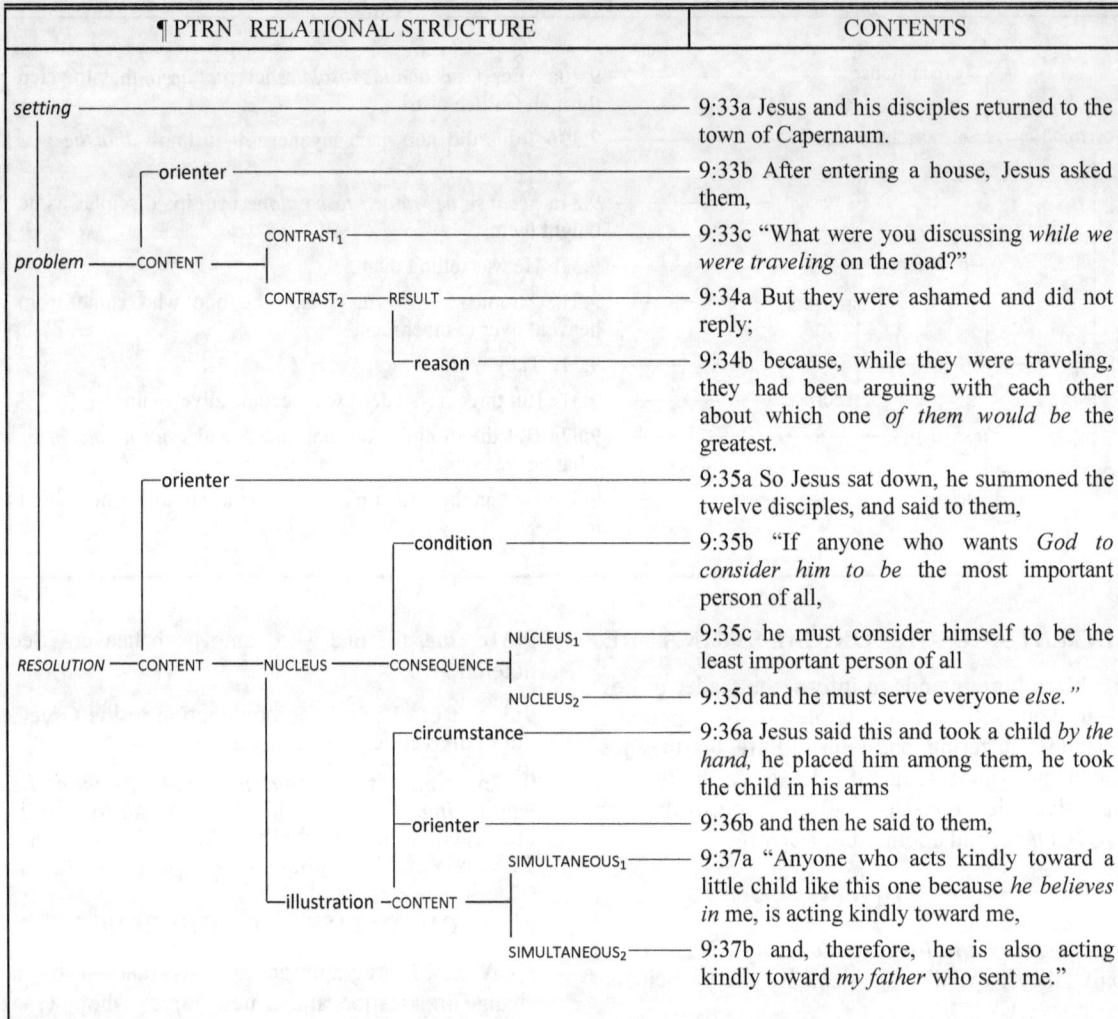

INTENT AND RHETORICAL STRUCTURE

In this episode, Jesus taught his disciples that they must serve one another.

As a solutionality type narrative it consists of a *setting*, a *problem*, and a *RESOLUTION*.

NOTES

9:33a Jesus and his disciples See note on 33a 11:19.

9:34b *which one of them would be the greatest* The text has only 'who would be the greatest' but 'of them' is implied, and supplied in CEV, NLT, JB, Williams. The Greek has the present tense, but most commentators say they were talking about future greatness. Several (e.g., Hiebert, Swete, and France) suggest they were arguing about the time that Jesus would be king.

9:35b *God to consider him* Humbling oneself is not the way to become great in the eyes of people; it is the way to become great in the sight of God. Therefore something like the wording in the display is implied.

9:36 *by the hand* The GNT has 'taking a child' and 'by the hand' is necessary to be understood to avoid wrong meaning.

9:37a *acts kindly toward* The word δέχομαι literally means 'welcome', but here it means to receive with a kindly welcome (Hiebert, L&N, and Guelich).

because *he believes in* me The text has 'in my name' and commentators vary greatly on what they think this expression means. The one that has the most votes is the wording in the display.

9:37b *my father* who sent me The text has only 'the one who sent me'; NLT also has "my Father who sent me".

BOUNDARIES AND COHERENCE

A new paragraph at v. 38 is marked by a question from John and Jesus' reply. Coherence within the 33–37 paragraph is shown by two occurrences of διαλογίζομαι 'argue'. Coherence is also seen in that Jesus taught his disciples as to whom God considers the most important.

PROMINENCE AND THEME

The theme is drawn from CONTRAST₁ of the *problem*, a condensation of the *orienter* and *condition* of the RESOLUTION, and a condensation of SIMULTANOUS₁ and SIMULTANEOUS₂ of the RESOLUTION.

SCENE CONSTITUENT 9:38–50 (Episode of 9:30–10:31)

THEME: *Jesus taught his disciples to not reject those who were performing miracles even if they were not accompanying him, to allow fellow believers who are in other groups to function without hindrance, to not cause fellow believers to sin, and to live peaceably with each other.*

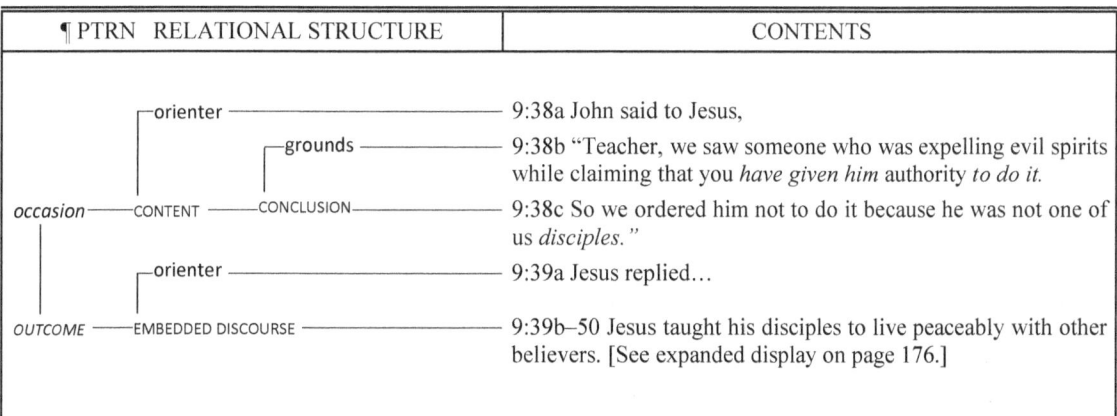

INTENT AND RHETORICAL STRUCTURE

This episode is the third of six in which Jesus teaches on various matters about his new order for God's ruling people. In this one, Jesus taught his disciples to live peaceably with other believers.

This unit consists of an *occasion* (9:38), and an OUTCOME (9:39). This demonstrates the unit's prominence structure and that it is a narrative.

Mark here intends to inform the reader of how Jesus kept preparing his disciples for his upcoming rejection, suffering, and return to life. As a causality type narrative it consists of an *occasion* and an OUTCOME.

There is a conversational exchange between Jesus and his disciples tying the *occasion* and the OUTCOME together.

The OUTCOME consists of an extended discourse of Jesus teaching his disciples. The display shows this as an embedded discourse.

The motif of 'expelling evil spirits' in v. 38 supplies proof that those in this other group were also Jesus' believers.

NOTES

9:38b while claiming that you *have given him* authority *to do it* The GNT has 'in your name'. Commentators who say his 'name' means 'authority' (i.e., as a metonymy) include Wessel, Gould, Hiebert, and Lane.

9:38c not one of us *disciples* The text has 'not following us', but as before, 'follow' is used in an extended sense meaning being someone's disciple (see note on 2:14). NLT has "isn't one of our group".

EXPANDED DISPLAY OF THE EMBEDDED HORTATORY DISCOURSE
9:39b–50 (HORTATORY DISCOURSE WITHIN THE EPISODE 9:38–50)

THEME: Jesus said to his disciples, "Do not hinder them from doing my work; do not cause a fellow-believer to sin; remain useful to God by living peacefully with other people who believe in me.

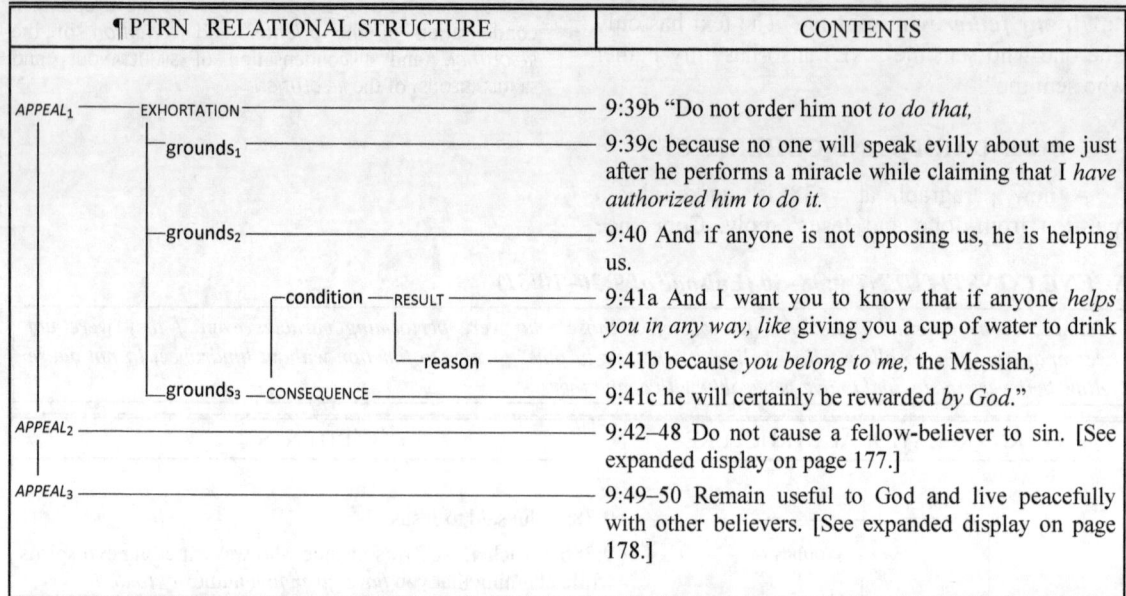

¶ PTRN RELATIONAL STRUCTURE	CONTENTS
APPEAL₁ — EXHORTATION	9:39b "Do not order him not *to do that*,
⎣ grounds₁	9:39c because no one will speak evilly about me just after he performs a miracle while claiming that I *have authorized him to do it.*
⎣ grounds₂	9:40 And if anyone is not opposing us, he is helping us.
condition — RESULT	9:41a And I want you to know that if anyone *helps you in any way, like* giving you a cup of water to drink
⎣ reason	9:41b because *you belong to me,* the Messiah,
⎣ grounds₃ — CONSEQUENCE	9:41c he will certainly be rewarded *by God*."
APPEAL₂	9:42–48 Do not cause a fellow-believer to sin. [See expanded display on page 177.]
APPEAL₃	9:49–50 Remain useful to God and live peacefully with other believers. [See expanded display on page 178.]

INTENT AND RHETORICAL STRUCTURE

This unit is an embedded hortatory paragraph in which Jesus taught his disciples to accept those who served others because of him. This is a causality type hortatory paragraph consisting of THREE APPEALS, each APPEAL unit consisting of a *grounds* and the EXHORTATION. Mark intends that the reader understand and obey Jesus' desire that his people accept each other even though not part of one's particular group, that one should not cause fellow believers to sin, and that we should live peacefully with other believers.

NOTES

9:40 he is helping us The GNT has 'is for us'; JBP has "is on our side". See also THM.

9:41a I want you to know This represents 'I tell you truly'.

helps you in any way, like The text says 'gives you a cup of water to drink' TN says such a deed "is used as an example here".

9:41b you belong to me, the Messiah The text has '*because you are* of the Christ'. 'Christ' here means 'Messiah'. NLT has "belongs to the Messiah"; CEV just has "belongs to me".

9:41c certainly be rewarded *by God* The text has 'will by no means lose his reward'. This is taken as a litotes, a means of emphasizing the positive by denying the negative. CEV also translates using an emphatic positive; see also CEV, NLT, and JBP. God is the implied agent of the rewarding; see TN.

EXPANDED DISPLAY OF EXHORTATION₂ 9:42–48 OF 9:38–50

RELATIONAL STRUCTURE	CONTENTS
EXHORTATION — CONSEQUENCE — NUCLEUS ┬ condition	9:42a But, if anyone causes *a person* who believes in me to sin,
	9:42b *God will severely punish him*, even if this person is *socially unimportant* like this little *child*.
└ amplification	9:42c If someone tied a very heavy stone around his neck and threw him into the sea *to punish him*, that would be a small *punishment. But the punishment God will give him* will be really terrible.
illustration₁ — CONTRAST₂ ┬ CONTRAST₁ ┬ MEANS	9:43a If you think about *using* your hand to *sin, get rid of those thoughts completely, because it would be good to avoid committing such a sin* [MTY]
└ purpose	9:43b in order to live *eternally*,
	9:43c rather than keep both hands *and commit that sin* and be thrown into hell [MET],
└ comparison	9:43d *just as* it would be better for you to cut off your hand *in order to save your life*.
illustration₂ — CONTRAST₂ ┬ CONTRAST₁	9:45a If you think about *using* your foot to *go somewhere* to sin, *get rid of those thoughts completely, because it would be good to avoid committing such a sin* [MTY]
	9:45b *rather than keep two feet and commit that sin,*
└ comparison	9:45c *just as* it would be better for you to cut off your foot *in order to save your life*.
illustration₃ — CONTRAST₂ ┬ CONTRAST₁	9:47a If you are thinking of *using* your eye to *look at something* that displeases God, *get rid of those thoughts completely, because it would be good to avoid committing such a sin* [MTY]
	9:47b rather than keep both eyes and *go to hell,*
└ comparison	9:47c *just as* it would be good for you to gouge out your eye *in order to save your life,*
grounds	9:48 *because* in hell people suffer eternally and the fires are never extinguished [MET].

NOTES

9:42a in me Some important manuscripts omit these words, but they are clearly implied anyway.

9:42b–c ***God will severely punish him*** This verse has several difficulties. The first is that the GNT says 'it would be better…' but only relatively so; being thrown in a lake with a millstone around one's neck is not 'good'. Secondly, throwing into the sea the person who sins thus is a punishment for what he has done; hence 'to punish him' in 42c.

is *socially unimportant* like this little *child* The text has 'one of these little ones'. Commentators say 'one of these little ones' refers to any believer who is "lowly" (Meyer), "insignificant" (Mann), "lowliest members of the community" (Taylor).

***But the punishment God will give him* will be really big** The text never answers the question, 'being thus thrown into the sea would be better than what?' The answer, which is not given in any of the versions except TfT, is supplied in the display: that would be a lighter punishment than the punishment he will receive from God.

9:43a–b This verse (and v. 45) are difficult. Much of the problem is caused by the figures of speech.

if you *think about using* your hand to *sin* 'If your hand causes you to sin' is a personification; hands are not sentient beings. Temptations to sin start in the brain; thus 'if you think about'. See Hiebert.

get rid of those thoughts completely The text says 'cut it off' which is both hyperbole and metaphor (Brooks, ESV footnote). Jesus did not mean his words to be taken literally (Lane, Taylor). But all versions (except TfT) translate it literally. Wessel says that this is a demand that we cease sinful activities associated with the hand. TRT is good, saying that it means "a person must get rid of the source of sin in his heart or mind".

in order to live *eternally* The text has 'enter life'; TN says it means "to enter eternal life in heaven with God".

9:44, 46 These two verses are omitted in the GNT with an A 'certain' rating. Some scribes inserted them here because the words are found in v. 48.

9:43c rather than keep both hands ***and commit that sin and* be thrown into hell** The GNT omits the implied reason for being thrown into hell: it is not having two hands but committing some sin with those hands.

9:43d ***just as* it would be better for you to cut off your hand** *in order to save your life* This retains the wording of 'cut off your hand' which is now the topic part of the metaphor, with 'to save your life' being the implied purpose of the action of that topic.

9:45, 47 See notes on v. 43.

EXPANDED DISPLAY OF EXHORTATION₃ 9:49–50 OF 9:38–50

RELATIONAL STRUCTURE	CONTENTS
grounds — NUCLEUS	9:49a Trials will come to everyone *in order to purify their lives.*
└ illustration	9:49b *It is like people put salt on sacrifices to purify them* [MET] *before they were burned in a fire.*
comparison	9:50a *Just as* salt is useful *to put on food,* but there is absolutely no way you can make it taste salty again if it becomes flavorless [MET],
EXHORTATION₁ — CONCLUSION	9:50b you must remain useful *to God,*
└ grounds	9:50c *because no-one can make you useful to God again if you become useless* [MET].
EXHORTATION₂	9:50c And you must live peacefully with each other.
comparison	

NOTES

9:49 Gould rightly says that this verse is one of the most difficult in the whole New Testament. There are at least three reasons for this: 1) the metaphors involving salt and fire, 2) the different suggestions for the points of comparison of those metaphors, and 3) there is nothing in the preceding context which points to the meaning of the metaphors.

9:49a–b Trials *will come to everyone in order to purify their lives. It is like people put salt on sacrifices to purify them before they were burned* in a fire Most scholars believe that Jesus was referring to Jewish sacrifices that were always salted and then burned on the altar (Lev. 2:13). The purpose of the salt was purification. That suggests the meaning of the metaphor is that we need to be purified. And for us, fire is a symbol of the trials and sufferings we all experience. See Gould, TRT, Brooks, Hendriksen, Taylor, Lane. Most versions are literal, but TEV's is a big step in the right direction: "Everyone will be purified by fire, as a sacrifice is purified by salt".

9:50a absolutely no way you can make it taste salty again The Greek has another rhetorical question: "by what will you season it?" It functions as emphatic negative statement. The display tries to capture this with 'absolutely no way'. All versions examined (except TfT) retain the question.

9:50b remain useful *to God* The text has 'have salt in yourselves' which is another metaphor. Commentators are very divided as to how believers are to be like salt. The display therefore is very generic, carrying over the word 'useful' from 50a as a quality that should apply to us as it applies to salt.

9:50c *because no-one can make you useful to God again if you become useless* This is the implied topic of the metaphor about losing saltiness in 50a. See Stein and Hooker.

BOUNDARIES AND COHERENCE

A new paragraph at 10:1 is shown by a change in location and a new topic: divorce. Coherence within the 38–50 unit is shown by one occurrence of 'in your name' and two of 'in my name', three occurrences of 'causes you to sin', and three occurrences of 'enter into life' Coherence is seen by Jesus teaching his disciples to live peaceably with other believers..

PROMINENCE AND THEME

The theme of the 9:38–50 paragraph is taken from a condensation of the EXHORTATION of *grounds*$_1$ and CONCLUSION of the *occasion*, EXHORTATION$_1$, a brief condensation of *illustration*$_1$, a brief condensation of APPEAL$_1$, plus summaries of APPEALS $_2$ and $_3$.

SCENE CONSTITUENT 10:1–12 (Episode of 9:30–10:31)

THEME: *Some Pharisees asked Jesus if the law permitted a man to divorce his wife. Jesus answered and supported his answer from scripture.*

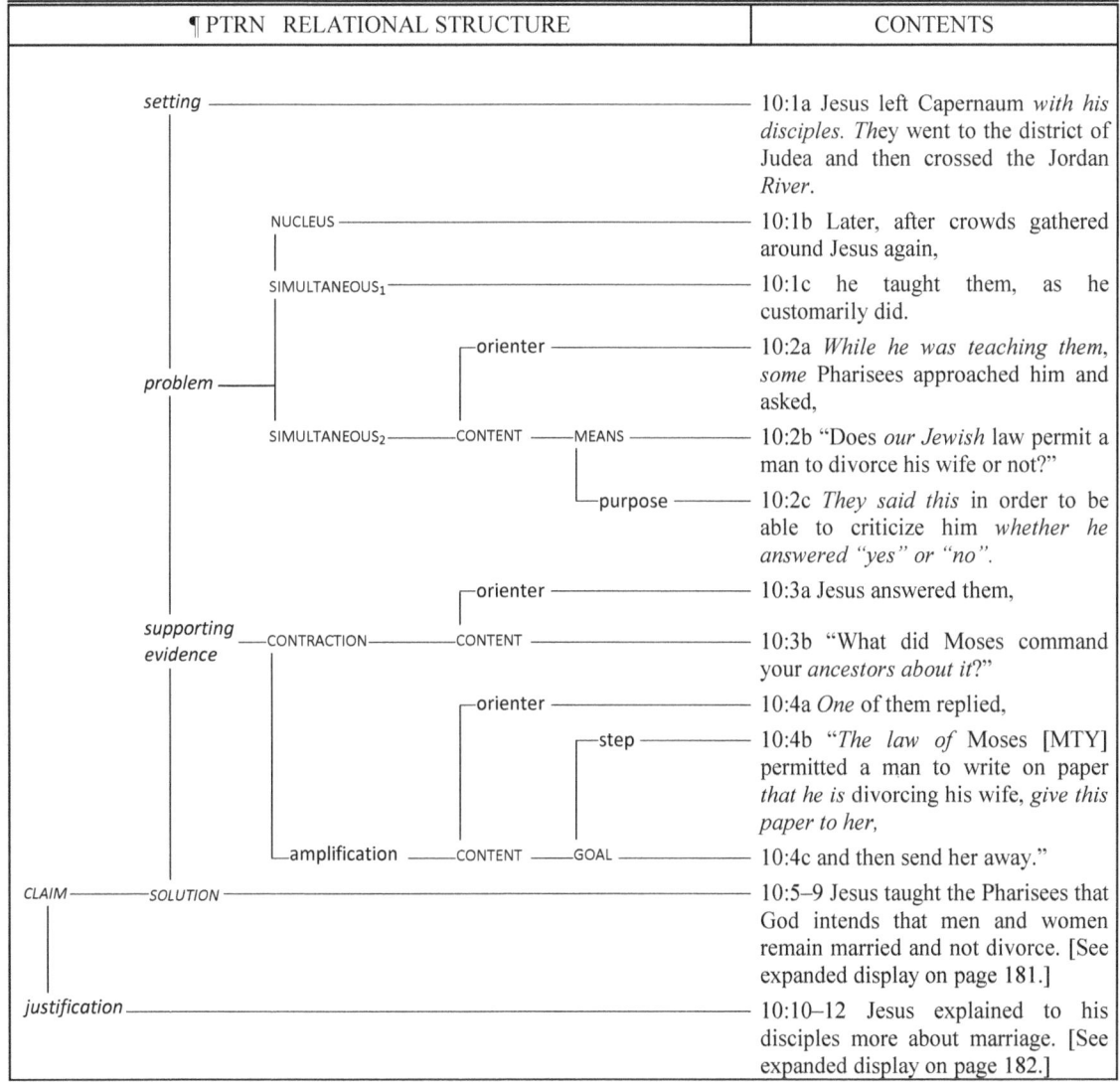

INTENT AND RHETORICAL STRUCTURE

This unit consists of two sub-episodes (10:1–9 and 10:10–12) closely linked by what Jesus said to the Jewish authorities and then to the disciples about divorce and marriage. This demonstrates that the unit is a narrative.

Mark here intends to inform the reader of how Jesus continued to prepare his disciples for his upcoming rejection, suffering, and return to life. Although this unit appears by its form to be a narrative, in its meaning structure it is an expositional unit consisting of a CLAIM (10:1–9), and a *justification* (10:10–12).

This entire unit is complex in that two units of CLAIM and *justification* each have embedded discourses. This seems to be a marked prominence device.

The CLAIM unit consists of a solutionality type exposition with a *problem* (10:1b–2), a *supporting evidence* (10:3–4), and a SOLUTION (10:5–6).

The justification unit consists of a causality type narrative with an *occasion* (10:10), and an OUTCOME (10:11–12).

NOTES

10:1 *with his disciples* TN says "it is clear from 10:10b that the disciples were with Jesus". See also the note on 5:21.

and then crossed the Jordan River 'River' is added as in TEV, NLT, CEV. The KJV follows manuscripts which have 'by the farther side of Jordan', which were introduced by copyists who could not understand the geographical problems.

10:2b *our Jewish* **law** The text has 'Is it permitted?' but what they were asking was whether their Jewish laws, specifically the laws given to Moses, permitted it.

10:2c *whether he answered "yes" or "no"* The text has 'testing him'. TEV has "to trap him," but in what way was their question a trap? The display tries to give help on that. Hiebert says "Either a 'yes' or a 'no' answer would be sure to arouse opposition by some part of the crowd."

10:3b **command** *your* **ancestors** *about it* The text has 'command you' but the command God gave Moses was to their ancestors (cf. TN), not to the Pharisees standing there.

10:4b *The law of* **Moses** They were referring to Deut. 24:1–4.

give this paper to her TN says "It is implied that the man gave the certificate of divorce to the woman".

EXPANSION OF CLAIM 10:5–9 IN MARK 10:1–12 DISPLAY

RELATIONAL STRUCTURE	CONTENTS
orienter	10:5a Jesus said to them,
CONTRAST₁ — reason	10:5b "It was because your ancestors stubbornly *refused to do what God desired*
CONTRAST₁ — RESULT	10:5c that Moses wrote that law for you.
grounds	10:6 But *it was also written in the Scriptures that, when God* first created *people*, he made them *one married couple*.
CONCLUSION₁ — CONTRAST₁	10:7a Therefore, *as the scriptures say*, a man and his wife shall no longer live with their fathers and mothers, *after they marry*;
CONTRAST₂ — step	10:7b instead, they shall live together,
CONTRAST₂ — GOAL	10:8a and the two of them shall be *very closely united so that they are like* one person [MET].
CONCLUSION₂ — concession	10:8b Therefore, although they were two *separate persons* before,
CONCLUSION₂ — CONTRAEXPECTATION	10:8c *God* regards them as one person now.
CONCLUSION₃	10:9 Therefore, a man must not separate *from the wife* God has joined to him."

(Outer structure: CONTENT with CONTRAST₁ and CONTRAST₂ branches)

NOTES

10:5b stubbornly *refused to do what God desired* The text has 'hardness of heart' which is an idiom meaning 'stubborn'. THM says specifically it means "their unwillingness to accept [God's] will in the matter".

10:6 *it was also written in the Scriptures that* What follows is a quote from Gen. 1:27. No versions (except TfT) make explicit this implied information, though RSV and TEV allude to it by putting the citation in single quotes.

God The Greek text has only 'he' but most versions supply 'God'.

one married couple The text has 'male and female' but that is ambiguous as to how many of each. An alternative to the wording in the display is 'one man and one woman'.

10:7a *as the scriptures say* What follows is again a quote from Genesis 2:24.

after they marry Most versions follow manuscripts which include the words 'and be joined to his wife'; JB is an exception. But that clause is implied anyway, and is represented here by 'after they marry'.

EXPANSION OF JUSTIFICATION 10:10–12 IN MARK 10:1–12 DISPLAY

RELATIONAL STRUCTURE	CONTENTS
circumstance — GOAL — step	10:10a When *Jesus and* his disciples were *alone* in the house,
	10:10b they asked him again about this.
SEQUENCE — CONTENT$_1$ — orienter	10:11a He said to them,
CONCLUSION — CONSEQUENCE	10:11b "A man is committing adultery
condition — NUCLEUS$_1$	10:11c if he divorces his wife
NUCLEUS$_2$	10:11d and then marries another *woman*
grounds	10:11e because God considers he is still married to his first wife,
CONTENT$_2$ — CONSEQUENCE	10:12a and *God considers* a woman to be committing adultery
condition — NUCLEUS$_1$	10:12b if she divorces her husband
NUCLEUS$_2$	10:12c and marries another *man*."

NOTES

10:10a *alone* This is implied; it is supplied in NLT.

10:11e *because God considers he is still married to his first wife* This supplies the grounds for the statement in v. 11b–c. "God still considers the first marriage to be valid" (TN).

BOUNDARIES AND COHERENCE

The start of a new paragraph at v. 13 is indicated by the introduction of new participants (children) and a new topic (Jesus welcomes children). Coherence in the 1–12 paragraph is provided by three occurrences of ἀπολύω 'send away', two occurrences of 'Moses', and two occurrences of μοιχάω 'commit adultery'. Its coherence is also seen in the two paragraphs all being on the subject of divorce.

PROMINENCE AND THEME

The theme is drawn from a condensation of the CLAIM.

SCENE CONSTITUENT 10:13–16 (Episode of 9:30–10:31)

THEME: Jesus became indignant when he saw his disciples scolding people for bringing children for him to bless, because it is people who trust like children who will be part of God's rule.

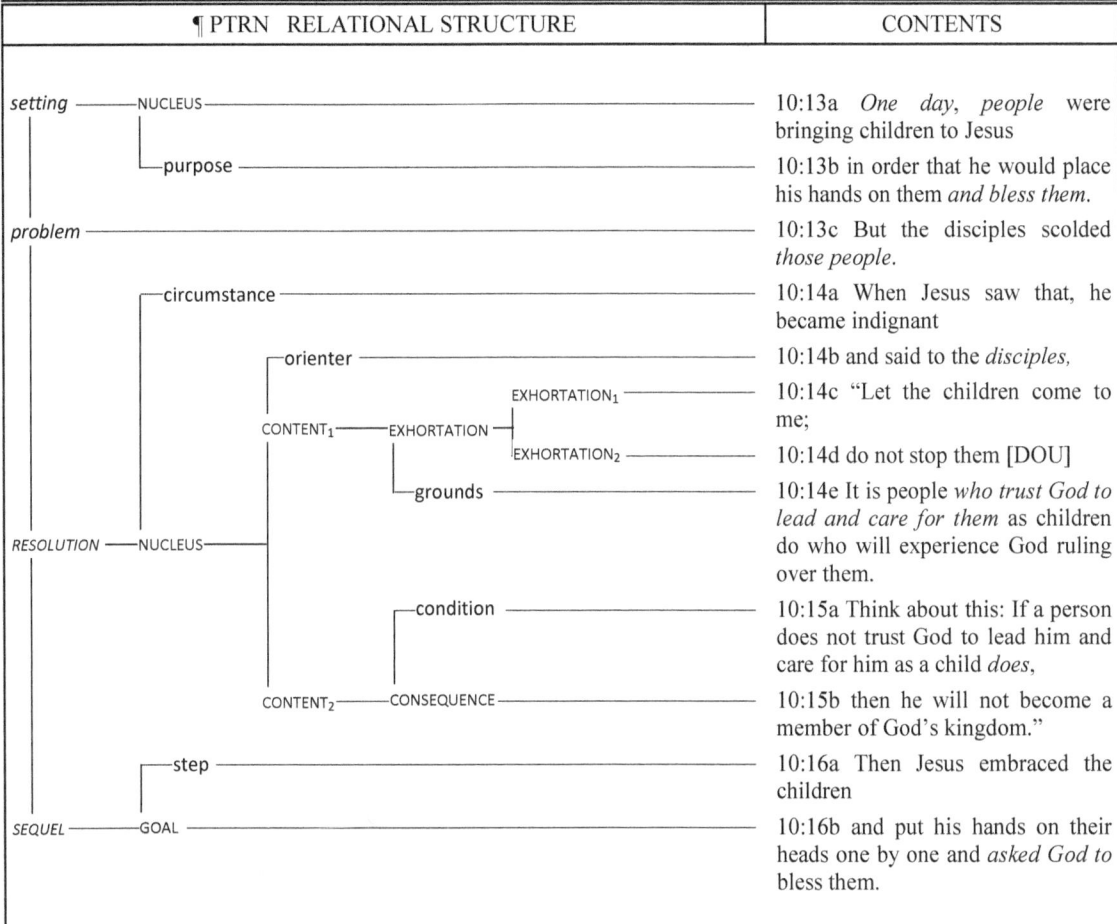

INTENT AND RHETORICAL STRUCTURE

This episode is the fifth of six in which Jesus teaches on various matters about his new order for God's ruling people. In this one, Jesus taught his disciples about trusting God to lead and care for them as a child does.

Mark here intends to inform the reader of how Jesus continued to prepare his disciples for his upcoming rejection, suffering, and return to life. This unit is a straight forward solutionality type narrative consisting of a *setting*, a *problem*, a RESOLUTION, and a SEQUEL.

NOTES

10:13a One day This gives the time setting; cf. NLT.

10:13b place his hands on them *and bless them* A host of commentators say that the Greek word ἅπτω 'touch' means to place one's hands on someone to bless that person; see also NLT and CEV.

10:13c scolded *those people* The original text has 'rebuked them', but some copyists changed it to 'rebuked those who brought them' to make clear who the 'them' referred to. This change is found in the KJV, and is implied anyway; thus the display supplies 'those people'.

10:14 c–d These two commands are considered a doublet; it is stated positively and then negatively to provide emphasis.

10:14e people *who trust God to lead and care for them* as children do who will experience God ruling over them This represents 'of such is the kingdom of God'. As previously, 'kingdom of God' is considered a metaphor referring to God's rule. But in the case of children, the point of comparison is considered to be leading, protecting, and taking care of (TN).

10:15a Think about this This represents 'I tell you truly', which is an idiomatic expression to emphasize what follows. See 9:41.

trust God to The text has 'receive the kingdom' but one cannot literally receive a kingdom; therefore 'trust God to'.

10:15b become a member of his kingdom The text has 'enter into', which "figuratively refers to belonging to God's kingdom" (TN).

10:16b *asked God to* **bless** See TN.

BOUNDARIES AND COHERENCE

A new paragraph starting at v. 7 is marked by the introduction of a new participant (a rich young man) and a new topic (riches). Coherence within the 13–16 paragraph is provided by two occurrences of παιδίον 'children' and two occurrences of 'kingdom of God', and by it being on the one topic of Jesus blessing little children.

PROMINENCE AND THEME

The theme is taken from a condensation of the two propositions of the *setting* and the *circumstance* of the RESOLUTION.

SCENE CONSTITUENT 10:17–31 (Episode of 9:30–10:31)

THEME: *A rich man ran to Jesus to ask what he should do in order to live eternally; After questioning the man, Jesus told him to sell all his possessions, which he refused to do, and the disciples were astonished that Jesus said that the rich had no advantage to be under God's rule.*

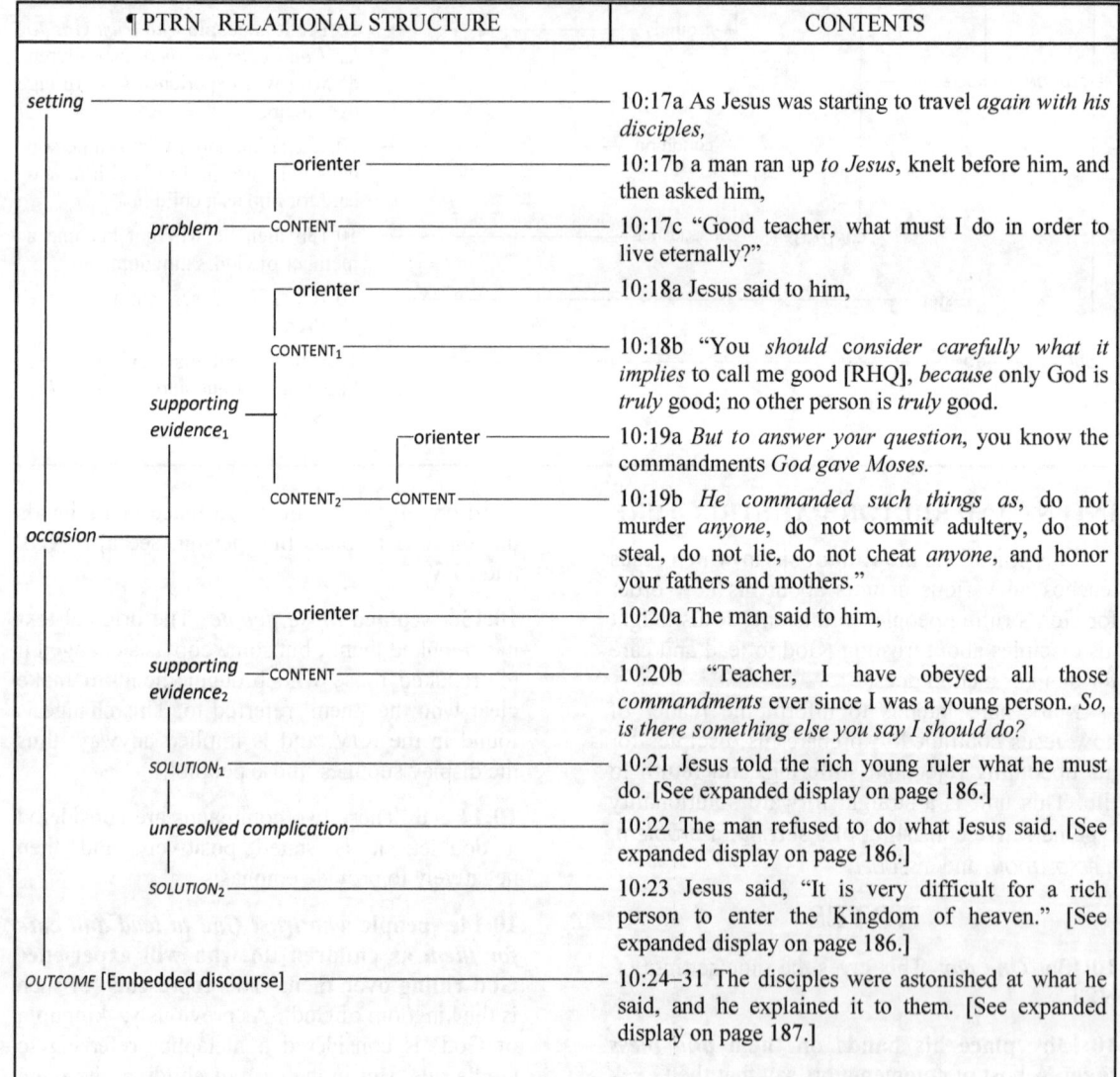

INTENT AND RHETORICAL STRUCTURE

This unit consists of *setting*, an *occasion*, and an OUTCOME, thus demonstrating that it is a narrative, and that the OUTCOME is the most prominent.

Mark here intends to inform the reader of how Jesus continued to prepare his disciples for his upcoming rejection, suffering, and return to life. This unit is a complex causality type narrative consisting of a *setting* (10:17a), an *occasion* with an embedded discourse (10:17b–23), and an OUTCOME also with an embedded discourse (10:24–31).

The embedded discourse of the *occasion* unit (10:17b–23) is a solutionality type exposition consisting of a *problem* (10:17b–c), a *supporting evidence*₁ (10:18–19)', a *supporting evidence*₂ (10:20), a SOLUTION₁ (10:21), an *unresolved complication* (10:22), and a SOLUTION₂ (10:23).

The embedded discourse of the OUTCOME unit (10:24–31) is also a solutionality type exposition consisting of a *problem* (10:24a), a *complication*₁ (10:24b–25), a *complication*₂ (10:26), a SOLUTION (10:27, and a *complication*₃ (10:28–31).

NOTES

10:17a *with his disciples* It is clear from v. 23 that Jesus was not traveling alone.

10:18b *should consider carefully what it implies* This represents a rhetorical question that begins with 'Why?' "It is a mild rebuke. It probably indicates that Jesus wanted the man to think about what it meant to say that Jesus was good" (TN; also Lenski).

10:19a *But to answer your question* Jesus' statement in 18b did not answer the man's question. The display makes clear that now Jesus will answer the question. NLT does likewise.

commandments *God gave Moses* The display specifies what commandments he was referring to.

10:19b *He commanded such things as* This is included to make clear that Jesus was not listing all the Ten Commandments. These commandments are cited from Ex. 20:3 and Deut. 5:17.

10:20b *So, is there something else you say I should do?* Commentaries support this. Hendriksen says, "He seems to be saying, 'What additional good deed must I be doing...?' "

EXPANSION OF SEQUENCES₄&₅ AND COMMENT 10:21–23 IN THE MARK 10:17–31 DISPLAY

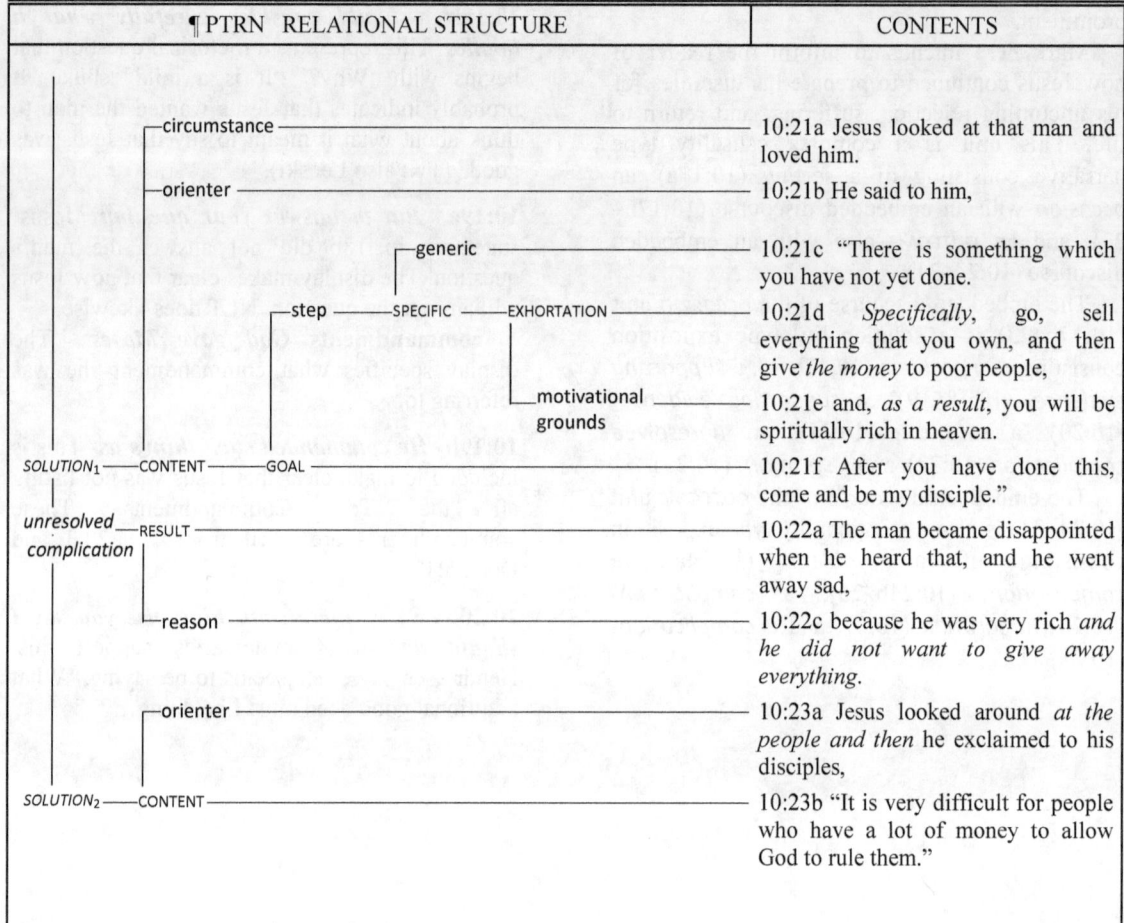

NOTES

10:21d give *the money* The text says 'give to the poor'; versions which supply 'money' include TEV, NLT, CEV, Beck, Williams, JB, and JBP.

10:21f come and be my disciple The text has 'come follow me'; but 'follow me' does not indicate what Jesus really meant. See note on 8:34.

10:22c *and he did not want to give away everything* The text says 'because he was very rich; but the reason he was sad was not that he was rich but that he did not want to part with his riches (see TN; Evans, Hiebert and Gould also sort of suggest the same thing).

10:23b to allow God to rule them Again, 'kingdom of God' is considered a metaphor, meaning 'God's rule', and entering the kingdom means "submitting to God's rule" (TRT).

EXPANSION OF OUTCOME 10:24–31 IN THE MARK 10:17–31 DISPLAY

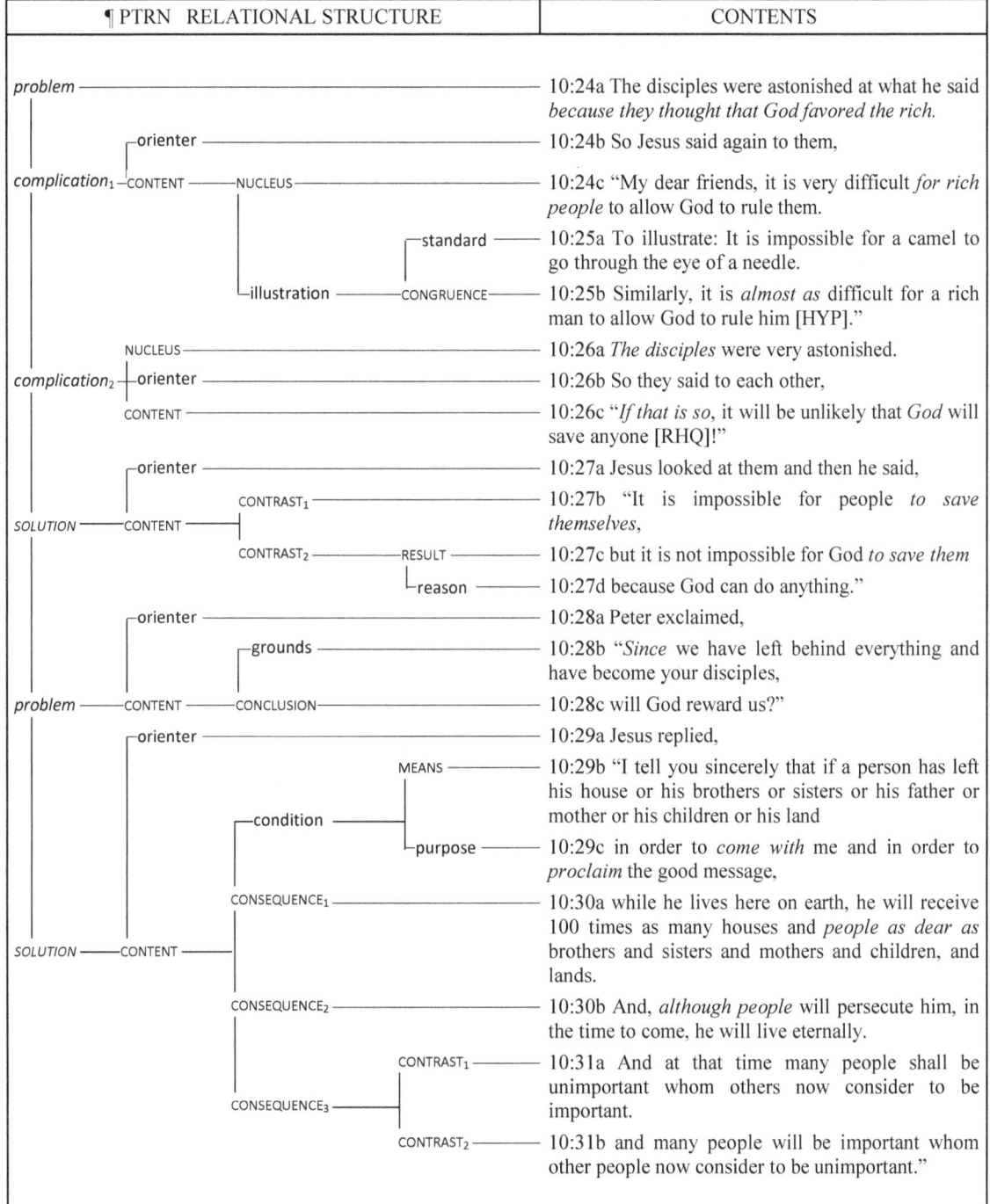

NOTES

10:24a *because they thought that God favored the rich* The first part of this implicit information is supported by the commentaries; e.g., Hendriksen "many people drew the wrong conclusion that individual prosperity was a sign of God's favor." The second part could be '*so, if the rich weren't able to go into God's kingdom, nobody could*'. the implied conclusion of the first part, and also explains 26b.

10:24c **My dear friends** The GNT has 'children' which is figurative, an expression for anyone "for whom there is a special relationship of endearment" (L&N).

difficult *for people* KJV follows some manuscripts which include the words 'for those who trust in riches' to make the statement fit the context better. The reading without those words is given a C rating.

10:25a–b *It is impossible...almost as difficult* Jesus' statement was hyperbole, to emphasize his point; camels do not go through eyes of needles. The display removes the hyperbole.

10:26c *If that is so* The Greek has 'And who can be saved?' Several versions have "Who then...?" but JB carries the force of the conjunction much more clearly with "In that case..."

it will be unlikely that anyone This is another rhetorical question. CEV conveys it with "How can...?" Some commentators (e.g., Hiebert, Hendriksen, Taylor) make it even stronger: 'then nobody can'.

10:27b **impossible for people** *to save themselves* The text has 'with men impossible' without specifying what is impossible. GW has the same wording as in the display.

10:28b **have become your disciples** The Greek has 'and followed you'; see note on 21d.

10:28c *will God reward us?* It seems clear that Peter's comment is more than just a statement of fact; cf. Matt 19:27; also Lane.

10:29c in order to come with me and in order to *proclaim* **the good message** See note on 8:35.

10:30a *people as dear as* **brothers** The text has 'a hundredfold... brothers...' which is hyperbole, speaking "about the extended family of the followers of Jesus" (France).

10:31a unimportant... important The text has 'first....last'. Lexicons (BAGD, L&N) make clear that the words mean 'most important...least important'.

BOUNDARIES AND COHERENCE

The start of a new paragraph at v. 32 is indicated by a change in location, and a new topic (another prediction of his death and resurrection). Coherence in the 17–31 paragraph is provided by two occurrences of 'kingdom of God' and occurrence of three terms denoting wealth. Coherence is also provided by the paragraph being on the topic of a rich young man asking Jesus about eternal life, Jesus' reply, and Jesus' subsequent interaction with his disciples on the subject of riches.

PROMINENCE AND THEME

The theme is taken from the *orienter* of the CONTENT of the *problem*, the EXHORTATION of the *step* of SOLUTION$_1$, of the RESULT of the *unresolved complication*, of the NUCLEUS and CONGRUENCE of *complication*$_1$ of the OUTCOME.

ACT CONSTITUENT 10:32–52 (Scene to Act II 9:30—10:52)

THEME: Jesus told them what was going to happen to him in Jerusalem. However, James and John asked to be the most important in his ruling kingdom. Then blind Bartimaeus asked Jesus to heal him, and Jesus enabled him to see again.

MACROSTRUCTURE	CONTENTS
occasion	10:32–34 As Jesus and his disciples and others were traveling toward Jerusalem, Jesus took the disciples aside and began to tell them again about what was going to happen to him.
OUTCOME₁	10:35–45 James and John requested to sit on the right and left of Jesus when he rules, and Jesus told them what will happen and how they should act.
OUTCOME₂	10:46–52 As Jesus passed by, a blind man called out asking Jesus to have mercy on him; Jesus called for him and healed him.

INTENT AND RHETORICAL STRUCTURE

This is the second episode cluster of ACT II in which even though Jesus explicitly taught his disciples that he must die in Jerusalem, they, even so, were vying for primary offices in his kingly rule.

In this cluster of episodes, Mark intends that the reader understand that Jesus and his disciples were journeying toward Jerusalem, and that Jesus taught his disciples about his coming suffering, dying, and return to life.

The structure of this unit consists of an initial *occasion* and TWO OUTCOMES. In all of the included episodes his disciples were involved, and Jesus spoke directly to his disciples.

BOUNDARIES AND COHERENCE

Both the initial and the closing boundaries coincide with the boundaries of the first and final included episodes. This unit is bound together by a series of teachings about Jesus' coming suffering and death in Jerusalem.

PROMINENCE AND THEME

The theme is a summary of the included episodes respecting the paragraph pattern prominence structure of this unit.

SCENE CONSTITUENT 10:32–34 (Episode of 10:32–52)

THEME: *As Jesus and his disciples and others were traveling toward Jerusalem, Jesus took the disciples aside and began to tell them again about what was going to happen to him.*

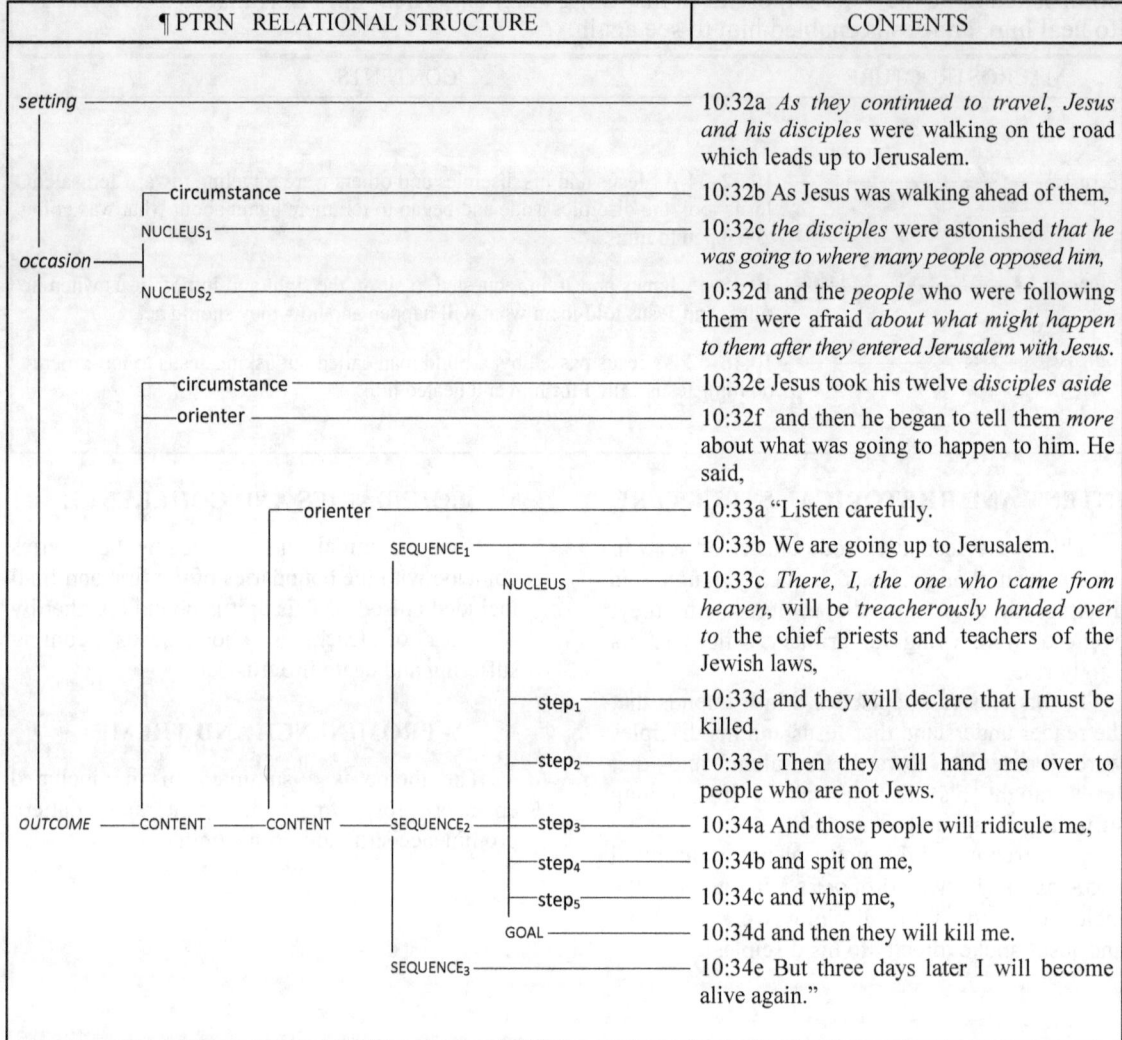

INTENT AND RHETORICAL STRUCTURE

This unit is a causality narrative consisting of a *setting*, an *occasion*, and an OUTCOME. This structure shows that this unit is a narrative.

Mark intends that the reader understand what he will suffer as the Messiah,

NOTES

10:32a *Jesus and the disciples* Again the display specifies the referent of the pronoun.

10:32c **astonished** *that he was going to where many people opposed him* Their astonishment is due to his "determined confrontation of the fate awaiting him in Jerusalem" (Gundry; see also TN).

10:32d **afraid** *about what might happen to them when they entered Jerusalem with Jesus* Hendriksen says they knew that "Going to Jerusalem in the company of Jesus is risky!"

10:32f *more* Jesus had already warned them once about what would happen to him in Jerusalem (8:35).

10:33c *I, the one who came from heaven* See note on 2:10.

treacherously *handed over to* The text has 'betrayed to'. 'Betray' means to "give someone to his enemies so that they can do whatever they want to him" (TN).

10:34e **three days later** KJV follows a few manuscripts which have 'on the third day' (as in

Matt. 20:19, Luke 18:33) instead of 'three days later'.

BOUNDARIES AND COHERENCE

The start of a new paragraph at v. 35 is marked by a request by two of his disciples. Coherence in the 32–34 paragraph is provided by two occurrences of the word 'Jerusalem', and by its being a second declaration by Jesus to his disciples of his coming death and resurrection.

PROMINENCE AND THEME

The theme is taken from the *setting*, the *circumstance* of the OUTCOME, and a very brief summary of the CONTENT of the OUTCOME.

SCENE CONSTITUENT 10:35–45 (Episode of 10:32–52)

THEME: James and John requested to sit on the right and left of Jesus when he rules, and Jesus told them what will happen and how they should act.

¶ PTRN RELATIONAL STRUCTURE	CONTENTS
setting — orienter	10:35a James and John, the sons of Zebedee, approached Jesus and said to him,
CONTENT	10:35b "Teacher, we want you to do something for us."
SEQUENCE — orienter	10:36a He said to them,
CONTENT	10:36b "What do you want me to do for you?"
problem — orienter	10:37a They said to him,
CONTENT — circumstance	10:37b "When *you rule* gloriously,
EXHORTATION	10:37c permit us *to sit* at your *most honored places: one* at your right side and one at your left side."
problem₁ — resolving incident — SEQUENCE₁ — orienter	10:38a But Jesus said to them,
CONTENT — MEANS	10:38b "You do not understand *what you must do*
purpose	10:38c *in order for me to grant* what you are requesting."
SEQUENCE₂ — orienter	10:38d *Then he asked them,*
CONTENT	10:38e "Will you be able to endure the kind of trials and suffering that I will endure?"
SEQUENCE₃ — orienter	10:39a They replied,
CONTENT	10:39b "*Yes,* we will be able *to do that.*"
RESOLUTION — orienter	10:39b Then Jesus said to them:
CONTENT — concession	10:39c "*It is true that* you will endure trials and suffering like I will endure.
CONTRA- EXPECTATION — RESULT	10:40a But it is not I who can permit you to sit where those *whom God will* honor the most *will sit, when I rule,*
reason	10:40b because *those places are* for those *people* for whom those places have been prepared."
problem₂ — reason	10:41a The *other* ten *disciples later* heard what James and John *had requested.*
RESULT	10:41b As a result, they were indignant *with them.*
RESOLUTION	10:42–45 Jesus explained more to his disciples. [See expansion on page 193.]

INTENT AND RHETORICAL STRUCTURE

In this unit, as in the previous episode, Mark comes back to Jesus telling his disciples in clear statements who he really is; the suffering, dying, and resurrecting savior of all humankind.

The basic communication relational structure of this unit consists of an *occasion* (10:35–40), and two OUTCOMES (10:41 and 10:42–45). This structure shows that this unit is a narrative and what its prominence structure is.

Mark intends that the reader understand that under God's ruling them the relationships between them should be of serving one another. There is a marked mismatch (skewing) between the basic structure and the meaning structure. Notice that according to the relational structure, one would expect this to be a causal type narrative, but the meaning structure as a solutionality type narrative accounts better for what is happening. There is a marked difference between the two outcomes, in that the second is more prominent than the first, and that the first supports the second. This unit is a solutionality type narrative consisting of a *problem*$_1$, a *problem*$_2$, and a RESOLUTION.

The *problem*$_1$ unit has an embedded narrative tied together by a long dialogue chain. This embedded narrative is a solutionality type consisting of a *setting* (10:35–36), a *problem* (10:37), a *resolving incident* (10:38–39b), and a RESOLUTION (10:39c–40).

Because of this unit's complex rhetorical structure, high prominence is focused on it. In the first half of the book there were no such complex structures. This seems to be a build up toward a climax in the book.

There are two motifs evident in this unit: 1) the 'rejection and suffering' motif in v, 38, and 2) the 'creating a new order' motif especially in vv. 42–45. This again brings marked focus on the unit.

NOTES

10:37b *you rule* **gloriously** The text has 'in your glory'; "This glory is that of the Messianic king" (Gould). Lenski and Swete point out that in the parallel passage in Matthew (20:20) the wording is 'in your kingdom'.

10:37c permit us *to sit* **at your** *most honored places:* **one** **at your right side and one at your left side** Most commentators agree that sitting on the right and the left side refers to the places of honor on each side of the royal throne.

10:38b–c *what you must do for me to grant what you are requesting* The text has 'You don't know what you are asking'. Jesus is saying that they had forgotten "that a request for glory is a request for suffering" (Hendriksen; see also Lane, France).

10:38e endure the kind of trials and suffering that I will endure The text has 'drink the cup that I drink'. This is a dead metaphor referring to his impending suffering; fourteen commentators support this interpretation. But all versions (except TfT) still retain the word 'cup'.

10:40a See note on 10:37c.

10:41a *other* **ten** *disciples later* **heard** The text has only 'the ten heard'; CEV has "the ten other disciples".

EXPANSION OF OUTCOME₂ 10:42–45 IN MARK 10:35–45 DISPLAY

RELATIONAL STRUCTURE	CONTENTS
orienter	10:42a Then, after Jesus called them all together, he said to them,
grounds₁ — CONTENT — orienter	10:42b "You know
SEQUENCE₁	10:42c that those non-Jewish people who rule others *enjoy* showing that they are powerful,
SEQUENCE₂	10:42d and that their high officials *enjoy* commanding *others to obey them*,
NEG EXHORTATION	10:43a but you should not act like them.
CONTENT — POS EXHORTATION — EXHORTATION₁ — condition	10:43b On the contrary, if anyone among you wants *God to consider him* to be great,
CONSEQUENCE	10:43c he must serve others;
EXHORTATION₂ — condition	10:44a and if anyone among you wants *God to consider him* to be the most important,
CONSEQUENCE	10:44b he must be *like* a slave to all others
grounds₂ — NEG NUCLEUS	10:45b because, *even though I am the one who has come from heaven*, I did not come for others to serve me;
POS NUCLEUS — MEANS	10:45c I came in order to serve *others* and to allow others to kill me,
purpose	10:45d in order that I will be a substitute to set *many people* free from being *condemned for their sins*."

NOTES

10:42c showing that they are powerful The GNT has 'lord it over them'; TN says the phrase here means "exercising control over others in a domineering or dictatorial way".

10:42d enjoy commanding *others to obey them* The text has 'exercise their authority over them'; NCV has "love to use all their authority" which is excellent; it is not just having authority, but loving to exercise it.

10:43a should not KJV, following the Textus Receptus, has the future tense "will not be" here. But even so, the future tense (i.e., a negative prohibition) is implied; cf. REB, CEV, NLT, JB, JBP, RSV.

10:43b wants *God to consider him* to be great The text has 'wants to be great' but the point is that greatness here is not as the world thinks of greatness, but what God considers to be greatness. Also in 44a.

10:44b *like* a slave This was not to be taken literally; a comparison is intended. NCV has "must serve all of you like a slave".

10:45b *even though I am the one who has come from heaven* This conveys the import of καί 'even'; Hendriksen says "he is the all-glorious one. Yet he humbles himself."

10:45d be a substitute to set many people free from being *condemned for their sins* This conveys 'as a ransom for many'. Originally the word λύτρον 'ransom' meant the price paid to secure the release of prisoners (Gundry, Hiebert, and Guelich), but came to mean 'redemption' or 'release' (THM). But release from what? Lenski says "Christ's ransom was paid for our sin and guilt;" hence from being condemned (or punished) for their sins.

BOUNDARIES AND COHERENCE

A new paragraph at v. 46 is indicated by a change in location and a new topic, the healing of a blind beggar. Coherence within the 35–45 unit is provided by two occurrences of the phrase 'right and left', two occurrences of ποτήριον 'cup', and two occurrences of the verb διακονέω 'serve' and one of the cognate noun διάκονος 'servant'. Coherence is also seen in the paragraph centering on the selfish request by James and John about occupying the most honored position with Jesus, the other disciples' reaction, and Jesus' statement that they needed to take lowly positions, not seek for the highest ones.

PROMINENCE AND THEME

The theme is drawn from the *orienter* (to identify the participants) and the two propositions of the *problem*, and the *orienter* and a condensation of the CONTENT of the RESOLUTION.

SCENE CONSTITUENT 10:46–52 (Episode of 10:32–52)

THEME: As Jesus passed by, a blind man called out asking Jesus to have mercy on him; Jesus called for him and healed him.

¶PTRN RELATIONAL STRUCTURE	CONTENTS
setting	10:46a *Jesus and his disciples* came to *the town of* Jericho.
problem — SIMULTANEOUS₁	10:46b Afterwards, while they were leaving Jericho along with a great crowd,
SIMULTANEOUS₂	10:46c a blind man *named* Bartimaeus, the son of Timaeus, who habitually begged *for money*, was sitting beside the road.
CIRCUMSTANCE	10:47a When he heard *people* say that Jesus, the man *who was from the town of* Nazareth, *was passing by*,
SIMULTANEOUS₃ — orienter	10:47b he shouted,
CONTENT	10:47c "Jesus, *you who are the Messiah* descended from *King David*, be merciful to me!"
complication — CONTRAST₁	10:48a Many *people* rebuked him and told him that he should be quiet.
orienter	10:48b But he shouted even more,
CONTRAST₂ — CONTENT	10:48c "You *who are the Messiah* descended from *King David*, be merciful to me *and help me*!
orienter	10:49a Jesus stopped *and* said *to someone*,
resolving incident₁ — SEQUENCE₁ — CONTENT	10:49b "Call him *to come over here*!"
orienter	10:49c The people there summoned the blind man, saying,
SEQUENCE₂ — CONTENT	10:49d "Cheer up and get up, because he is calling you!"
step	10:50a The blind man threw off his cloak *so that he could run faster*.
resolving incident₂ — GOAL	10:50b He jumped up and came to Jesus.
orienter	10:51a Jesus asked him,
move₁ — CONTENT	10:51b "What do you want me to do for you?"
orienter	10:51c The blind man said,
move₂ — CONTENT	10:51d "Master, *I want you to enable me* to see."
orienter	10:52a *Jesus said to him*,
move₃ — CONTENT	10:52b "You may go. *I am* healing you because you believed *in me*."
RESOLUTION — ACCOMPLISHMENT — OUTCOME₁	10:52c He could see immediately,
OUTCOME₂	10:52d and he went with *Jesus* along the road.

INTENT AND RHETORICAL STRUCTURE

The author here intends that the reader understand that although the man was blind, he knew that Jesus was the promised ruling Messiah, and after Jesus healed him, he went with Jesus.

This unit is a solutionality type narrative consisting of a *problem*, a *complication*, a *resolving incident₁*, a *resolving incident₂*, and a RESOLUTION.

NOTES

10:47c *you who are the Messiah descended from King David* The GNT reads 'Son of David'. The Greek word 'Son' here means 'descendant'. 'David' refers to King David. But 'Son of David' was a Messianic title (so 11 commentators examined). No versions (except TfT) make that clear; all translate it literally.

10:48c *be merciful to me and help me* The GNT has only 'be merciful to me'; the words 'and help me' make more specific what the man wanted.

10:50a *so that he could run faster* This may be needed if readers do not know why he threw down his cloak.

10:51d *I want you to enable me to see* The text has 'that I may see'; the display makes it a full sentence. The verb ἀναβλέπω can mean either "to see or 'to regain one's sight'" (BAGD). Versions are divided.

10:52b *I am healing you because you believed in me* The text has 'your faith has healed you' which is a personification; Jesus was the healer. The display follows the second suggested translation in TN.

10:52d *went with Jesus* As before, in the N.T. 'follow' usually means 'to accompany'; see note on 1:18.

BOUNDARIES AND COHERENCE

A new paragraph at 11:1 is marked by a further change in location and a new topic, Jesus' entry into Jerusalem. Coherence within the 10:46–52 unit is provided by three occurrences of τυφλός 'blind man' and two occurrences of the phrase ἐλεέω 'pity me'. It is also provided by it being one problem-RESOLUTION episode of Jesus healing blind Bartimaeus.

PROMINENCE AND THEME

The theme is taken from a condensation of the TWO SIMULTANEOUS propositions of the *problem*, the *orienter* and CONTENT of SIMULTANEOUS₃, the CONTENT of *resolving incident₁*, and a rephrasing of *move₃* of the RESOLUTION.

PART CONSTITUENT 11:1—13:37 (Act III of Part II 8:31—16:8)

THEME: When Jesus entered Jerusalem as Israel's king, he had a final conflict with the Jewish authorities. Then, he foretold what would happen to Jerusalem before he returned later.

MACROSTRUCTURE	CONTENTS
occasion	11:1—12:12 Jesus entered Jerusalem as a king, cursed Israel (symbolized by the fig tree), cleansed the temple. The Jewish authorities asked Jesus by what authority he had done these things. When the fig tree that Jesus cursed withered, Jesus taught his disciples to expect God to do what they asked him to do.
OUTCOME₁	12:13–44 Jesus had a final conflict with the Jewish authorities, and warned his disciples to not follow the haughty way of these authorities.
OUTCOME₂	13:1–37 Jesus foretold events that will happen to Jerusalem and the temple, and warned his disciples to always believe him and be ready for his return.

INTENT AND RHETORICAL STRUCTURE

This ACT III (11:1—13:37) is the third unit of the second book of Mark (8:31—16:18). Mark presents, here, that Jesus and his disciples enter Jerusalem as Israel's popular king, and prophesied about the future of the city and its inhabitants.

The paragraph structure consists of an *occasion* and two OUTCOMES.

BOUNDARIES AND COHERENCE

Both the initial and the closing boundaries coincide with the boundaries of the first and final included episodes. The scope of this unit is that Jesus demonstrates to his disciples that he controls and knows all about what will happen to Jerusalem, the temple, and its inhabitants.

PROMINENCE AND THEME

The theme consists of a summary of the three structural units maintaining structural prominence.

ACT CONSTITUENT 11:1—12:12 (Scene of 11:1—13:37)

THEME: *Jesus entered Jerusalem as a king, cursed Israel (symbolized by the fig tree), cleansed the temple. The Jewish authorities asked Jesus by what authority he had done these things. When the fig tree that Jesus cursed withered, Jesus taught his disciples to expect God to do what they asked him to do.*

MACROSTRUCTURE	CONTENTS
occasion₁	11:1–11 Jesus sent two disciples to get a young donkey, which they brought to him; then people threw their cloaks on it, and Jesus mounted it and rode to Jerusalem with people shouting praise to him.
occasion₂	11:12–14 Jesus cursed the fig tree as a sign of what would happen to the people of Israel.
OUTCOME₁	11:15–19 Jesus and his disciples went to the temple in Jerusalem, and there Jesus expelled those who were buying and selling goods in the temple and taught that the temple was to be a place of prayer. These actions angered the priests and teachers of the Jewish laws who, then, looked for a way to kill Jesus.
OUTCOME₂	11:20–25 The next day when Jesus and his disciples passed the fig tree that Jesus had cursed, they saw that it had withered. Jesus used this as an illustration for trusting God to answer prayer.
SEQUEL	11:27—12:12 The chief priests, teachers of the Jewish laws and elders asked Jesus by what authority he was doing these things. He, then, asked them a question which they would not answer; so he did not answer theirs.

INTENT AND RHETORICAL STRUCTURE

This is the first of three episode clusters included in ACT III, where Mark presents that Jesus entered Jerusalem, and prophesized about the future of the city and its inhabitants. In this unit Mark gives the details of Jesus entering Jerusalem. This unit consists of *two occasions* and THREE OUTCOMES.

Mark presents the structure of this unit (11:1—12:12) as follows[2]:

[A] Jesus entered Jerusalem as the *people acclaim* him to be the Messiah (11:1–11)
  [B] Jesus cursed the *fig tree* (11:12–14) figuratively cursing Israel.
    [C] Jesus cast out all the temple merchants (11:15–19)
  [B'] The *fig tree* withered and died (11:20–25) figuratively prophesying Israel's future
[A'] Jesus left Jerusalem, after the *Jewish authorities rejected* Jesus by asking him by what authority he was doing these things (11:26—12:12)

Here a chiastic structure focuses prominence on the [C] central unit.

---

[2] Edwards recognizes the inclusio represented here as ['B,C,B'].

BOUNDARIES AND COHERENCE

Both the initial and the closing boundaries coincide with the boundaries of the first and final included episodes. In this unit Mark presents the details of Jesus and his disciples entering Jerusalem,

PROMINENCE AND THEME

The theme statement is derived from a summary of the included units reflecting the prominence of the chiastic structure.

SCENE CONSTITUENT 11:1–11 (Episode of 11:1—12:12)

THEME: Jesus sent two disciples to get a young donkey, which they brought to him; then people threw their cloaks on it, and Jesus mounted it and rode to Jerusalem with people shouting praise to him.

¶PTRN STRUCTURE	CONTENTS
setting	11:1a When they came near to Jerusalem, *they came* to *the villages of* Bethphage and Bethany near Olive *Tree Hill*.
occasion	11:1b–3 Jesus sent two disciples to bring a young donkey to him. [See expanded display on page 198.]
OUTCOME₁	11:4–7a The two disciples went and brought back a young donkey to him. [See expanded display on page 199.]
OUTCOME₂	1:8–11a Jesus and many people had a procession into Jerusalem proclaiming him the Messiah. [See expanded display on page 199.]
OUTCOME₃	11:11b–f Jesus entered Jerusalem and the temple area. He had a good look around, then left for Bethany where he and his disciples spent the night.[See expanded display on page 199.]

INTENT AND RHETORICAL STRUCTURE

Here, Mark presents Jesus entering Jerusalem acclaimed by the people as the Messiah King of Israel.

The author here intends that the reader understand that the people thought Jesus was going to Jerusalem to become their Messiah King to deliver them from Roman rule.

This unit is causality type narrative consisting of a *setting*, an *occasion*, and FOUR OUTCOMES.

NOTES

11:1a *villages of* **Bethphage and Bethany** The display identifies these as villages, as does Hiebert. TEV and NLT say they are towns.

Olive *Tree Hill* TN says it was a hill, and "people called it the Mount of Olives because it had olive trees growing on it".

EXPANSION OF OCCASION 11:1b–3d IN MARK 11:1–11 DISPLAY

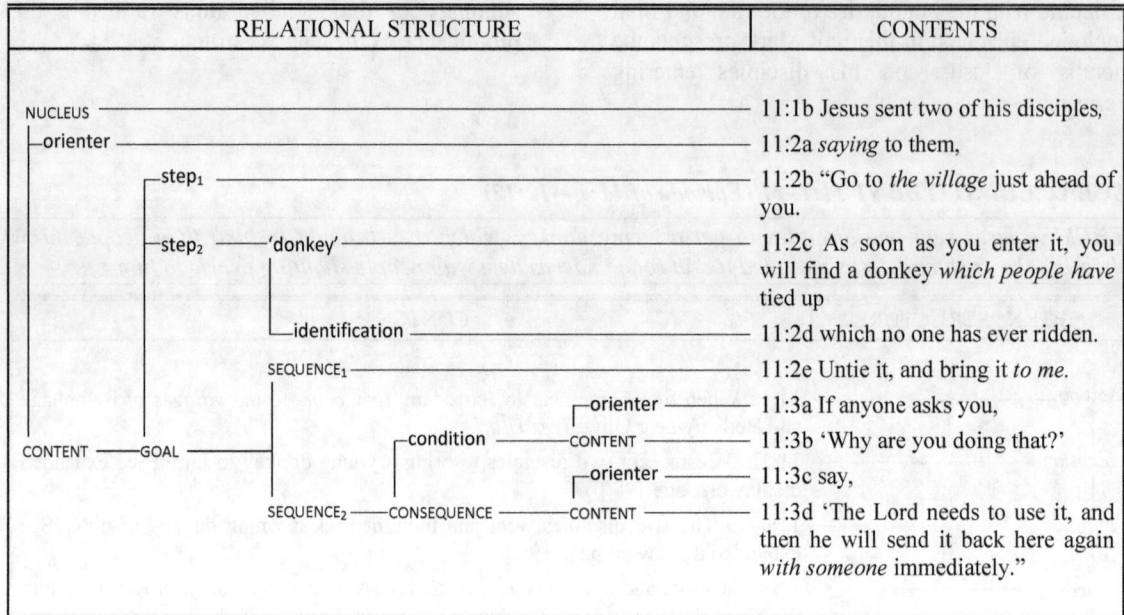

NOTES

11:2c a donkey The GNT says 'colt', which in Biblical times could refer to the young of several animals. However, the parallel passages in Matthew and John specify that it was a donkey.

EXPANSION OF OUTCOME₁₋₃ AND GOAL 11:4–11 IN MARK 11:1–11
DISPLAY

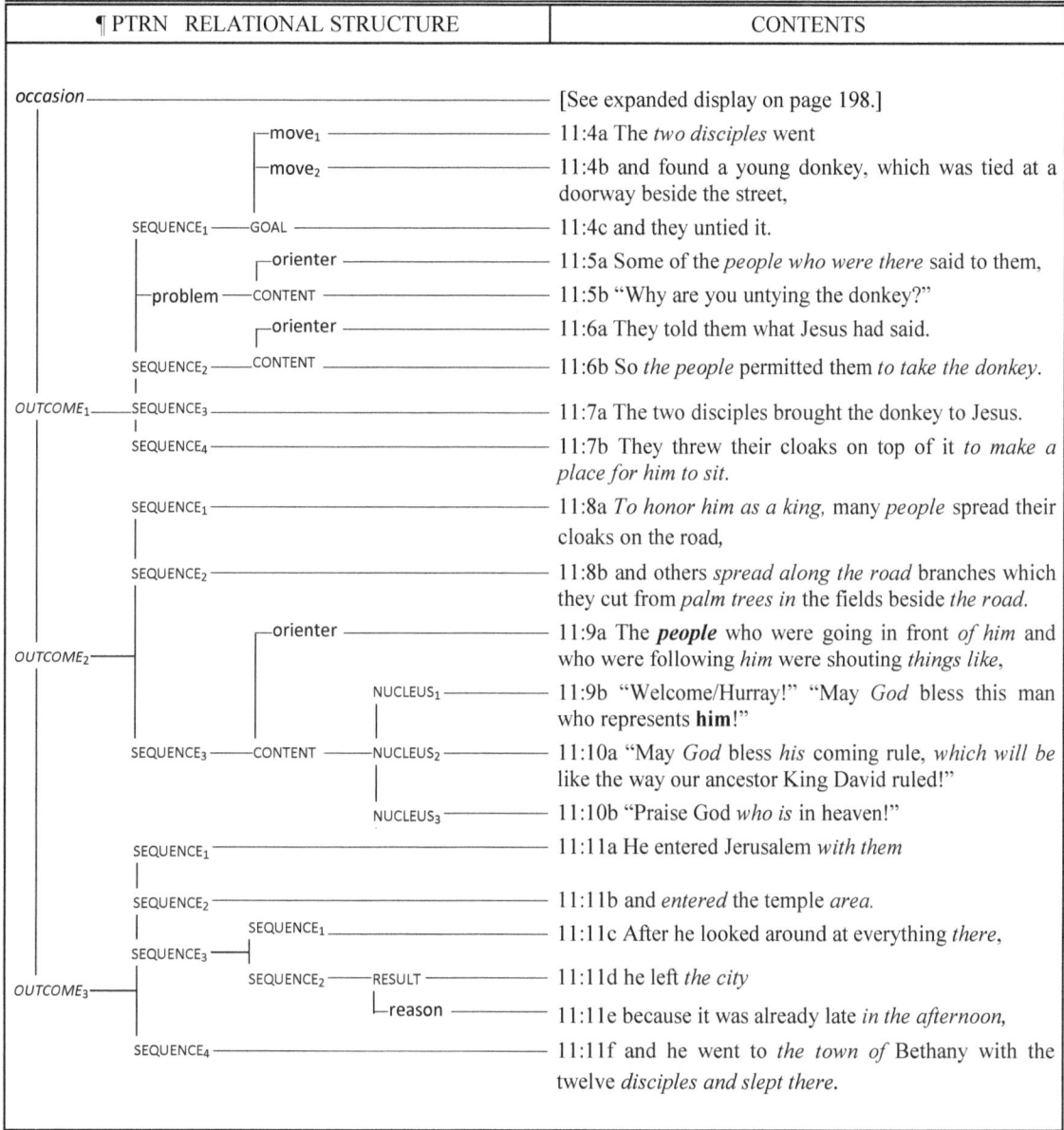

NOTES

11:7b *to make a place for him to sit* The italicized words indicate the purpose of the action.

11:8a *To honor him as a king* These words indicate the function of the actions of v. 8a–b.

11:8b **cut from** *palm trees* Lenski, THM and TRT say these were palm fronds.

11:9a *things like* These words are included to indicate that various ones shouted various things.

11:9b **Welcome/Hurray!** Many commentators agree that the word 'Hosanna' is an expression of praise, but others also add that it was a shout of welcome to the pilgrims coming to Jerusalem for a festival.

this man who represents <u>him</u> The GNT has 'him who comes in the name of the Lord'. Both THM and TRT say this means "the one who represents the Lord". Commentators are divided as to whether the expression means 'God has blessed' or 'may God bless'; most versions have chosen the latter.

11:10a *his* **coming rule**, *which will be* **like the way our ancestor** *King* **David ruled** The Greek text has 'the coming kingdom of our father David'. As before, 'kingdom' is considered a figure of speech indicating 'rule'. 'Father' here means 'ancestor' (as in CEV, NLT). 'David' is identified as King David.

11:10b Praise God *who is* in heaven The text has 'Hosanna in the highest'. For 'Hosanna' see the note on 9b. Some commentators say this is a prayer for God to save the nation, but it seems best to say that 'Hosanna' has the same meaning here as in 9b (so THM). 'In the highest' is a metonymy, standing for the one who is in the highest place, i.e., who is in heaven (BAGD, NCV, NLT, CEV).

11:11b the temple *area* This was the area surrounding the temple (BAGD, L&N), not the temple itself.

11:11e late *in the afternoon* The GNT has 'the hour was late', which meant 'late in the day' (so TEV, CEV, JBP.) NLT has "late in the afternoon".

11:11f *and slept there* This is implied from the next verse.

BOUNDARIES AND COHERENCE

A new paragraph at v. 12 is indicated by a change in time and location, and a new topic: the cursing of the fig tree. Coherence within the 1–11 paragraph is seen in four occurrences of πῶλος 'colt', two of ἱμάτιον 'garments', and two of λύω 'untie'. Coherence is also seen in its being the one episode of Jesus entering Jerusalem on a donkey.

PROMINENCE AND THEME

The theme is taken from the NUCLEUS in v. 1b, an abbreviation of *step*$_1$ in v. 2b, *step*$_3$, and a summary of SEQUENCE$_3$ in *step*$_4$.

SCENE CONSTITUENT 11:12–14 (Episode of 11:1—12:12)

¶PTRN RELATIONAL STRUCTURE	CONTENTS
THEME: *Jesus cursed the fig tree as a sign of what would happen to the people of Israel.*	
setting	11:12 The next day, as *Jesus and his disciples* were leaving Bethany, Jesus was hungry.
⎡ step₁	11:13a He saw from a distance a fig tree which was covered with leaves, *so it should have had figs on it.*
⎢ step₂	11:13b So he went *to it in order to see* if he could find any *figs* on it.
problem ⎯ NEG GOAL ⎯ RESULT	11:13c But when he came to it, he found only leaves on it.
⎣ reason	11:13d This was because it was not *yet* time when *normal* fig trees have figs.
⎡ orienter	11:14a *To illustrate how God would soon punish the nation of Israel,* he said to it,
RESOLUTION ⎯ CONTENT	11:14b "No one shall ever eat figs from you again *because you will no longer bear figs.*"
COMMENT	11:14c The disciples heard *what he said.*

INTENT AND RHETORICAL STRUCTURE

This is the second of five episodes that form a chiastic structure in the ACT about Jesus going to Jerusalem, telling about his activities and teachings concerning Jerusalem. Here, Mark presents Jesus returning to Jerusalem and finding no fruit on a fig tree. Jesus then says that the tree will never bear fruit again. This was said as a prophecy regarding the nation of Israel.

The paragraph pattern structure of this unit consists of a *setting* (11:12), a *problem* (11:13), a RESOLUTION (11;14a–b), and a COMMENT (11:14c).

The author intends that the reader understand that Jesus used the fig tree as a parable of what will happen to the nation of Israel.

This second episode (11:12–14) is paired with the fourth episode (11:20–25) in the chiasmus.

NOTES

11:13a *so it should have had figs on* Hendriksen says, it "was most likely in full foliage, and could therefore be expected to have fruit."

11:13d *not yet* The normal time for ripe figs was June, and this was still late March or early April.

11:14a *To illustrate how God would soon punish the nation of Israel, he said to it* Hendriksen says, "He was predicting the downfall of unfruitful Israel." Without such an explanation of Jesus words, it appears that Jesus was just expressing his anger at not finding any figs to eat.

11:14b *because you will no longer bear figs* The text says 'may no one any longer eat your fruit'. But this is a metonymy, the effect standing for the cause: it "means that the tree would never again produce fruit" (TN).

BOUNDARIES AND COHERENCE

A new paragraph at v. 15 is marked by a change in location and a new topic: chasing money-changers and sellers out of the temple. Coherence within the 12–14 paragraph is seen in occurrences of συκῆ 'fig tree' and καρπός 'fruit', and two occurrences of φύλλον 'leaves'. Coherence is also seen in it being the account of Jesus cursing the unfruitful fig tree.

PROMINENCE AND THEME

The theme is taken from the *orienter* in 14a, plus the implied connotation of the RESOLUTION in 14b.

SCENE CONSTITUENT 11:15–19 (Episode of 11:1—12:12)

THEME: Jesus and his disciples went to the temple in Jerusalem, and there Jesus expelled those who were buying and selling goods in the temple and taught that the temple was to be a place of prayer. These actions angered the priests and teachers of the Jewish laws who, then, looked for a way to kill Jesus.

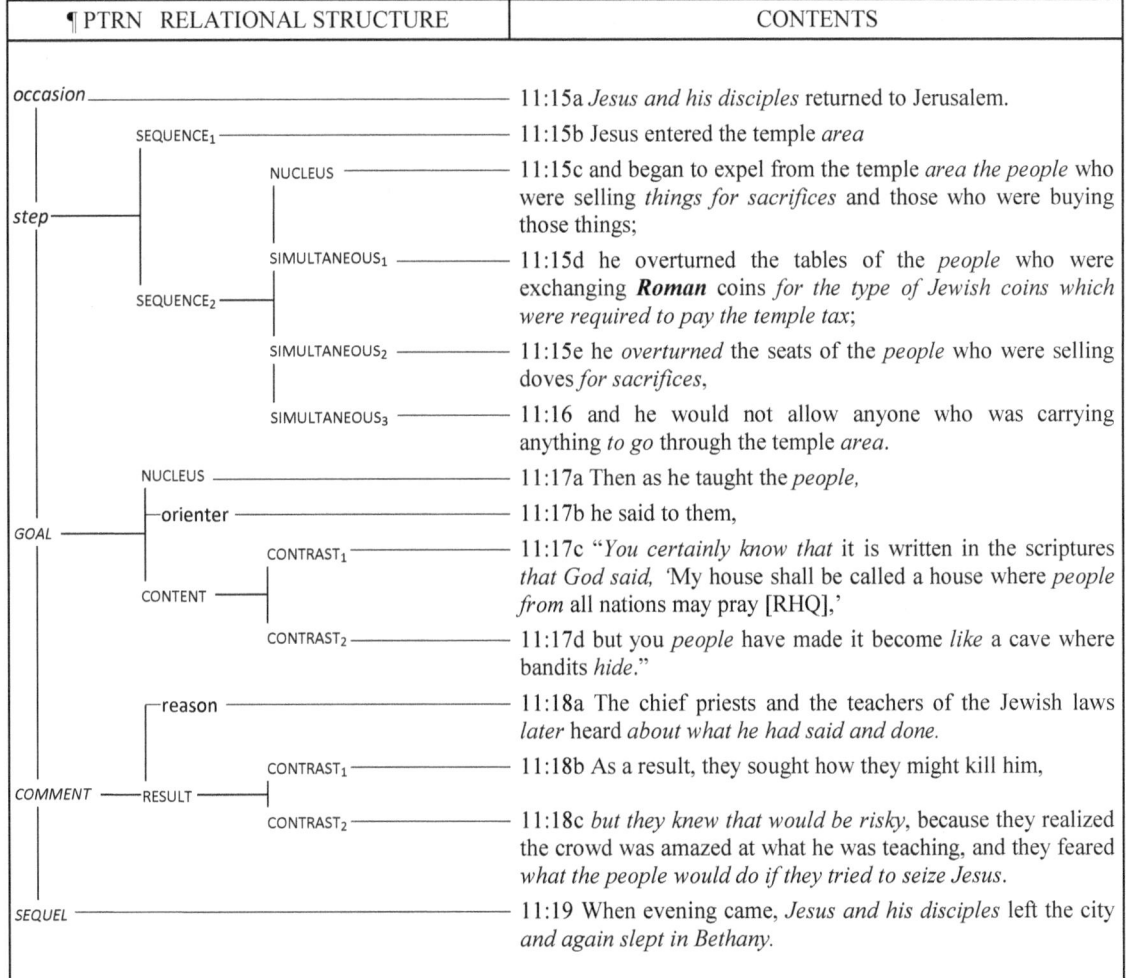

INTENT AND RHETORICAL STRUCTURE

This is the third and middle episode of the five that form a chiastic structure in the ACT about Jesus going to Jerusalem, telling about his activities and teachings concerning Jerusalem. Here, Mark presents Jesus expelling all the merchants from the temple compound. This is the focal episode of this chiasmus and the ACT unit.

The paragraph pattern structure of this unit consists of a *setting* (v. 15a), a *step* (vv. 15b–16), a GOAL (v. 17), an OUTCOME (v. 18), and a SEQUEL (v. 19). This structure demonstrates that the unit is an objective type narrative with a GOAL, a COMMENT, and a SEQUEL as the naturally prominent units.

The author intends that the reader understand that Jesus drove out the merchants from the temple area, thus enraging the Jewish authorities to the point of them making plans to kill Jesus.

The motif of 'praying' to God is explicitly stated in the prominent unit of the GOAL in v. 15.

NOTES

11:15c selling *things for sacrifices* See Gould, Lane, Swete, Taylor, and THM. These things would include salt, olive oil, wine, and animals.

11:15d exchanging <u>Roman</u> coins *for the type of Jewish coins which were required to pay the temple tax* The Greek word is κολλυβιστής 'moneychangers'. For the meaning of the word see THM and Hiebert.

11:15e doves *for sacrifices* See Gould, Lane, THM, and Guelich.

11:17c *You certainly know that* The text here has a rhetorical question, 'Is it not written…?' which functions as an emphatic positive statement. CEV, NLT, and TEV render it as a positive statement. Jesus was referring to Is. 56:7.

11:17d bandits *hide* CEV renders the genitive phrase 'den of robbers' as "a place where robbers hide". The word λῃστής means more 'bandit' than 'robber'.

11:18a heard *about what he had said and done* The GNT text has only 'heard' but the display supplies the content. NLT has "heard what Jesus had done".

11:18b *were very angry at this challenge to their authority* This is the implied reason for their desire to kill him; cf. Hiebert, Strauss.

11:18c *but they knew that would be risky* The GNT here begins with γάρ 'because' followed by 'they were afraid', which does not cohere semantically as introducing the reason for what precedes it. The words in italics supply the implied result for the reason that follows: they knew it would be difficult because the crowds were amazed at Jesus' teaching.

they feared *what the people would do if they tried to seize* Jesus The text says 'they were afraid of him', but afraid of what? Gundry suggests "Because disturbing the crowd by arresting him might incite a riot," and in the context, this seems to be correct.

11:19 *Jesus and his disciples* left the city *and again slept in Bethany* See note on 1:11f. The KJV has a singular verb 'he left', but it is clearly implied that Jesus <u>and</u> the disciples left Jerusalem.

BOUNDARIES AND COHERENCE

A new paragraph at v. 20 is marked by a change in time and a new topic: praying in faith. Coherence within the 15–19 paragraph is provided by two occurrences of ἱερόν 'temple' and two occurrences of πωλέω 'selling'. Coherence is also provided by the paragraph telling of Jesus 'cleansing' the temple, and the reaction of the Jewish leaders to his doing that.

PROMINENCE AND THEME

The theme is taken from the *setting* in 15a, the NUCLEUS of SEQUENCE$_1$ of the *step*, the NUCLEUS of the *GOAL*, CONTRAST$_1$ of the CONTENT of the *GOAL*, and CONTRAST$_1$ of the OUTCOME.

SCENE CONSTITUENT 11:20–25 (Episode of 11:1—12:12)

THEME: *The next day when Jesus and his disciples passed the fig tree that Jesus had cursed, they saw that it had withered. Jesus used this as an illustration for trusting God to answer prayer.*

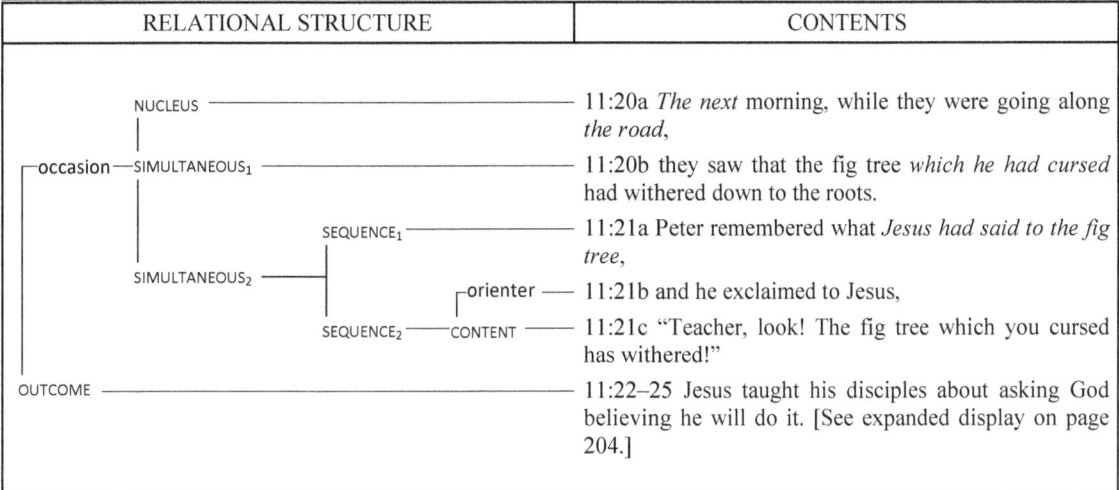

RELATIONAL STRUCTURE	CONTENTS
NUCLEUS	11:20a *The next* morning, while they were going along the road,
occasion—SIMULTANEOUS₁	11:20b they saw that the fig tree *which he had cursed* had withered down to the roots.
SIMULTANEOUS₂ — SEQUENCE₁	11:21a Peter remembered what *Jesus had said to the fig tree*,
orienter	11:21b and he exclaimed to Jesus,
SEQUENCE₂ — CONTENT	11:21c "Teacher, look! The fig tree which you cursed has withered!"
OUTCOME	11:22–25 Jesus taught his disciples about asking God believing he will do it. [See expanded display on page 204.]

INTENT AND RHETORICAL STRUCTURE

The author intends that the reader understand that Jesus used the fig tree incident to teach the disciples that they must believe that God will do what they ask for.

This unit is a causality type narrative consisting of a *occasion* and an OUTCOME.

NOTES

11:20a *The next* **morning** The text has only 'early' which means 'the next morning' (NLT, CEV) or 'early the next morning'.

11:20b **tree** *which he had cursed* The display specifies what tree was being referred to.

11:21a **remembered what** *Jesus had said to the fig tree* All the text has is 'Peter remembered', which requires some semantic content. TEV has "remembered what had happened", and CEV supplies "what Jesus had said to the tree".

EXPANSION OF OUTCOME 11:22–25 IN MARK 11:20–25 DISPLAY

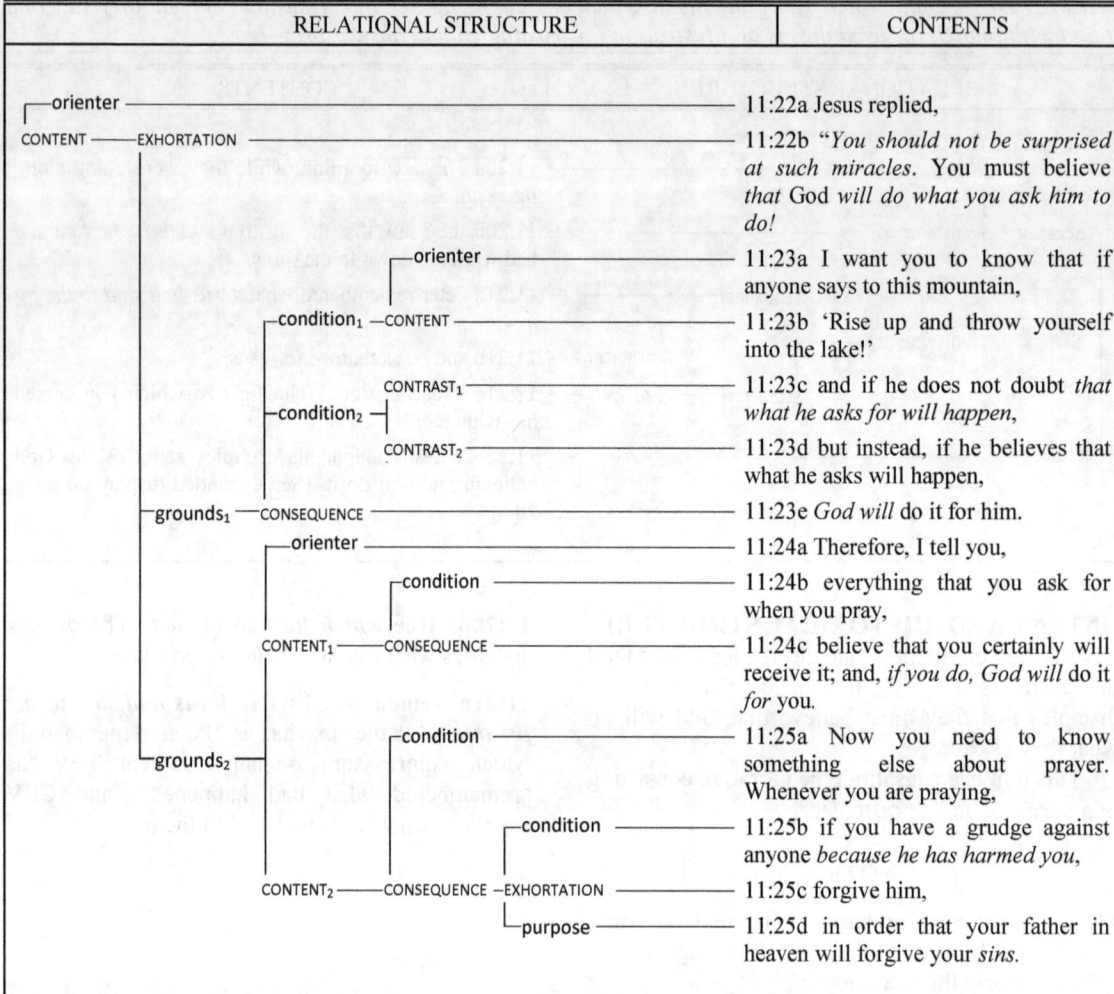

NOTES

11:22b *You should not be surprised at such miracles* The GNT has only 'have faith in God'. What the disciples said (v. 12) obviously expresses their surprise. Jesus' reply here is both a rebuke to the disciples with this implied negative command plus the stated positive command: 'You shouldn't be surprised; on the contrary, you should…' Commentaries do not recognize this.

believe *that* **God** *will do what you ask him to* All Jesus said was 'have faith of God', but in the context, which is not about faith in general, it means exactly what these implied words say; cf. suggestion in TN. Some manuscripts have the sentence introduced by 'if', and this shows up in TEV, but the form without 'if' is given a B 'almost certain' rating.

11:23a I want you to know This represents 'I tell you truly'; see note on 9:41.

doubt *that what he asks for will happen* 'Doubt' semantically requires a content of what is doubted. See suggestion in TN.

11:25a *Now there is something* **else** *you need know about prayer* The conjunction καί 'and' introduces a completely different comment about prayer. The display states this clearly.

11:26 There is very poor support for the inclusion of this verse, which was added due to influence from Matt. 6:15.

BOUNDARIES AND COHERENCE

A new paragraph as v. 27 is marked by a change in location and a couple questions hurled at Jesus by the Jewish religious leaders. Coherence within the 20–25 paragraph is provided by two further occurrences of 'fig tree', two of ῥίζα 'withered', two of the verb πιστεύω 'believe', and one of the cognate noun πίστις 'faith'. Coherence is also provided by the paragraph consisting solely of Jesus' teaching on praying with faith and with forgiveness.

PROMINENCE AND THEME

The theme is taken from the NUCLEUS in v. 20a to give an orientation regarding the time of this interchange, SIMULTANEOUS₁ of the OCCASION, the *orienter* of the OUTCOME, and a rephrasing of the EXHORTATION in v. 22b.

SCENE CONSTITUENT 11:27—12:12 (Episode of 11:1—12:12)

THEME: *The chief priests, teachers of the Jewish laws and elders asked Jesus by what authority he was doing these things. He, then, asked them a question which they would not answer; so he did not answer theirs. Instead Jesus accused the Jewish authorities of planning to kill him.*

¶PTRN RELATIONAL STRUCTURE	CONTENTS
setting — circumstance — SIMULTANEOUS	11:27a Jesus and his disciples arrived in Jerusalem again.
	11:27b While Jesus was walking in the temple *area, some of* the chief priests, teachers of the Jewish laws, and elders came to him
problem — orienter — CONTENT — NUCLEUS₁	11:27c and said to him,
	11:28a "By whose authority are you doing these things?
NUCLEUS₂	11:28b Who authorized you to do things like those you did here yesterday?"
complication — problem — orienter — CONTENT₁ — SEQUENCE₁	11:29a Jesus said to them,
	11:29b "I will ask you something, and then,
condition	11:29c if you answer me,
SEQUENCE₂ — CONSEQUENCE	11:29d I will tell you who authorized me to do these things.
CONTENT₂	11:30 Did God or people authorize John to baptize people? Answer me [MTY]."
NEG RESOLUTION	11:31–33b The authorities did not answer because they feared the people. [See expanded display on page 207.]
NEG RESOLUTION	11:33c–d Jesus did not answer their question either. [See expanded display on page 208.]
POSITIVE RESOLUTION	12:1–11 Jesus told the Jewish authorities a parable accusing them of wanting to kill him.. [See expanded display on page 208.]
OUTCOME	12:12 The Jewish authorities knew that Jesus was teaching about them, but because of fear of the people they did nothing. [See expanded display on page 211.]

INTENT AND RHETORICAL STRUCTURE

This is the last of five episodes that form a chiastic structure in the ACT about Jesus going to Jerusalem, telling about his activities and teachings concerning Jerusalem. Here, Mark presents Jesus in sharp opposition to the Jewish authorities by them questioning Jesus about his expelling the merchants from the temple area, upon which Jesus tells them a parable about the vineyard tenants killing the son, the heir of the vineyard.

The basic communication relational structure of this unit consists of a *circumstance*, THREE SEQUENCES, and an OUTCOME. This structure demonstrates that the unit is a narrative one.

The author, here, intends that the reader understand that the Jewish authorities were very angry with Jesus and questioned him as to who gave him the authority to expel the merchants from the temple area.

This unit is a solutionality type narrative consisting of a *setting/problem*, a NEG-RESOLUTION, a POSITIVE RESOLUTION, and an OUTCOME.

The POSITIVE RESOLUTION unit (12:1–12) is unusually long in comparison to the main unit. It is not an episode in itself since it has no narrative characteristics; it only consists of an *orienter*-CONTENT unit. Also, the CONTENT is a full narrative on its own consisting of a *setting* (11:27a–b), a *problem* (11:27c–28), a *complication* (11:29–33b), a NEG RESOLUTION (11:33c–d), a POS RESOLUTION (12:1–11), and an OUTCOME (12:12).

NOTES

11:27a The display again specifies the referent of the pronoun 'they'.

11:28a **By whose authority** The GNT has 'by what authority'. LB has 'Who gave you the authority?'

11:28b *like those you did here yesterday* The GNT has only 'these things'. The display specifies from the preceding context what things they were referring to; cf. LB's "to drive out the merchants". Hendriksen says there is "a wide difference of opinion among commentators here." Lane says it refers to "the expulsion of the merchants from the temple, with the popular response to Jesus' ministry." But it is very difficult to see how the people's response is something that Jesus did. Hooker says these words "clearly refer to Jesus' actions in the temple on the previous day." Evans says similarly, they "must have referred directly to what Jesus had just done in the temple precincts." Hiebert says "The primary reference seems to be His work of cleansing the temple the previous day."

EXPANSION OF NEG-RESOLUTION OF THE COMPLICATION 11:31–33b IN MARK 11:27—12:12 DISPLAY

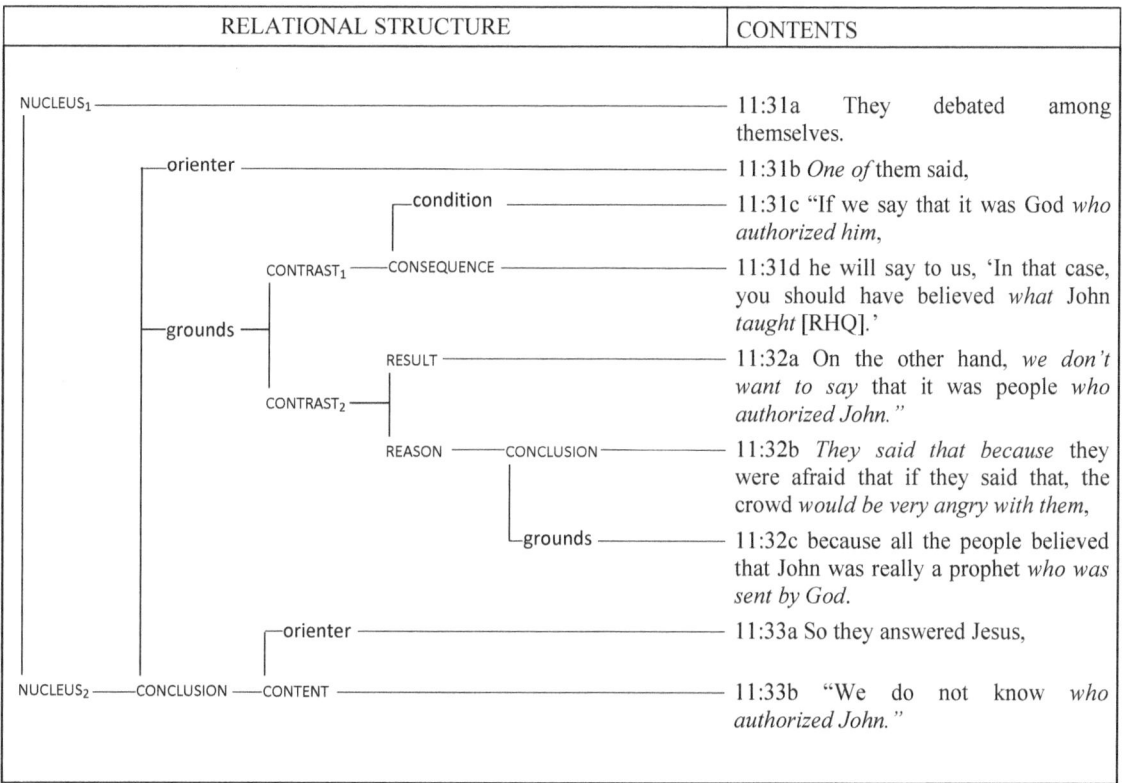

NOTES

11:31b *One of* **them said** Since they did not all say the same thing at once, the display has 'one of them said'.

11:31c Some manuscripts have the words 'What shall we say?' and these are found in TEV and NEB, but the evidence for the shorter text is considerably stronger. It is given a C 'difficulty in deciding' rating.

God *who authorized him* The display makes a full sentence; the text simply has 'from heaven', which is a metonymy, 'heaven' standing for the One who lives there.

11:31d *what* **John** *said* The text has only 'him' but it is referring to his message, not to putting faith in John; see TN.

11:32a *we don't want to say* **that it was people** *who authorized John* The text has only an abbreviated statement, 'but if we say "from men..." ' which can be a conditional clause or a question, and there is good support for each in both commentaries and versions. The display makes it a full sentence with the implied negative.

11:32b *They said that because* These words are supplied to give a suitable conclusion to the words that follow which give the reason.

afraid *that if they said that, the crowd would be very angry with them* The text has only 'they feared the crowd'. The display makes clear what about the crowd they feared; NLT has "afraid that the people would start a riot".

11:32c prophet *who was sent by God* The GNT has only 'a prophet', but in the context, where Jesus asked them if John's ministry was authorized by God, the words in italics are clearly implied.

11:33b know *who authorized John* The text has only 'we do not know'; the display supplies from the context the content of what they did not know.

EXPANSION THE NEG-RESOLUTION 11:33c–d IN MARK 11:27—12:12
DISPLAY

RELATIONAL STRUCTURE	CONTENTS
NEG RESOLUTION — orienter	11:33c So Jesus said to them,
— CONTENT	11:33d *"Because you did not answer my question, I will not tell you who authorized me to do these things."* [See the basic display on page 205.]

NOTES

11:33d ***Because you did not answer my question*** These words spell out the meaning of 'neither'. It could be expressed very idiomatically by 'In that case…'

EXPANSION OF POSITIVE RESOLUTION 12:1–12 IN MARK 11:27—12:12
DISPLAY

THEME: Jesus told the Jewish authorities a story as an analogy of what they had done to God's messengers and to himself.

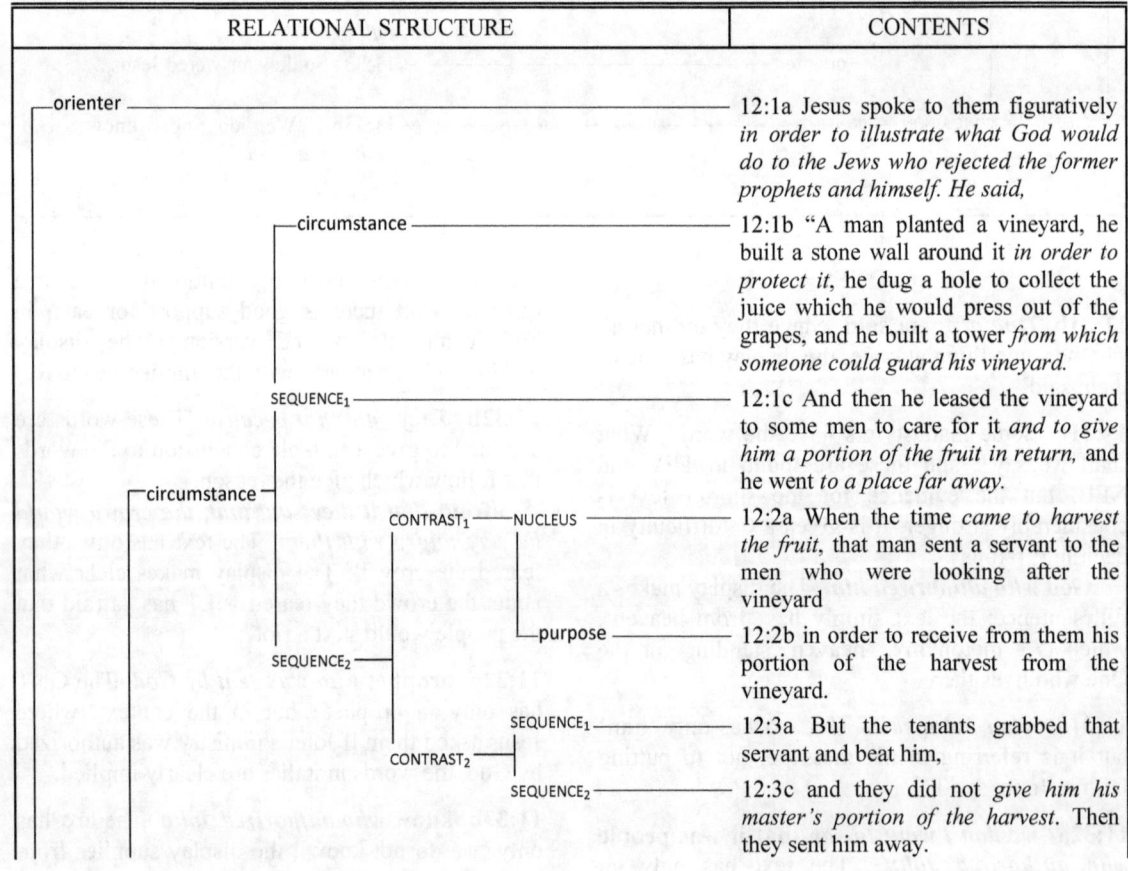

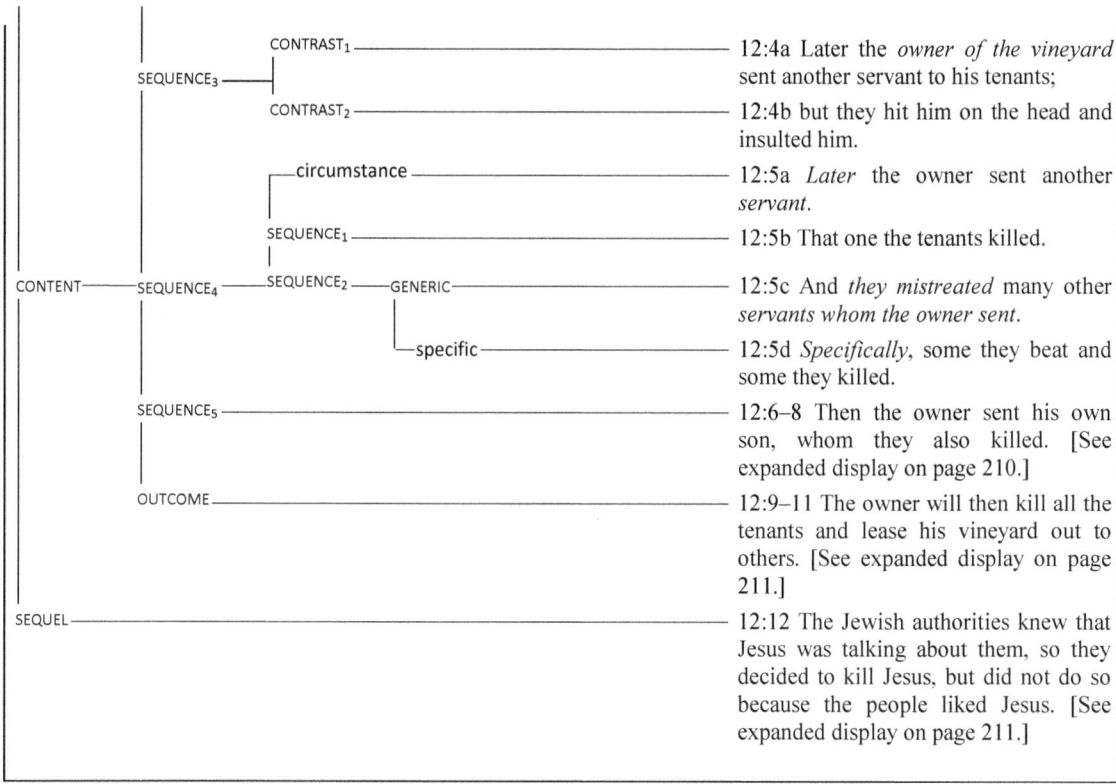

NOTES

12:1a *in order to illustrate what God would do to the Jews who rejected the former prophets and himself* What follows is a parable. The display supplies the topic of the parable; Jesus did not state it, but he expected his hearers to understand it, and from their reaction, it is clear that they did.

12:1b *from which someone could guard his vineyard* These clauses give the implied purposes of these two actions.

12:1c *and to give him his master's portion of the harvest* This was a part of the rental agreement, and is crucial to be understood for the rest of the parable.

12:2a *time came to harvest the fruit* The text has only 'at the time'; versions which specify what time is meant include TEV, NIV, CEV, and NLT.

12:3c *not give him any fruit* This represents the Greek word κενός 'empty'. Many versions use the English idiom 'empty-handed'.

EXPANSION OF SEQUENCE₅ 12:6–8 IN MARK 12:1–12 DISPLAY

RELATIONAL STRUCTURE	CONTENTS
circumstance GENERIC	12:6a *The man who owned this vineyard* still had one *other person with him*.
⸺ specific	12:6b *Specifically*, he had his son *with him* whom he loved very much.
CONTRAST₁ ⸺ RESULT	12:6c Finally, he sent his son to his tenants
⸺ reason	12:6d because he said, 'Surely they will respect my son!'
⸺ orienter	12:7a But the men who were taking care of the vineyard said to each other, *after the son arrived*:
⸺ grounds	12:7b 'This man is the one who will own this land *when his father dies*.
step ⸺ CONTENT ⸺ CONCLUSION ⸺ MEANS	12:7c For this reason let's kill the son
⸺ purpose	12:7d in order that this vineyard will be ours.'
CONTRAST₂ ⸺ GOAL	12:8 They seized him, killed him, and then threw his *body* outside the vineyard.

NOTES

12:6a one *other person with him* The text has 'he still had one'; several versions have 'one left to send'.

12:7a *after the son arrived* This states the intervening action.

12:7b the one who will own this land *when his father dies* The Greek has κληρονόμος 'the heir'; the display spells out the meaning of the word. It also makes clear the time when the inheritance goes into effect (see TN).

12:8 threw his *body* outside The text says 'threw him out', but in many languages one cannot refer to a corpse by a pronoun.

EXPANSION OF COMMENT 12:9–11 IN MARK 12:1–12 DISPLAY

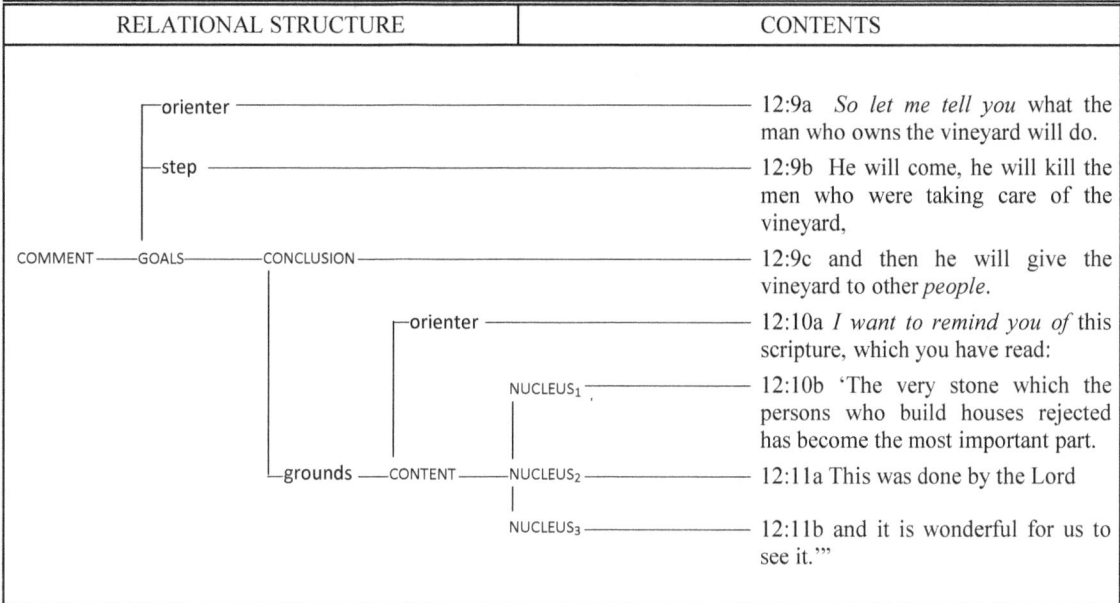

NOTES

12:9a *So let me tell you* The text has a rhetorical question, 'What will the owners do?' Jesus framed it as a question, "It makes them think. about what the owner in the parable should do" (TN).

12:10a *I want to remind you of* **this scripture** The text has another rhetorical question, 'Have you not read...?' THM says "The form of the question implies that they had undoubtedly read this particular Scripture passage." CEV has "You surely know..." Jesus quoted from Psalm 118:22–23.

12:10b has become the most important part Commentators are divided as to whether the word κεφαλή means 'cornerstone' or 'capstone of an arch'. The display attempts to be neutral by expressing the connotation. TEV and CEV do likewise.

EXPANSION OF COMMENT 12:12 IN MARK 12:1–12 DISPLAY

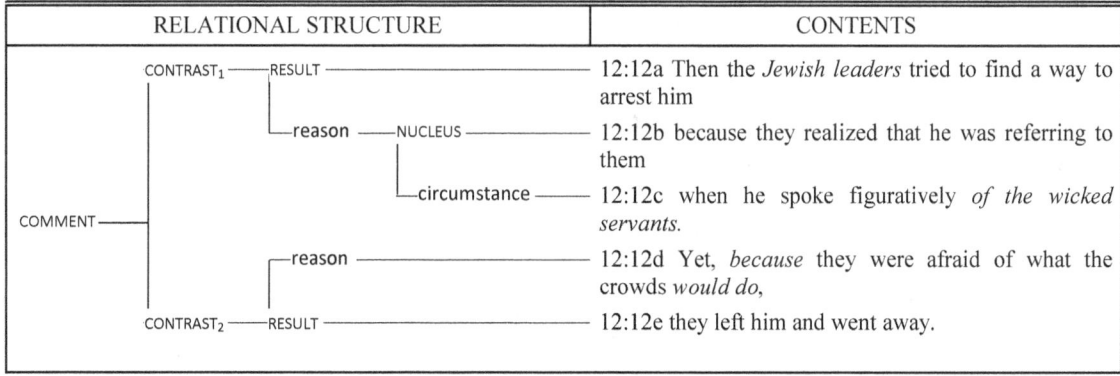

NOTES

12:12c *when he spoke figuratively of the wicked servants* The display specifies what specifically in the parable made them so angry.

12:12d what the crowds *would do* See note on 11:32.

BOUNDARIES AND COHERENCE

Regarding the embedded narrative (12:1–12): A new paragraph at v. 13 is marked by new participants (Pharisees and Herodians) and a new topic (paying taxes to the government). Coherence in the 12:1–12 narrative is provided by 4 occurrences of ἀμπελών 'vineyard', three occurrences of ἀποκτείνω 'kill' and two of γεωργός 'tenants'. Coherence is also seen in it being one parable by Jesus pointing to the religious leaders arranging for Jesus to be executed.

PROMINENCE AND THEME

Regarding the embedded narrative (12:1–12): The theme is taken from prominent units in this narrative: a condensation of the *orienter*, of the *circumstance*, and of the SEQUENCE₄.

BOUNDARIES AND COHERENCE

Regarding the episode 11:27—12:12: A new paragraph at 12:13 is marked by Jesus telling the religious leaders about paying taxes to the Roman government. Coherence within the 11:27–12:12 paragraph is shown by two occurrences of the phrase ἐξ οὐρανοῦ 'from heaven', two occurrences of ἐξουσία 'authority', three occurrences of ἀμπελών 'vineyard' and two of γεωργός 'tenants'. Coherence is also provided by the dialogue between Jesus and the religious leaders on the subject of Jesus' authority and John the Baptizer's authority.

THEME AND PROMINENCE

Regarding the episode 11:27—12:12: The theme is a condensation of the *setting*, the *problem*, the NEGATIVE AND POSITIVE RESOLUTIONS.

ACT CONSTITUENT 12:13–44 (Scene of 11:1—13:37)

THEME: Jesus had a final conflict with the Jewish authorities, and warned his disciples to not follow the haughty way of these authorities.

MACROSTRUCTURE	CONTENTS
occasion	12:13–34 The Jewish authorities took an aggressive role, but Jesus cleverly foiled various attempts by the Jewish authorities to trap him into saying something that would incriminate himself.
OUTCOME	12:35–44 Jesus now takes the aggressive role by teaching publicly in the temple. Jesus warned the people and his disciples to avoid the teachers of the Jewish laws' haughty actions. Jesus said that he was more than just King David's descendant. Jesus also taught that God highly values a widow's unnoticed offering rather than the haughty actions of the Jewish authorities.

INTENT AND RHETORICAL STRUCTURE

This is the second of three scenes included in ACT III, where Mark presents that Jesus entered Jerusalem, and prophesized about the future of the city and its inhabitants. In this unit Mark gives the details of Jesus' final conflict with the Jewish religious authorities. This unit consists of an *occasion* and an OUTCOME.

Here Mark intends that the reader understand that the Jewish religious authorities tried to trap Jesus into saying something that would condemn him both religiously and politically, but they completely failed. So Jesus started teaching publicly that these authorities were an evil influence among the people of Israel.

BOUNDARIES AND COHERENCE

Both the initial and the closing boundaries coincide with the boundaries of the first and final included episodes. In this unit Mark presents the details of the conflict between Jesus and the Jewish religious authorities.

PROMINENCE AND THEME

The theme statement is derived from a summary of the included units reflecting the prominence of the *occasion-OUTCOME* structure.

SCENE CONSTITUENT 12:13–34 (Episode Cluster of 12:13–44)

THEME: The Jewish authorities took an aggressive role, but Jesus cleverly foiled various attempts by the Jewish authorities to trap him into saying something that would incriminate himself. Jesus cleared himself of all further accusation by defending the two most important commandments of the Mosaic law.

MACROSTRUCTURE	CONTENTS
initiation	12:13–17 Jesus cleverly foiled the Jewish leaders' attempt to trap him about the question of paying taxes to the Roman government.
build-up	12:18–27 Jesus showed from Scripture that the Sadducees were wrong to ridicule the idea of life after death.
CLIMAX	12:28–34 Jesus commended a teacher of the Jewish laws who accepted Jesus' assessment of the two greatest commandments, after which they asked Jesus no more questions to try to trap him.

INTENT AND RHETORICAL STRUCTURE

This is the first of two sub- episode clusters included in *EPISODE CLUSTER* (12:13–34) where Mark gives the details of Jesus' final conflict with the Jewish religious authorities. This unit consists of an *initiation*, a *build-up*, and a CLIMAX.

Here Mark intends that the reader understand that the Jewish religious authorities tried to trap Jesus into saying something that would condemn him both religiously and politically, but they completely failed. So they decided to take action toward killing Jesus.

BOUNDARIES AND COHERENCE

Both the initial and the closing boundaries coincide with the boundaries of the first and final included episodes. In this unit Mark presents the details of the conflict between Jesus and the Jewish religious authorities.

PROMINENCE AND THEME

The theme statement is derived from a summary of the included units reflecting the prominence of its rhetorical structure.

EPISODE CLUSTER CONSTITUENT 12:13–17 (EPISODE of 12:13–34)

THEME: Jesus cleverly foiled the Jewish leaders' attempt to trap him about the question of paying taxes to the Roman government.

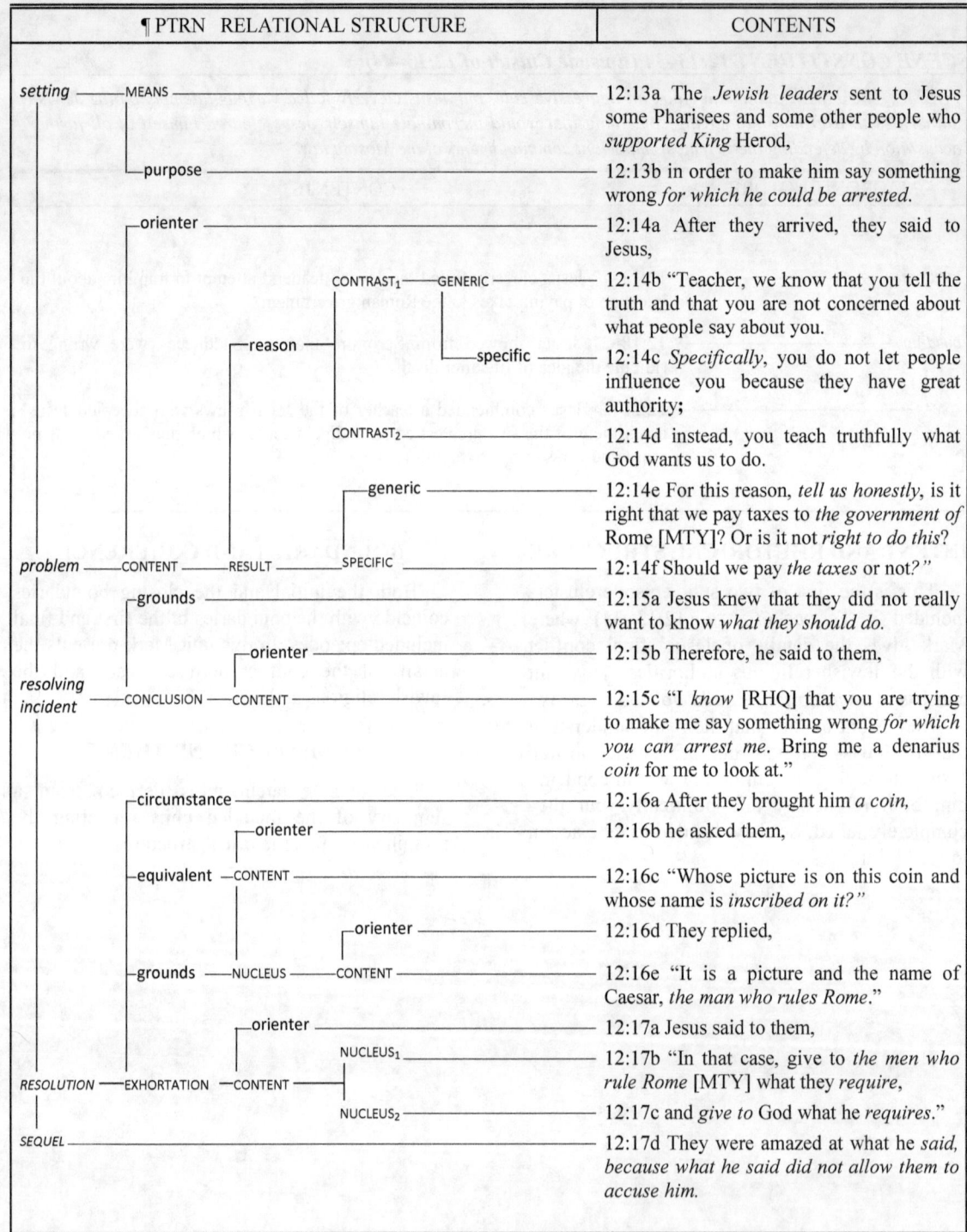

INTENT AND RHETORICAL STRUCTURE

The author intends that the reader understand that Jesus saw through the evil intent of the Jewish authorities to trap him into saying something for which they could accuse him before the Roman authorities. This is a solutionality type narrative consisting of a *setting*, a *problem*, a *resolving incident*, a RESOLUTION, a SEQUEL.

NOTES

12:13a The *Jewish leaders* sent The text has 'they sent'; the display identifies who 'they' refers to. NLT has "the leaders".

supported King **Herod** This explicates the word 'Herodians'. See note on 3:6a.

12:13b say something wrong *for which he could be arrested* The text has 'catch him in a word'. CEV's wording is good: "trick him into saying something wrong"; NLT's is even better: "trap Jesus into saying something for which he could be arrested".

12:14b say about you The text has 'to you about anyone'. JBP has "not swayed by men's opinion of you".

12:14c do not let people influence you because they have great authority The text literally has 'you do not look at the face of men'. CEV has "you pay no attention to a man's status".

12:14e to *the government of* Rome This is a metonymy; 'Caesar' stands for the government which he heads. NLT also has "the Roman government".

12:14f Should we pay *the taxes or not?* This can be considered a doublet with the preceding clause. It could be eliminated if the speakers of the receptor language object to repetition.

12:15a not really want to know *what they should do* The display spells out the meaning of the words, 'their hypocrisy'.

12:15c I *know* that The text has a rhetorical question introduced by 'why?' which is conveying a rebuke (TN).

trying to make me say something wrong *for which you can arrest me* The text has 'are you testing me'; the sense is almost exactly the same as that in 13b.

12:16c are *inscribed on this coin* The text has 'whose image is this and superscription?' NLT has "are stamped on it".

12:16e Caesar, *the man who rules Rome* The text has only 'of Caesar'. The words in italics are supplied to make Jesus' reply in 17b fit better.

12:17b *the men who rule Rome* This again spells out the metonymy of the word 'Caesar'.

12:17b–c they *require*...he *requires* The text has only genitive constructions, 'the things of Caesar... the things of God'. But tax money doesn't belong to the government until we pay it; they require it.

12:17d *because what he said did not allow them to accuse him* This supplies the reason that the people were amazed; so say Guelich, Gould, and Hiebert.

BOUNDARIES AND COHERENCE

A new paragraph at v. 18 is indicated by a switch from a question by the Pharisees and Herodians to a question by Sadducees. Coherence within the 13–17 paragraph is shown by four occurrences of 'Caesar'. Cohesion is also given by the paragraph being one episode regarding the paying of taxes.

PROMINENCE AND THEME

The theme is drawn from a portion of 13a (to identify participants), 13b, and 14e, plus an implied result of the EXHORTATION of the RESOLUTION.

EPISODE CLUSTER CONSTITUENT 12:18–27 (EPISODE of 12:13–34)

THEME: Jesus showed from Scripture that the Sadducees were wrong to ridicule the idea of life after death.	
MACROSTRUCTURE	CONTENTS
occasion	12:18–23 The Sadducees tried to trap Jesus on whether there was life after death. [See expanded display on page 217.]
OUTCOME	12:24–27 Jesus replied that they were wrong to suppose that people will not become alive again, and showed them that Scripture proved this. [See expanded display on page 218.]

INTENT AND RHETORICAL STRUCTURE

Mark here intends that the reader understand that Jesus proved by quoting Scriptures that there is life after death.

This episode is a causality type narrative. It consists of an *occasion* and an OUTCOME.

BOUNDARIES AND COHERENCE

A new paragraph at v. 28 is marked by a teacher of the Jewish law asking Jesus a question. Coherence within the 18–27 paragraph is seen in two occurrences of ἀδελφός 'brother', three occurrences of τέκνον 'children', two of 'Moses', three occurrences of 'God of', and two of νεκρός 'dead ones'. Coherence also is provided by the paragraph dealing with only the subject of resurrection.

PROMINENCE AND THEME

The theme is drawn from the OUTCOME of the unit.

EXPANSION OF OCCASION 12:18a–23 IN DISPLAY OF MARK 12:18–27

RELATIONAL STRUCTURE	CONTENTS
NUCLEUS — orienter	12:18a *Some* Saducees, who deny that dead people come alive again, came to Jesus,
	12:18b *and in order to ridicule the idea that dead people will become alive again,* they asked him,
standard — condition	12:19a "Teacher, Moses wrote for us *Jews* that if a man who has no children dies,
CONSEQUENCE₁	12:19b his brother should marry that man's widow
CONSEQUENCE₂	12:19c and then he should produce and raise children to be his *dead* brother's heirs.
grounds — SEQUENCE₁ — circumstance	12:20a *Well*, there were seven brothers.
concession	12:20b Although the oldest *brother* married a woman,
CONTRA-EXPECTATION	12:20c when he died, he and his wife had not borne any children.
SEQUENCE₂ — occasion	12:21a The second *brother obeyed this law,* married that woman,
OUTCOME	12:21b and he, too, had no children before he died.
SEQUENCE₃	12:21c The third *brother* did likewise.
SEQUENCE₄ — concession	12:22a Although all seven *brothers married that woman* one by one,
CONTRA-EXPECTATION	12:22b they had no children and they all died.
SEQUENCE₅	12:22c Afterwards the woman died, too.
CONTENT — CONGRUENCE — CONCLUSION — CONCLUSION — CONSEQUENCE — condition	12:23a Therefore, *if it were true what some people say, that* people will become alive again,
CONSEQUENCE	12:23b whose wife will *that woman* be, when people become alive again?
grounds	12:23c *It will be very difficult to decide this* because she was married to all seven brothers."

NOTES

12:18b *in order to ridicule the idea that dead people will become alive again* This clause is included to make clear the intent of the Sadducees' question in 23b. Hendriksen says the purpose of their question was "to ridicule his faith in the afterlife."

12:19a Moses wrote They were referring to Deut. 25:5.

12:19c to be his dead brother's heirs The text has 'seed to his brother'. NLT has "who will be his brother's heir".

12:20a *Well* This word is inserted to mark the transition from a discussion of Moses' law to their story about the seven brothers. NLT does the same.

12:21a second brother obeyed this law The text has 'the second took her' but from the

12:23a *if it were true what some people say*
The text has 'in the resurrection' which sounds as though they believed in the resurrection of the dead. The words in italics make their skepticism clear.

There are several important manuscripts that do not have the words 'when they rise'. The reason is no doubt that they seem superfluous. They are omitted in RSV, NLT, NCV, NIV, GW, CEV, and in this analysis.

12:23c *It will be very difficult to decide this*
The text here has a γάρ 'because' but there is no result to go with the reason clause. The display supplies a suitable result clause. CEV points in the direction of the display by supplying "After all,…"

EXPANSION OF OUTCOME 12:24–27 IN DISPLAY OF MARK 12:18–27

RELATIONAL STRUCTURE	CONTENTS
CONTENT₁ — orienter	12:24a Jesus replied to them,
CONTRAST₁ — CONCLUSION	12:24b "You are certainly wrong;
grounds	12:24c you do not know *what is written in* the Scriptures *about this*, and you do not know the power of God *to make people alive again after they die*.
CONTRAST₂ — OUTCOME — occasion	12:25a When *people* have become alive again after they have died,
CONTRAST₁	12:25b instead of men and women being married,
CONTRAST₂	12:25c they will be like the angels in heaven *who do not marry*.
CONTENT₂ — CONTENT — orienter	12:26a Furthermore, in the books which Moses wrote, there is something which I am certain that you have read, about dead people being alive again.
grounds — CONTENT — orienter	12:26b *When Moses was standing near the bush which was burning,* God said,
CONTENT	12:26c 'I am the God whom Abraham *worships* and the God whom Isaac *worships* and the God whom Jacob *worships*.'
CONCLUSION — grounds — CONTRAST₁	12:27a *Therefore, because* God is surely not *one whom* dead people worship,
CONTRAST₂	12:27b he is the God *whom living people worship*;
CONCLUSION	12:27c therefore *the spirits of Abraham, Isaac, and Jacob must still be alive, even though they died long before Moses lived.*
CONTENT₃	12:27d Therefore, you Sadducees are very wrong, *claiming that dead people do not become alive again*."

NOTES

12:24b You are certainly wrong This represents a rhetorical question, 'Are you not wrong?' which semantically is expressing an emphatic positive statement (Gundry, Hiebert, Meyer, Swete, and Taylor). CEV also renders it as a statement: "You are completely wrong!" and NEB, TEV do also.

12:24c *what is written in* the Scriptures *about this* The text has 'you do not know the Scriptures', but what Jesus meant was that they did not understand what the Scriptures said about life after death (so Lenski, Hendriksen).

power of God *to make people alive again after they die* The text has only 'the power of God' but in this context it refers to his power to produce life after death (see Stein, TN).

12:25a This verse begins with γάρ, which is introducing an amplification of the subject of life after death, not a reason.

12:25b *men* and women being married The text has 'they neither marry nor are given in marriage', which reflects Jewish marriage customs. Many English versions reduce it to one clause (e.g., TEV, JB, NEB, NLT, CEV, and Beck).

12:25c *who do not marry* This is the point of comparison of the simile. Cf. Cranfield, Gould, Hiebert, Lenski, France, and Taylor.

12:26a I am certain that you have read This is another rhetorical question, 'have you not read…?' which has the force of an emphatic positive statement; CEV and NCV also render it as a declaration. The Sadducees had read it but not realized its implications.

12:26c Abraham *worships* The text has three genitive constructions, starting with 'the God of Abraham'. The display supplies the verb 'worship' to convey the meaning of the genitive; CEV does likewise. See also TN. The same word is supplied in 27a–b.

12:27c therefore *the spirits of Abraham, Isaac, and Jacob must still be alive, even though they died long before Moses lived* This is the implied conclusion of Jesus' argument. See Cranfield and Strauss.

BOUNDARIES AND COHERENCE

The start of a new paragraph at v. 28 is indicated by a switch from questions intended to trap Jesus to a genuine question by one individual. Coherence within the 18–27 paragraph is shown by four occurrences of ἀποθνῄσκω 'die' and three of the cognate words νεκρός 'dead ones', plus five occurrences of ἀδελφός 'brother'. Coherence is seen in the discussion between Jesus and Sadducees about the resurrection.

PROMINENCE AND THEME

The theme for this paragraph is drawn from 18a (to identify the participants), 18b, and a condensation of CONTRAST₁ of CONTENT₁ of the *OUTCOME*.

EPISODE CLUSTER CONSTITUENT 12:28–34 (EPISODE of 12:13–34)

THEME: *Jesus commended a teacher of the Jewish laws who accepted Jesus' assessment of the two greatest commandments, after which they asked Jesus no more questions to try to trap him.*

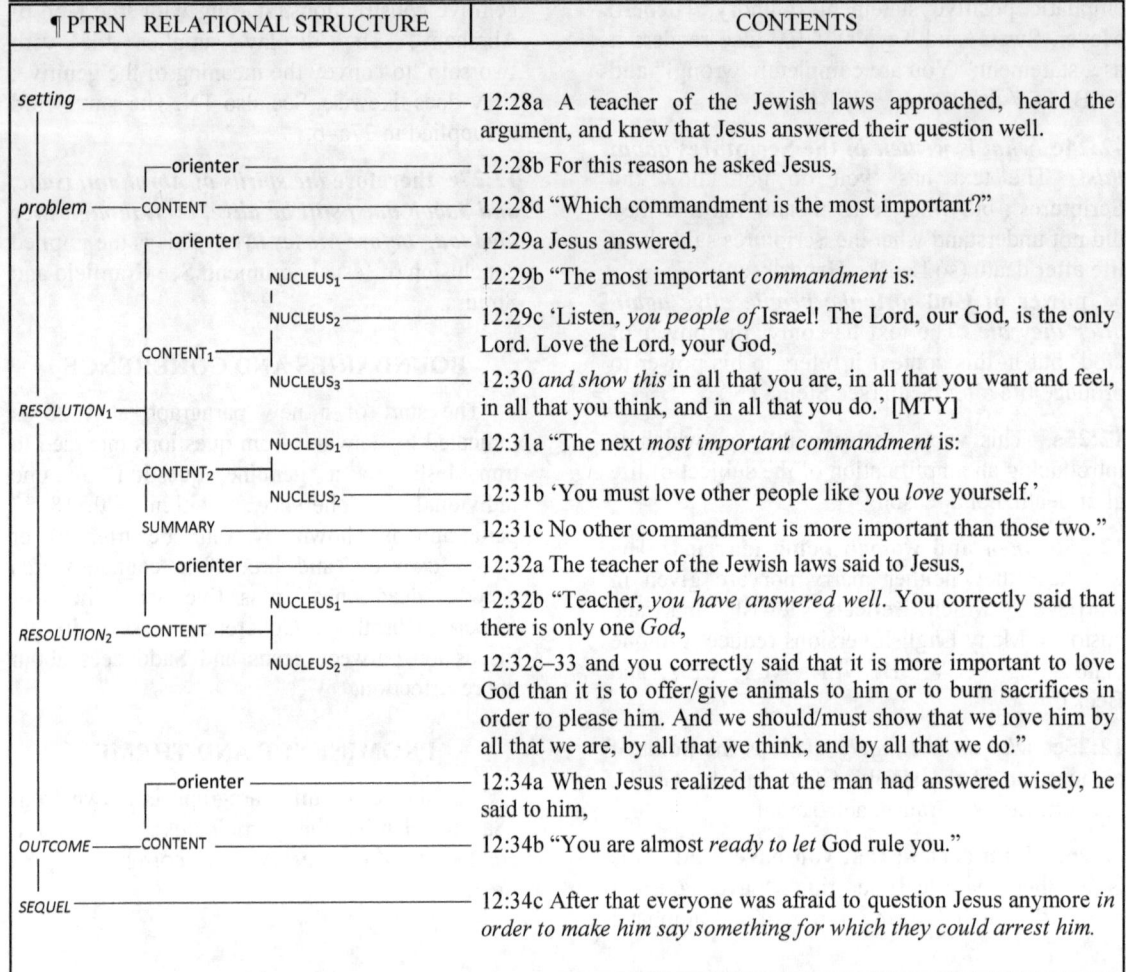

INTENT AND RHETORICAL STRUCTURE

Mark here intends that the reader understand that Jesus said that the most important commands were to love God with our whole being, and to love our fellow-humans as we love ourselves.

This episode is a solutionality type narrative. The paragraph consists of a *setting*, a *problem*, a RESOLUTION$_1$, a RESOLUTION$_2$, an OUTCOME, and a SEQUEL.

NOTES

12:29c *you people of* **Israel** The text has only 'Israel', which is an apostrophe. CEV also has "People of Israel". Jesus cited this from Deut. 6:4–5.

12:30 *and show this* **in all that you are, in all that you want and feel, in all that you think, and in all that you do** The text has 'with all your heart and with all your soul and with all your mind and with all your strength'. This is a series of four metonymies, four body parts standing for the actions associated with them.

12:31b Jesus cited this from Lev. 19:18.

12:34b *almost ready to let* **God rule you** The text has 'not far from the kingdom of God'. This would seem to imply a physical distance, whereas Jesus was implying a spiritual distance. For the rendering in the display see BAGD. As before, 'kingdom' is considered to refer to God's ruling of people's lives; see note on 1:15.

12:34c *in order to make him say something for which they could arrest him* The phrase 'no more questions' means no one "questions to try to trick him" (TN).

BOUNDARIES AND COHERENCE

A new paragraph at v. 35 is indicated by a switch from questions to Jesus to one by him. Coherence in the 28–34 paragraph is provided by the clauses 'love the Lord... love your neighbor' occurring twice. Coherence is also provided by it being a dialogue between Jesus and one of the teachers of the Jewish laws on the subject of which commandment is the greatest.

PROMINENCE AND THEME

The theme is drawn from a portion of 28a (to identify participants), a condensation of 29b and 31a of the CONTENT of the SOLUTION, plus a condensation of the SEQUEL.

SCENE CONSTITUENT 12:35–44 (Episode Cluster of 12:13–44)

THEME: *Jesus now takes the aggressive role by teaching publicly in the temple. Jesus warned the people and his disciples to avoid the teachers of the Jewish laws' haughty actions. Jesus said that he was more than just King David's descendant. Jesus also taught that God highly values a widow's unnoticed offering rather than the haughty actions of the Jewish authorities.*

MACROSTRUCTURE	CONTENTS
basis₁	12:35–37 Jesus showed from Scripture that the Messiah must be David's Lord as well as his descendant.
APPEAL	12:38–40 Jesus warned the people about the teachers of the Jewish laws' haughty actions.
basis₂	12:41–44 Jesus told them that a poor widow's unnoticed offering was worth more in God's sight than large amounts of money from rich people.

INTENT AND RHETORICAL STRUCTURE

This is the last of two EPISODE CLUSTERS included in SCENE (12:13–44) where Mark gives the details of Jesus' final conflict with the Jewish religious authorities. In this unit (12:35–44) Mark presents the details of Jesus' publicly rebuking the Jewish religious authorities while teaching in the temple area. This unit consists of a *basis*, an APPEAL, and a second *basis*.

Here Mark intends that the reader understand that Jesus was very displeased with the pompous leadership of the Jewish religious authorities.

BOUNDARIES AND COHERENCE

Both the initial and the closing boundaries coincide with the boundaries of the first and final included episodes. In this unit Mark presents the details of Jesus' disapproval of the religious authorities.

PROMINENCE AND THEME

The theme statement is derived from a summary of the included units reflecting the prominence of its rhetorical structure.

EPISODE CLUSTER CONSTITUENT 12:35–37 (Episode of 12:35–44)

THEME: *Jesus showed from Scripture that the Messiah must be David's Lord as well as his descendant.*

¶ PTRN RELATIONAL STRUCTURE	CONTENTS
occasion	12:35a In response to this, while Jesus was teaching in the temple area,
OUTCOME	12:35b–37b he showed that the Messiah is not only the descendant of King David, but that he must also be David's Lord. [See expanded display on page 222.]
SEQUEL	12:37c The large crowd listened to him gladly.

INTENT AND RHETORICAL STRUCTURE

The author intends that the reader understand that Jesus showed that he, the Messiah, was greater than his ancestor King David. This is a causality type narrative consisting of an *occasion*, an OUTCOME, and a SEQUEL.

BOUNDARIES AND COHERENCE

A new paragraph at v. 38 is shown by a switch from a comment about the Jewish leaders having a wrong understanding about the Messiah to a thorough exposing of the hypocrisy of those same men. Coherence in the 35–37 paragraph is shown by three occurrences of the name 'David' and three of the word 'Lord'. Coherence is seen in Jesus teaching that the Messiah must be David's lord as well as his descendant.

PROMINENCE AND THEME

The theme is taken from a portion of 35a of the *occasion* (to identify participants) plus the CONCLUSION of CONTENT₂ of the OUTCOME.

EXPANSION OF OUTCOME 12:35b–37b IN DISPLAY OF 10:46—13:37

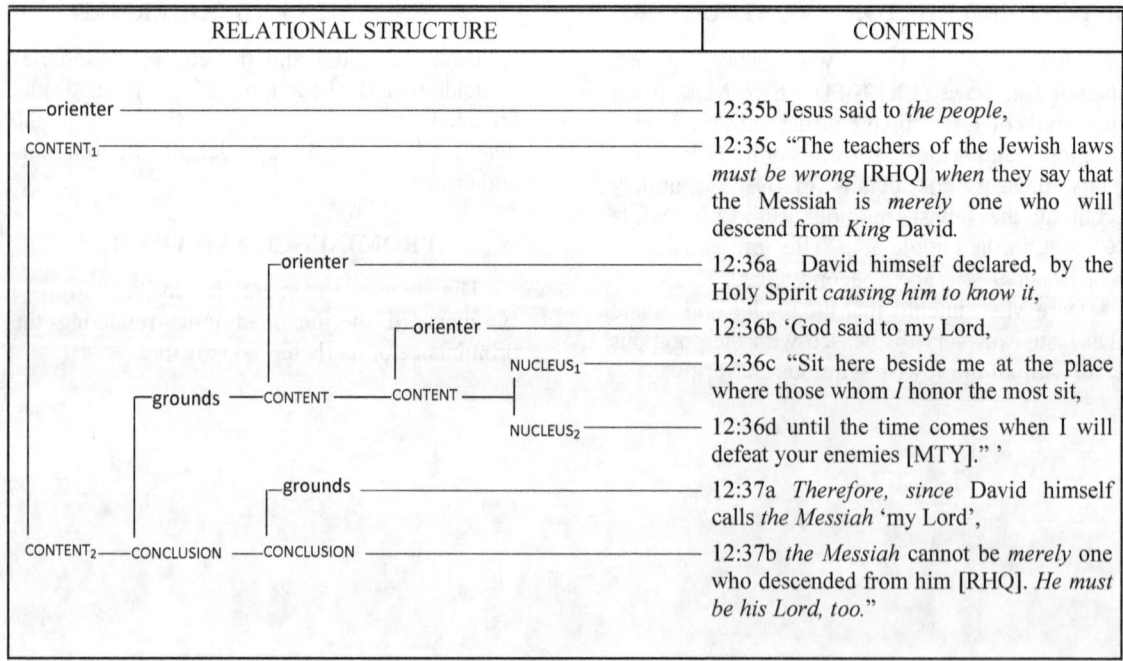

NOTES

12:35c The teachers of the Jewish laws *must be wrong when* they say The text has a rhetorical question, 'How do the scribes say…?' The purpose of the question was to make the listeners think carefully about this passage from Psalm 110:1, and to realize that their conclusion was wrong.

merely The Messiah WAS descended from King David, but he was more than that. See Hendriksen. Similarly in 37b.

12:36a by the Holy Spirit *causing him to know it* The text has 'by the Holy Spirit'. TEV has "the Holy Spirit inspired", and NLT's and LBP's renderings are almost the same.

12:36c the place where those whom *I* honor the most sit The text has 'at my right hand'. See notes on 10:37. Jesus quoted here from Psalm 110:1.

12:36d defeat your enemies The text has 'put your enemies under your feet'. This is figurative, indicating "that he has conquered the enemy" (TN).

12:37a–b *the Messiah…the Messiah* The text has only a third person singular pronoun twice; the display makes clear that they refer to the Messiah (CEV translates likewise).

12:37b *He must be his Lord, too* This is the positive conclusion in contrast to the negative conclusion that precedes it. See TN.

BOUNDARIES AND COHERENCE

A new paragraph starting at v. 38 is marked by Jesus' comment about a poor widow's offering. Coherence within the 35–37 paragraph is provided by three occurrences of the name 'David' and two of υἱός 'son'. Coherence is also seen in it being a teaching by Jesus that the Messiah must be King David's lord as well as his descendant.

PROMINENCE AND THEME

The theme is taken from the *orienter* plus the CONCLUSION of CONTENT$_2$ (v. 37b).

EPISODE CLUSTER CONSTITUENT 12:38–40 (Episode of 12:35–44)

Theme: *Jesus warned the people about the teachers of the Jewish laws' haughty actions.*

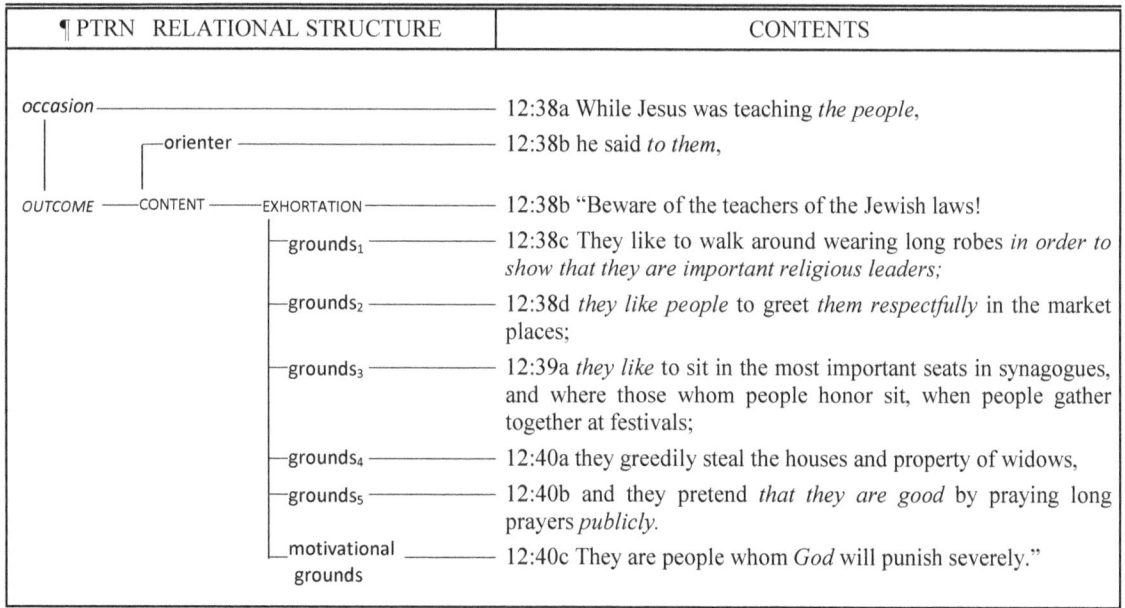

INTENT AND RHETORICAL STRUCTURE

The author intends that the reader understand that Jesus showed that he knew well the hypocritical character of the Jewish authorities, and so warned the people about it. This is a causality type narrative consisting of an *occasion* and an OUTCOME.

NOTES

12:38c *in order to show that they are important religious leaders* The long robes were worn "to show off their status as religious leaders" (Strauss).

12:40a greedily steal The text has 'devour' which is very figurative; Evans says that there are six different explanations of what is meant by devouring. NLT says they "shamelessly cheat widows out of their property".

12:40b pretend *that they are good* This wording clarifies the abstract noun πρόφασις 'under pretense'. CEV has "just to show off".

12:40c *God* **will punish** The display supplies the agent of the punishment.

BOUNDARIES AND COHERENCE

A new paragraph at v. 41 is indicated by a new topic: sacrificial giving. Coherence within the 38–40 paragraph is provided by descriptions of five activities of the teachers of the Jewish laws. Coherence is also seen in it consisting of a rebuke by Jesus of the teachers of the Jewish laws for their hypocrisy.

PROMINENCE AND THEME

The theme is taken from a portion of 38a of the *occasion* (to identify participants) plus the EXHORTATION of the OUTCOME.

EPISODE CLUSTER CONSTITUENT 12:41–44 (Episode of 12:35–44)

THEME: *Jesus told them that a poor widow's unnoticed offering was worth more in God's sight than large amounts of money from rich people.*

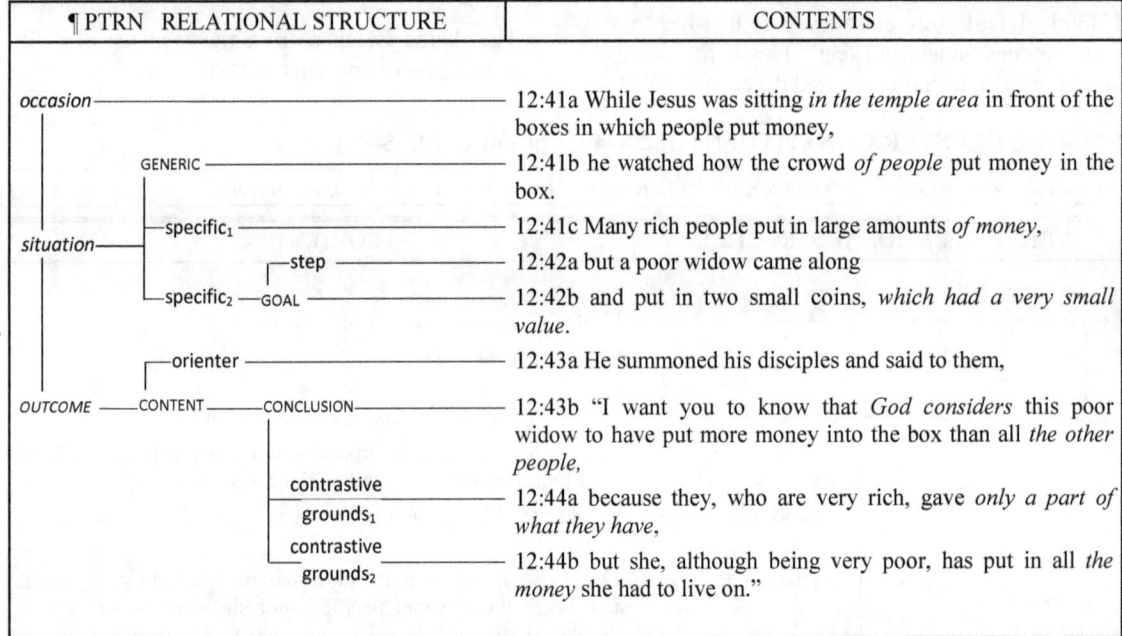

INTENT AND RHETORICAL STRUCTURE

The author intends that the reader understand that Jesus knew well the hypocritical character of the Jewish authorities, and so pointed out a case in point.

Although the basic structure is narrative, the meaning structure is descriptive, in that Jesus observes an event and then reacts to it. This is a causality type descriptive paragraph consisting of a *circumstance*, a *situation*, and a REACTION.

NOTES

12:41a Jesus The best manuscripts do not have the word 'Jesus', but it is clearly implied as the identification of 'he', and included in many versions.

the boxes in which people put money This spells out the word γαζοφυλάκιον 'treasuries'. CEV has "offering box" but there were several boxes.

12:42b two small coins, *which had a very small value* The Greek text has 'two lepta, which is a 'quadrans'. TEV has "two little copper coins, worth about a penny", which is good only if one is familiar with pennies. The wording in the display will be suitable anywhere.

12:43b I want you to know This represents 'I tell you truly', which introduces statements that Jesus wanted to emphasize.

God considers Something like this must be understood to avoid the wrong meaning of a literal translation: she did not put in more than the others. No version examined except TfT makes this clear.

12:44a gave *only a part of what they have* The text has only 'put'. TEVs rendering supplies the content of the verb well: "put in what they had to spare".

BOUNDARIES AND COHERENCE

A new paragraph at v. 13:1 is marked by a comment by the disciple about the magnificent stones in the temple and Jesus' reply. Coherence in the 12:41–44 paragraph is provided by two occurrences of the phrase χήρα πτωχός 'poor widow' and two of γαζοφυλάκιον 'treasury'. Coherence is also seen in it being a brief episode of Jesus commending a poor widow for her sacrificial giving.

PROMINENCE AND THEME

The theme is taken from the CONCLUSION of the REACTION of the episode.

ACT CONSTITUENT 13:1–37 (Scene of 11:1—13:37)

THEME: Jesus foretold events that will happen to Jerusalem and the temple, and warned his disciples to always believe him and be ready for his return.

MACROSTRUCTURE	CONTENTS
occasion	13:1–2 Jesus prophesied that the temple would be completely destroyed.
OUTCOME	13:3–37 Jesus prophesied about the events that would precede his return, and commanded his disciples to be prepared for his return.

INTENT AND RHETORICAL STRUCTURE

This is the last of three episode clusters included in ACT III, where Mark presents that Jesus entered Jerusalem, and prophesied about the future of the city and its inhabitants. In this unit Mark gives the details of Jesus telling his disciples about the destruction of the temple and the events before his return to earth. This unit consists of an *occasion* and an OUTCOME.

Here Mark intends the reader to understand that Jesus prophesied future events about Jerusalem and the temple.

BOUNDARIES AND COHERENCE

Both the initial and the closing boundaries coincide with the boundaries of the first and final included episodes. In this unit Mark presents the details of what Jesus prophesied about Jerusalem and the temple.

PROMINENCE AND THEME

The theme statement is derived from a summary of the included units respecting the prominence of the *occasion-OUTCOME* structure.

SCENE CONSTITUENT 13:1–2 (Episode of 13:1–37)

THEME: *Jesus prophesied that the temple would be completely destroyed.*

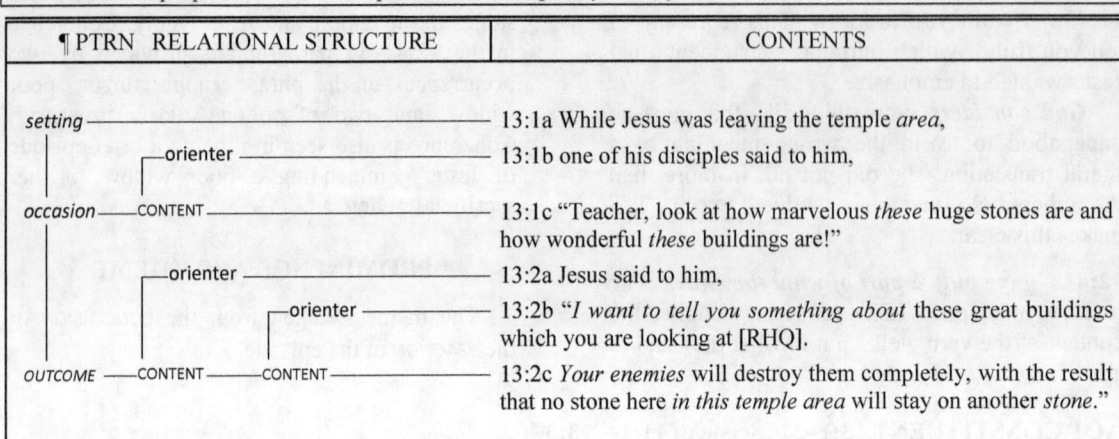

¶PTRN RELATIONAL STRUCTURE	CONTENTS
setting	13:1a While Jesus was leaving the temple *area*,
orienter	13:1b one of his disciples said to him,
occasion—CONTENT	13:1c "Teacher, look at how marvelous *these* huge stones are and how wonderful *these* buildings are!"
orienter	13:2a Jesus said to him,
orienter	13:2b "*I want to tell you something about* these great buildings which you are looking at [RHQ].
OUTCOME—CONTENT—CONTENT	13:2c *Your enemies* will destroy them completely, with the result that no stone here *in this temple area* will stay on another *stone*."

INTENT AND RHETORICAL STRUCTURE

Mark intends the reader to understand that great disaster will come to Jerusalem and the whole temple area will be totally destroyed.

This unit consists of a *setting*, an *occasion*, and an OUTCOME.

NOTES

13:2b *I want to tell you something about* The text has a rhetorical question, 'Do you see…?' The purpose of the question was to prepare them for what he was about to say about the buildings. NLT omits the question.

13:2c *Your enemies* **will destroy them completely** The text has a passive construction; the display supplies a suitable agent.

BOUNDARIES AND COHERENCE

A new paragraph at v. 3 is indicated by a change in location and questions by the disciples. Coherence within the 1–2 paragraph is provided by three occurrences of λίθος 'stones' and two of οἰκοδομή 'buildings', and by a short quote of Jesus predicting the destruction of the temple.

PROMINENCE AND THEME

The theme is taken from the *orienter* in 2a (to identify the speaker) and the CONTENT of the OUTCOME in 2c.

SCENE CONSTITUENT 13:3–37 (Episode of 13:1–37)

THEME: *Jesus prophesied about the events that would precede his return, and commanded his disciples to be prepared for his return.*

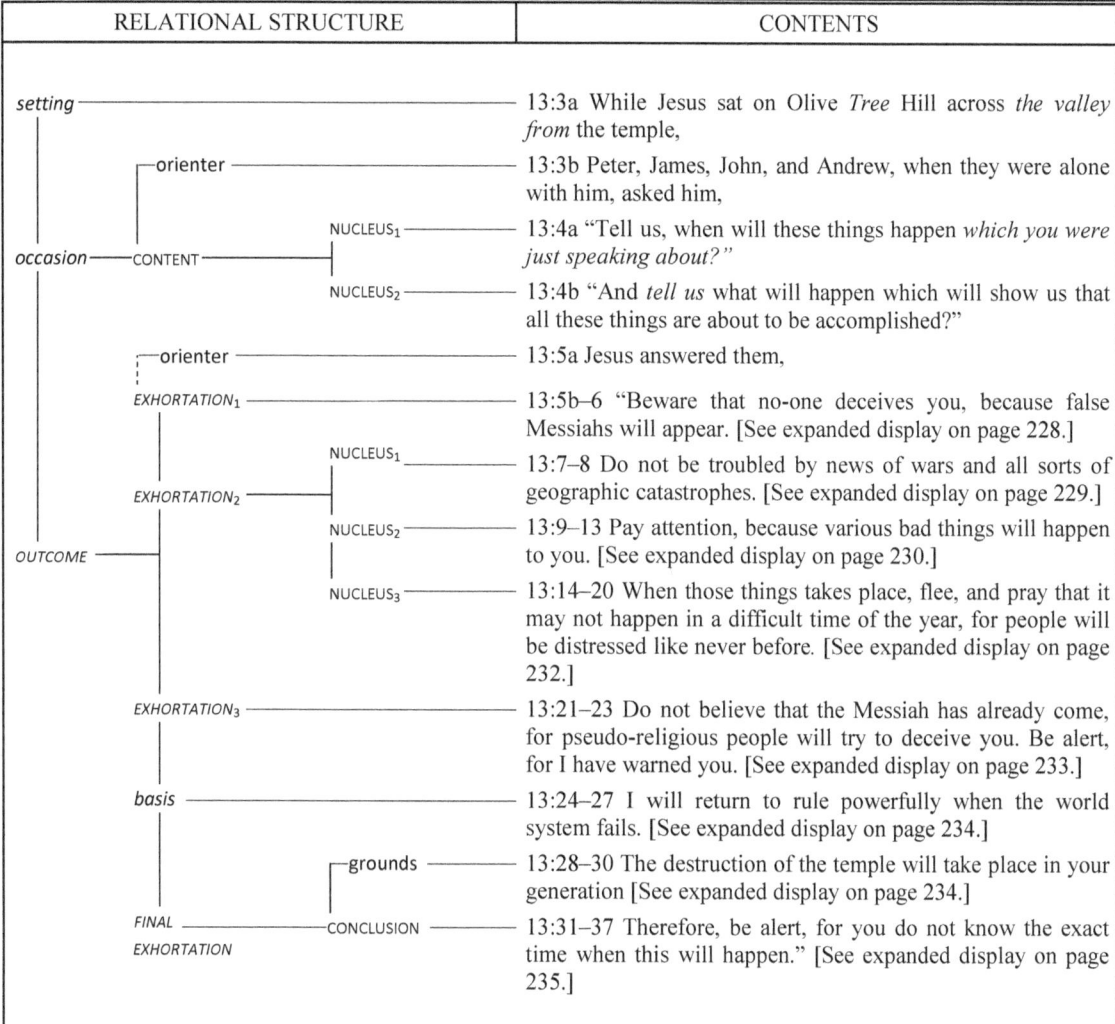

INTENT AND RHETORICAL STRUCTURE

Mark's intent is to affect the reader's behavior to be on the alert, by quoting Jesus' exhortation about the events that would come before his return to earth.

This unit consists of a *setting*, an *occasion*, and an OUTCOME.

This discourse unit (13:5–37) has the simultaneous structure of an extended chiasmus consisting of:

[A] An exhortation, to be aware of deceivers and false Messiahs (13:5b–6)
  [B] Don't be alarmed by the suffering and persecution, but remain faithful to me (13:7–20)
    [C] Beware of false Messiahs (13:21–23)
  [B'] Events that will precede Jesus' return (13:24–27)
[A'] A final exhortation, to be alert (13:28–37)

The two units [B] and [B'] directly answer the two questions that the disciples posed by asking 'what' and 'when'. Jesus answers their questions also in chiastic order. [B] answers their second question of 'when' will these things happen, while [B'] answers their first question of 'what' will be the signs of Jesus' return.

NOTES

13:3a Olive *Tree* Hill The hill was famous for its olive trees, not just for its olives.

13:4a *which you were just speaking about* The text has 'these things'; the display makes clear what things they were referring to.

EXPANSION OF CONTENT₁ 13:5b–6 OF MARK 13:3–37 DISPLAY

RELATIONAL STRUCTURE	CONTENTS
EXHORTATION	13:5b "Beware that no one deceives you *concerning what will happen*,
┌─ generic	13:6a *since* many people will come *while* pretending to be me.
│ ┌─ orienter	13:6b *Specifically, various ones will say*,
│ ┌─ means ─ CONTENT	13:6c 'I am *the Messiah.*'
└─ grounds ─ SPECIFIC ─ RESULT	13:6d *By doing this*, they will deceive many *people*.

NOTES

13:5b *concerning what will happen* Jesus was warning them not about deception in general but about the coming events.

13:6a *pretending to be me* The GNT has 'in my name'; this is a metonymy, the name standing for the person who has that name. CEV has "and claim to be me".

13:6c I am *the Messiah* The GNT has only 'I am'. NLT also has "the Messiah".

13:6d By doing this The Greek conjunction καί here is conveying a means-RESULT relationship between the two clauses; see the suggested translations in TN.

EXPANSION OF NUCLEUS₁ 13:7–8 OF MARK 13:3–37 DISPLAY

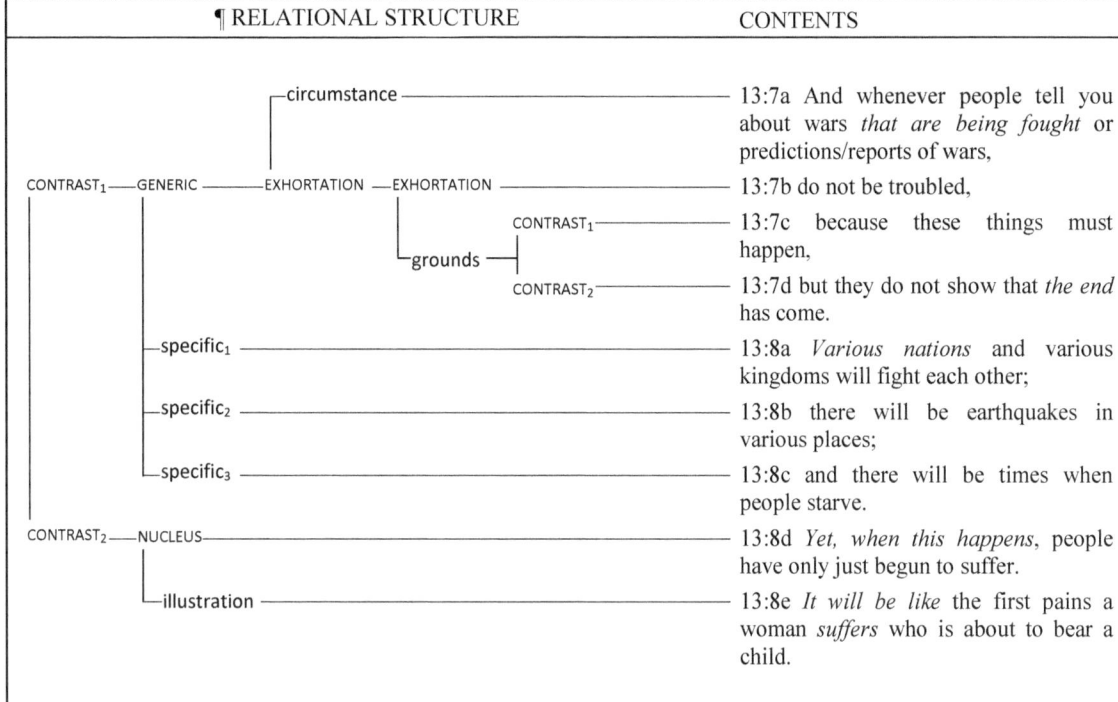

NOTES

13:7a **wars** *that are being fought* **or predictions/reports of wars** The text has 'wars and rumors of wars'. Commentators are divided as to whether the 'rumors' refers to wars which people expect to begin in the future or to wars that are already underway but far away. The display supplies both.

13:8c Some manuscripts have 'and troubles' after 'earthquakes', and those words are found in the KJV, but they have very poor manuscript support; the shorter text is given a B 'almost certain' rating.

13:8e *It will be like* The text has a metaphor, 'these are the beginning of birth-pangs'. The display indicates that a comparison is intended.

EXPANSION OF NUCLEUS₂ 13:9–13 IN THE 13:3–37 DISPLAY

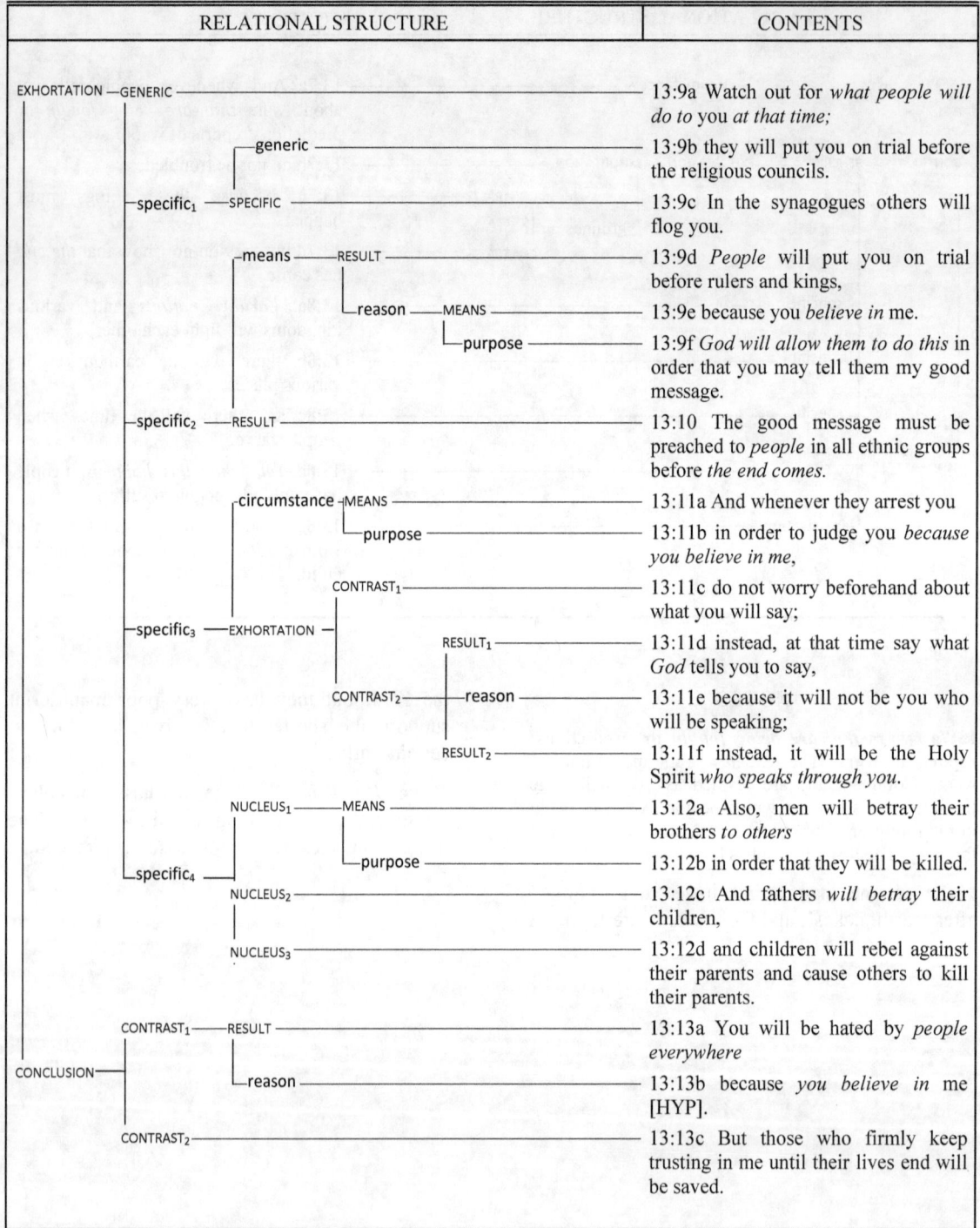

NOTES

13:9a Watch out for *what people will do to you* *at that time* This states more clearly the wording in the text, 'watch out for yourselves.'

13:9b put you on trial The Greek word means 'handed over', but here it means to judge in a court. CEV has "be taken to courts".

13:9e because *you believe in* me The text has 'for my sake' which is ambiguous. Some verb is implied; NCV has "because you follow me".

13:9f tell them my good message The text has 'for a testimony to them'; TEV has "to tell them the Good News".

13:10 all ethnic groups The Greek word ἔθνος means ethnic groups, not political entities.

   before *the end comes* The text has 'first'; CEV and TEV also have "before the end comes"; NCV has "before these things happen".

13:11b judge you *because you believe in me* Something like the words in italics may need to be supplied; it is not referring to being arrested for committing some crime.

13:11d what *God* tells you to say The text has 'what is given you'. The implied agent of the passive is 'God'. For 'given' NLT also has "say what God tells you to".

13:13a by *people everywhere* The text has 'by all men' which is hyperbole (TN). No versions consulted (except TfT) tone down the hyperbole.

13:13b because *you believe in* me See note on 13:9.

13:13c those who The Greek has 'the one who', but the sense is generic. NLT has "those who"; TEV has "whoever".

   keep trusting in me The text has 'endures', but the sense is as in the display. NCV has "keep their faith until the end".

EXPANSION OF NUCLEUS₃ 13:14–20 IN THE 13:3–37 DISPLAY

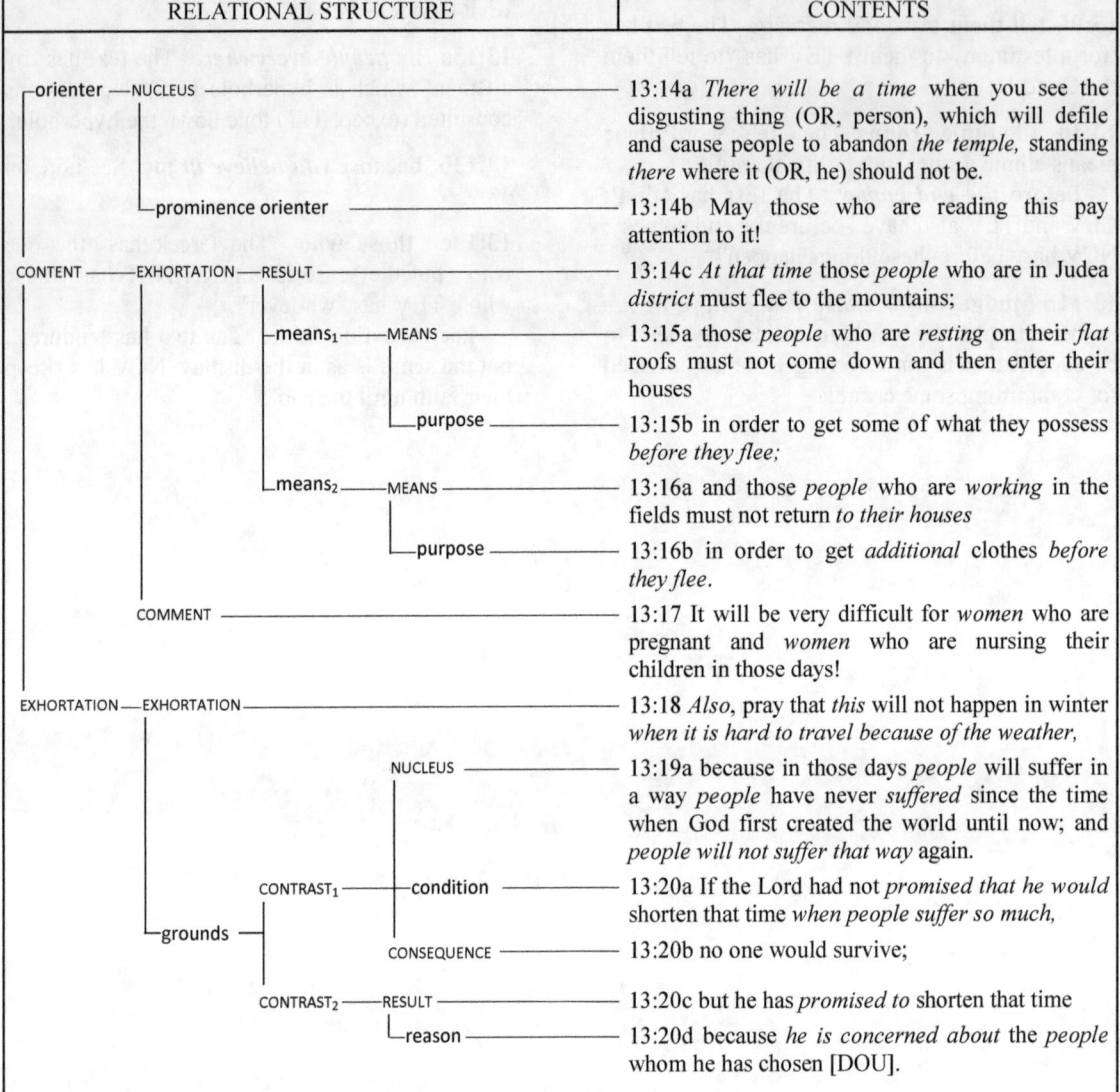

NOTES

13:14a the disgusting thing (OR, person) The grammar here is unclear, with the result that the majority of commentators say the reference is to a person, but the majority of versions say it refers to a thing. The display gives both alternatives.

which will defile and cause people to abandon *the temple* The text has 'the abomination of desolation'. The display replaces the abstract nouns with simpler words. It also spells out the sense of the genitive construction 'of desolation' with a causative construction, 'cause people to abandon'.

the temple The text does not state what will be defiled and abandoned, but it is clear from the parallel passage in Matthew as well as the book of Daniel (9:24–27, 11:31, 12:11) that the temple is meant.

13:14b Almost all commentators say this is a comment by Mark to his readers. If so, how is it that Matthew (24:15) makes the same parenthetical comment?

those who See note on 13c. Also in 15a.

13:15a *resting* on their *flat* roofs The text has 'the one on the roof'. This was very understandable in 1st century Israel, but seems very strange in most cultures today. So the display spells out the needed cultural information.

13:15b *before they flee* The point is that they must flee immediately, and not waste time retrieving possessions. TEV points in the right direction by rendering 'must not waste time'. Also in 16b.

13:16b get *additional* clothes *before they flee* The word 'additional' is needed to avoid the implication that they were working in the fields naked.

13:18 winter *when it is hard to travel because of the weather* Commentators agree that this refers to the cold and wet conditions of winter.

13:20a not *promised that he would* shorten The problem here is that "the whole verse conforms to the Hebrew prophetic style by speaking of the matter as if it were in the past" (THM). The solution is either to follow the display (and NCV), or to make it future tense in both parts of the verse (e.g., "if the Lord doesn't make the time shorter... he will make the time shorter" (CEV).

13:20d because *he is concerned about* The Greek has only διά 'on account of'. NCV has "to help".

the *people* whom he has chosen The text has 'the chosen whom he has chosen' which is a doublet (TN). It is represented by only one phrase in TEV, NLT, JBP, 20th Century, and Beck.

EXPANSION OF CONTENT₃ 13:21–23 IN THE 13:3–37 DISPLAY

RELATIONAL STRUCTURE	CONTENTS
┌circumstance ───────────────	13:21a At that time, if anyone says to you, 'Look, here is the Messiah!' *or if someone says*, 'Look, there *he is*!'
EXHORTATION─EXHORTATION──────	13:21b do not believe *it*,
└grounds ──MEANS ────────	13:22a because false Messiahs and false prophets will appear and will perform many kinds of miracles [DOU]
└purpose ────────	13:22b in order to deceive the *people* whom *God* has chosen, if they would be able to.
CONCLUSION ───────────────	13:23 So, be alert, because I have warned you about all *this* before *it happens*.

NOTES

13:22a many kinds of miracles The text has 'signs and miracles' which is also considered a doublet to emphasize the variety of miracles. The LB has "wonderful miracles". See also suggestion in TN. Evidence that it is a doublet is that this doublet occurs fourteen times in the New Testament.

13:22b if they would be able to Nine commentators say that the word 'if possible' indicates that it will not be possible. Therefore the display uses the contrafactual form (as do NIV, JB, and NEB).

EXPANSION OF CONTENT₄ 13:24–27 IN THE 13:3–37 DISPLAY

RELATIONAL STRUCTURE	CONTENTS
circumstance	13:24a During that time, after the time when people suffer,
┌ specific₁	13:24b the sun will become dark,
├ specific₂	13:24c the moon will not shine,
├ specific₃	13:25a stars will fall from the sky,
move — GENERIC	13:25b and *God will cause the powerful things* in the sky to shake.
SEQUENCE₁ — GOAL	13:26 And then *people* will see *me*, the one who came from heaven, coming through the clouds powerfully and gloriously.
SEQUENCE₂ — MEANS	13:27a Afterwards, I will send out the angels
└ purpose	13:27b in order that they gather the *people* whom *God has* chosen from everywhere, *that is*, even from all the most remote places there are on earth [IDI] [DOU].

NOTES

13:25b the powerful things in the sky The text has 'the powers in the heavens'. Commentators are divided as to whether this refers to stars or to supernatural forces.

13:26 For 'Son of Man' see note on 2:10.

13:27b from everywhere, *that is***, even from all the most remote places there are on earth** The text has 'from the four winds, from the extremity of earth to the extremity of heaven'. Mann notes that the phrases about the winds and the extremities both have the same meaning. The doublet is for emphasis. CEV renders them as 'from all over the earth"; see also TRT.

EXPANSION OF CONTENT₅ 13:28–30 IN THE 13:3–37 DISPLAY

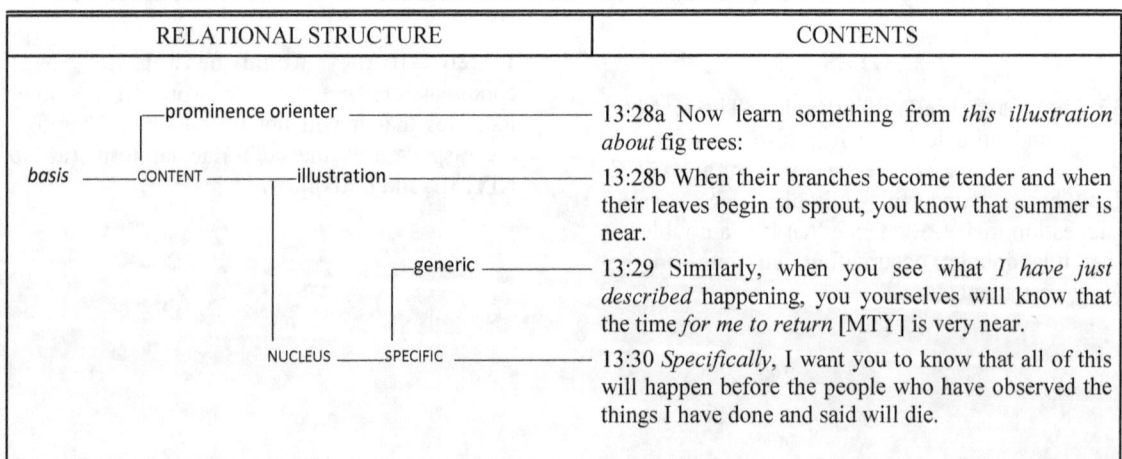

NOTES

13:28a learn something The text has 'learn the parable', which means 'learn something from this illustration'.

13:29 what *I have just described* The display specifies what the words 'these things' refer to.

time for me to return The text has only 'is near' without specifying what is near. Seven versions state that the subject is 'he'. LB is more specific: "my return is very near".

13:30 I want you to know For 'I tell you truly' see note on 9:41.

the people who have observed the things I have done and said For 'this generation' see note on 8:12.

EXPANSION OF CONCLUSION 13:31–37 IN THE 13:3–37 DISPLAY

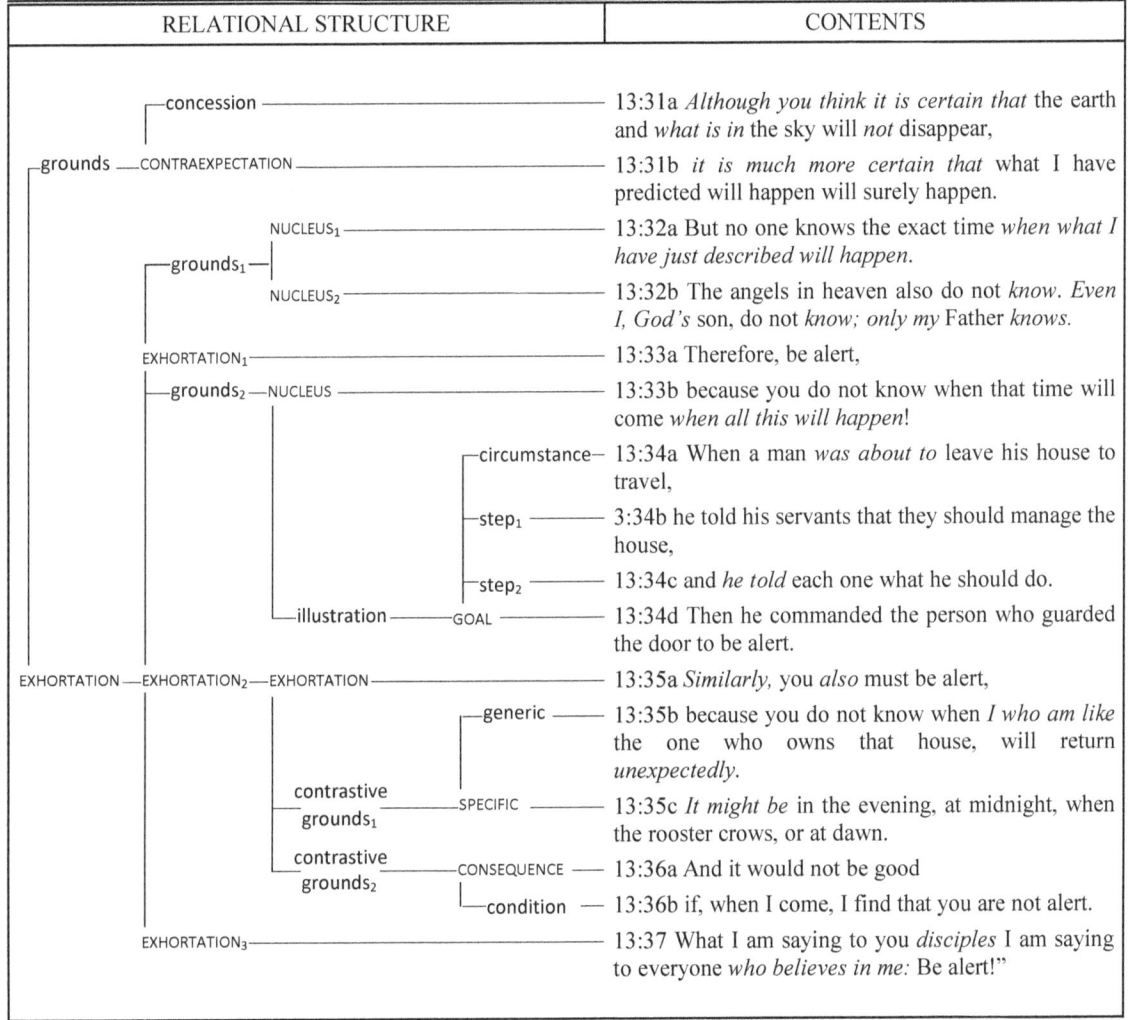

NOTES

13:31a–b *Although you think it is certain that* **the earth and** *what is in* **the sky will** *not* **disappear,** *it is much more certain that* **what I have predicted will happen will surely happen** What Jesus meant by the words, 'heaven and earth will disappear, but my words will not disappear', is not clear. The display follows TN: "Jesus indicated what he said was more reliable than heaven and earth were".

13:32a the exact time *when what I have just described will happen* The text has 'the day or the hour'. This is a metonymy and a doublet, a time standing for the events that will occur then.

NLT has "when these things will happen"; see also JBP and JB. Also In v. 33.

13:32b The display fills in a number of ellipses concerning 'know'.

son...Father See note 1:1a.

13:33 be alert Some manuscripts have in addition 'and pray', and they are found in the KJV, but they were probably added by some copyist who saw those words in 14:38.

13:35b *I who am like* **the one who owns that house** Jesus continued with the parable, without stating that by 'the owner of the house' he was referring to himself. The display makes this clear.

13:36b when I come The display continues to make clear that Jesus was referring to himself.

13:37 you *disciples*... everyone *who believes in me* The display makes clear who the 'you'(plural) and 'all' refer to. Cranfield, France, and Guelich state that the 'all' refers to the whole Christian church throughout the ages.

BOUNDARIES AND COHERENCE

A new paragraph at 14:1 is indicated by an initial reference to the Feast of Unleavened Bread. Coherence within the 13:1–37 unit is provided by the words 'day', 'hour', and 'time' and three occurrences of ἀγρυπνέω 'be on guard', and two of οἰκία 'house'. Coherence is also provided by the whole unit being about events that will occur in the end times and a warning that his disciples must be on guard and ready for his return.

THEME AND PROMINENCE

The theme consists of a brief summary of the three EXHORTATIONS and a rephrasing of the CONCLUSION of the FINAL EXHORTATION.

PART CONSTITUENT 14:1—16:8 (Act IV of Part II 8:31—16:8)

THEME: The Jewish authorities and the Roman authorities executed Jesus. He suffered, died, and came back to life again, just as he said he would.

MACROSTRUCTURE	CONTENTS
initiation	14:1–31 A woman and the Jewish leaders and Jesus himself foreshadowed his imminent death.
build-up	14:32—15:41 Jesus enemies, the Jewish authorities and the Roman authorities, arrested Jesus, tried him, and then crucified him.
anti-climax	15:42–47 Several women watched as Joseph and others buried Jesus' body in a cave after getting permission from Pilate.
CLIMAX	16:1–8 Two days later, several women were astonished to find Jesus' tomb empty, but an angel told them Jesus was alive again.

INTENT AND RHETORICAL STRUCTURE

This ACT IV (14:1–16:8) is the last unit of the second part of Mark (8:31—16:18), where Mark presents that Jesus suffered, died, and rose again.

The macro-structure consists of an *initiation, a build-up, an anti-climax,* and a CLIMAX.

BOUNDARIES AND COHERENCE

Both the initial and the closing boundaries coincide with the boundaries of the first and final included episodes. Coherence is seen in the topic of Jesus suffering, dying, and becoming alive again.

PROMINENCE AND THEME

The theme consists of a summary of the four structural units maintaining structural prominence.

ACT CONSTITUENT 14:1–31 (Scene of 14:1—16:8)

THEME: A woman and the Jewish leaders and Jesus himself foreshadowed his imminent death.	
MACROSTRUCTURE	CONTENTS
┌ contraction	14:1–11 A woman beautifully symbolized Jesus being buried, while the Jewish authorities plotted with Judas to arrest Jesus without causing a riot.
└ AMPLIFICATION	14:12–31 Jesus instructed two disciples to prepare the Passover meal. While eating the Passover, Jesus predicted that someone would betray him. He also changed the significance of that meal to be that God now accepts people because of Jesus' dying. Later he predicted that Peter would deny that he knew Jesus.

INTENT AND RHETORICAL STRUCTURE

This is the first of four scenes included in ACT IV, where Mark presents that a woman symbolized Jesus' burial, while the Jewish authorities plotted with Judas how to arrest Jesus without causing a riot, and Jesus predicted that one of his disciples would betray him to the authorities, all foreshadowing Jesus' eminent death. This unit consists of a *contraction* and an AMPLIFICATION.

BOUNDARIES AND COHERENCE

Both the initial and the closing boundaries coincide with the boundaries of the first and final included episodes. In this unit Mark presents the events which foreshadowed Jesus' death.

PROMINENCE AND THEME

The theme statement is derived from a summary of the included units reflecting the prominence of the *contraction*-AMPLIFICATION structure.

SCENE CONSTITUENT 14:1–11 (Episode Cluster of 14:1–31)

THEME: A woman beautifully symbolized Jesus being buried, while the Jewish authorities plotted with Judas to arrest Jesus without causing a riot.	
MACROSTRUCTURE	CONTENTS
[A]	14:1–2 The Jewish leaders planned how they could seize Jesus without starting a riot.
[B]	14:3–9 Jesus commended a woman who extravagantly anointed Jesus in anticipation of his death.
[A']	14:10–11 After Judas negotiated with the religious authorities to help them seize Jesus

INTENT AND RHETORICAL STRUCTURE

There are three episodes in which Jesus' death is imminent. The Jewish authorities and Judas planned to arrest him without causing a riot, but a woman symbolically prepared Jesus for his burial.

These three episodes form a chiasmus. The first and last episodes (14:1–2 and 14:10–11) are about making plans to seize Jesus. The middle and prominent episode is about the woman who anointed Jesus (14:3–9).

This scene unit presents a foreshadowing of Jesus' eminent death by the authorities plotting his death, a woman anointing Jesus in preparation for his death, and Judas agreeing to betray Jesus in such a way that the authorities could arrest him without causing a riot.

BOUNDARIES AND COHERENCE

Both the initial and the closing boundaries coincide with the boundaries of the first and final included episodes. In this unit Mark presents the details concerning Jesus' imminent death.

PROMINENCE AND THEME

The theme statement arises from the prominence structure of the three chiastic episodes.

EPISODE CLUSTER CONSTITUENT 14:1–2 (Episode of 14:1–11)

THEME: The Jewish leaders planned how they could seize Jesus without starting a riot.

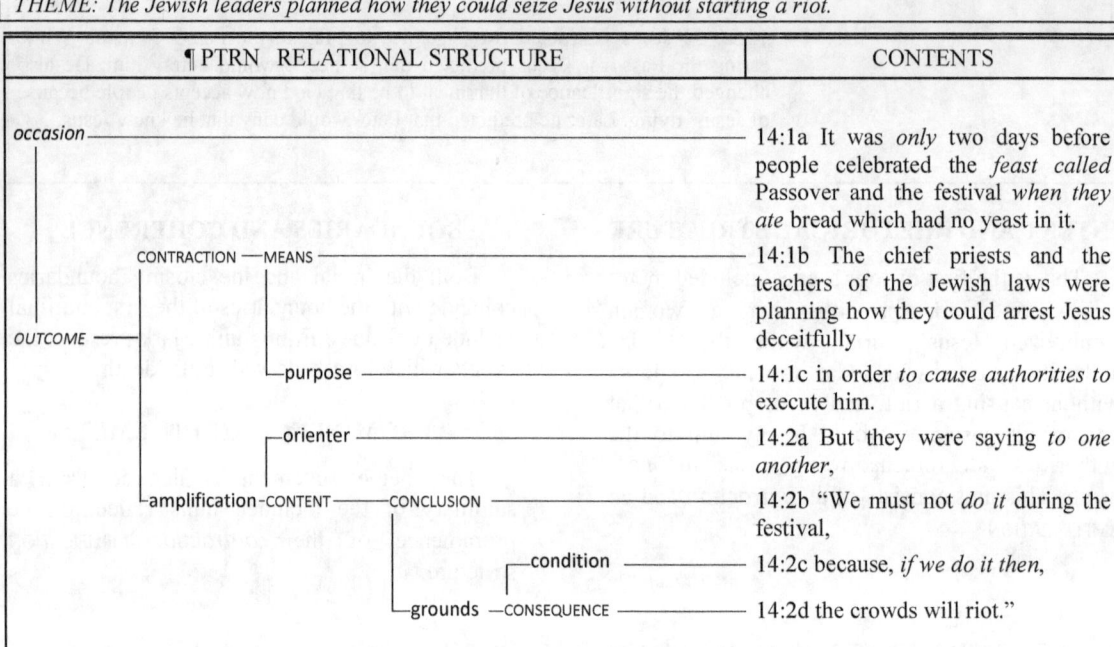

INTENT AND RHETORICAL STRUCTURE

The episode structure of this unit consists of an *occasion* and an OUTCOME.

Mark intends that the reader understand that the Jewish authorities had decided to arrest Jesus and have him killed.

NOTES

14:1a *only* two days NIV and NEB both include 'only'. If the Jewish leaders wanted to get rid of Jesus before the festivals, they had to act quickly.

***festival when they ate* bread which had no yeast in it** This spells out the one Greek word ἄζυμος 'unleavened'.

14:1c *to cause authorities to* execute him The Greek has 'they might kill' but the Jewish leaders knew they could not do it themselves.

BOUNDARIES AND COHERENCE

A new paragraph at v. 3 is indicated by a new location and a new topic: the anointing of Jesus. Coherence within the vv. 1–2 paragraph is shown by the words ἄζυμος '(feast of) unleavened bread' and ἑορτή 'festival', and by the deliberation by the religious leaders on how to do away with Jesus.

PROMINENCE AND THEME

The theme is drawn from a contraction of the OUTCOME in v. 1b and the CONSEQUENCE of the *grounds* v. 2d of the *amplification* of the OUTCOME.

EPISODE CLUSTER CONSTITUENT 14:3–9 (Episode of 14:1–11)

THEME: Jesus commended a woman who extravagantly anointed Jesus in anticipation of his death.	
¶ PTRN RELATIONAL STRUCTURE	CONTENTS

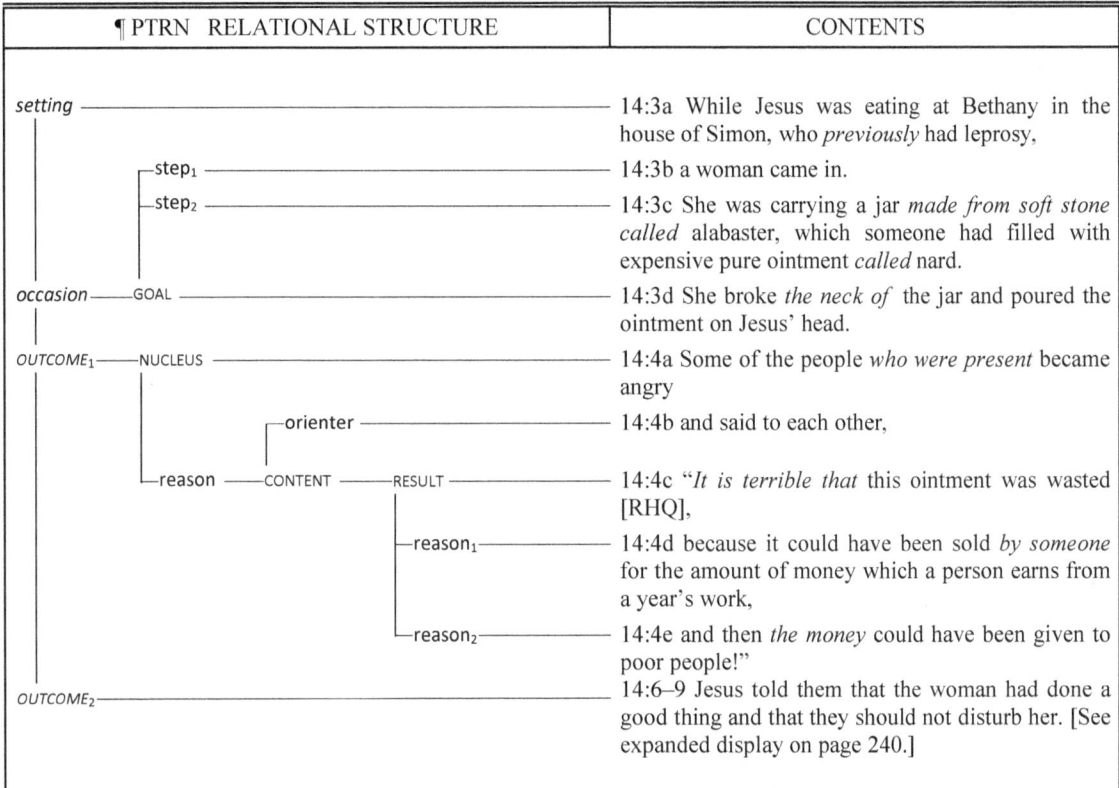

INTENT AND RHETORICAL STRUCTURE

This unit consists of an *occasion* and TWO OUTCOMES. Mark intends that the reader understand that a woman greatly honored Jesus just shortly before his death. The paragraph consists of a *setting*, an *occasion*, an OUTCOME$_1$, and an OUTCOME$_2$.

NOTES

14:3a who *previously* had leprosy Since lepers were not allowed to be near other people, he must have already been healed (see Stein, Hiebert, Lenski, Evans, and TRT).

14:3c jar *made from soft stone called* alabaster This spells out 'alabaster' which will be unfamiliar to most readers.

14:3d opened the jar The text says 'breaking'. It meant she broke the narrow neck of the jar and then poured out the contents (see JBP).

14:4c *It is terrible that* The text has a rhetorical question beginning with 'why?' which expresses strong disapproval.

14:4d amount of money which a person earns from a year's work The text has 'three hundred denarii'. A denarius was a standard day's wage, so NIV wisely renders the phrase as "a year's wages".

EXPANSION OF OUTCOME₂ 14:6–9 OF 14:3–9 DISPLAY

RELATIONAL STRUCTURE	CONTENTS
orienter	14:6a But Jesus said,
EXHORTATION	14:6b "Don't disturb her! I don't want [RHQ] you to bother her,
grounds — SPECIFIC — grounds₁	14:6c because she has done for me *what I consider* to be delightful.
reason	14:7a Poor *people* will always be among you,
grounds₂ — RESULT — CONTRAST₁	14:7b and, *as a result*, you can help them whenever you want to,
CONTRAST₂	14:7c but I will not *be here among* you forever.
amplification — generic	14:8a *It is appropriate that* she has done what she was able *to do:*
SPECIFIC — MEANS	14:8b *specifically, it is as if* she has anointed my body before *I die*
purpose	14:8c *in order to prepare it* before someone buries it.
COMMENT — reason	14:9a I want you to know that, wherever the good message is preached *by people* throughout the world, what she has done *to me* will be told,
RESULT	14:9b and *as a result, people* will remember her."

NOTES

14:6b I don't want you to The text has another rhetorical question starting with 'why?', expressing a rebuke.

14:8a Therefore, it is appropriate that she has done what she was able to do The text is literally 'what she had, she did'. The notion that this was appropriate, since the Messiah was soon to die, is conveyed by Cranfield and Lane.

14:8b it is as if The display makes it clear that she was not literally pouring perfume on Jesus' corpse.

14:9a I want you to know that See note on 9:41.

BOUNDARIES AND COHERENCE

A new paragraph at v. 10 is indicated by the account of Judas going to the chief priests. Coherence within the 3–9 paragraph is provided by two occurrences of μύρον 'ointment' and one of the cognate verb μυρίζω 'anoint'. Coherence is also provided by it being an incident of a woman pouring ointment on Jesus.

PROMINENCE AND THEME

The theme is taken from part of the orienter (to identify the speaker), a rephrasing of the *grounds* of EXHORTATION₁, the GOAL of the *occasion*, a condensation of the OUTCOME, and the NUCLEUS of RESULT₁.

EPISODE CLUSTER CONSTITUENT 14:10–11 (Episode of 14:1–11)

THEME: After Judas negotiated with the religious authorities to help them seize Jesus, he began to plan a way to do it.

RELATIONAL STRUCTURE	CONTENTS
occasion — CONTRA-EXPECTATION — MEANS	14:10a Then Judas Iscariot went to the chief priests
└ purpose	14:10b in order to *talk to them* about enabling them to seize Jesus.
└ concession	14:10c *He did that even though* he was one of the twelve *disciples*.
NUCLEUS₁	14:11a When they heard *what he said,* they were very happy,
OUTCOME₁ — ┌ orienter	14:11b and they promised
NUCLEUS₂ — CONTENT	14:11c that they would give him money *for doing that*.
OUTCOME₂	14:11d As a result, he began planning a convenient way to enable them to seize Jesus.

INTENT AND RHETORICAL STRUCTURE

This unit consists of an *occasion* and two OUTCOMES, demonstrating that this is a narrative.

Mark intends that the reader understand that the Jewish authorities were very happy that Judas offered to help them seize Jesus.

NOTES

14:10b enabling them to seize This conveys the sense of the word παραδίδωμι 'betray'.

14:10c *He did that even though* he was one of the twelve *disciples* The question here is, why does Mark mention this when he has already mentioned it in 3:19? Strauss says these words "magnify the crime." The wording here follows that in TfT and suggested in TN.

BOUNDARIES AND COHERENCE

A new paragraph at v. 12 is marked by an indication of time and a new theme, preparation for celebrating the Passover. Coherence within the 10–11 paragraph is seen in several references to Judas and the chief priests, and by the account of Judas going to the chief priests to talk about enabling them to seize Jesus.

PROMINENCE AND THEME

The theme is taken from a condensation of the two propositions of the *occasion* and the two OUTCOMES.

SCENE CONSTITUENT 14:12–31 (Episode Cluster of 14:1–31)

THEME: Jesus instructed two disciples to prepare the Passover meal. While eating the Passover, Jesus predicted that someone would betray him. He also changed the significance of that meal to be that God now accepts people because of Jesus' dying. Later he predicted that Peter would deny that he knew Jesus.

MACROSTRUCTURE	CONTENTS
occasion	14:12–17 Two disciples followed Jesus' instructions and prepared the Passover meal.
OUTCOME₁	14:18–26 During the Passover meal, Jesus prophesied that one disciple would betray him. He gave his disciples bread and wine which represented his body and blood which would be sacrificed to establish the new agreement with many people.
OUTCOME₂	14:27–31 Jesus predicted that Peter would deny three times that he knew him.

INTENT AND RHETORICAL STRUCTURE

This is the scene in which Jesus predicts that Judas will betray him and that Peter will deny that he knew him.

This unit consists of an *occasion* and two OUTCOMES. Mark intends that the reader understand the events of preparing the Passover meal, its significance, and that Judas would betray him, while Peter would deny that he knew him.

BOUNDARIES AND COHERENCE

Both the initial and the closing boundaries coincide with the boundaries of the first and final included episodes. In this unit Mark presents the details of Jesus' eating the Passover meal with his disciples.

PROMINENCE AND THEME

The theme statement arises from the prominence structure of the *occasion* and two OUTCOMES.

EPISODE CLUSTER CONSTITUENT 14:12–17 (Episode of 14:12–31)

THEME: *Two disciples followed Jesus' instructions and prepared the Passover meal.*

¶ PTRN RELATIONAL STRUCTURE	CONTENTS
occasion	14:12a *It was now* the first day of the festival *when people ate* bread which had no yeast and when they used to kill lambs *in order to celebrate that festival.*
SEQUENCE₁ — CONTENT — orienter	14:12b Jesus' disciples said to him,
⎣ MEANS	14:12c "Where do you want us to go and prepare the Passover meal
⎣ purpose	14:12d in order that you can eat it *with us*?"
orienter	14:13a So Jesus chose two of his disciples and said this to them:
step₁	14:13b "Go into the city *of Jerusalem*.
step₂	14:13c A man will meet you, who will be carrying a large jar full of water.
step₃	14:13d Follow him.
step₄ — orienter	14:14a When he enters a house, say to the person who owns the house,
⎣ CONTENT	14:14b 'The teacher wants to know, "Where is the room where I *arranged* to eat the meal of the Passover with my disciples?'
OUTCOME₁ — SEQUENCE₂ — CONTENT — GOAL — NUCLEUS₁	14:15a He will show you a large room which is on the upper *floor of* the house and which is furnished and ready *for us to eat a meal in it.*
⎣ NUCLEUS₂	14:15b And prepare *the meal* there for us."
step₁	14:16a The two disciples left.
step₂	14:16b They went into the city.
step₃	14:16c They found everything *to be* like Jesus had told them.
SEQUENCE₃ — GOAL	14:16d So they prepared the meal of the Passover, *and then returned to Jesus.*
OUTCOME₂	14:17 When it was evening, Jesus arrived *at that house* with the twelve disciples.

INTENT AND RHETORICAL STRUCTURE

Mark intends that the reader understand that Jesus knew exactly what would take place. The paragraph is a causality type narrative consisting of an *occasion*, an OUTCOME$_1$, and a second OUTCOME$_2$.

NOTES

14:12a kill a lamb *in order to celebrate that festival* This represents 'they sacrificed the passover'. Here the word 'passover' means the lambs killed for that festival. TEV has "the lambs for the Passover meal were killed". There is a lot of implicit information from Exodus 12 regarding the word 'Passover' but it is not needed here, except perhaps as a footnote.

14:13a Jesus chose The GNT has 'Jesus sent' but the sending comes in v. 16; the instructions to them come first. Cf. CEV.

14:13c large jar These were made from clay. Many commentators point out that this would be surprising, because normally only women carried such jars.

14:14b he *arranged* **to eat** Some commentators think that knowing about this place was supernatural knowledge on Jesus' part, but the great majority say it was prearranged by Jesus.

14:15a ready *for us to eat a meal in it* The words in italics spell out what is meant by 'ready'. CEV has "ready for you to use".

14:17 *and then returned to Jesus* The next verse says that Jesus came with the twelve. It must therefore be assumed that when the meal was ready, the two disciples returned to where Jesus and the others were.

BOUNDARIES AND COHERENCE

A new paragraph at v. 18 is marked by references to their eating the Passover meal. Coherence within the 12–17 episode is provided by two occurrences of πάσχα 'Passover' and two of ἑτοιμάζω 'prepare'. It is also provided by it being on the preparations for their eating the Passover meal.

PROMINENCE AND THEME

The theme is taken from a condensation of the two propositions of the *occasion,* NUCLEUS$_2$ of SEQUENCE$_2$, and a condensation of the GOAL of SEQUENCE$_3$ of OUTCOME$_1$.

EPISODE CLUSTER CONSTITUENT 14:18–26 (Episode of 14:12–31)

Theme: During the Passover meal, Jesus prophesied that one disciple would betray him. He gave his disciples bread and wine which represented his body and blood which would be sacrificed to establish the new agreement with many people.

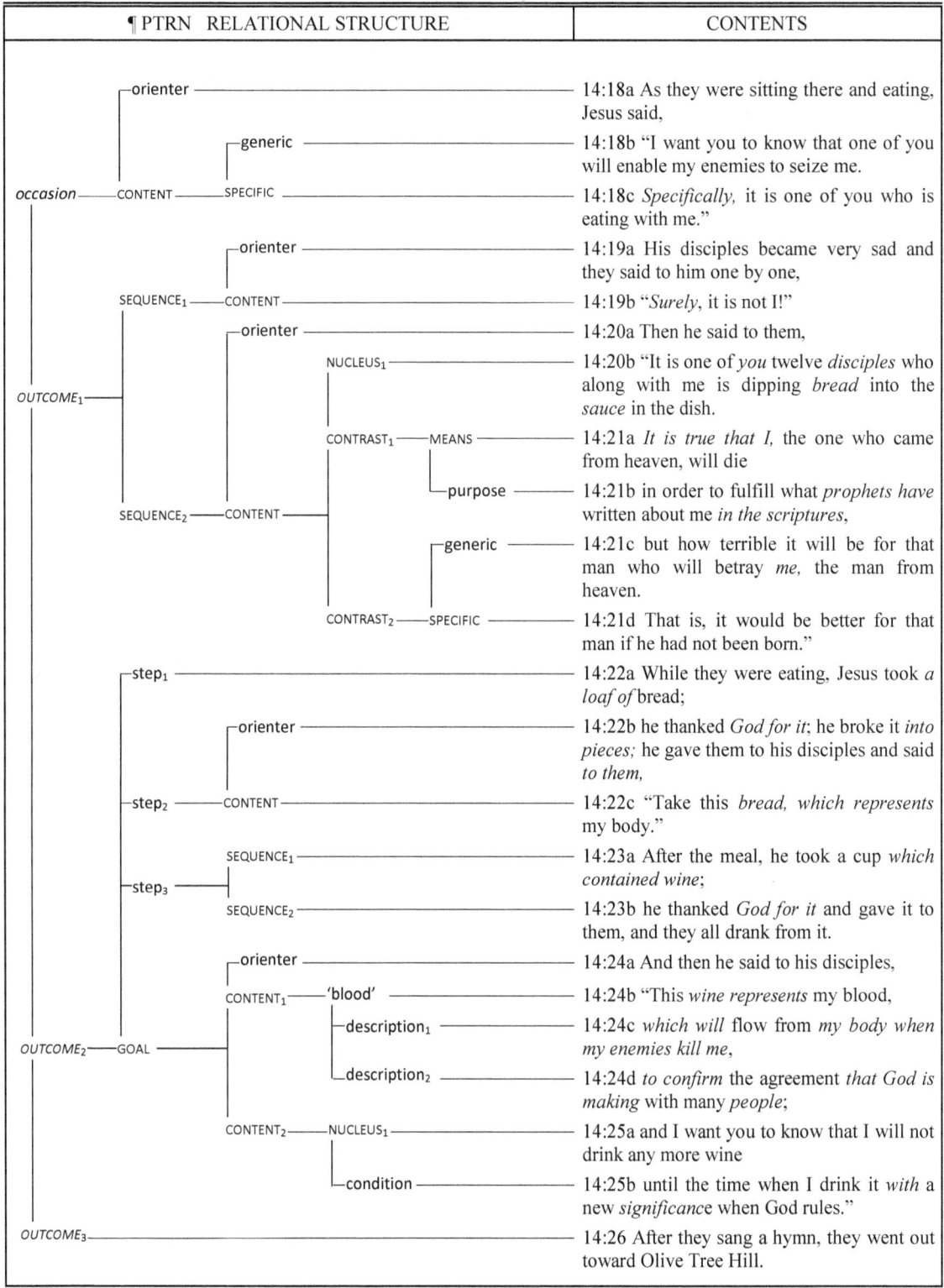

INTENT AND RHETORICAL STRUCTURE

The pattern structure of this narrative unit consists of an *occasion*, and three OUTCOMES.

Mark intends that the reader understand that Jesus knew exactly what would take place, and that he ate the Passover meal with his disciples.

NOTES

14:18b I want you to know See note on 14:9a and 9:41.

14:20b dipping *bread* into the *sauce* in the dish The text has 'dipping in the dish'; several versions (e.g., NIV, TEV, Williams, 20th Century) specify 'bread'. Marcus notes that dipping food in bowls of sauces and relishes was a common feature of meals.

14:21a will die The text has 'is going' which is a euphemism; versions which say 'die' include CEV, TEV, and NLT.

14:21b *in the scriptures* The words 'it is written' imply 'in the Scriptures'; see note on 9:12c. Versions which include the word 'scriptures' include TEV, CEV, NLT, Williams, 20th Century, NEB, JBP, and JB.

14:21c how terrible it will be This represents the word 'woe'. CEV's rendering is very similar to that in the display; see also TEV.

14:22c, 24b which represents my body... represents my blood Translators need to consult the local churches before deciding to follow the display. Many, but not all, churches believe that the references to body and blood are metaphorical. No version except TfT makes this clear.

14:23a cup *which contained wine* The text says only 'cup'. CEV, Williams, and NLT all have "cup of wine".

14:24d *to* confirm the agreement that God is making This spells out the meaning of the words 'of the covenant'. TEV has "which seals the covenant". NLT is clearer with "sealing the covenant between God and his people".

Following the Byzantine text form, some versions include the word 'new' before the word 'agreement'. Its addition in some manuscripts was probably motivated by the wording in Luke 22:20 and 1 Cor. 11:25. Its omission is given a B 'almost certain' rating.

14:25a I want you to know See note on 18b.

14:25b drink it *with* a new *significance* The text has 'I drink it new'. Commentators are about equally divided as to the meaning. Some say it functions adjectivally, to describe the fruit as being a new kind; see also TEV, NJB, GW, and CEV. The others say it functions adverbially, with the sense of 'anew' = again. The wording in the display seems to make the most sense (see suggestion in TN).

when God rules See previous notes about 'kingdom' (e.g., 1:15).

BOUNDARIES AND COHERENCE

A new paragraph at v. 27 is marked by an interchange between Peter and Jesus. Coherence is provided by two occurrences of 'the Twelve', two of παραδίδωμι 'betray', and by the paragraph giving what Jesus said and did during that Passover meal.

PROMINENCE AND THEME

The theme is taken from a rephrasing of the *occasion*, the generic proposition of the CONTENT of the *occasion*, the CONTENT of $step_2$ and a condensation of the two propositions v. 23a–b of $step_3$ of $OUTCOME_2$.

EPISODE CLUSTER CONSTITUENT 14:27–31 (Episode of 14:12–31)

Theme: Jesus predicted that Peter would deny three times that he knew him.

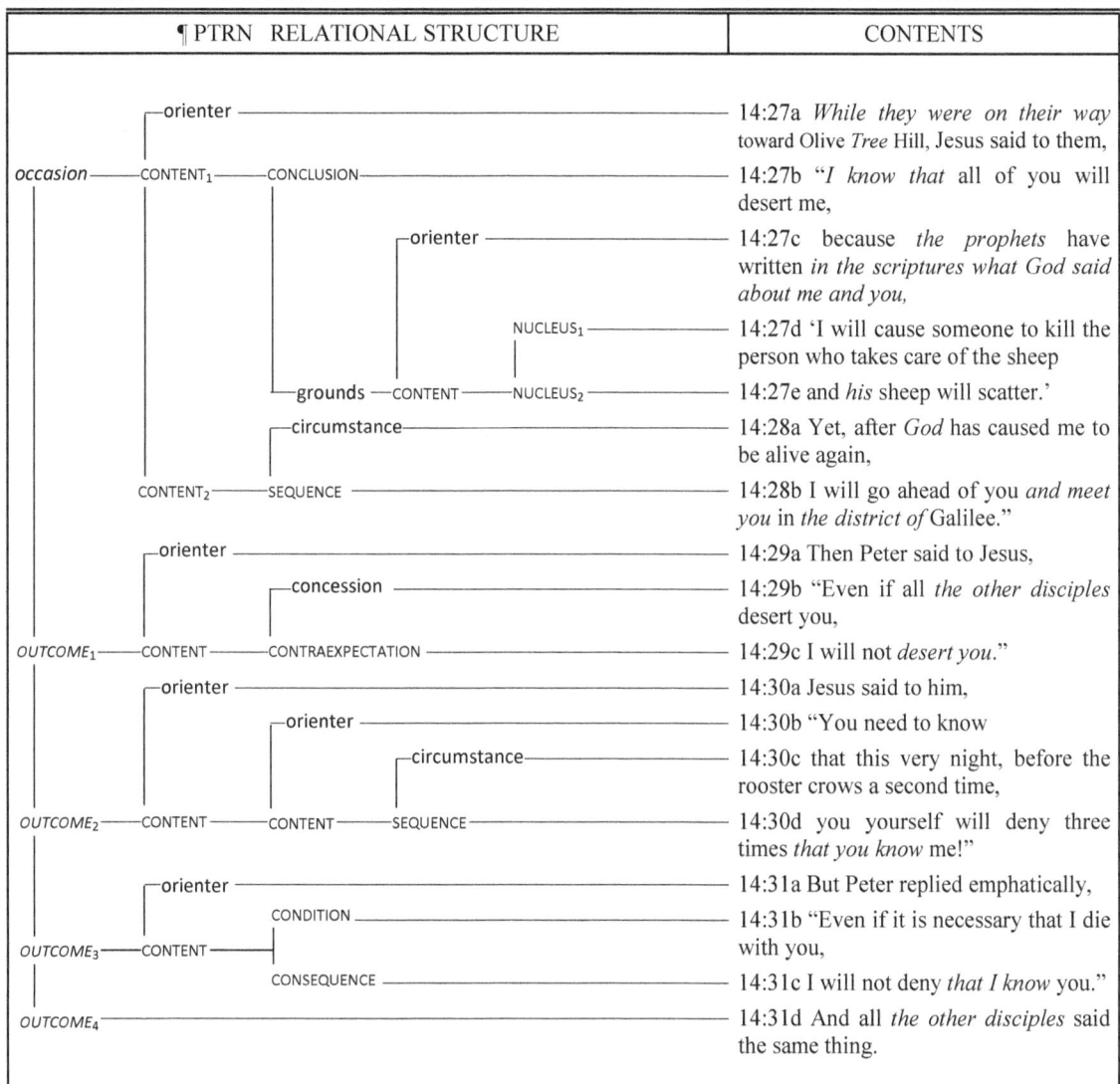

INTENT AND RHETORICAL STRUCTURE

This episode tells about Jesus predicting that Peter would deny three times that he knew him.

Mark intends that the reader understand that Jesus knew exactly what would take place, and that Peter would deny that he knew him three times. The episode is a causality type narrative consisting of an *occasion*, and four OUTCOMES.

NOTES

14:27a *While they were on their way* Lenski says "Jesus makes this disclosure on the way to Gethsemane." See also Strauss, Hiebert, TN.

14:27c *the prophets* **have written** *in the scriptures* For 'in the scriptures', see note on 14:21b. The display also supplies the implied agent of the passive 'is written'.

***what* God said** This supplies the referent of the pronoun 'I' in 27d. NLT and TEV make this clear by rendering "God will strike" in 27d.

14:27f *And those words apply to me and you disciples* This proposition supplies the topic of the metaphor: Jesus was saying that in the passage he quoted, the shepherd referred to himself and the sheep referred to his disciples.

14:27a ***While they were on their way*** Lenski says "Jesus makes this disclosure on the way to Gethsemane." See also Strauss, Hiebert, TN.

14:27b ***I know that*** 14:27c starts with 'because', providing the reason for 27a. But it makes much more sense to say that the scripture quoted here (from Zech. 13:7) provides the reason that Jesus <u>knew</u> they would all desert him, rather than the reason they would desert him.

14:27c ***the prophets*** **have written** ***in the scriptures*** For 'in the scriptures', see note on 14:21b. The display also supplies the implied agent of the passive 'is written'.

what God said This supplies the referent of the pronoun 'I' in 27d. NLT and TEV make this clear by rendering "God will strike" in 27d.

14:27d Jesus was quoting from Zech. 13:7.

14:27f ***And those words apply to me and you disciples*** This proposition supplies the topic of the metaphor: Jesus was saying that in the passage he quoted, the shepherd referred to himself and the sheep referred to his disciples.

14:29b **Even if** What Peter was saying was, 'If the other disciples desert you, you would expect that I would, too, but I will not'.

all the other disciples The words in italics specify who Peter meant by 'all'. TEV has "all the others".

14:30b **you need to know** This again represents 'I tell you truly'; see note on 9:14.

14:30c **a second time** There is a textual question here: the word meaning 'a second time' does not occur in some manuscripts. It is included in the UBS with a C "difficult to decide" rating.

14:30d deny...*that you know* **me** The text has 'deny me'. The display makes the meaning clear. CEV has "say that you don't know me".

14:31d all *the other disciples* See note on 29b.

BOUNDARIES AND COHERENCE

The start of a new paragraph at v. 32 is marked by a change in location and a new topic: Jesus' prayers in Gethsemane. Coherence within the 27–31 paragraph is provided by two occurrences of ἀπαρνέομαι 'deny', and by Jesus saying that Peter would deny that he knew him.

PROMINENCE AND THEME

The theme is taken from the *orienter* in 30a (to identify the speaker) and v. 14:30d sequence$_2$ of OUTCOME$_2$.

ACT CONSTITUENT 14:32—15:41 (Scene of 14:1—16:8)

THEME: Jesus enemies, the Jewish authorities and the Roman authorities, arrested Jesus, tried him, and then crucified him.

MACROSTRUCTURE	CONTENTS
initiation	14:32–52 Jesus' disciples slept while they were supposed to be on guard. Judas came with an armed crowd and arrested Jesus. All the disciples and even Mark ran away.
build-up	14:53—15:20 The Jewish authorities had an illegal mock trial of Jesus. Incidentally, Peter denied Jesus just as Jesus said he would. The Roman authority had a trial, but was swayed by the crowd so that he ordered Jesus to be executed. Then the Roman soldiers mocked Jesus as if he were a king.
CLIMAX	15:21–41 After the soldiers crucified Jesus, they gambled for his clothing, other people insulted him, and then Jesus died; the temple curtain split in two, and a Roman officer declared that Jesus was the Son of God.

INTENT AND RHETORICAL STRUCTURE

This is the second of four scenes included in ACT IV, where Mark presents that Jesus suffered, died, and rose again. In this unit Mark gives the details of Jesus' arrest, trial, and execution. This unit consists of an *initiation, a build-up,* and a CLIMAX.

Here Mark intends that the reader understand that Jesus was crucified by the Jewish and Roman authorities as he said would happen.

BOUNDARIES AND COHERENCE

Both the initial and the closing boundaries coincide with the boundaries of the first and final included episodes. In this unit Mark presents the details of Jesus' death.

PROMINENCE AND THEME

The theme statement is derived from a summary of the included units reflecting the prominence of the rhetorical structure.

SCENE CONSTITUENT 14:32–52 (Episode Cluster of 14:32—15:41)

THEME: *Jesus' disciples slept while they were supposed to be on guard. Judas came with an armed crowd and arrested Jesus. All the disciples and even Mark ran away.*

MACROSTRUCTURE	CONTENTS
problem	14:32–42 While the disciples slept, Jesus prayed that God would spare him from the coming suffering.
RESOLUTION	14:43–49 Judas betrayed Jesus, and the armed crowd arrested Jesus.
SEQUEL	14:50–52 Mark ran away.

INTENT AND RHETORICAL STRUCTURE

This is the first episode cluster of the scene in which Jesus is crucified and died. In this unit the Jewish authorities arrest Jesus. These three episodes consist of a *problem*, a RESOLUTION, and a SEQUEL.

BOUNDARIES AND COHERENCE

Both the initial and the closing boundaries coincide with the boundaries of the first and final included episodes. In this unit Mark presents the details of Jesus' arrest.

PROMINENCE AND THEME

The theme statement arises from the prominence structure of the three episodes.

EPISODE CLUSTER CONSTITUENT 14:32–42 (Episode of 14:32–52)

THEME: While the disciples slept, Jesus prayed that God would spare him from the coming suffering. Then he awoke them before he was seized.

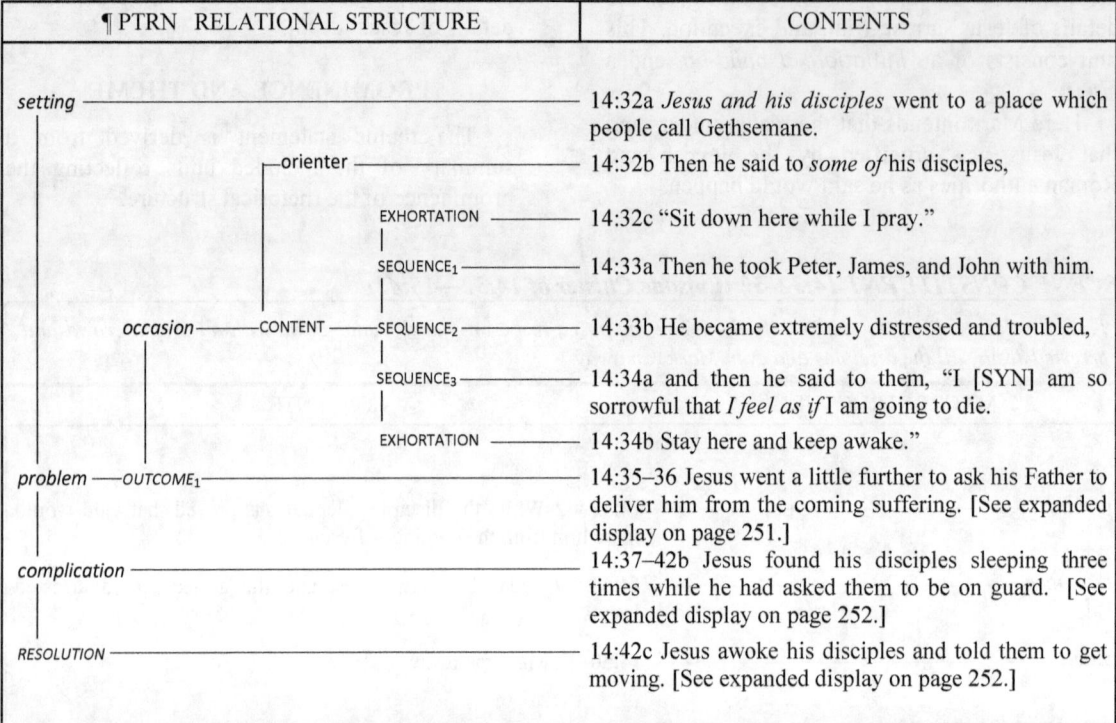

¶PTRN RELATIONAL STRUCTURE	CONTENTS
setting	14:32a *Jesus and his disciples* went to a place which people call Gethsemane.
orienter	14:32b Then he said to *some of* his disciples,
EXHORTATION	14:32c "Sit down here while I pray."
SEQUENCE₁	14:33a Then he took Peter, James, and John with him.
occasion — CONTENT — SEQUENCE₂	14:33b He became extremely distressed and troubled,
SEQUENCE₃	14:34a and then he said to them, "I [SYN] am so sorrowful that *I feel as if* I am going to die.
EXHORTATION	14:34b Stay here and keep awake."
problem — OUTCOME₁	14:35–36 Jesus went a little further to ask his Father to deliver him from the coming suffering. [See expanded display on page 251.]
complication	14:37–42b Jesus found his disciples sleeping three times while he had asked them to be on guard. [See expanded display on page 252.]
RESOLUTION	14:42c Jesus awoke his disciples and told them to get moving. [See expanded display on page 252.]

INTENT AND RHETORICAL STRUCTURE

Mark intends that the reader understand that Jesus agonized praying while his disciples could not stay awake as he told them to. This episode consists of a *setting*, a *problem*, a *complication*, and a RESOLUTION.

NOTES

14:32a *Jesus and the disciples* The display identifies the referent of 'they'; CEV does likewise.

14:32b **some of his disciples** It is clear from v. 33 that he did not say this to all the disciples.

14:34a so that *it is as if* I were going to die CEV similarly has "I feel as if I am dying".

EXPANSION OF PROBLEM 14:35–36 IN THE 14:32–42 DISPLAY:

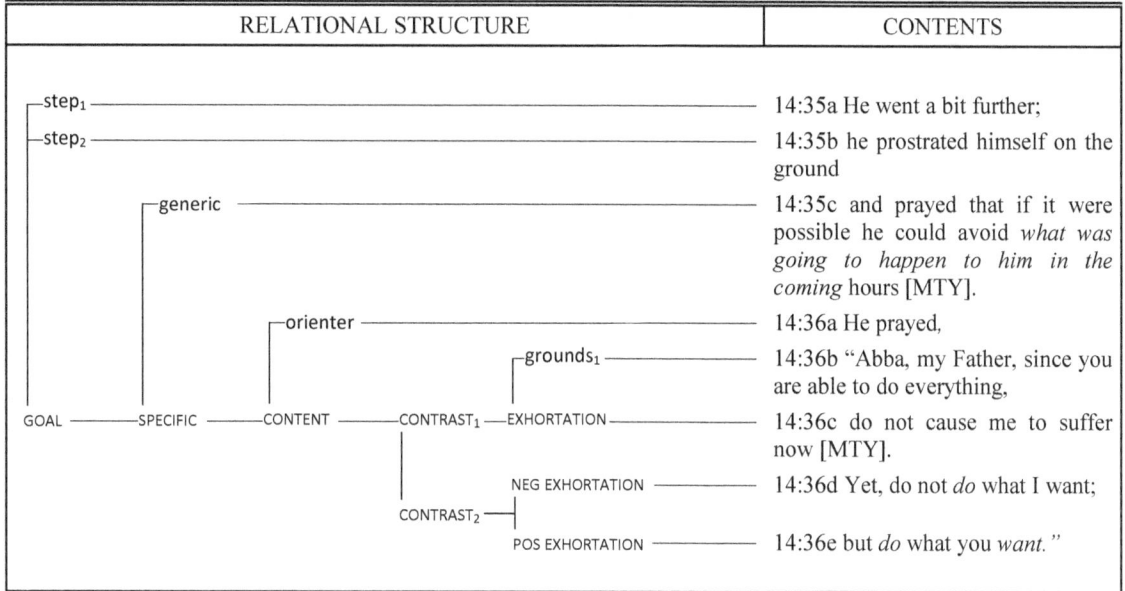

NOTES

14:35c *what was going to happen to him in the coming* hours The GNT has 'the hour might pass away from him'. This is a metonymy: a time standing for the events that would occur during that time. TEV has "he might not have to go through that time of suffering". See also GW and NCV.

14:36c do not cause me to suffer now The text has 'take this cup from me'; 'cup' is a dead metaphor referring to suffering. See L&N. All versions examined except TfT retain the word 'cup', but dead metaphors should never be retained in a translation.

EXPANSION OF COMPLICATION 14:37–42 IN THE 14:32–42 DISPLAY:

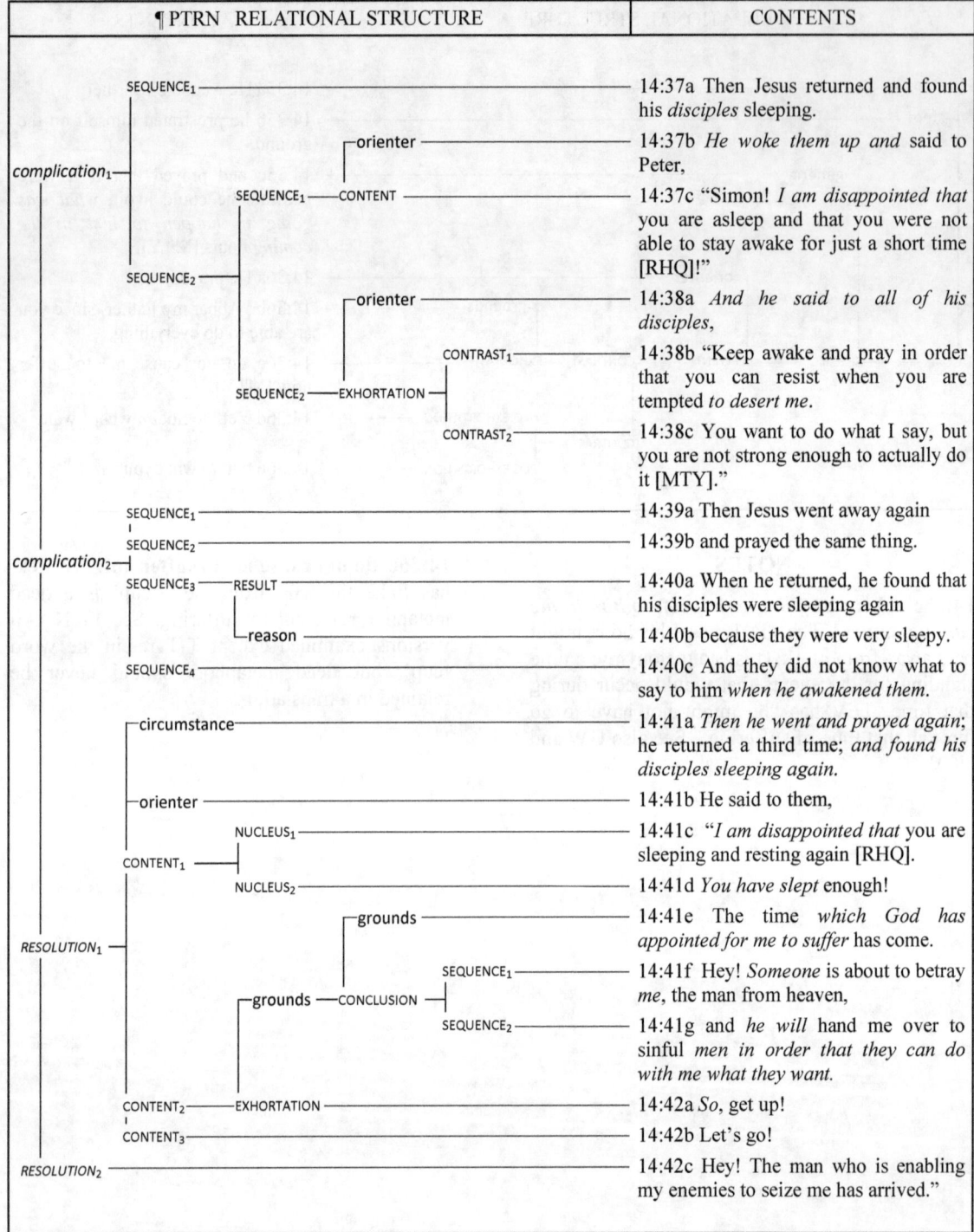

NOTES

14:37b *He woke them up and* **said** This is implied; he couldn't talk to Peter if Peter were still asleep.

14:37c *I am disappointed that* The words 'Are you asleep?' are a rhetorical question that both expresses disappointment and constitutes a rebuke.

14:38a *And he said to all of* **his disciples** The exhortations in 38b are in the 2nd person plural; the words in italics indicate this transition. TEV starts the verse with "And he said to them".

14:38b tempted *to desert me* The problem here is, what temptation was Jesus referring to? The display follows France, Strauss, Lane and Gundry.

14:38c you want *to do what I say***, but you are not strong** *enough to actually do it* This represents the cryptic saying, 'the spirit is willing but the flesh is weak'. CEV's rendering is quite good: "You want to do what is right, but you are weak".

14:40c *when he awakened them* This the implied intervening action which must be understood. See TN.

14:41a *Then he went and prayed again;* **he returned a third time;** *and found his disciples sleeping again* The material in italics again states the intervening actions.

14:41c *I am disappointed that* This is another rhetorical question with the same force as that in 37c.

14:41d You have slept enough The text has only the word 'enough'. The display provides a brief complete clause; see TN and L&N.

14:41e There is somewhat of a textual problem here, but the wording here is given a B 'almost certain' rating in the GNT.

The time *which God has appointed for me to suffer* **has come** This is again considered a metonymy in which a time stands for the events that will occur during that time.

14:41g sinful *men in order that they can do with me what they want* Something like this may be needed to indicate the purpose of the 'handing over'.

14:42c enabling my enemies to seize me See note on 3:19 regarding 'betray'.

BOUNDARIES AND COHERENCE

A new paragraph at v. 43 is marked by the arrival of Judas and those accompanying him, and a new topic; the seizure of Jesus. Coherence within the 32–42 unit is seen in three occurrences of the verb ἀπαρνέομαι 'pray' and three occurrences of καθεύδω 'sleep'. Coherence is also seen in the paragraph giving further events of Jesus' praying in the garden of Gethsemane and his interaction there with the sleeping disciples.

PROMINENCE AND THEME

The theme of this paragraph is taken from SEQUENCE₁ and the *specific* of the GOAL of COMPLICATION₁ and the *RESOLUTION*.

EPISODE CLUSTER CONSTITUENT 14:43–49 (Episode of 14:32–52)

THEME: *Judas betrayed Jesus, and the armed crowd arrested Jesus.*

¶ PTRN RELATIONAL STRUCTURE	CONTENTS
setting	14:43a While he was still speaking, Judas Iscariot, who was one of the twelve *disciples*, arrived.
occasion — NUCLEUS₁ — 'crowd'	14:43b With him *came* a crowd who carried swords and clubs,
└ identification	14:43c *who had been sent* by the chief priests, teachers of the Jewish laws, and elders.
NUCLEUS₂ — CONTENT — circumstance	14:44a *Before that, in order that they would know which man to arrest, Judas*, who was going to enable them to seize Jesus,
orienter	14:44b had told *this crowd*,
EXHORTATION — grounds	14:44c "The man whom I shall kiss is *the one you want to arrest*.
SEQUENCE₁	14:44d Therefore, seize him
SEQUENCE₂	14:44e and lead him away *while you guard him* carefully."
OUTCOME₁ — SEQUENCE₁ — NUCLEUS₁ — GOAL — step₁	14:45a So, when Judas arrived,
step₂	14:45b he immediately went up to Jesus
step₃ — orienter	14:45c and said,
CONTENT	14:45d "My teacher!"
GOAL	14:45e And he kissed Jesus *on the cheek*.
NUCLEUS₂	14:46a Then the *crowd* seized Jesus and they held him securely.
SEQUENCE₂ — STEP	14:47a One of the *disciples* who was standing nearby drew his sword
GOAL — MEANS	14:47b and struck the servant of the Supreme Priest *with it;*
purpose	*14:47c he intended to kill the man,* but missed and only cut off his ear.
concession — CONTENT — orienter	14:48a Jesus responded by saying to the crowd,
CONCLUSION	14:48b "*It is ridiculous that* you have come here to capture me with swords and clubs, as if I were a bandit [RHQ],
grounds — CONTRAST₁	14:49a *because* day after day I was with you in the temple *while I* taught *people*
CONTRAST₂	14:49b and you did not seize me.
OUTCOME₂ — CONTRAEXPECTATION	14:49c But, *this is happening* in order that *what is written in* the scriptures *about me* may happen."

INTENT AND RHETORICAL STRUCTURE

Mark intends that the reader understand that the armed crowd sent by the Jewish authorities were able to arrest Jesus by Judas betraying him.

This is a causality type narrative consisting of a *setting*, an *occasion*, an OUTCOME, and a second OUTCOME.

NOTES

14:43a one of the twelve *disciples* The question again arises, why is Judas again identified as being one of the twelve disciples? Hiebert and Gould both say it emphasizes the ignominy of Judas' action. See note on 14:10.

14:43b a crowd The reading 'large crowd' is very poorly supported, but is found in the KJV.

14:44a *Before that, in order that they would know which man to arrest* This is supplied to provide the implied purpose of Judas kissing Jesus. See TN.

14:44c is the one *you want to arrest* The text has only the words 'he is'. TEV has "is the one you want".

14:44e *while you guard him* carefully The text has 'securely'. TEV and NLT have "under guard".

14:45e *on the cheek* This was the cultural way of kissing between friends; it may be needed to avoid wrong meaning.

14:47c *he intended to kill the man but missed and only* cut off his ear See Lenski; without this information readers would likely assume that slicing off the man's ear was all that was intended.

14:48b *It is ridiculous that* The text has a rhetorical yes/no question. It again conveys a rebuke but also expresses ridicule.

14:49c But, *this is happening* in order that *what is written in* the scriptures *about me* may happen The text is only a partial sentence, 'in order that the Scriptures may be fulfilled'. NLT has "But these things are happening..." The other bits in italics are contextually implied; NLT also has "about me".

BOUNDARIES AND COHERENCE

A new paragraph at v. 50 is marked by the topic of all Jesus' disciples running away. Coherence within the 43–49 paragraph is provided by two occurrences of φιλέω 'kiss', two of ξύλον 'clubs' and three of μάχαιρα 'sword'. Coherence is also provided by the paragraph narrating the account of Jesus being seized.

PROMINENCE AND THEME

The theme is taken from a rephrasing of the circumstance of the *occasion* and the GOAL of SEQUENCE₁ of the OUTCOME.

EPISODE CLUSTER CONSTITUENT 14:50–52 (Episode of 14:32–52)

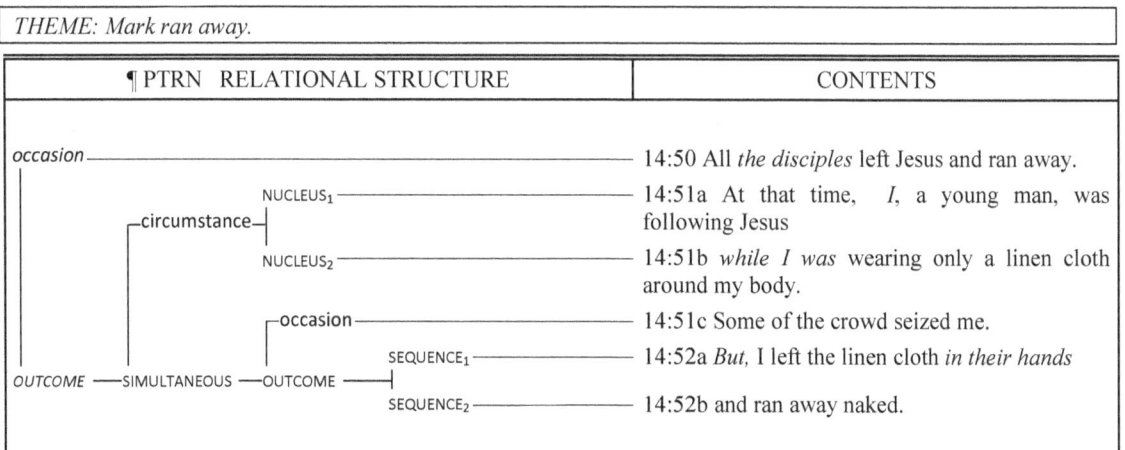

INTENT AND RHETORICAL STRUCTURE

Mark intends that the reader understand that he ran away.

This is a causality type narrative consisting of an *occasion* and an OUTCOME.

NOTES

14:51a *I, a young man* Hendriksen says that although there are commentators who say that the identification of the young man is impossible, the majority say that it was Mark. Hendriksen presents three good reasons for saying it was Mark. For this writer, the strongest reason is that it doesn't make any sense to be stated if it was anyone else; but for Mark, it was an inconspicuous way of 'leaving his own footprints' in the narrative.

14:52a cloth *in their hands* This is implied; he did not lay it carefully on the ground. JB and JBP also include "in their hands".

BOUNDARIES AND COHERENCE

The new paragraph starting at v. 53 is marked by their taking Jesus to a new location, and the topic of his trial before the religious authorities. Coherence within the 50–52 paragraph is seen in two occurrences of σινδών 'nightgown' and two of γυμνός 'naked', and by it being the brief account of the young man fleeing the scene.

PROMINENCE AND THEME

The theme is taken from SEQUENCE$_2$ of the OUTCOME.

SCENE CONSTINUENT 14:53—15:20 (Episode Cluster of 14:32—15:41)

THEME: *The Jewish authorities had an illegal mock trial of Jesus. Incidentally, Peter denied Jesus just as Jesus said he would. The Roman authority had a trial, but was swayed by the crowd so that he ordered Jesus to be executed. Then the Roman soldiers mocked Jesus as if he were a king.*

MACROSTRUCTURE	CONTENTS
move$_1$	14:53–65 After witnesses accusing Jesus contradicted each other, Jesus said that he was the Son of God, the Messiah, after which the Jewish leaders decided that Jesus must be executed.
observation	14:66–72 As Jesus predicted, Peter denied three times that he knew Jesus.
move$_2$	15:1–5 In the governor Pilate's presence Jesus refused to answer accusations against him.
GOAL	15:6–15 At the crowd's insistence (instigated by the Jewish religious authorities), Pilate released a criminal and ordered that Jesus be crucified.
SEQUEL	15:16–20 The soldiers ridiculed Jesus as being a king.

INTENT AND RHETORICAL STRUCTURE

This is the second episode cluster of the scene in which Jesus is crucified. In this unit the Jewish and Roman authorities conduct the trials of Jesus. These five included episodes consist of two *moves* (14:53–56 and 15:15), an author *observation* (14:66–72), a GOAL (15:6–15), and a SEQUEL (15:16–20).

BOUNDARIES AND COHERENCE

Both the initial and the closing boundaries coincide with the boundaries of the first and final included episodes. In this unit Mark presents the details of Jesus' trials.

PROMINENCE AND THEME

The theme statement arises from the prominence structure of the five episodes.

EPISODE CLUSTER CONSTITUENT 14:53–65 (Episode of 14:53—15:20)

Theme: After witnesses accusing Jesus contradicted each other, Jesus said that he was the Son of God, the Messiah, after which the Jewish leaders decided that Jesus must be executed.

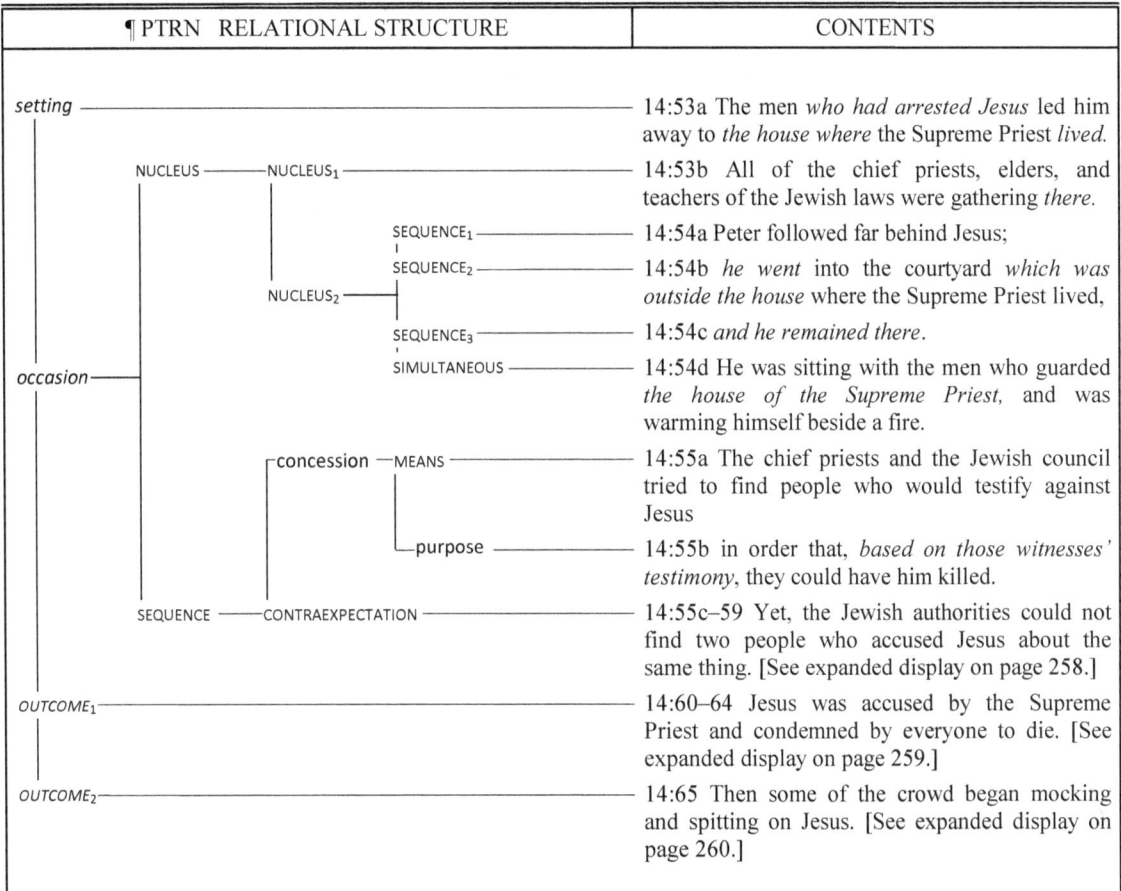

INTENT AND RHETORICAL STRUCTURE

This is the first of five episodes in the scene about Jesus being tried by the authorities. This one is specifically about Jesus being tried by the Jewish authorities.

This is a causality type narrative consisting of a *setting* (14:53a), an *occasion* (14:53b–59), an OUTCOME₁ (14:60–64), and an OUTCOME₂ (14:65).

Mark intends that the reader understand that Jewish authorities tried Jesus according to their laws.

There is a dialogue chain between the Supreme Priest and Jesus that ties the FIRST OUTCOME together.

The motif of 'rejection and suffering' is central to this entire episode.

NOTES

14:53a The men *who had arrested Jesus* The display identifies the referent of the pronoun 'they'.

14:54b courtyard *which was outside the house* The text has 'courtyard of the high priest'. CEV and TEV have "courtyard of the high priest's house".

Supreme Priest The word ἀρχιερεύς is usually rendered as 'high priest' but 'high' is ambiguous. See note on 2:26a.

14:54d guarded *the house of the Supreme Priest* The text has 'guards'; the display makes clear what kind of guards they were.

14:55b *based on their testimony*, they could have him killed The text has 'so that they could put him to death'. This omits the intervening action: that the result of what they would testify against Jesus would be that they could present this evidence to the Roman authorities, who alone had the power to execute criminals.

EXPANSION OF CONTRAEXPECTATION 14:55c–59 IN THE 14:53–65 DISPLAY

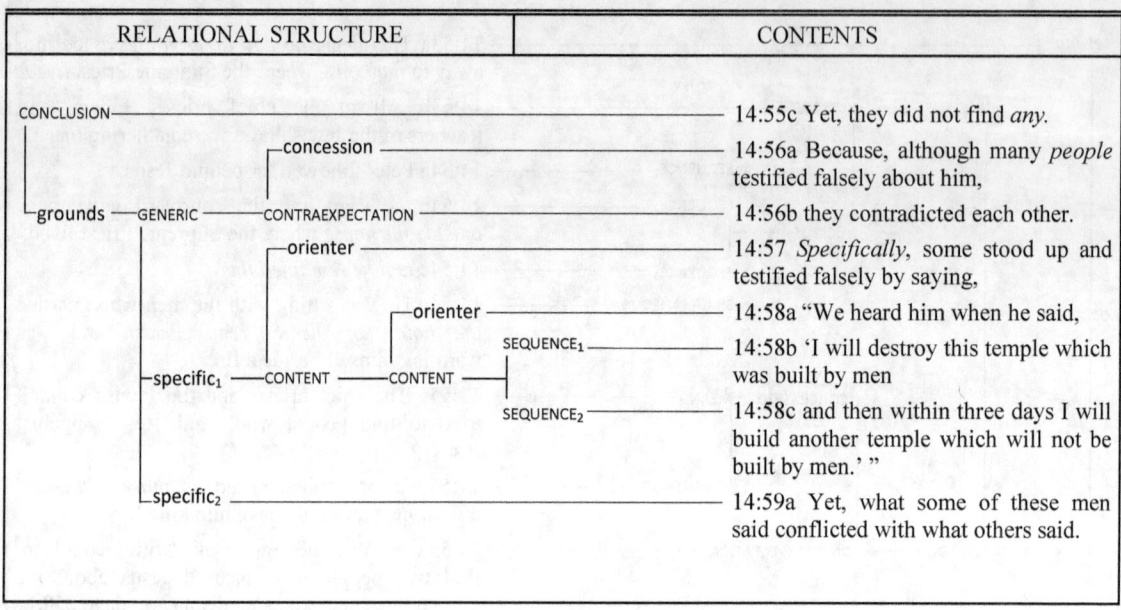

EXPANSION OF OUTCOME₁ 14:60–64 IN THE 14:53–65 DISPLAY

RELATIONAL STRUCTURE	CONTENTS
step₁ — concession — orienter	14:60a The Supreme Priest stood up in front of the Council and said to Jesus,
concession — CONTENT	14:60b *"Are you not going to reply to* everything that they *are saying* as they accuse you?"
CONTRAEXPECTATION	14:61a But *even though he was not guilty*, he did not reply [DOU].
step₂ — SEQUENCE₁ — orienter	14:61b The Supreme Priest asked him another question,
SEQUENCE₁ — CONTENT	14:61c "Are you the Messiah, the one *who is* the Son of God {MNG: here the focal concepts are the man who will rule over all Israel, and the man who is also God}?"
SEQUENCE₂ — orienter	14:62a Jesus said,
NUCLEUS₁	14:62b "I am.
SEQUENCE₂ — CONTENT — NUCLEUS₂ — generic	14:62c Furthermore you will see *me*, the one who came from heaven, sitting where the one who is honored most sits,
NUCLEUS₂ — SPECIFIC	14:62d, beside *God, who is* completely powerful,
NUCLEUS₃	14:62e and *you will also see me* come down through the clouds."
step₁	14:63a The Supreme Priest tore his clothes *in order to comply with Jewish law and show that he was horrified by what Jesus had said about God*,
orienter	14:63b and then he said *to the Council*,
grounds — CONCLUSION	14:63c "We certainly do not need any more people who will testify against him! [RHQ]
grounds	14:64a You have heard what he said; *that is, he claimed to be equal with God.*
step₂ — CONTENT — CONCLUSION	14:64b Therefore, what have you all decided?"
GOAL — GOAL	14:64c They all said that Jesus was guilty and that he deserved to be killed.

NOTES

14:61a ***even though he was not guilty*** In some cultures this will need to be included, because readers will assume that Jesus' silence was proof of his guilt.

14:61c **the Son of God** See note on 1:1a.{**MNG: here the focal concept is the man who is also God**}

14:62c **where the one who is honored most sits** The text has 'at the right hand'. See the notes on 10:37 and 12:36.

14:63a *in order to comply with Jewish tradition to show that he was horrified by what Jesus had said about God* NLT adds "to show his horror", but THM points out that what the Supreme Priest did was mostly for show, a ritual "minutely prescribed by tradition". Hendriksen says it was hypocrisy.

14:63c We certainly do not need The text has a rhetorical question, 'What need have we...?' which functions semantically as an emphatic negative statement. TEV also renders it as a negative statement.

14:64a *that is, he claimed to be equal with God* The text has 'the blasphemy'. The display spells out exactly what that meant. CEV similarly renders "heard him claim to be God."

EXPANSION OF OUTCOME₂ 14:65 IN THE 14:53–65 DISPLAY

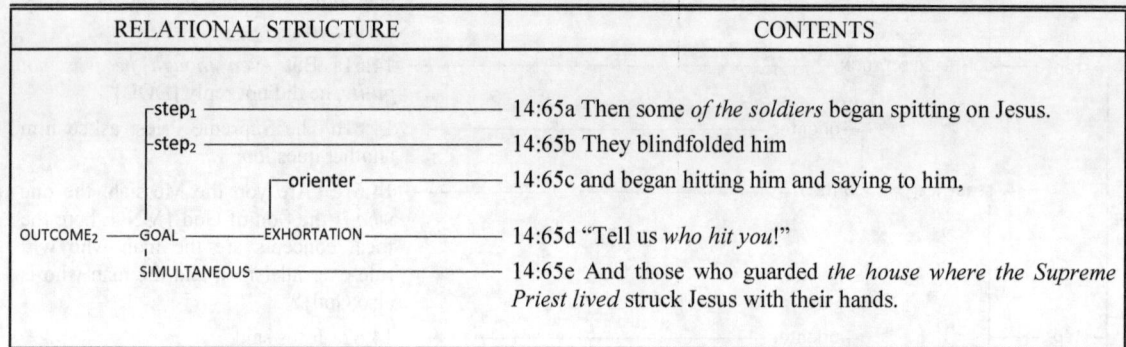

RELATIONAL STRUCTURE	CONTENTS
OUTCOME₂ — GOAL — step₁	14:65a Then some *of the soldiers* began spitting on Jesus.
step₂	14:65b They blindfolded him
orienter	14:65c and began hitting him and saying to him,
EXHORTATION	14:65d "Tell us *who hit you!*"
SIMULTANEOUS	14:65e And those who guarded *the house where the Supreme Priest lived* struck Jesus with their hands.

NOTES

14:65d Tell us *who hit you* The Greek has 'prophesy!' but the sense is as in CEV, "Tell us who hit you!" See also TEV, JBP, and NLT.

BOUNDARIES AND COHERENCE

The occurrence of a new paragraph at v. 66 is marked by the topic of Peter's denial that he knew Jesus. Coherence within the 53–65 episode is provided by five occurrences of ἀρχιερεύς 'chief priest' and two of ἀποκρίνομαι 'answer'. It also is seen in its being the account of Jesus' illegal trial before the religious leaders.

PROMINENCE AND THEME

The theme is taken from the CONTRAEXPECTATION of the *occasion*, NUCLEUS₁ and NUCLEUS₂ of SEQUENCE₂ of *step*₂ of the OUTCOME₁, and the GOAL of OUTCOME₁.

EPISODE CLUSTER CONSTITUENT 14:66–72 (Episode of 14:53—15:20)

THEME: As Jesus predicted, Peter denied three times that he knew Jesus, and later remembered what Jesus had said, then cried bitterly.

¶PTRN RELATIONAL STRUCTURE	CONTENTS
occasion	14:66 While Peter was *outside the house* in the courtyard, one of the girls who worked for the Supreme Priest came near *Peter*.
OUTCOME₁	14:67–71 Peter denied three times that he knew Jesus. [See expanded display on page 261.]
OUTCOME₂	14:72a–c Peter later remembered what Jesus said about him denying Jesus. [See expanded display on page 262.]
OUTCOME₃	14:72d–e Peter cried bitterly. [See expanded display on page 262.]

INTENT AND RHETORICAL STRUCTURE

This is the second of five episodes in the scene about Jesus being tried by the authorities. This one is specifically about Peter denying three times that he knew Jesus.

This causality type narrative which consists of an *occasion* (14:66), an OUTCOME₁ (14:67–71), and an OUTCOME₂ (14:72a–c), and a third OUTCOME₃ (14:72d–e).

Mark intends that the reader understand that Peter denied he knew Jesus, just as Jesus had foretold he would.

There is a dialogue chain between the Supreme Priest's servant girl and Peter throughout the FIRST OUTCOME where Peter denied Jesus.

The motif of 'denial' is central to this entire episode.

EXPANSION OF OUTCOME₁ 14:67–71 IN THE 14:66–72 DISPLAY

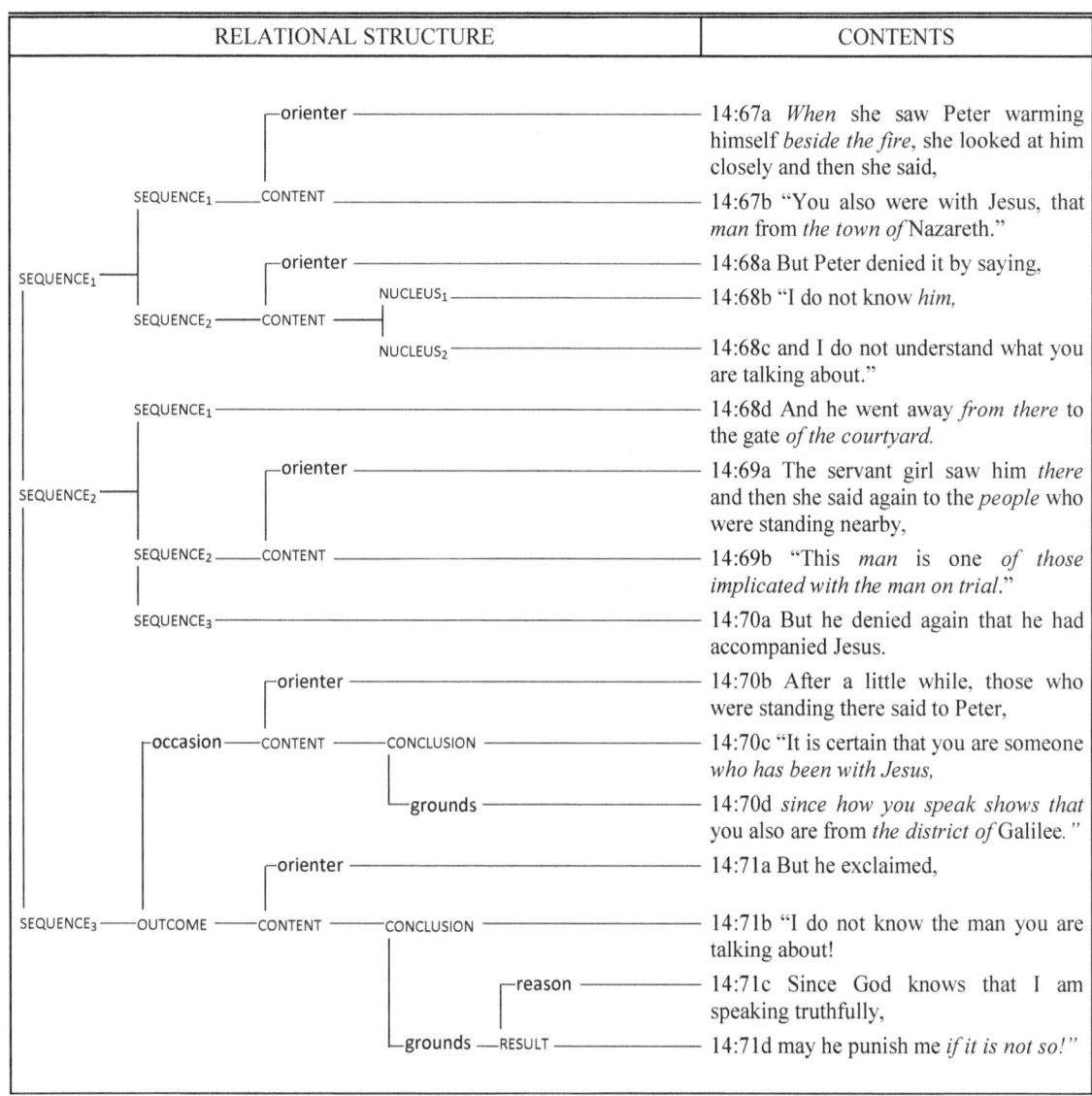

NOTES

14:67a warming himself *beside the fire* The text just has 'warming himself'. CEV has "warming himself by the fire". NLT's wording is almost the same.

14:68d At the end of this verse, some manuscripts have 'and a rooster crowed'. It is very difficult to determine whether these words were added because of what Jesus said in v. 30, or whether they were omitted to make this account agree with the accounts in the other gospels. English versions are divided; some put these words in a footnote.

14:69b one *who has accompanied* The text has simply 'is of them'. The display spells out who 'them' refers to. Also in 70c.

14:70d *since how you speak shows that* The text has 'for indeed you are a Galilean'. The display supplies the evidence for that conclusion; see Matt. 26:73.

14:71c–d Since God knows that I am speaking truthfully, may he punish me *if it is not so!* The text has 'he began to curse and swear'. The 'speaking truthfully' clause represents 'swear', and the 'punish me' clause represents 'curse'. See a host of commentators. NLT has "I swear by God".

EXPANSION OF OUTCOME₂&₃ 14:72 IN THE 14:66–72 DISPLAY

RELATIONAL STRUCTURE	CONTENTS
OUTCOME₂ — SEQUENCE₁	14:72a Immediately the rooster crowed a second time.
SEQUENCE₂ — orienter	14:72b Peter remembered what Jesus had said to him *before*,
— CONTENT	14:72c "Before the rooster crows a second time, you will deny three times *that you know* me."
— circumstance	14:72d *When* Peter realized *what he had done*,
OUTCOME₃ — NUCLEUS	14:72e he started crying bitterly.

NOTES

14:72a a second time A few manuscripts omit these words, to make Mark's account agree with the other gospels.

14:72d Peter realized *what he had done* The text has 'and thinking about it he cried'. Some manuscripts replace 'thinking about it' with 'he began to', but the wording followed here is given a B 'almost certain' rating.

14:72e he started crying about it bitterly The text has a word which commentators say that there is no agreement on how to translate it. Several versions have 'broke down' but that is very idiomatic.

BOUNDARIES AND COHERENCE

A new unit at 15:1 is marked by a change in time and a new topic: taking Jesus to Pilate. Coherence within the 66–72 episode is seen in four occurrences of the name 'Peter', two of ἀλέκτωρ 'rooster', two of παιδίσκη 'maidservant', and two of ἀπαρνέομαι 'deny'. Coherence is also provided by it being the account of Peter denying three times that he knew Jesus.

PROMINENCE AND THEME

The theme is simply a very brief summary of the three OUTCOMES.

EPISODE CLUSTER CONSTITUENT 15:1–5 (Episode of 14:53—15:20)

THEME: *In the governor Pilate's presence Jesus refused to answer accusations against him.*

¶ PTRN RELATIONAL STRUCTURE	CONTENTS
occasion — SEQUENCE₁ — MEANS	15:1a Early the *next* morning the chief priests met together with the elders, teachers of the Jewish laws, and the Jewish council,
purpose	15:1b in order to decide *what to do with Jesus*.
SEQUENCE₂ — SEQUENCE₁ — SIMULTANEOUS₁	15:1c They bound Jesus,
SIMULTANEOUS₂	15:1d took him away,
SEQUENCE₂	15:1e and handed him over to Pilate, *the Roman who ruled Judea*.
OUTCOME₁ — SEQUENCE₁ — orienter	15:2a Pilate asked Jesus,
CONTENT	15:2b "Are **you** the king *of* the Jews?"
SEQUENCE₂ — orienter	15:2c Jesus answered *him*,
CONTENT	15:2d "It is as you yourself have said."
OUTCOME₂ — RESULT — reason	15:3 Then the chief priests claimed that Jesus had done many *evil* things.
CONTENT — orienter	15:4a So Pilate asked him again,
NUCLEUS₁	15:4b "Don't you have anything to reply?
NUCLEUS₂	15:4c Listen to how many *evil* things they are claiming that you *have done*!"
OUTCOME₃ — RESULT — reason	15:5a But Jesus did not say anything more,
	15:5b with the result that Pilate was very surprised.

INTENT AND RHETORICAL STRUCTURE

This is the third of five episodes in the scene about Jesus being tried by the authorities. This one states specifically that Jesus refused to answer accusations against him in the presence of the governor, Pilate.

This is a causality type narrative which consists of an *occasion*, and several OUTCOMES.

Mark intends that the reader understand that Jesus was being tried before the Roman governor, but he refused to answer the unfounded accusations by the Jewish authorities.

There are two reported dialogues between governor Pilate and Jesus. In both cases the governor initiates the dialogue, then Jesus leaves the governor in an awkward situation.

The motif of 'rejection and suffering' is central to this entire episode.

NOTES

15:1a Early the *next* morning The text has 'immediately early'; CEV also renders it as "early the next morning".

15:1b decide *what to do with Jesus* The word συμβούλιον means 'held a consultation'. L&N say the word denotes a session to devise a plan of action. NCV also has "decided what to do with Jesus".

15:1e Pilate, *the Roman who ruled Judea* Since this is the first mention of Pilate, an identification is important. NLT has "the Roman governor".

15:2b you The pronoun is emphatic in Greek; this emphasis is shown by bolding in the display.

15:2c It is as you yourself have said The text has 'you are saying'. Commentators have given it various interpretations. But Hendriksen says, "This can mean no less than 'it is even as you have stated.' " He cites the parallel passages in Matthew (26:25) and John (18:37) as proof.

15:3 many *evil* things The GNT has only 'many things', so 'evil' is clearly implied. Also in 4c. NLT has "crimes", CEV has "charges".

BOUNDARIES AND COHERENCE

A new paragraph at v. 6 is indicated by a discussion regarding the prisoner Barabbas. Coherence within the 15:1–5 episode is seen in three occurrences of the name 'Pilate' and two of ἀρχιερεύς 'chief priests'. Coherence is also seen in the paragraph consisting of their taking Jesus to Pilate, and Pilate's initial questioning of Jesus.

PROMINENCE AND THEME

The theme is taken from v. 1e of the *occasion* and a summary of the three OUTCOMES.

EPISODE CLUSTER CONSTITUENT 15:6–15 (Episode of 14:53—15:20)

Theme: At the crowd's insistence (instigated by the Jewish religious authorities), Pilate released a criminal and ordered that Jesus be crucified.

¶PTRN RELATIONAL STRUCTURE	CONTENTS
problem	15:6–8 The Jewish religious authorities asked Pilate, the Roman governor, to release a prisoner. [See expanded display on page 265.]
complication	15:9–14 The Roman governor released Barabbas but decided that 'the king of the Jews' should be crucified. [See expanded display of page 266.]
RESOLUTION	15:15 The Roman governor ordered that Jesus be flogged and crucified. [See expanded display on page 267.]

INTENT AND RHETORICAL STRUCTURE

This is the fourth of five episodes about Jesus' trial. This episode focuses on the trial before the Roman governor. As the story line progresses toward the climax of this ACT IV, there develops a turbulence in the structure of the episodes. Although this episode consists of a *problem*, *complication*, and RESOLUTION, the internal structure of each constituent unit is mixed:

- The *problem* is a causality type exposition in which the Jewish religious authorities make a proposal to Pilate that he should release a prisoner.

- The *complication* is a dickering exchange between the crowd (motivated by the Jewish religious authorities) as to which one should be released and what to do with the other. This conversational exchange can be observed in the display.

- The RESOLUTION is a causality type exposition of why the Roman governor released Barrabas and ordered that 'the king of the Jews' be executed.

Mark intends that the reader understand that the Roman authority condemned Jesus to die by crucifixion.

This is a solutionality type narrative which consists of a *problem* (5:6–8), a *complication* (15:9–14), and a RESOLUTION (15:15).

There is a dialogue chain between Pilate and the Jewish crowd in the *complication* binding the unit together.

The motif of 'Jesus' rejection and suffering is central to this entire episode.

EXPANSION OF THE PROBLEM 15:6–8 IN THE 15:6–15 DISPLAY

¶ PTRN RELATIONAL STRUCTURE	CONTENTS
problem—CONGRUENCE—standard—NUCLEUS—circumstance-SPECIFIC—generic	15:6a *Each year* during the *time when the Jews celebrated the* Passover festival, *Pilate* would release a person who had been put in prison.
(circumstance-SPECIFIC)	15:6b *Specifically, he would release* whichever *person the people* requested.
NUCLEUS	15:7 Well, there was a *man* called Barabbas, who had been put in prison with *other* men who had murdered *some people* when they rebelled against *the Roman rulers.*
CONGRUENCE—NUCLEUS	15:8a A crowd approached *Pilate*
[PROPOSAL]	15:8b and asked him *to release someone,*
standard	15:8c just like he customarily did for them *during the Passover festival.*

NOTES

15:6a Each year The text has only 'at a feast'. NLT has "each year". TEV has "every Passover Feast".

15:7 Well This word is inserted to mark the transition from generic background information to specific background information pertinent to the narrative. NEB marks it with "As it happened,…"

rebelled against *the Roman rulers* The text has 'in the rebellion'. Scholars do not know what rebellion was being referred to. Lane says that rebellions were common at that time, but the definite article suggests that it must have been very recent and well-known.

15:8a approached The KJV follows a few manuscripts which have a verb, 'cry out', which is similar to the form in the display, which is given a B rating.

15:8b–c asked him *to release someone* just like he customarily did for them *during the Passover festival* The text has only 'asked as he used to do for them'. The display supplies the content of what they asked. CEV includes "to set a prisoner free;" NLT has "to release a prisoner". The display also specifies when this request was made.

EXPANSION OF COMPLICATION 15:9–14 IN THE 15:6–15 DISPLAY

RELATIONAL STRUCTURE	CONTENTS
SEQUENCE₁ — SEQUENCE₁ — [COUNTER-PROPOSAL] — CONCLUSION — orienter	15:9a Pilate answered them,
	15:9b "Do you want me to release for you *the man who you say is* the king of the Jews?"
grounds — CONTENT — orienter	15:10a *He asked this* because he realized that
	15:10b the chief priests had turned Jesus over to him because they were jealous of Jesus.
SEQUENCE₂ — [COUNTER-PROPOSAL] — orienter	15:11a But the chief priests urged the crowd *to request*
	15:11b that *Pilate* release Barabbas for them instead *of Jesus*.
SEQUENCE₂ — SEQUENCE₁ — [QUESTION] — orienter	15:12a Pilate spoke to them again, saying,
	15:12b "*If I release Barabbas*, what *do you want* me to do with the *man* whom you call the king *of* the Jews?"
SEQUENCE₂ — [PROPOSAL] — orienter	15:13a Then they shouted,
	15:13b "*Command* soldiers to crucify him!"
SEQUENCE₃ — SEQUENCE₁ — [QUESTION] — orienter	15:14a Then Pilate said to them,
	15:14b "Why? What wrong has he done?"
SEQUENCE₂ — [PROPOSAL] — orienter	15:14c But they shouted even louder,
	15:14d "*Command soldiers to* crucify him!"

NOTES

15:9b *the man who you say is* **the king** *of the* **Jews** The text has 'the king of the Jews'. But Pilate did not think Jesus was a king (see Lenski), and the crowd certainly did not, either. To avoid these wrong meanings, the display has 'the man who says he is'.

15:12b *do you want* Many good Greek manuscripts omit this word, and it is omitted in NIV, NLT, JBP, RSV, JB and NEB. But there is very little meaning difference.

15:12f *If I release Barabbas* The text has 'what therefore…?' NLT also has "If I release Barabbas".

15:13b *Command that* **soldiers crucify him** The text has 'crucify him' but it was the soldiers, not Pilate, who carried out executions.

EXPANSION OF RESOLUTION 15:15 IN THE 15:6–15 DISPLAY

¶ PTRN RELATIONAL STRUCTURE	CONTENTS
RESOLUTION—RESULT—reason	15:15a Because Pilate wanted to satisfy the crowd,
SEQUENCE₁	15:15b he released Barabbas for them.
SEQUENCE₂—[ACT₁]	15:15c He *commanded his soldiers* to flog Jesus
[ACT₂]—MEANS	15:15d and then Pilate told *the soldiers to take him away*
purpose	15:15e in order to crucify him.

NOTES

15:15c *commanded his soldiers* to flog The text has 'having flogged', but again, it was the soldiers, not Pilate, who did the flogging. Hendriksen says that flogging was a punishment using a whip "the end equipped with pieces of lead or brass and with sharply pointed bits of bone".

15:15d told *the soldiers to take him away* The text has 'delivered Jesus'. The display specifies who he delivered Jesus to.

BOUNDARIES AND COHERENCE

A new paragraph at v. 16 is indicated by a change in location and new participants, Roman soldiers, and a new topic: the soldiers mocking Jesus. Coherence within the 6–15 paragraph is shown by five occurrences of the name 'Pilate', three of the name 'Barabbas', three occurrences of σταυρόω 'crucify', and four occurrences of ἀπολύω 'release'. Coherence is also provided by the paragraph consisting of the account of the crowd insisting that Pilate release a criminal and sentence Jesus to be crucified.

PROMINENCE AND THEME

The theme consists of a condensation of the most prominent NUCLEUS of the *problem*, a condensation of the *complication* and of the RESOLUTION.

EPISODE CLUSTER CONSTITUENT 15:16–20 (Episode of 14:53—15:20)

THEME: The soldiers ridiculed Jesus as being a king. Then they led him away to be crucified.

¶ PTRN RELATIONAL STRUCTURE	CONTENTS
occasion — SEQUENCE₁ — NUCLEUS₁	15:16a Then the soldiers took Jesus into the courtyard *of the house where Pilate lived*, which is called the Praetorium,
NUCLEUS₂	15:16b and they summoned the whole troop *of soldiers*.
SEQUENCE₂	15:17a *After the soldiers gathered together*, they put a purple *robe* on Jesus
SEQUENCE₃	15:17b and then they placed on his head a crown *made from branches of* thorn bushes, *in order to ridicule him by pretending he was a king*.
OUTCOME₁ — SEQUENCE₁ — orienter	15:18a Then they saluted Jesus *like they would salute a king, in order to ridicule him*, saying,
CONTENT	15:18b "Cheers to the King *of* the Jews!"
SEQUENCE₂	15:19a They repeatedly struck Jesus' head with a cane rod;
SEQUENCE₃	15:19b they spat on him;
SEQUENCE₄	15:19c and, by kneeling down, they *pretended to* honor him.
OUTCOME₂ — SEQUENCE₁ — circumstance	15:20a And when they had finished ridiculing him,
	15:20b they snatched off the purple *robe*;
SEQUENCE₂	15:20c put his own clothes on him,
SEQUENCE₃ — MEANS	15:20d and led him away (OR, outside *of the city*)
purpose	15:20e to crucify him.

INTENT AND RHETORICAL STRUCTURE

This is the last of five episodes in the scene about Jesus being tried by the authorities. This one states specifically that the Roman soldiers ridiculed Jesus, mocking him as king of the Jews.

This is a causality type narrative which consists of an *occasion* (15:16–17), an OUTCOME₁ (15:18–19), and another OUTCOME₂ (15:20).

Mark intends that the reader understand that the Roman soldiers mocked Jesus as being king of the Jews.

The motif of 'rejection and suffering' is central to this entire episode.

NOTES

15:16a *the house where Pilate lived* REB has "the governor's residence, the Praetorium." See also NCV, NET, and TEV.

15:16b **troop** The GNT has σπεῖρα 'cohort', but that word is not well known in English. The word refers to a Roman military unit which ordinarily consisted of six hundred soldiers.

15:17a *purple* **robe** The Greek simply has the word 'purple'.

15:17b *in order to ridicule him by pretending he was a king* A NET footnote says the soldiers did this to mock Jesus' claim to be a king.

15:18a **salute him** *like they would salute a king, in order to ridicule him* See Stein, Hiebert.

15:18b **Cheers** This is an expression wishing well for some authority.

15:19c **they** *pretended to* **honor him** The Greek word means 'worshiped', and CEV renders it as "knelt down and pretended to worship him". NLT's rendering is very similar.

15:20d **away (OR, outside** *of the city*) The text has 'led him out', which is ambiguous as to where they led him out of. Most versions have 'led him away', but Swete suggests it means 'out of the city', and cites Heb. 13:12 as support.

BOUNDARIES AND COHERENCE

A new paragraph at v. 21 is indicated by a move to a new location, and a new topic: the crucifixion. Coherence is within the 16–20 episode is seen in two occurrences of πορφύρα 'purple robe'. Coherence also seen in the episode consisting of the account of the Roman soldiers making fun of Jesus.

PROMINENCE AND THEME

The theme is from the v. 18a–b of OUTCOME$_1$, and v. 20d–e of SEQUENCE$_2$ of OUTCOME$_2$.

SCENE CONSTITUENT 15:21–41 (Episode Cluster of 14:32—15:41)

THEME: After the soldiers crucified Jesus, they gambled for his clothing, other people insulted him, and then Jesus died; the temple curtain split in two, and a Roman officer declared that Jesus was the Son of God.

MACROSTRUCTURE	CONTENTS
occasion$_1$	15:21–24 After the soldiers crucified Jesus, they gambled for his clothing.
occasion$_2$	15:25–32 People passing by, as well as the Jewish leaders and two criminals being crucified with Jesus, insulted him.
OUTCOME	15:33–41 As several women who had accompanied Jesus watched, he died, after which the temple curtain was torn in two, and a Roman officer declared that Jesus was the Son of God.

INTENT AND RHETORICAL STRUCTURE

This is the last episode cluster of the scene in which Jesus is crucified and died. In this unit the Roman soldiers crucified Jesus. This is the first climax in this last PART of Mark. These three included episodes consist of two *occasions* (15:21–24 and 15:2532), and an OUTCOME (15:33–41).

BOUNDARIES AND COHERENCE

Both the initial and the closing boundaries coincide with the boundaries of the first and final included episodes. In this unit Mark presents the details of Jesus' crucifixion.

PROMINENCE AND THEME

The theme statement arises from the prominence structure of the three episodes.

EPISODE CLUSTER CONSTITUENT 15:21–24 (Episode of 15:21–41)

THEME: After the soldiers crucified Jesus, they gambled for his clothing.

¶ PTRN RELATIONAL STRUCTURE	CONTENTS
occasion — occasion — NUCLEUS	15:21a *After Jesus became too tired from carrying his cross*, the soldiers compelled a man named Simon to carry the cross *for Jesus*.
identification	15:21b He was from *the city of* Cyrene, the father of Alexander and Rufus, who was passing by *while he* was returning *home* from outside *the city*.
OUTCOME	15:22 The soldiers brought Jesus to a place *called in the Aramaic language*, Golgotha, which means, "a place like a skull."
OUTCOME₁ — occasion — CONTRAST₁	15:23a Then they tried to give Jesus wine which had been mixed with *medicine called* myrrh *to reduce the pain when they crucified him*,
CONTRAST₂	15:23b but he did not drink it.
OUTCOME	15:24a And then they nailed him to a cross.
OUTCOME₂	15:24b Afterwards, they divided his clothes among themselves by gambling with *something like* dice *in order to determine* which *piece of clothing* each one would get.

INTENT AND RHETORICAL STRUCTURE

This (15:21–24) is the first of three episodes in the scene about Jesus being crucified. This specifically is that the Roman soldiers crucify Jesus and gamble for his clothes.

This is a causality type narrative which consists of an *occasion* (15:21–22), an OUTCOME₁ (15:23–24a), and another OUTCOME₂ (15:24b).

Mark intends that the reader understand that the Roman soldiers crucified Jesus.

The motif of 'rejection and suffering' is central to this entire episode.

NOTES

15:21a *After Jesus became too tired from carrying his cross* This is implied; it is needed to avoid a contradiction with John 19:17.

15:23a *medicine called* **myrrh** These words are supplied to identify 'myrrh'. TEV has "a drug called myrrh".

to reduce the pain when they crucified him This expresses the implied purpose. CEV has "to ease the pain".

15:24b **gambling with** *something like* **dice** The text has 'casting a lot'; the display uses more commonly known words. It is not certain whether they actually used dice; NLT says 'dice' while CEV resolves the uncertainty by just saying "gambled". This action fulfilled what was written in Psalm 22:18.

in order to determine **which** *piece of clothing* **each one would get** The display makes clear the sense of the text which has only 'which one might take'.

BOUNDARIES AND COHERENCE

A new paragraph at v. 25 is introduced by a noting of the time, and a new topic: the insults hurled at Jesus while he was on the cross. Coherence within the 21–24 paragraph is shown by the word σταυρός 'cross' and the cognate verb σταυρόω 'crucify'. Coherence is also seen in the topic of the soldiers crucifying Jesus.

PROMINENCE AND THEME

The theme is taken from OUTCOME₁ and a condensation of OUTCOME₂.

EPISODE CLUSTER CONSTITUENT 15:25–32 (Episode of 15:21–41)

THEME: People passing by, as well as the Jewish leaders and two criminals being crucified with Jesus, insulted him.

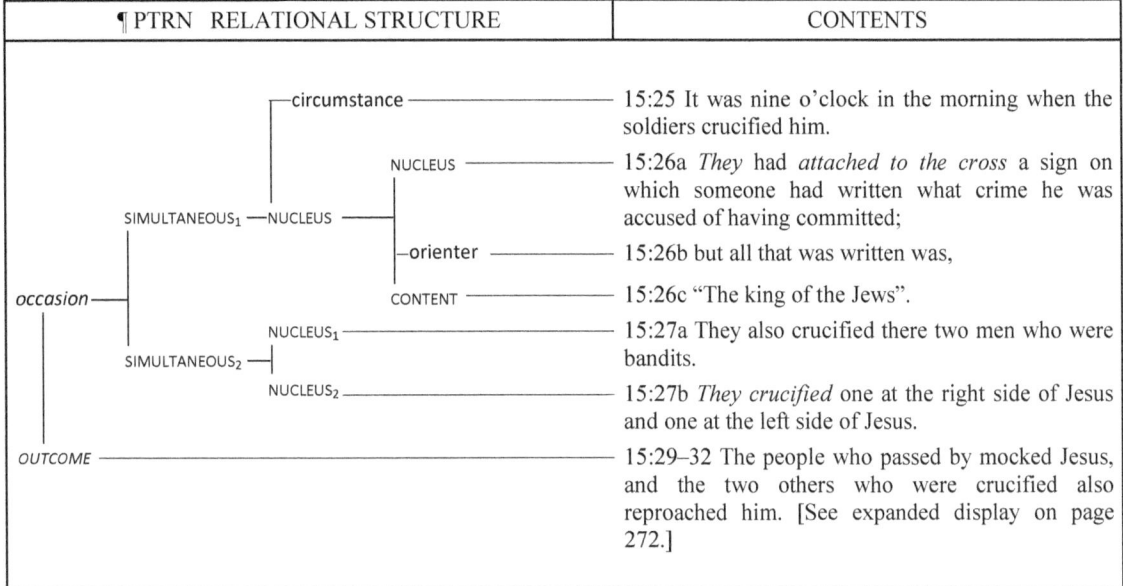

INTENT AND RHETORICAL STRUCTURE

This is the second of three episodes in the scene about Jesus being crucified. This one is specifically about people, the Jewish leaders, and the two criminals being crucified with Jesus, all insulting him.

This is a causality type narrative which consists of an *occasion*, and an OUTCOME.

Mark intends that the reader understand that many people insulted Jesus.

The motif of 'rejection and suffering' is central to this entire episode.

NOTES

15:26a They had *attached to the cross* a sign The text has 'the written notice'. NLT is extremely clear: "a sign-board was fastened to the cross above Jesus' head."

what crime he was accused of having committed This conveys the sense of 'his accusation' without using an abstract noun.

15:26b *but all that was written was* These words are supplied because being 'The King of the Jews' is hardly a crime. See Hendriksen and Gundry.

15:28 The earliest and best manuscripts lack v. 28, which probably was added because of its occurrence in Luke 22:37. No versions except KJV include it (except in a footnote).

EXPANSION OF THE OUTCOME 15:29–32 IN THE 15:25–32 DISPLAY

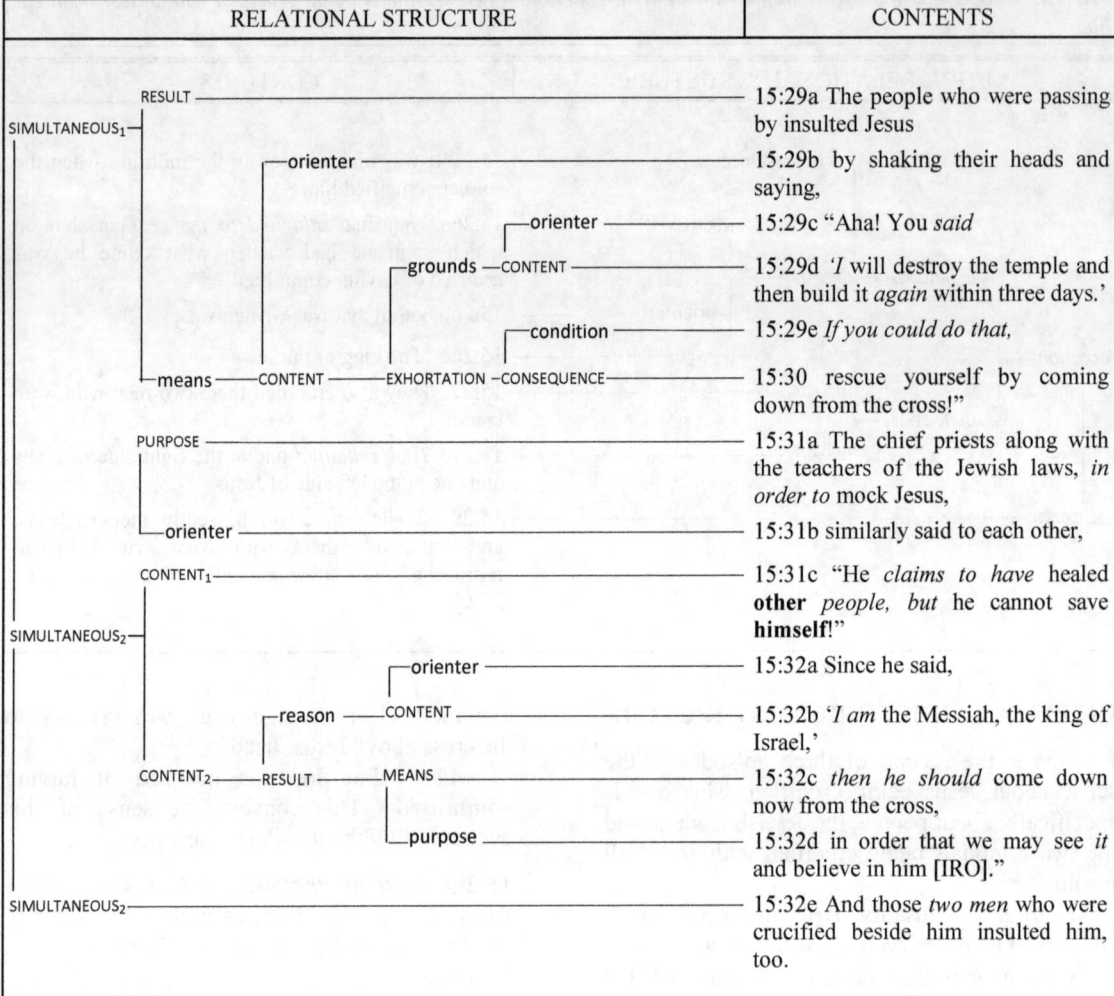

NOTES

15:29b shaking their heads There seems to be an allusion to Psalm 109:25.

15:29c–d You *said*, *'I will destroy* The text has 'you who destroys the temple' which omits crucial bits of information. CEV's rendering, "You're the one who claimed you could tear down", is excellent.

15:29e *If you could do that* These words supply the implied grounds for the exhortation that follows. NLT carries the sense with "Well then,…"

15:31c *claims to have* healed The text says 'he saved' but it is very dubious that they admitted that was true. Lenski says, "it is…a denial that he really ever saved others". See also Guelich.

Other people … himself Both of these words are emphasized in the Greek; this emphasis is indicated by bold type in the display.

15:32a–b *Since he said*, *'I am* the Messiah The words in italics are not in the text. Several versions have 'Let the Messiah…' but such wording fails to recognize that their words were spoken in irony. See Hendriksen, Lenski, Lane, and Hiebert.

15:32e those *two* men The Greek has only 'those', but TEV, NLT, and CEV have "two".

BOUNDARIES AND COHERENCE

A new paragraph at v. 33 is marked by two more indications of time and a new topic, Jesus' death. Coherence within the 25–32 episode is shown by two occurrences of the clause 'come down from the cross' and two verbs which express the concept of 'insult'. Coherence also consists of the account of various ones insulting Jesus while he hung on the cross.

PROMINENCE AND THEME

The theme is taken from the OUTCOME: the RESULT of SIMULTANEOUS$_1$, the PURPOSE of SIMULTANEOUS$_2$, and SIMULTANEOUS$_3$.

EPISODE CLUSTER CONSTITUENT 15:33–41 (Episode of 15:21–41)

THEME: As several women who had accompanied Jesus watched, he died, after which the temple curtain was torn in two, and a Roman officer declared that Jesus was the Son of God.

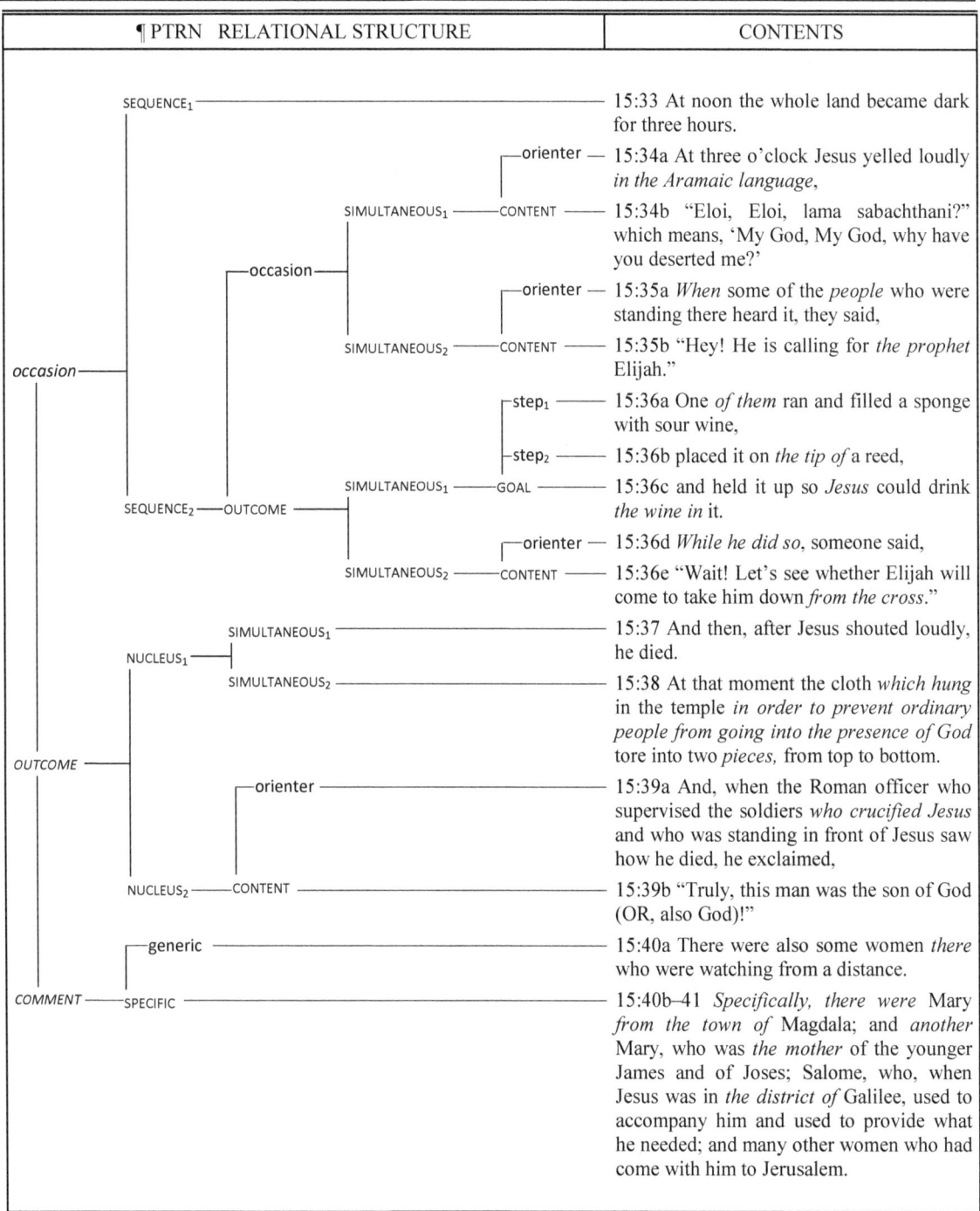

INTENT AND RHETORICAL STRUCTURE

This is the last of three episodes in the scene about Jesus being crucified. This one states specifically that several women watched Jesus die, the temple curtain tore in two, and the Roman officer declared that Jesus was the Son of God.

This is a causality type narrative which consists of an *occasion*, an OUTCOME, and a COMMENT.

Mark intends that the reader understand that many people saw Jesus die, and that the curtain in the temple tore in two.

The people continued to insult Jesus even when he shouted to God. This is the only dialogue in this unit.

The motif of 'rejection and suffering' is central to this entire episode.

NOTES

15:34a *in the Aramaic language* TN says "there is much discussion in the commentaries about whether Mark's original text is a transliteration of this quote from Aramaic or Hebrew, or a mix of the two," but most say it was Aramaic. Jesus quoted from Psalm 22:1.

15:34b eloi Of the modern versions, only NEB has eli, as is found in Matt. 27:46.

15:35b *the prophet* **Elijah** The words in italics identify Elijah; NLT also has "the prophet Elijah".

15:36a–c This action fulfilled what was written in Psalm 69:21.

15:38 cloth *which hung* in the temple *in order to prevent ordinary people from going into the presence of God* Commentators agree that this was the significance of the curtain being torn, but no version (except TfT) states it; however, see the footnote in ESV.

15:39a the Roman officer who supervised the soldiers *who crucified Jesus* This spells out the meaning of 'centurion'.

Many manuscripts lack the word 'cried out'. Most versions omit it, and assume it was added later because of the wording in Matt. 27:50.

15:40b *from the town of* **Magdala** The text has 'the Magdalene' which means 'from the town of Magdala'; see THM, BAGD.

BOUNDARIES AND COHERENCE

A new paragraph at v. 42 is marked by another indication of time and a new topic: Jesus' burial. Coherence within the 33–41 episode is shown by two occurrences of the name 'Elijah'. Coherence is also provided by a narration of the events immediately preceding and immediately following Jesus' death.

PROMINENCE AND THEME

The theme is taken from the *generic* proposition of the COMMENT, the two SIMULTANEOUS propositions of NUCLEUS$_1$ of the OUTCOME, and a condensation of NUCLEUS$_2$ of the OUTCOME.

ACT CONSTITUENT 15:42–47 (Episode of 14:1—16:8)

THEME: Several women watched as Joseph and others buried Jesus' body in a cave after getting permission from Pilate.

¶PTRN RELATIONAL STRUCTURE	CONTENTS
setting — RESULT ┬ reason	15:42a When evening was *near*, because it was *Friday*, the day when people prepared *for the Sabbath*,
└ RESULT ┬ reason	15:42b and the Jewish law required that bodies of people who died be buried before sundown on that day,
├ 'Joseph'	15:43a Joseph *from the town of* Arimathea came *to where they were crucifying Jesus*.
├ identification₁	15:43b He was one of the Jewish council, who was respected *by the people*,
└ identification₂	15:43c and who, *like other people*, was waiting expectantly for the time when God would rule as king.
move₁ ┬ SEQUENCE₁	15:43d He became courageous and went to Pilate
└ SEQUENCE₂ ┬ orienter	15:43e and asked Pilate
└ CONTENT	15:43f to permit him to take the body of Jesus *down from the cross so he could bury it*.
move₂ ┬ SEQUENCE₁	15:44a Pilate was surprised *when he heard* that *Jesus* was already dead.
├ SEQUENCE₂	15:44b So he summoned the one who led the soldiers *who crucified Jesus*
└ SEQUENCE₃	15:44c and asked him if *Jesus* had already died.
move₃ ┬ circumstance	15:45a When the soldier confirmed *that Jesus was dead*,
└ NUCLEUS	15:45b Pilate allowed Joseph to take Jesus' body.
GOAL ┬ GOAL ┬ step₁	15:46a After Joseph bought a linen cloth,
├ step₂	15:46b he and others took *Jesus'* body down from the cross,
├ step₃	15:46c wrapped it in the linen cloth,
├ SEQUENCE₁	15:46d laid it in a tomb which *previously* had been cut in the side of the cliff,
└ SEQUENCE₂	15:46e and rolled a *huge* stone in front of the entrance to the tomb.
COMMENT	15:47 Mary *from the town of* Magdala and Mary *the mother* of Joses were watching where those men placed Jesus' *body*.

INTENT AND RHETORICAL STRUCTURE

This is the only episode about how Jesus was buried; all as part of the ACT of how the Jewish authorities rejected Jesus as their Messiah and had him put to death.

Mark intends that the reader understand that several men and women observed or were involved in taking the body of Jesus down from the cross and burying it in a stone tomb.

This is an objective type narrative which consists of *three moves*, a GOAL, and an author's COMMENT.

NOTES

15:42a *Friday*, **the day when people prepared for the Sabbath** The text has only 'preparation'. NLT also states it was Friday.

15:42b **and the Jewish law required that bodies of people who died be buried before sundown on that day** This explains why Joseph could not waste any time.

15:43c **who** *like other people* **was waiting** The word in italics explain more clearly the Greek 'Joseph himself'. CEV's rendering, 'also', is similar with "waiting expectantly for the time when God would rule as king". The Greek has 'expecting the kingdom of God'. Some versions have 'waiting for the kingdom of God to come', but kingdoms do not literally 'come'. As previously, 'kingdom of God' is considered a metaphor standing for God's rule.

15:43e–f **asked Pilate** *to permit him to take* **the body of Jesus** *down from the cross so he could bury it* The text has only 'asked for the body of Jesus'. See TN.

15:44b **one who led the soldiers** *who crucified Jesus* See note on 39a.

15:45a **confirmed** *that Jesus was dead* This represents 'knowing from the centurion'.

15:46b **he** *and others* Most versions do not recognize that moving a corpse was not a one-man job. See Lane.

took *Jesus' body down from the cross* This makes clear the text which has only 'taking him down'.

15:46e *huge* **stone** CEV has "big stone". TEV has "large stone".

BOUNDARIES AND COHERENCE

A new paragraph at 16:1 is marked by an indication of time, new participants, and a new topic: the empty tomb. Coherence within the 15:42–47 episode is shown by two occurrences of the name 'Pilate' and two of the name 'Joseph', two occurrences of 'tomb' and two of κεντυρίων 'centurion'. Coherence is also provided by the paragraph providing the events concerning Jesus' burial.

PROMINENCE AND THEME

The theme is taken from a condensation of the *moves* and of the GOAL, and the COMMENT.

ACT CONSTITUENT 16:1–8 (Episode of 14:1—16:8)

THEME: Two days later, several women were astonished to find Jesus' tomb empty, but an angel told them Jesus was alive again.

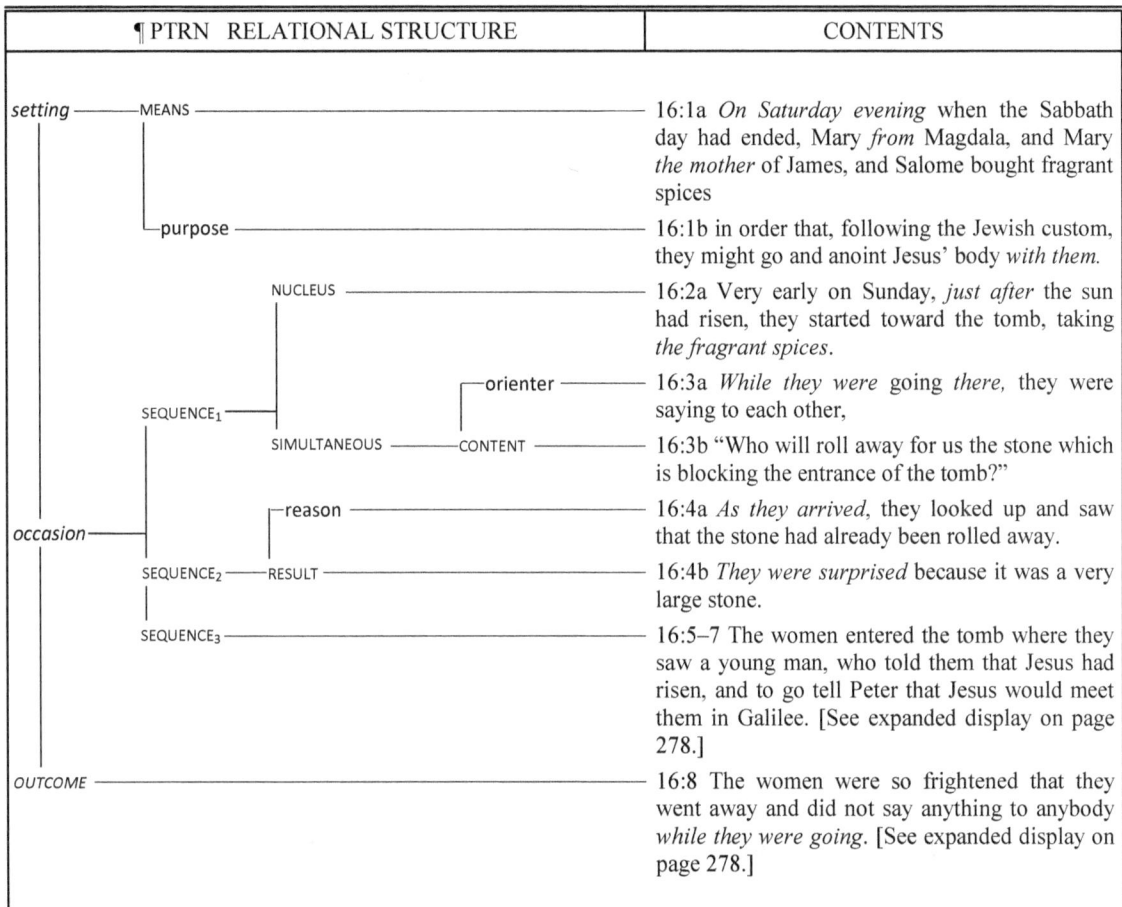

¶PTRN RELATIONAL STRUCTURE	CONTENTS
setting — MEANS	16:1a *On Saturday evening* when the Sabbath day had ended, Mary *from* Magdala, and Mary *the mother* of James, and Salome bought fragrant spices
purpose	16:1b in order that, following the Jewish custom, they might go and anoint Jesus' body *with them*.
NUCLEUS	16:2a Very early on Sunday, *just after* the sun had risen, they started toward the tomb, taking *the fragrant spices*.
SEQUENCE₁ — orienter	16:3a *While they were* going *there,* they were saying to each other,
SIMULTANEOUS — CONTENT	16:3b "Who will roll away for us the stone which is blocking the entrance of the tomb?"
occasion — reason	16:4a *As they arrived,* they looked up and saw that the stone had already been rolled away.
SEQUENCE₂ — RESULT	16:4b *They were surprised* because it was a very large stone.
SEQUENCE₃	16:5–7 The women entered the tomb where they saw a young man, who told them that Jesus had risen, and to go tell Peter that Jesus would meet them in Galilee. [See expanded display on page 278.]
OUTCOME	16:8 The women were so frightened that they went away and did not say anything to anybody *while they were going*. [See expanded display on page 278.]

INTENT AND RHETORICAL STRUCTURE

Mark intends that the reader understand that two women found the tomb empty, and an angel told them that Jesus was alive.

This is an objective type narrative which consists of a *setting*, an *occasion*, and an *OUTCOME*.

NOTES

16:1a *On Saturday evening* This makes clear just the time meant by 'when the Sabbath ended'.

16:2a **Sunday** The text has 'the first day of the week', but in some cultures Sunday is not the first day of the week. TEV, NEB, Beck, NLT and CEV have "Sunday".

16:4a **saw** The text has 'looked up and saw'. No commentaries suggest that this is a Hebrew doublet. Strauss says the words 'looking up' "heightens the drama."

16:4b *They were surprised because* The γάρ 'because' introduces a reason, but there is no result clause to accompany it. The display supplies one which fits the context.

EXPANSION OF SEQUENCE₃ 16:5–7 IN THE 16:1–8 DISPLAY

RELATIONAL STRUCTURE	CONTENTS
┌─ NUCLEUS ───────────────────────────	16:5a They entered the tomb
┌─ occasion ─┤ ┌─ reason ────────────	16:5b and saw a young man, who was sitting at the right side *of the* tomb wearing a white robe,
│ SIMULTANEOUS ─ RESULT ─────	16:5c so they were very astonished.
│ ┌─ orienter ────────────────	16:6a The *young man* said to them,
│ EXHORTATION₁ ────────────────	16:6b "Do not be astonished;
│ ┌─ identification ─	16:6c Jesus, *the man* from Nazareth whom you are looking for, who was crucified,
│ NUCLEUS₁ ─ NUCLEUS ───	16:6d has become alive again.
OUTCOME ─ CONTENT ─ grounds ─ NUCLEUS₂ ─ CONCLUSION ───	16:6e He is not here!
│ └─ grounds ────────	16:6f Look! *Here is* the place where they laid his *body*.
│ ┌─ orienter ────────────────	16:7a But, instead *of remaining here*, go! Tell Jesus' disciples, particularly Peter,
│ EXHORTATION₂ ─ CONTENT ──────	16:7b that Jesus is going ahead of them to *the district of* Galilee, and that they will see him there, just like he told them *previously*."

NOTES

16:7a instead *of remaining here* The Greek conjunction ἀλλά means 'instead of'. TN states it clearly: "he told them not to stay there but to go and tell the news to others".

EXPANSION OF OUTCOME 16:8 IN THE 16:1–8 DISPLAY

¶ PTRN RELATIONAL STRUCTURE	CONTENTS
┌─ NUCLEUS ────────────	16:8a *The women* went outside and fled from the tomb;
┌─ NUCLEUS₁ ─┤	
OUTCOME ─┤ └─ SIMULTANEOUS ────	16:8b they were trembling *because they were* awestruck.
└─ NUCLEUS₂ ───────────────	16:8c And they did not say anything to anyone *while they were going*, because they were afraid.

NOTES

16:8b trembling *because they were awestruck* Many commentators state that this was the cause of their trembling.

BOUNDARIES AND COHERENCE

A new paragraph at 16:9 is marked by a repetition of Jesus' appearance to Mary Magdalene and several statements of unbelief about Jesus' resurrection. Coherence within the 1–8 paragraph is provided by two occurrences of μνημεῖον 'tomb' and two of λίθος 'stone', and the verb ἀποκυλίω 'roll away'. Coherence is also seen in the paragraph consisting of the account of several women going to the tomb and what an angel told them there.

PROMINENCE AND THEME

The theme is taken from a condensation of SEQUENCE₂ of the *occasion*, and the *grounds* of EXHORTATION₁ of the OUTCOME v. 6c–f.

[It seems that perhaps the original end of Mark's gospel was lost or destroyed long ago. There are four different endings that are found in various manuscripts, but it is clear from internal evidence that they were not written by Mark. The longest of those endings is found in the KJV and RSV and is given below.]

BOOK CONSTITUENT 16:9–20 (Part III: Conclusion of the Book 1:1—16:20)

THEME: After Jesus arose from being dead on Sunday morning, his disciples did not believe he was alive. So, Jesus rebuked them for not believing and commanded them to preach the good news throughout the world. Jesus then ascended to heaven, and his disciples started telling God's message everywhere.

¶ PTRN RELATIONAL STRUCTURE	CONTENTS
setting	16:9a When Jesus became alive again early on Sunday *morning*,
occasion — SEQUENCE₁ — SEQUENCE₂ — SEQUENCE₁	16:9b he appeared first to Mary *from* Magdala, from whom he had *previously* expelled seven evil spirits.
NUCLEUS	16:10a She went
SIMULTANEOUS	16:10b and told *what happened* to those who had been with Jesus, while they were mourning and crying.
concession	16:11a *Yet*, even though they heard that Jesus was alive *again*, and that she had seen him,
SEQUENCE₃ — CONTRAEXPECTATION	16:11d they did not believe *it*.
SEQUENCE₂ — SEQUENCE₁	16:12 After that, Jesus, who *now* looked very different, appeared to two *men who had accompanied him*, while they were walking along from Jerusalem into the *surrounding* country.
SEQUENCE₂ — step	16:13a They both went back *to Jerusalem*
GOAL	16:13b *and told the others who had been with him what had happened*,
SEQUENCE₃	16:13c but they did not believe it.
OUTCOME₁ — NUCLEUS₁ — circumstance	16:14a Later Jesus appeared to the eleven *disciples* themselves while they were eating.
RESULT	16:14b He rebuked them
reason₁ — NUCLEUS₁	16:14c because they did not believe *that he had become alive again*,
NUCLEUS₂	16:14d and because they were stubborn,
reason₂	16:14e because they did not believe *what* those who saw him after he had become alive again *had reported to them.*
NUCLEUS₂	16:15–18 Jesus commanded his disciples to preach the good message throughout the world. [See expanded display on page 280.]
OUTCOME₂	16:19–20 After Jesus ascended to heaven, and his disciples preached everywhere, God confirmed their message by performing miracles. [See expanded display on page 281.]

INTENT AND RHETORICAL STRUCTURE

The scribe who authored this episode intends the reader to understand that there needed to be a closure to this Gospel.

This is an objective type narrative which consists of a *setting*, an *occasion*, and two OUTCOMES.

NOTES

16:9a *Sunday morning* See note on 2a.

16:12 *who had accompanied him* The text has 'of them'; the display specifies who 'them' refers to. NIV has "those who had been with him"; see also CEV, JB, and JBP.

16:13b *the others who had been with him* The text has only 'the others'; the display specifies who the others were.

16:14c *not believe what those who saw him after he had become alive again had reported to them* The text has 'their disbelief'; the display removes the abstract noun and supplies the content of what they did not believe.

EXPANSION OF NUCLEUS₂ 16:15–18 IN THE 16:9–18 DISPLAY

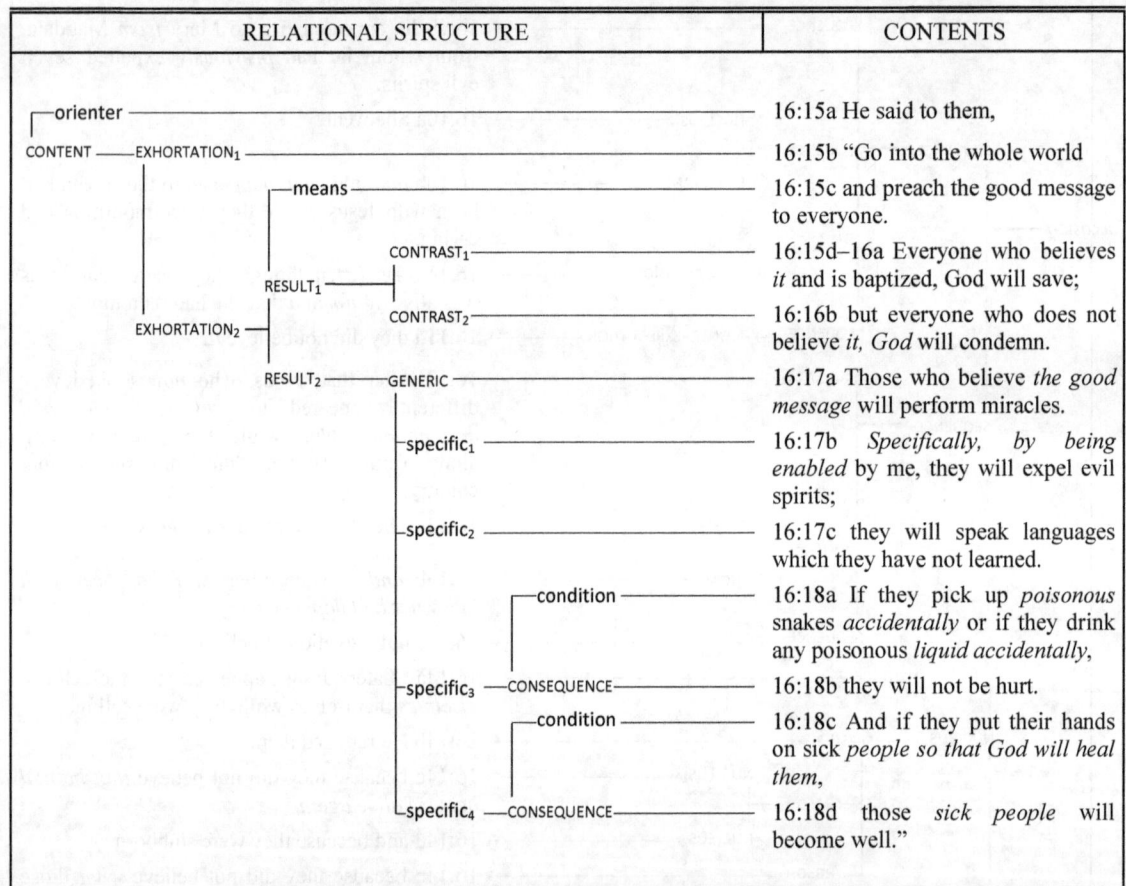

NOTES

16:17b *by being enabled by me* The text has 'in my name'. 'Name' is a metonymy, standing for the ability or authority of the person who has that name. LB has "use my authority".

16:17c *speak languages which they have not learned* The text has 'speak with new tongues' which is a metonymy, 'tongue' standing for the ability to speak. The word 'new' means 'new to them; i.e., that they had not spoken before.

16:18a *poisonous snakes accidentally* There are two crucial bits of implied information here: first, that the snakes were poisonous, and secondly, that it is not talking about picking them up deliberately.

Some manuscripts include the words 'with their hands', probably in view of Acts 28:3–6, and that wording is found in NIV and JB, but even if it were in the original manuscript, it contributes nothing to the meaning.

16:18c *so that God will heal them* This supplies the purpose of laying on of hands; see 6:5a, 7:32b.

EXPANSION OF OUTCOME 16:19–20 (SUMMARY OF 16:9–20)

RELATIONAL STRUCTURE	CONTENTS
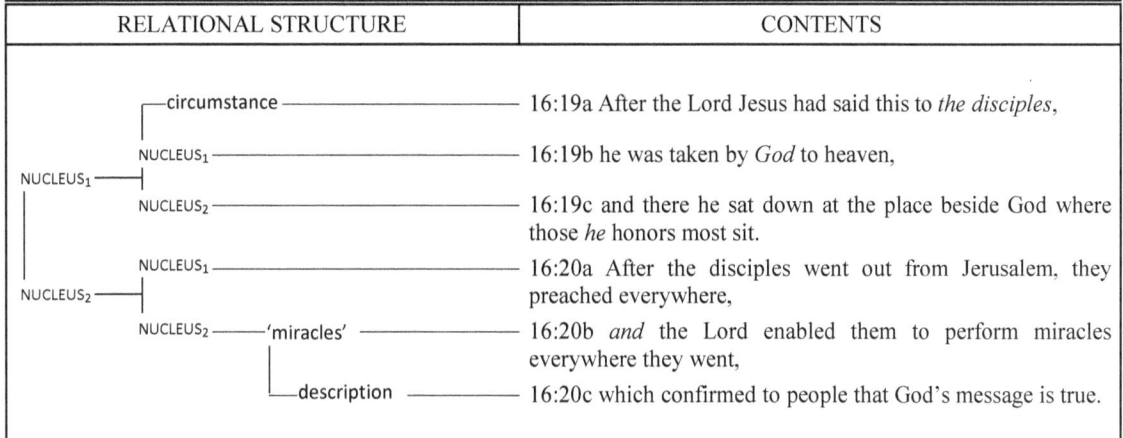	16:19a After the Lord Jesus had said this to *the disciples*,
	16:19b he was taken by *God* to heaven,
	16:19c and there he sat down at the place beside God where those *he* honors most sit.
	16:20a After the disciples went out from Jerusalem, they preached everywhere,
	16:20b *and* the Lord enabled them to perform miracles everywhere they went,
	16:20c which confirmed to people that God's message is true.

NOTES

16:19a the Lord Jesus Some manuscripts omit the word 'Jesus' (as in the KJV), but this appears to be due to influence by the church in later centuries.

16:19c place beside God where those *he* honors most sit See notes at 12:36, 14:62.

16:20 Most manuscripts have the word 'amen' at the end, and occurs in KJV and RSV, but it is clear that this was added in later centuries because of liturgical use of the gospel.

BOUNDARIES AND COHERENCE

Coherence within the 9–20 paragraph is provided by three occurrences of words or phrases meaning 'not believe' and two of the verb 'believe' in the positive sense, and two of σημεῖον 'miracles'. Coherence consists of this being the account of Jesus' final instructions to his disciples, his ascent to heaven, and what happened when the disciples' carried out his instructions.

PROMINENCE AND THEME

The theme is drawn from the prominence structure of the episode.

Thus ends this scribe's analysis of the Gospel of Mark

REFERENCES

Commentaries and other references

Anderson, Hugh. *The Gospel of Mark*. The New Century Bible Commentary. Grand Rapids: Eerdmans, 1976.

Bauer, Walter A . Greek-English Lexicon of the New Testament and Other Early Christian Literature. Second Edition. Chicago: The University of Chicago Press. 1979. (cited as BAGD)

Beekman, John, John C. Callow and Michael F. Kopesec, *The Semantic Structure of Written Communication*, 5th rev.; Dallas, Summer Institute of Linguistics; 1981

Bilezikian, Gilbert G. *The Liberated Gospel: a comparison of the Gospel of Mark and Greek tragedy*. Grand Rapids: Baker Book House, 1977. Print.

Billingham, Anthony. *The pattern of Mark's gospel.* Ipswich: Coverdale Cottage Publications, 1978. Print.

Blight, Richard C. *An Exegetical Summary of Mark 1–8*. Dallas: SIL International Publications. 2012.

Blum, Julia. *The hidden saviour in heaven.* Blog post on Jewish studies blog: Official forum of Israel Institute of Biblical Studies. 2016.

Bock, Darrell L. *Mark: New Cambridge Bible commentary.* New York, NY : Cambridge University Press. 2015.

Boltz, David H. *The foundation for a discourse analysis of the gospel of Mark.* 1976. Print.

Booth, Steve. *Selected peak marking features in the Gospel of John.* Series: American university studies. Series VII, Theology and religion. v. 178 New York: Peter Lang Publishing Inc. 1996.

Bratcher, Robert G. and Eugene A. Nida. *A Translator's Handbook on the Gospel of Mark*. London: United Bible Societies. 1961. (cited as THM)

Brooks, James A. *Mark*. The New American Commentary, Nashville, Tenn. Broadman, 1991.Bruce , Alexander Balmain. *The Synoptic Gospels.* Expositor's Greek New Testament, vol.1. 1910. Reprint. Grand Rapids: Eerdmans. 1980.

Callow, Kathleen, *Man and Message: A Guide to Meaning-Based Text Analysis*; Lanham, MD/Dallas, University Press of America and Summer Institute of Linguistics; 1998

Cole, R. Alan. *The Gospel According to Mark: An Introduction and Commentary.* 2nd ed., Tyndale New Testament Commentaries. Leicester, England: Inter-Varsity Press, 1989.

Cook, John G. *The structure and persuasive power of Mark: a linguistic approach*. Atlanta Ga.: Scholars Press, 1995. Print.

Cranfield, C.E.B. *The Gospel According To Saint Mark*. Cambridge: Cambridge University Press. 1959

Danove, Paul L. *Linguistics and exegesis in the Gospel of Mark : applications of a case frame analysis*. Sheffield, England: Sheffield Academic Press, 2001. Print.

Donahue, John R. and Daniel J. Harrington. *The Gospel of Mark*. Collegeville, MN.: The Liturgical Press. 2002.

Edwards, James R. *The Gospel according to Mark: The Pillar New Testament Commentary.* William B. Eerdmans Publishing Company, Grand Rapids, Michigan. 2002.

Evans, Craig A. *Mark 8:27–16:20.* Word Biblical Commentary, Vol. 34B. Nashville: Thomas Nelson. 2001.

Follingstad, Carl M. *An intent analysis of the gospel of Mark* . MA thesis for University of Texas at Arlington. 1986.

France, R.T. *The Gospel of Mark*. Grand Rapids: Wm. B. Eerdmans Publishing Co. 2002.

Gould, Ezra P. *A Critical and Exegetical Commentary on the Gospel According to St. Mark*. Edinburgh: T. & T. Clark. 1896.

Groff, Randy and Linda Neeley. *Translator's Notes on Mark 1–8*. Dallas: SIL International. 2008. (cited as TN)

Groff, Randy and Linda Neeley. *Translator's Notes on Mark 9–16*. Dallas: SIL International. 2008. (cited as TN)

Guelich, Robert A. *Mark 1–8:26*. Volume 34, Word Biblical Commentary. Dallas: Word Books. 1989.

Gundry, Robert H. *Mark: A Commentary on His Apology for the Cross*. Grand Rapids: Wm. B. Eerdmans Publishing Co. 1993.

Hendriksen, William. *Exposition of the Gospel According to Mark*. New Testament Commentary. Grand Rapids: Baker Book House. 1975.

Hiebert, D. Edmond. *The Gospel of Mark: An Expositional Commentary*. Greenville, S.C.: Bob Jones University Press. 1994.

Hooker, Morna D. *The Gospel according to Saint Mark*. Black's New Testament Commentary. London: A & C. Black Limited. 1991

Kopesec, Michael F. *Preliminary observations on the genre of Mark and some implications for discourse analysis*. 1978. Print.

Lane, William L. *The Gospel According To Mark*. New International Commentary on the New Testament. Grand Rapids: Wm. B. Eerdmans. 1974.

Larson, Mildred L. *The gospel of Mark, 1:1–3:6*. SIL International. n.d.

Lenski, R.C.H. *The Interpretation of St. Mark's Gospel*. Minneapolis: Augsburg Publishing House. 1946.

Levinsohn, Stephen H. *The function of de in the narrative of Mark 14:1–16:8*. SIL International. 1977.

Louw, Johannes P. and Eugene A. Nida. *Greek-English Lexicon of the New Testament Based on Semantic Domains*. Vol. 1. New York: United Bible Societies. 1988. (cited as L&N)

Mann, C.S. *Mark: A New Translation with Introduction and Commentary*. The Anchor Bible. New York: Doubleday. 1986.

Marcus, Joel. *Mark 1–8. A New Translation with Introduction and Commentary*. The Anchor Bible. New York: Doubleday. 2000.

Metzger, Bruce M. *A Textual Commentary on the Greek New Testament*. United Bible Societies. 1971.

Meyer, Heinrich August Wilhelm. *Critical and Exegetical Handbook to the Gospels of Mark and Luke*. Translated and revised by William Dickson. New York: Funk and Wagnalls, 1884.

Nicoll, W. Robertson, Bruce and Alexander Balmain. *The Expositor's Greek Testament*. Grand Rapids, MI: Eerdmans. 1980. (cited as EGT)

Nineham, D.E. *The Gospel of St Mark*. Pelican New Testament Commentaries. Harmondsworth, UK/New York. Penguin, 1963.

Patte, Daniel and Aline Patte. *Structural exegesis : from theory to practice : exegesis of Mark 15 and 16, hermeneutical implications*. Philadelphia: Fortress Press. 1978.

Stein, Robert H. *Mark*. Baker. *Exegetical Commentary on the New Testament*. Grand Rapids: Baker. 2008.

Strauss, Mark L. *Mark: Zondervan Exegetical Commentary on the New Testament*. Zondervan. Grand Rapids. 2014

Swete, Henry Barclay. *The Gospel According to St Mark*. Grand Rapids: Wm. B. Eerdmans Publishing Company.. 1956.

Taylor, Vincent. *The Gospel according to St. Mark: the Greek text with introduction, notes, and indexes.* New York: St Marin's press, 1966.

Wallis, Ethel E. "Mark's goal-oriented plot structure" in *Journal of Translation and Textlinguisitics Vol 10.* SIL, Dallas. 1998.

Wessel, W. and M. L. Strauss. "Mark," in *The Expositor's Bible Commentary*, vol.9. Revised edition, Grand Rapids: Eerdmans, 2001.

Versions

Anderson, Richie. The Gospel of Mark (Simplified Translation of Mark). Unpublished: no date

Beck, William F. The New Testament in the Language of Today. St. Louis: Concordia Publishing House. 1963.

Carlton, Matthew E. *The Translator's Reference Translation of the Gospel of Mark.* Dallas: SIL International. 2001. (cited as TRT)

The New Testament of our Lord and Saviour Jesus Christ. 1611. (cited as KJV)

New American Standard Bible. The Lockman Foundation, La Habra, CA. 1963. (cited as NASB)

A Translation for Translators of the New Testament. Deibler, Ellis W., Jr. Ann Arbor, MI: Cummins Works. 2008. (cited as TfT)

The Greek New Testament. Fourth Revised Edition. Stuttgart: Deustche Bibelgesellschaft. 1993. (cited as GNT)

God's Word. Grand Rapids: World Publishing. 1995. (cited as GW)

Holy Bible: New Living Translation. Carol Stream, Il: Tyndale House Publishers. 2004. (cited as NLT)

New Century Version. Dallas: Word Publishing; 1991. (cited as NCV)

The HOLY BIBLE: Contemporary English Version. New York: American Bible Society. 1995. (cited as CEV)

The Jerusalem Bible. Garden City, NY: Doubleday & Company, Inc. 1966. (cited as JB)

The Living Bible. Wheaton, IL: Tyndale House Publishers. 1971. (cited as LB)

The Message. Eugene H. Peterson. Colorado Springs: NavPress: 2002

The New International Version Interlinear Greek-English New Testament. Grand Rapids: Zondervan Publishing House. 1976.

The New English Bible. New York: Oxford University Press. 1972. (cited as NEB)

The New English Translation, Bible. Spokane, Wash.: Biblical Studies Press, 1998. (cited as NET)

The New Revised Standard Version. Grand Rapids, MI: Zondervan Bible Publishers, c1990 (cited as NRSV)

The New Testament in Modern English. J.B. Phillips. New York: Macmillan. 1958. (cited as JBP)

The New Testament of our Lord and Savior Jesus Christ, King James Version. Norwalk, CT: The C. R. Gibson Co. 1611.

The NIV Study Bible, New International Version. Grand Rapids: The Zondervan Corporation. 1985.

The Revised English Bible. New York: Oxford University Press. 1989.

The True Servant: Mark's story about Jesus. Toronto: The Full Gospel Publishing House. 1959.

The Twentieth Century New Testament: a translation into modern English. Lincoln, NB: Back to the Bible Publishers. 1961. (cited as 20th Century)

Today's English Version. New York: American Bible Society. 1976. (cited as TEV)

Williams, Charles B. The New Testament in the Language of the People. Chicago: Moody Press. 1937.

www.ingramcontent.com/pod-product-compliance
Lightning Source LLC
Chambersburg PA
CBHW080935300426
44115CB00017B/2827